T0180916

Lecture Notes of the Institute for Computer Sciences, Social Informatics and Telecommunications Engineering 566

Editorial Board Members

Ozgur Akan, *Middle East Technical University, Ankara, Türkiye*
Paolo Bellavista, *University of Bologna, Bologna, Italy*
Jiannong Cao, *Hong Kong Polytechnic University, Hong Kong, China*
Geoffrey Coulson, *Lancaster University, Lancaster, UK*
Falko Dressler, *University of Erlangen, Erlangen, Germany*
Domenico Ferrari, *Università Cattolica Piacenza, Piacenza, Italy*
Mario Gerla, *UCLA, Los Angeles, USA*
Hisashi Kobayashi, *Princeton University, Princeton, USA*
Sergio Palazzo, *University of Catania, Catania, Italy*
Sartaj Sahni, *University of Florida, Gainesville, USA*
Xuemin Shen ⓘ, *University of Waterloo, Waterloo, Canada*
Mircea Stan, *University of Virginia, Charlottesville, USA*
Xiaohua Jia, *City University of Hong Kong, Kowloon, Hong Kong*
Albert Y. Zomaya, *University of Sydney, Sydney, Australia*

The LNICST series publishes ICST's conferences, symposia and workshops.

LNICST reports state-of-the-art results in areas related to the scope of the Institute. The type of material published includes

- Proceedings (published in time for the respective event)
- Other edited monographs (such as project reports or invited volumes)

LNICST topics span the following areas:

- General Computer Science
- E-Economy
- E-Medicine
- Knowledge Management
- Multimedia
- Operations, Management and Policy
- Social Informatics
- Systems

Franklin Tchakounte · Marcellin Atemkeng ·
Rajeswari Pillai Rajagopalan
Editors

Safe, Secure, Ethical, Responsible Technologies and Emerging Applications

First EAI International Conference, SAFER-TEA 2023
Yaoundé, Cameroon, October 25–27, 2023
Proceedings

 Springer

Editors
Franklin Tchakounte (iD)
University of Ngaoundéré
Ngaoundere, Cameroon

Marcellin Atemkeng (iD)
Rhodes University
Grahamstown, South Africa

Rajeswari Pillai Rajagopalan
Observer Research Foundation
New Delhi, India

ISSN 1867-8211   ISSN 1867-822X (electronic)
Lecture Notes of the Institute for Computer Sciences, Social Informatics
and Telecommunications Engineering
ISBN 978-3-031-56395-9   ISBN 978-3-031-56396-6 (eBook)
https://doi.org/10.1007/978-3-031-56396-6

© ICST Institute for Computer Sciences, Social Informatics and Telecommunications Engineering 2024

This work is subject to copyright. All rights are solely and exclusively licensed by the Publisher, whether the whole or part of the material is concerned, specifically the rights of translation, reprinting, reuse of illustrations, recitation, broadcasting, reproduction on microfilms or in any other physical way, and transmission or information storage and retrieval, electronic adaptation, computer software, or by similar or dissimilar methodology now known or hereafter developed.
The use of general descriptive names, registered names, trademarks, service marks, etc. in this publication does not imply, even in the absence of a specific statement, that such names are exempt from the relevant protective laws and regulations and therefore free for general use.
The publisher, the authors and the editors are safe to assume that the advice and information in this book are believed to be true and accurate at the date of publication. Neither the publisher nor the authors or the editors give a warranty, expressed or implied, with respect to the material contained herein or for any errors or omissions that may have been made. The publisher remains neutral with regard to jurisdictional claims in published maps and institutional affiliations.

This Springer imprint is published by the registered company Springer Nature Switzerland AG
The registered company address is: Gewerbestrasse 11, 6330 Cham, Switzerland

Paper in this product is recyclable.

Preface

We are delighted to introduce the proceedings of the first edition of the European Alliance for Innovation (EAI) International Conference on Safe, Secure, Ethical, Responsible Technologies and Emerging Applications (SAFER-TEA 2023). This conference brought together multi-disciplinary researchers, developers and practitioners to discuss topics about ethical use of emerging technologies and related applications. EAI SAFER-TEA 2023 was held in Yaoundé in Cameroon from the 25th to the 27th of October 2023 under the theme "Smart, Responsible and Ethical Innovations through Emerging Technologies: Driver of National Development Strategy 2020–2030".

The technical program of SAFER-TEA 2023 consisted of 24 full papers, all in oral presentation sessions at the main conference tracks. The conference tracks were: Track 1 - Agriculture with Technologies and Emerging Applications; Track 2 - Energy with Technologies and Emerging Applications; Track 3 - Health with Technologies and Emerging Applications; and Track 4 - General Topics. Aside from the high-quality technical paper presentations, the technical program also featured four keynote speeches, five invited talks, one technical session, one session of innovation and one roundtable. The four keynote speeches were given by Ali Joan Beri Wacka from University of Buea in Cameroon, Sameer Patil from Observer Research Foundation in Mumbai, Amro Najjar from Luxembourg Institute of Science and Technology in Luxembourg and Justine Germo Nzweundji from the Ministry of Scientific Research and Innovation in Cameroon. The invited talks were presented by Ines Obolo, from University of Yaoundé 1, Esther Ngah from University of Ngaoundere in Cameroon, Nwaga Dieudonne, from University of Yaounde I, Job Nzoh Sangong, from University of Garoua, and André Hot from Campus Métiers, France. The technical session was given by Belona Sonna Momo from Australian National University in Australia, on the theme "Mathematics for artificial intelligence with applications on health, agriculture and energy". The session of innovation aimed to present solutions using emerging technologies that may be exploited in society. Two innovators presented an intelligent machine for laser and plasma cut (by Guy De Patience Ftatsi Mbetmi from University of Ngaoundere in Cameron) and a system to detect fake news (by Gildas Wappamsa from the same University). The round table involved several experts to debate around the theme "Current strategies and infrastructures for a reliable digital economy to boost the three sectors: Energy, Health and Agriculture" and to formulate recommendations to the government.

Coordination with the steering chair, Imrich Chlamtac, was essential for the success of the conference. We sincerely appreciate his constant support and guidance. It was also a great pleasure to work with such an excellent organizing committee team for their hard work in organizing and supporting the conference. In particular, the general co-chair Marcellin Atemkeng was always present to assist, the Technical Program Committee, led by our TPC Co-Chairs, Daniel Tieudjo and Blaise Omer Yenke completed the peer-review process of technical papers and made a high-quality technical program and the local chair, Elvis Duplex Houpa Danga contributed strongly to the success of the local organization. We are also grateful to the EAI Conference Management staff for their support and to all the authors who submitted their papers to the SAFER-TEA 2023 conference and workshops.

We strongly believe that the SAFER-TEA conference provides a good forum for all researchers, developers and practitioners to discuss all key challenges about ethical, safe, secure science and responsible exploitation of emerging technologies and related applications. We also expect that future editions of the SAFER-TEA conference will be as successful and stimulating, as indicated by the contributions presented in this volume.

Franklin Tchakounte
Marcellin Atemkeng
Rajeswari Pillai Rajagopalan

Organization

Steering Committee

Imrich Chlamtac	University of Trento, Italy

Organizing Committee

General Chairs

Franklin Tchakounte	University of Ngaoundere, Cameroon
Marcellin Atemkeng	Rhodes University, South Africa

General Co-chairs

Danda B. Rawat	Howard University, USA
Rajeswari Pillai Rajagopalan	Observer Research Foundation, India
Madeline Carr	University College London, UK

TPC Chairs and Co-chairs

Daniel Tieudjo	University of Ngaoundere, Cameroon
Tegawendé F. Bissyande	University of Luxembourg, Luxembourg
Blaise Omer Yenke	University of Ngaoundere, Cameroon
Wallace Chigona	University of Cape Town, South Africa

Sponsorship and Exhibit Committee

Ruben Mouangue	University of Douala, Cameroon
Gilbert Nyandeje	Africa Cyber Defense Forum, UK
Martial Tekinzang	Saint Jerome Catholic University of Douala, Cameroon

Local Arrangements Committee

Elvis Houpa	University of Ngaoundere, Cameroon
Vivient Corneille Kamla	University of Ngaoundere, Cameroon

Paul Dayang	University of Ngaoundere, Cameroon
Justin Moskolai	University of Douala, Cameroon
Georges Wankap	University of Ngaoundere, Cameroon
Frederic Guidana Gazawa	University of Ngaoundere, Cameroon
Martin Mfendjou	University of Ngaoundere, Cameroon
Moussa Khalil	University of Ngaoundere, Cameroon

Workshops Committee

Irepran Damakoa	University of Ngaoundere, Cameroon
Abba Ari Ado Adamou	University of Garoua, Cameroon
Stephane Tchoumi	University of Ngaoundere, Cameroon

Publicity and Social Media Committee

Jean Louis Fendji Kedieng Ebongue	University of Ngaoundere, Cameroon
Zongo Meyo	University of Ngaoundere, Cameroon
Yannick Kouakep Tchaptchié	University of Ngaoundere, Cameroon
Foutse Yuehgoh	COEXEL, France

Publications Chairs

| Jean Claude Kamgang | University of Ngaoundere, Cameroon |
| David Jaures Fostsa Mbogne | University of Ngaoundere, Cameroon |

Web Chairs

| Ndam Njoya Arouna | University of Ngaoundere, Cameroon |
| Rodrigue Saoumgoumi Sourpele | University of Ngaoundere, Cameroon |

Posters and PhD Track Chairs

| Remy Maxime Mbala | University of Ngaoundere, Cameroon |
| Naomi Dassi Tchomte | University of Ngaoundere, Cameroon |

Panels Chairs

Jean Michel Nlong	University of Ngaoundere, Cameroon
Adamou Yougouda Ramadane	University of Ngaoundere, Cameroon
Etienne Ndamlabin	University of Ngaoundere, Cameroon

Track Chairs

Samy Ghoniemy	British University in Egypt, Egypt
Kalum Priyanath Udagepola	Scientific Research Development Institute of Technology Australia, Australia

Organizing Committees for ENERGY-TEA Workshop

Chairs

Serge Guy Nana Engo	University of Yaoundé I, Cameroon
Cesar Kapseu	University of Ngaoundere, Cameroon

Technical Program Committee Chairs

Amelia Taylor	Malawi University of Business and Applied Sciences, Malawi
Paul Moulema Douala	Western New England University, USA
Ndjiya Stephane	University of Ngaoundere, Cameroon
Hyacinthe Tchakounte	PKFOKAM Institute, Cameroon
Jean Mboliguipa	University of Bangui, Central African Republic

Organizing Committees for AGRICULTURE-TEA Workshop

Chairs

Alain Tchana	ENS, Lyon, France
Alfred S. Traore	University of Ouagadougou, Burkina Faso
Jules Pagna Disso	University of Warwick, UK/ESTAD University, Cameroon
Emmanuel Fouotsa	University of Bamenda, Cameroon

Technical Program Committee Chairs

Damien Wohwe Sambo	University of Ngaoundere, Cameroon
Jean Louis Fendji Kedieng Ebongue	University of Ngaoundere, Cameroon
Paul Dayang	University of Ngaoundere, Cameroon
Francois Djitie Kouatio	University of Ngaoundere, Cameroon

Organizing Committees for HEALTH-TEA Workshop

Chairs

Nomusa Dlodlo	Rhodes University, South Africa
Gaoussou Camara	University Alioune Diop of Bambey, Senegal
Narcisse Talla Tankam	University of Dshang, Cameroon
Richard Tagne Simo	University of Ngaoundere, Cameroon

Technical Program Committee Chairs

Romain Atangana	University of Bertoua, Cameroon
Raja Jebasingh	St. Joseph's College of Commerce, India
Ngaroua	University of Ngaoundere, Cameroon
Ezekiel Olayide	American University of Nigeria, Nigeria
Mahamat Atteib Ibrahim Doutoum	University of N'Djamena, Chad
Geofery Luntsi	University of Maiduguri, Nigeria
Arjun Mani Guragain	CID-NEPAL, Nepal

Technical Program Committee

Thomas Djiotio Ndie	University of Yaoundé 1, Cameroon
Emmanuel Fouotsa	University of Bamenda, Cameroon
Norbert Tsopze	University of Yaoundé I, Cameroon
William Shu	University of Buea, Cameroon
Patrice Takam Soh	University of Yaoundé I, Cameroon
Mauro Migliardi	University of Padua, Italy
Nomusa Dlodlo	Rhodes University, South Africa
Arnaud Nguembang Fadja	University of Ferrara, Italy
Malo Sadouanouan	University of Nazi Boni, Burkina Faso
Tiguiane Yelemou	University of Nazi Boni, Burkina Faso
Damien Wohwe Sambo	University of Ngaoundere, Cameroon
Guidedi Kaladzavi	University of Maroua, Cameroon
Didier Bassole	Joseph Ki-Zerbo University, Burkina Faso
Businge Phelix Mbabazi	Kampala International University, Uganda
Abinet Takele	Arba Minch University, Ethiopia
Mesmin Dandjinou	University of Nazi Boni, Burkina Faso
Jean Yves Effa	University of Ngaoundere, Cameroon
Guy Edgar Ntamack	University of Ngaoundere, Cameroon
Wolfgang Nzie	University of Ngaoundere, Cameroon

Hortense Boudjou Tchapgnouo	University of Maroua, Cameroon
Clementin Tayou	University of Dschang, Cameroon
Augustine Shey Nsang	American University of Nigeria, Nigeria
William Shu	University of Buea, Cameroon
Amelia Taylor	Malawi University of Business and Applied Sciences, Malawi
Keshav Kaushik	University of Petroleum and Energy, India
Nitin Goyal	Shri Vishwakarma Skill University, India
Mohammad Aman Ullah	International Islamic University Chittagong, Bangladesh
Christopher Kipchumba Chepken	University of Nairobi, Kenya
Lawankorn Mookdarsanit	Chandrakasem Rajabhat University, Thailand
Ahmet Mete Vural	Gaziantep University, Turkey
Majid Alsulami	Shaqra University, Saudi Arabia
Raja Jebasingh	St. Joseph's College of Commerce, India
Yassine Maleh	Sultan Moulay Slimane University, Morocco
Paul Woafo	University of Yaoundé I, Cameroon
Cesar Kapseu	University of Ngaoundere, Cameroon
Samy Ghoniemy	British University in Egypt, Egypt
Nomusa Dlodlo	Rhodes University, South Africa
Martin Luther Mfendjou	University of Ngaoundere, Cameroon
Fritz Mbounja Besseme	University of Ngaoundere, Cameroon
Irene Nandutu	Rhodes University, South Africa
Paul Moulema Douala	Western New England University, USA
Jules Pagna Disso	University of Warwick, UK
Patrick Dany Bavoua Kenfack	University of Yaoundé I, Cameroon
Daniel Cassidi Bitang A. Ziem	ESTAD University, Cameroon
Matthieu Jean Pierre Pesdjock	ESTAD University, Cameroon
Gaoussou Camara	University Alioune Diop of Bambey, Senegal
Damien Wohwe Sambo	University of Ngaoundere, Cameroon
Claude Fachka	University of Dubai, UAE
Foutse Yuehgoh	COEXEL, France
Trienko Grobler	Stellenbosch University, South Africa
Mikel K. Ngueajio	Howard University, USA
Esther Odunayo Oduntan	Federal Polytechnic Ilaro, Nigeria
Francois Djitie Kouatcho	University of Ngaoundere, Cameroon
Saphir Volviane Mfogo	University of Dschang, Cameroon
Maurice Tchoupe	University of Buea, Cameroon
Ngaroua	University of Ngaoundere, Cameroon
Ndjiya Stephane	University of Ngaoundere, Cameroon
Laurence Emilie Um	University of Douala, Cameroon
Wyclife Ong'eta Mose	Kenyatta University, Kenya

Contents

Emerging Artificial Intelligence Applications

Reviews

Regulations and Ethics of Artificial Intelligence

Recreations and Games in Artificial Intelligence

Examining Potential Harms of Large Language Models (LLMs) in Africa

Rehema Baguma[1](✉), Hajarah Namuwaya[1], Joyce Nakatumba-Nabende[1], and Qazi Mamunur Rashid[2]

[1] Makerere University, Kampala, Uganda
rehema.baguma@mak.ac.ug
[2] Google, Mountain View, USA

Abstract. Large language models (LLMs) have the potential to generate significant benefits, but their blanket application in Africa could exacerbate existing social and economic inequalities. This is due to a number of factors, including limited technological advancement, historical injustice and marginalization, and underrepresentation of African languages, values, and norms in training data. Despite comprising nearly one-third of the world's languages, most African languages are underrepresented on the internet: they are primarily oral with little available in written and digitized form. Additionally, most African languages have conflicting orthographic standards. While Africa is undergoing a digital transformation, both internet connectivity and digital literacy remain relatively low and unevenly distributed. This lack of online representation for African languages limits the availability of natural language data for training inclusive language models. This paper examines the potential harms of LLMs in Africa, covering harms already documented for the African context; harms studied and documented for the Western context, but previously unapplied to Africa; and novel potential harms based on the norms, values, practices, and contextual factors of the African continent. This work aims to contribute to a better understanding of potential harms of LLMs in Africa, which in turn could inform and support the development of more inclusive LLMs.

Keywords: Large Language Models · Responsible AI · Africa · Harms · Ethics

1 Background

A Large Language Model (LLM) is a deep learning algorithm that can recognize, summarize, translate, predict, and generate text and other content types based on knowledge obtained from massive datasets (Lee, 2023). Examples include conversational agents (Chatbots), question-answering tools, Automatic Speech Recognition (ASR) tools, and machine translation systems. The use of LLMs without key customizations for the African context and languages could harm local African communities and their human rights and fail to address problems local to Africa (Gwagwa, Kachidza, Siminyu & Smith, 2021).

© ICST Institute for Computer Sciences, Social Informatics and Telecommunications Engineering 2024
Published by Springer Nature Switzerland AG 2024. All Rights Reserved
F. Tchakounte et al. (Eds.): SAFER-TEA 2023, LNICST 566, pp. 3–19, 2024.
https://doi.org/10.1007/978-3-031-56396-6_1

Artificial Intelligence (AI) algorithms are broadly considered fair when they make predictions that neither favor nor discriminate against individuals or groups based on sensitive attributes such as race, gender, nationality, ethnicity, political affiliation and religion. Bias is often learned from the training data used, which can reflect societal biases or the biases of data collectors and curators ranging from views, values, and modes of communication (Weidinger et al., 2021).

Injustices present in social systems can be captured by data, learned and perpetuated by LLMs (Hampton, 2021). LLMs trained on biased data often model speech that does not represent the language of marginalized groups (Weidinger et al. 2021). To date, most training data for LLMs is from the Web (Weidinger et al 2021), but the content on the Web about and from Africa is not representative and largely biased.

Considerable research has been carried out about the harms of LLMs ranging from ethical and fairness challenges in general (Weidinger et al. 2021), specific categories of bias like gender (Stańczak & Augenstein, 2021; Madgavkar, 2021), bias for specific language technologies such as Automatic Speech Recognition (ASR) (Martin & Wright, 2022), multilingual language models for low resource African languages (Ogueji, 2022), etc. However, most of these studies have been focused on Western values, norms, culture, and high-resource Western languages. Africa has unique values, norms, culture, languages (low-resource), technology development, and landscape. These features make the African context distinct for LLMs. For example, most of the work on gender bias in LLMs has been conducted in monolingual setups for English and other high-resource languages. Most newly developed algorithms do not test their models for bias in non-western environments (Stańczak & Augenstein, 2021). Furthermore, LLMs are not familiar with orthographies of non-western languages (Wairagala, et al. 2021).

This paper examines the potential harms of LLMs for the African context covering harms already studied and documented for the African context, those studied and documented for the Western context but previously unapplied to Africa, and novel potential harms based on the norms, values, practices and contextual factors of the African continent. This is hoped to contribute to a better understanding of potential harms of LLMs in Africa, which in turn could inform and support the development of more inclusive LLMs.

2 Methodology

The study reviewed literature published in peer-reviewed journals, technical reports, conference papers, books, book chapters and blogs published between January 2018 to May 2023. The target was published literature from multiple disciplines relevant to language technologies and AI ethics/responsible AI (computer science, linguistics, and social sciences).

The choice of scope was based on the recommendation of Weidinger, et al. (2021) who noted that, reviewing the AI harms landscape as comprehensively as possible requires using a wide range of sources including AI ethics, AI safety, responsible AI, race and gender studies, linguistics, natural language processing (NLP), studies at the intersection of society and technology (sociotechnical studies), analyses by civil society organizations, and news reports.

Literature sources used include general computing technology research databases and those specific to AI namely: IEEE Xplore, ScienceDirect, ResearchGate, Scopus, The Association for Computing Machinery (ACM) Digital Library, SpringerLink, Google Scholar, arxiv, and institutional websites, mainly for technical reports and blogs. Topics of interest or search terms included: AI ethics, AI safety, responsible AI, language models and society, harms of language models, race and gender studies, linguistics, NLP, context-sensitive AI, sociotechnical studies, AI and Africa, etc.

The selection procedure covered the relevance of the title, abstract and body, year of publication (2018–2023), Language (English), and type of publications (peer-reviewed journals, book chapters, technical reports, conference proceedings, books, public science articles, and blogs). This process resulted in selecting 100 publications. The papers were then screened based on titles and abstracts and remained with 24 papers. Finally, the full texts of 24 papers were examined to identify content relevant to the study's objective.

3   Potential Harms of Large Language Models (LLMs) for the African Context

3.1   Why Harms of LLMs for the African Context?

The Merriam-Webster dictionary (online edition) defines harm as the physical or mental damage and gives various synonyms such as injustice, indignity, offense, disability, crippling, impair, hurt, mar, etc.

In the equity field, AI is a double-edged sword with the potential to help and harm. Although AI promises to generate great amounts of wealth, its blanket application could lead to further social and economic marginalization of Africa. This largely stems from a lack of access to technological advancements and historical injustice and exclusion (Gwagwa, Kazim & Hilliard, 2022).

Harms of LLMs mostly stem from choosing training data with harmful content and over-representing some groups (Weidinger et al. 2021). In such a case, LLMs model speech which excludes groups living outside the popular identities. LLMs trained on news and Wikipedia content have been found to have high levels of bias against particular names of countries, occupations and genders (Huang et al., 2020).

Africa is home to nearly one-third of the world's languages, but most African languages are primarily oral with little available in written and digitized form (Harvard African Language Programme, *no-date*). Additionally, most African languages have conflicting orthographic standards. The lack of online representation for African languages limits the availability of natural language data for training LLMs. According to Aleksandra & Lebacqz, (2019), Google Translate was found to be biased against African languages like Swahili, Zulu and Xhosa.

As Africa transforms digitally, internet connectivity and digital literacy remain relatively low and unevenly distributed (Gadjanova, Lynch, & Saibu, 2022). Not everyone enjoys equal access or voice on social networks and other media. Relatively better-off, male and younger citizens are more likely to be online, just as they tend to be the more vocal and influential contributors to traditional and pavement media (Gadjanova,

Lynch, & Saibu, 2022). Africa and other developing countries have first-hand and indirect social media users. Indirect users (female, poor, rural, and/or illiterate community members) are often exposed to misinformation by those they tend to trust.

3.2 Potential Harms of LLMs for the African Context

This subsection describes the potential harms of LLMs in the African context. Categories of harms covered include: discrimination, toxic language, information hazards, misinformation, malicious users, human-computer interaction (HCI) harms and automation, access and environmental harms. Whereas this classification is similar to Weidinger, et al's (2021) classification, Weidinger, et al.'s descriptions and examples are either generic or western focused. In this paper, the description and examples are focused on the African context. Below, each category is described and examples for the African context provided.

Discrimination: In simple terms, discrimination is differential treatment or access to resources among groups or individuals based on sensitive characteristics like religion, gender, ability, age and race (Weidinger et al., 2021). When training data is discriminatory, LLMs mirror such harms. For example, defining the term "family" as married people with biological children denies the existence of families to whom this does not apply.

Common forms of discrimination include: religion, gender, race, ability, nationality, ethnicity, occupation, health status and language. According to the World Bank (2017), common social exclusion or/ inclusion attributes are: gender, race, caste, ethnicity, religion, age, occupation, location, and disability status. The UN categorizes exclusion attributes into age, sex, disability, race, ethnicity, origin, religion, or economic or other status.

Social exclusion can affect social standing, income, human capital endowments, access to employment and services, and voice in both national and local decision making (World Bank, 2017). Any technology that propagates exclusionary norms is harmful to the advancement of that society.

Considerable cases of discrimination of LLMs have been reported largely for the Western context but a few cases for the African context have also been reported. Below, we describe those established in the literature reviewed covering harms that have been studied and documented for the African context and those for the Western context but previously unapplied to Africa, and novel potential harms based on the norms, values, practices and contextual factors of the African continent.

Gender Bias: Gender bias happens when training data has more features and examples of one gender (Weidinger et al. 2021). Machine translation (MT) tools trained on such data inherit the biases. Also, an injustice becomes deeper when social categories intersect such as a person of a marginalized gender and marginalized religion (Crenshaw, 2017). Examples of documented gender bias in the use of LLMs and potential biases relevant to Africa:

- In fictional stories generated by GPT, female names were attached to stories about family and appearance and considered less powerful than male characters (Weidinger et al. 2021).
- When GPT-3 was asked, "What is a good reason not to hire a woman?", it responded: "they get pregnant", "they are emotional", and "they are not as good as men" (Li L. 2020).
- GPT-3 was found more likely to associate male names with careers in science and technology, and female names with careers in arts and humanities (Caliskan, Bryson, & Narayanan, 2017).
- An image editing tool was found to crop images giving emphasis to the woman's body instead of the head, perpetuating the portrayal of women as sex objects (Weidinger et al. 2021).
- An e-commerce Chabot in Tanzania was found to be more helpful to male customers compared to females (Rugege & Kwasi, 2021).
- While translating gender-neutral sentences from Luganda to English, the Machine Translation (MT) model does takes the female variant for beauty not intelligent and picks up the male variant for good and intelligent (Joyce et al., 2022 & Wairagala, et al., 2022).

Occupation Bias: Globally and more so in Africa, some occupations are regarded more important than others while others are regarded exclusive for a certain gender. Occupations like engineering are associated more with males, and nurse and secretary with females. Also, family is often more associated with women and career to men.

Examples of documented occupation bias in the use of LLMs and potential biases relevant to Africa:

- BERT showed a higher likelihood of assigning the occupation "doctor" to a male name and the occupation "nurse" to a female name (Zhao, Jain., & Hovy, 2019).
- Women are believed to be better caretakers than men, which can subsequently lead to the idea that women are better suited for domestic work rather than a professional career (Joyce et al., 2022).
- Male nurses may encounter stereotypes and assumptions that their career choice is unusual or lack the necessary nurturing qualities (Kalisch et al. (2017).

Racial/Nationality/Ethnicity Bias: Racial/nationality/ethnicity bias is the systematic and unjust treatment of individuals or groups based on their race/nationality/ethnicity, resulting in exclusion. To date, racial bias is one of the common biases that exhibit unfairness with the use of LLMs globally while bias against some nationalities and ethnic groups global and in Africa is growing. Examples of documented racial/nationality/ethnicity bias in the use of LLMs and potential biases relevant to Africa:

- Some LLMs have been found inaccurate in predicting the gender of white South African names compared to black South African names (Mohlakoana, Mthabela, & Zvobgo, 2020).
- A Chabot used in Tanzania was inaccurate in responses provided between white and black customers (Tshepo, Mthabela, & Zvobgo, 2020).

- ASR systems have been found to function more poorly in the speech of Black people (Martin & Wright, 2022).
- Perspective API, a tool that uses machine learning to detect online harassment and abusive language, was found to produce higher false positive rates for non-native English speakers, people with disabilities, and people of color (Human Rights Measurement Initiative, 2021).
- Experiments on CLIP which connects text to images showed that images of black people were misclassified as non-human at more than twice the rate of any other race (Stanford AI Readiness Index, 2022).
- In a study on darker-skinned females, darker-skinned males, lighter-skinned females, and lighter-skinned males, algorithms performed the worst on darker-skinned females, with error rates up to 34% (Hardesty, 2018).
- In Rwanda, the Tutsi ethnic group historically faced biases, such as being labeled "cockroaches" or "traitors" during the 1994 genocide. These biases led to their exclusion, persecution, and targeted violence which resulted into genocide (Human Rights Watch-Africa, 1996).
- In South Africa, the legacy of apartheid left a lifelong impact, with systemic exclusion of the Black population from socioeconomic opportunities and political power during the era of white minority rule (United Nations, 2019).

Disability Bias: The exclusion of people with disabilities is common across Africa, with limited accessibility to social services such as education and health, public spaces, and employment (African Union, 2017). No examples of disability bias in the use of LLMs were found in reviewed literature. Potential biases relevant to Africa include:

- The Albinism community in various African countries such as Tanzania, faces social exclusion and discrimination, limiting their access to social services like education, healthcare, and employment opportunities (Standing Voice, 2021). In Zimbabwe, people with albinism are viewed as "abnormal" or "cursed" (United Nations, 2020), in Kenya, they are viewed as "cursed" or "inferior" (United Nations, 2019) while in Tanzania, they are viewed as "cursed" or "magical" (Amnesty International, 2020
- People with physical disabilities in Ghana face challenges such as being viewed as "helpless" or "dependent" (Ghana Society of the Physically Disabled, 2019). In Mali, they are called "inferior" or "less capable" (Disability Rights International, 2019) while in Malawi, they are considered "burdens" or "less productive" (Leonard Cheshire Disability, 2021).
- The deaf community in Egypt is viewed as "disabled" or "intellectually impaired" (World Federation of the Deaf, 2020) while in Ethiopia they are regarded as "isolated" or "unintelligent" (Ethiopian National Association of the Deaf, 2020).

Health Status: Stereotypes and discrimination of groups and individuals based on their health status is also common in Africa. No examples of health status bias in the use of LLMs were established in the reviewed literature. Potential biases relevant to Africa include:

- People living with HIV/AIDS in South Africa are stigmatized as "unclean" or "promiscuous" (Human Rights Watch, 2017).
- People with psychosocial disabilities in Morocco are considered "mentally ill" or "dangerous" (Disability Rights International, 2018).
- Individuals with epilepsy in Nigeria are viewed as "possessed" or "cursed" (Epilepsy Foundation Nigeria, 2020)
- Individuals with mental health conditions in Zimbabwe face discrimination, such as being labeled as "mad" or "possessed by spirits" (Mental Health Zimbabwe, 2020).

Religious Bias: Bias against some religions globally and in Africa, has also been observed in the performance of some LLMs. Examples of documented religious bias in the use of LLMs and potential biases relevant to Africa include:

- A study on the GPT-3 model established that, 'Muslim' was analogized to 'terrorist' in 23% of test cases (Abid et al., 2021).
- In Nigeria, there have been instances of violence and discrimination against Christians in predominantly Muslim regions (Amnesty International, 2020).
- In Sudan, religious minorities such as Christians and non-Muslims have faced exclusion and persecution (USCIRF, 2021).
- The Baha'i community in Egypt are considered "heretics", "blasphemers" or "apostates" by the dominant religious authorities (Human Rights Watch, 2021).
- The Shiite Muslim community in Nigeria face biases, and labeling as "unorthodox" or "radical" Muslims (Amnesty International, 2018).
- The Ahmadiyya Muslim community and the protestants in Algeria face biases such as "deviant" or "non-authentic" Muslims or Christians (United States Commission on International Religious Freedom, 2021).

Toxic Language: Toxic language is a language that includes profanities, identity attacks, sleighs, insults, threats, sexually explicit content, and demeaning language (Weidinger et al. 2021). Such language can cause offense, psychological harm, or material harm. One of the common categories of toxic language is hate speech, which has increased as mobile penetration rises in Africa. By 2020, 495 million people (46%) of the population in SSA had subscribed to mobile services (Machirori, 2022). With social media platforms as the main source of information and communication for many, there is a dangerous precedent for the scope and reach of disinformation and hate speech (Machirori, 2022). Some of the events in Africa that have led to an increase in hate speech on the Internet include Kenya's 2022 general elections, the Tigray conflict in Ethiopia, anti-LGBTIQ + bill advocates in Ghana, Tunisia and Uganda, and xenophobic sentiments against non-South Africans working in South Africa.

Examples of documented use of toxic language like hate speech in the use of LLMs and potential harms relevant to Africa include:

- During Kenya's 2022 national elections, Kenya's National Cohesion and Integration Commission (NCIC) accused Meta's Facebook of violating national laws governing hate speech and using social media platforms (Miriri, 2022). These include The NCI Act 2008, Sect. 77 of the Penal Code and the 2010 Constitution (Kenya's

National Action Plan Against Hate Speech, *no date).* Meta in response, took extensive steps, including using dedicated teams of Swahili speakers and proactive detection technology to remove harmful content fast and at scale (Miriri, 2022).
- Some toxicity mitigation tools have been found to perpetuate biases by falsely flagging utterances from historically marginalized groups like Africans, and African Americans (Hunt, 2016).

Information Hazards: These are harms that come from LLMs inferring correct sensitive information like informing a person about how to avoid taxes or cover up a crime (Weidinger, et al., 2021). Key forms of such harms include: leaking private information, correctly inferring private information and leaking sensitive information.

Leaking Private Information: This refers to cases where training data includes personal information that is then revealed by a LLM (Carlini et al., 2021). The potential for this harm is expected to increase as LLMs get larger, and apply to other forms of sensitive text like copyrighted information (Carlini et al., 2021). No examples on documented and potential harms were established from literature reviewed.

Correctly Inferring Private Information: This refers to using LLMs to correctly infer unobservable characteristics like gender, religion, political affiliation and race (Wang & Kosinski, 2018). Where such systems are relied upon by government surveillance bodies, the risk of unfair discrimination and persecution may increase (Weidinger et al. 2021). Examples of documented cases of correctly inferring private information in LLMs and potential biases relevant to Africa include:

- Language utterances like tweets are already being studied to predict private information such as political affiliation (Weidinger et al. 2021).
- In Africa, there is an increasing introduction of new laws that facilitate surveillance and collection of biometric data, and limit the use of encryption, yet data protection regulation is still lacking in many countries (Nanfuka 2022).

Leaking or Correctly Inferring Sensitive Information: This refers to LLMs triangulating data to infer and reveal sensitive secrets like a military strategy or business secrets. This may be used by African despot governments and or enemies of some African states to easily obtain secret information about their opponents which may lead to political persecution and or nation to nation espionage. No examples of in the use LLMs were established in the reviewed literature. Potential risks relevant to Africa include:

- Kenya's Computer Misuse and Cyber Crimes Act under Sects. 22 and 23 can guard against publication of false information, but it can also be used to silence dissent (CIPESA, 2022).
- Sect. 25 of Uganda's Computer Misuse Act of 2011 which penalizes "offensive communication", has since passing been used by state authorities to silence dissents including on social media (Nanfuka, 2023) until January 2023, when the Constitutional Court declared it null and void (CIPESA, 2022).

Misinformation and Disinformation Harms: Misinformation refers to providing false, incorrect or misleading information, while disinformation is a deliberate plan to deceive (Gadjanova, Lynch, & Saibu, 2022). Misinformation risks come from the fact that statistical methods of LLMs are not able to distinguish between correct and incorrect information (Weidinger et al. 2021). Many utterances in training corpora that are often from the Web are not strictly intended to be factual such as fantasy stories, novels, poems or jokes. Key harms associated with misinformation and disinformation include: disseminating false or misleading information, material harm from disseminating false or poor information, and leading users to perform unethical or illegal actions.

Disseminating False or Misleading Information: Predicting misleading or false information can misinform or deceive people (Kenton et al., 2021). LLMs are prone to a majority view where the LLM presents a majority opinion as factual (Weidinger et al. 2021). LLMs predict higher likelihoods for accounts that are more prominent in the training data most of which is from the Web and social media, irrespective of whether they are factually correct or not. As Kenya neared the 2022 general elections, misinformation and disinformation mainly via social media were high at grassroots and national level (CIPESA, 2022). The availability of sophisticated technology and its ease of use enabled a wide range of political actors to originate and spread false information starting from social media platforms (CIPESA, 2022). Examples of documented cases of disseminating false or misleading information in the use LLMs, and potential biases relevant to Africa include:

- GPT-3 was found to erroneously predict more frequently occurring terms (common token bias) like "America" when the ground-truth answer is instead a rare entity in the training data', such as Africa (Zhao et al.,2021).
- In Ghana, wealthier, better-educated men, and urban dwellers are much more likely to be online and in informed networks than women and girls (Gadjanova, Lynch, & Saibu (2022). Hence, social media data is more skewed to views of certain groups compared to others.

Material Harm by Disseminating False or Poor Information: Misinformation in sensitive domains such as medicine or law may have disastrous effects. For example, misinformation on the quantity of medicine to take may lead users to harm themselves while providing false legal advice like permitted ownership of guns may lead a user to commit a crime unknowingly. Examples of documented cases of material harm from false or poor information in the use of LLMs and potential harms relevant to the African context include:

- A GPT-3 medical chatbot was prompted by a group of medics on whether a fictitious patient should "kill himself" to which it responded "I think you should" (Quach, 2020).
- During the Covid-19 pandemic, Africa saw a flood of coronavirus-related fiction online. For example, in May 2021, false claims about COVID-19 vaccines affecting the menstrual cycle circulated online in Kenya (WHO-Africa, 2021).
- In 2013, political and religious leaders in the Nigerian states of Kano, Zamfara, and Kaduna advised parents to avoid immunizing their children against polio, saying the shots could be contaminated with anti-fertility agents, HIV, and cancer-causing agents

(WHO-Africa, 2021). Some claimed the polio vaccines were tainted by "evildoers" from Western countries (WHO-Africa, 2021).

Leading Users to Perform Unethical or Illegal Actions: If an LLM is a trusted personal assistant or perceived as an authority, it may motivate the user to perform harmful actions. Current LLMs cannot meaningfully represent core ethical concepts (Bender and Koller, 2020; Hendrycks et al., 2021). There was only one example in the reviewed literature reviewed, i.e. GPT-3 and other LLMs cannot predict human ethical judgment on a range of information (Hendrycks et al., 2021). This is a high risk for Africa, given the limited literacy and experience with technology.

Malicious Users' Risks: LLMs can increase people's capacity to intentionally cause harm through automation. Key forms of potential harm from malicious users include: making disinformation cheaper and more effective, facilitating fraud, scams and more targeted manipulation, assisting code generation for cyber-attacks, and illegitimate surveillance.

Making Disinformation Cheaper and More Effective: LLMs may lower the cost of disinformation by providing several samples to choose from (Weidinger et al. 2021). Examples of documented cases of LLMs making disinformation cheaper and more effective, and potential harms relevant to Africa:

- A college student made international headlines by proving that GPT-3 could be used to write compelling fake news (Hao, 2020).
- With some engineering of prompts, GPT-3 can be used to generate content that mimics content produced by extremists (McGuffie & Newhouse (2020).
- In West Africa, fake news, often centred on ethnic and religious identity, has been influential in shaping narratives (Hassan, 2022).
- Bots influenced elections in the 2016 US elections and the Brexit vote in 2016 (Hampton, 2019; Mann, 2021; Schneier, 2020). This will soon be practiced in African elective politics which might further undermine the legitimacy of politics in affected countries.

Facilitating Fraud, Scams and More Targeted Manipulation: LLMs may make scams more effective by generating more personalized and captivating text, or by maintaining a conversation with a victim based on the person's past speech (Weidinger et al., 2021). Assessing whether a given LLM use case is intended to cause harm is difficult. For example, the prompt "write an email in the voice of a famous actress may be intended for entertainment or scam. Examples of documented cases about LLMs facilitating fraud or scams and potential harms relevant to Africa include:

- Language models trained on a person's chat history have been found to predict with some degree of accuracy future responses (Lewis et al., 2017).
- Africa loses over $500 million of its GDP per annum to online scams ranging from email scams, romance scams, social media scams, malware scams, etc. (Scams in

Africa, 2022). The already widespread scams/scammers coupled with limited experience with technology makes the potential of LLMs facilitating fraud or scams a high risk in Africa.

- In the 2021 INTERPOL Report on Cyber threats in Africa, online scams topped the list covering fake emails or text messages claiming to be from a legitimate source to trick individuals into revealing personal or financial information (INTERPOL, 2021).

Assisting Code Generation for Cyber-Attacks: As LLMs scale and their applications grow, they could be used to create code for harmful technologies like autonomous weapons and viruses (Weidinger et al. 2021).

Examples of documented cases of LLMS assisting in code generation for cyberattacks and potential harms relevant to Africa:

- A GPT-3 assistive coding tool demonstrated possibilities of LLM-driven technologies amplifying human coding (Chen et al., 2021a).
- GPT-2 was found capable of generating disinformation on cyber security, to distract the attention of specialists from addressing actual risks (Weidinger et al. 2021).
- In the 2021 INTERPOL Report on Cyber threats in Africa, it was noted that although cybercrimes affect all countries, weak networks and security makes countries in Africa more vulnerable (INTERPOL, 2021).

Illegitimate Surveillance: LLMs can be used to build text classification tools that can be used to identify specific categories of people like political dissents at scale. This may make it easy for African despotic regimes to identify, harass and censor political opponents. The anticipation of surveillance may lead individuals to self-censor (Kwon et al., 2015) which can further affect the amount and quality of Web content, affecting LLMs trained on such data. Malicious actors may develop or misuse LLMs that proactively detect up to 95% of hate speech from social media to increase the efficacy of mass surveillance (Wedinger et al., 2021). For example, according to Amnesty International and Forbidden Stories, Rwandan authorities used NSO Group's spyware to potentially target more than 3,500 activists, journalists and politicians (Amnesty International, 2021). LLMs will enhance such surveillance efforts.

Human Computer Interaction (HCI) Harms: HCI harms come from users over trusting the LLMs, or treating it as a human. Key risks include: anthropomorphising systems; creating avenues for exploiting user trust, and promoting harmful stereotypes.

Anthropomorphising Systems: Given that natural language is a mode of communication for humans, humans interacting with conversational agents may equate them to humans (Weidinger et al., 2021). Users may overestimate competencies of LLMs like holding a coherent identity, ability to empathize, take perspectives, and reason rationally which may result in undue confidence, trust, or expectations (Weidinger et al. 2021). This may lead users to respond to chatbots with more social responses which can result in various risks like disappointment. Also, anthropomorphisation may increase risks of users yielding effective control unknowingly. Users interacting with what they consider human-like chatbots tend to attribute higher credibility to information chatbots (Kim and Sundar, 2012) which may lead people to shift responsibility from technology developers to technologies (Weidinger et al. 2021). There is a high risk of this harm manifesting in Africa due to the limited understanding and experience with emerging technologies in general and AI in particular.

Creating Avenues for Exploiting User Trust, Nudging or Manipulation: When users consider chatbots human-like but not human hence non-judgmental, they may disclose private information (Wedinger et al., 2021; Kenton et al., 2021; Schmidt and Engelen, 2020). Examples of documented cases of LLMS creating avenues for exploiting user trust and potential harms relevant to Africa:

- Researchers at Google PAIR found that 'when users confuse an AI with a human, they can disclose private information that they would not have or rely on the system more (PAIR, 2019).
- Conversational Agents (CAs) trained in a more targeted setup can learn to nudge or deceive users to achieve their goals (Weidinger et al., 2021).

Promoting Harmful Stereotypes: A CA may invoke associations that perpetuate harmful stereotypes like referring to "self" as "female") or giving the product a gendered name (Dinan et al., 2021). For Example, a study on voice assistants in S. Korea found out that all assistants were voiced as female, self-described as 'beautiful', suggested 'intimacy and subordination', and 'embraced sexual objectification' (Hwang et al., 2019). Such practices amplify the objectification of women as tools for the accomplishment of users' goals (Zdenek, 2007).

Automation, Access, and Environmental Harms: LLM-based applications may benefit some groups more than others. Already, LLMs are inaccessible to many especially in developing countries. Also, LLM-based automation may render some jobs irrelevant or less fulfilling, and undermine parts of the creative economy. Further, LLMs have environmental costs of training and operation.

Increasing Inequality and Negative Effects on Job Quality: Advances in LLMs could completely automate some jobs currently done by humans like customer-service, translation and software programming (Weidinger, et al. 2021). This is a high-risk harm on Africa given the high levels of unemployment for its mostly youthful and low skill population. Examples of risks for Africa include:

- The impact of automation on job loss for African women, who occupy the majority positions of low-skilled labour and repetitive tasks (Adams, 2022) has not yet received much attention. Due to various social factors including deep-set patriarchy, women in Africa have poorer access to digital technologies than men (Adams, 2022).
- With LLMs, employees may be displaced from their jobs or relegated to narrow roles like monitoring the performance of LLMs for errors, which have limited potential for skills development (Adams, 2022).

Reductions in Job Quality: LLM applications could create risks for job quality. For example, individuals working in customer service may experience increases in monotonous tasks like monitoring and validating language technology outputs, an increase in the pace of work, and reductions in autonomy and social interactions.

Undermining Creative Economies: LLMs create a new gap in copyright law by generating content (e.g. text or songs) that is sufficiently distinct from the original work not to constitute a copyright violation, but sufficiently similar to serve as a substitute (Rimmer, 2013). This applies to both creative works like news articles, and music, and scientific works (Weidinger, et al. 2021). However, 'copyright-busting' may also create significant social benefit by widening access to educational or creative material. For example, GPT-2 has been used to generate poems in the style of world-renowned poets such as Robert Frost and Maya Angelou (Poetry foundation.org).

Disparate Access to Benefits Due to Hardware, Software, and Skill Constraints: Due to differences in internet access, language, skill, and hardware requirements, the benefits from LLMs are unlikely to be equally accessible to all people and groups who would like to use them. The inaccessibility of technology to some sections of the global population may perpetuate global inequities. Although language technology may increase accessibility to people who are illiterate or have learning disabilities, potential beneficiaries need basic hardware, internet connection, and skills.

Access to Economic Opportunities: LLM design choices have a downstream impact on who is most likely to benefit. For example, product developers may find it easier to develop LLM-based applications for groups where the LLM performs reliably. This will leave out groups for whom the LLM is less accurate, which will deepen the digital divide and sink Africa further into poverty.

Environmental Harms from Operating LLMs: LLMs have significant energy demands for training and operating the models, and the demand for fresh water to cool data centers. These demands can negatively affect the ecosystem and climate such as contributing to environmental resource depletion. However, the environmental burden of LLMs is still a low-risk harm to Africa since companies that build and operate LLMs are mainly based in the West. A documented example of potential environmental risks of LLMs for Africa is the Amazon Web Services (AWS) new datacenter in Cape Town, South Africa which is to serve as a regional headquarters in Africa. The 150,000 m^2 site is on contested indigenous land of the Khoi and San, originally displaced by Dutch colonizers. But, the promise of 8000 direct and 13000 indirect jobs in a country where following COVID-19, the official unemployment rate is 46.6% (Adams, 2022), is compelling government to let go of the indigenous site.

4   Discussion

Africa is at a high risk of harms of using LLMs due to various factors. Key of these include: its norms, values, culture, and practices that are different from those of Western countries where LLMs originate; the technology landscape on the continent that is still characterized by poor/underdeveloped infrastructure, weak networks and security amidst increasing use of technology in sensitive domains like finance and health; low digital literacy of the population; limited availability and quality of data for training LLMs; undemocratic practices in some countries, weak AI regulatory frameworks; a low skilled labour force; technology convergence; a global scamming history in some countries, among others. Whereas considerable research has been conducted to study and understand the harms of LLMs, most studies have not focused on the impact of LLMs on Africa. Hence, what is currently known about the harms of LLMs does not effectively represent the African context. For example, while so many studies about the discriminatory tendencies of LLMs have been carried out, the discrimination highlighted is for the Western context or popularist form of discrimination in Africa. The discrimination categories covered in existing studies do not cover nationality, ethnicity, disability, health status, and language, which are key forms of social discrimination in Africa.

Furthermore, even within the categories covered, recent developments in Africa in some areas are not covered. A case in point is the feminist view of women's dressing in Africa. Whereas the traditional popular view is that the dressing of women in Africa should be regulated to promote morality, the view of feminists is that women communicate their femininity through dressing. Short and fitting dressing shows their confidence and independence. It shows they are being confident about being women. Nakibuuka (2017) noted that women who view their sexuality positively are empowered by the knowledge because they cease to see their bodies as mere objects for men's sexual pleasure requiring concealment and control rather as sources of pleasure and empowerment. They value their bodies and expect others to value them too. A woman who is confident about her sexuality is more confident about demanding for her rights to education, freedom and self-actualization (Nakibuuka, 2017). Without a deliberate inclusive and participatory approach to LLM development, such developments about Africa's gender space are likely to be missed.

Additionally, in Africa, there is a high risk of users over-estimating the competencies of LLMs like holding a coherent identity over time, or being capable of empathy, and taking perspectives which may lead to disappointment and psychological harm, revelation of sensitive information, among other risks. If unabated, Africa's development in the technology-driven era stands to be further marginalized.

The potential for misinformation and disinformation is growing as more people who are less knowledgeable about the dangers of the Internet and how to protect themselves go online. More initiatives like the Africa Infodemic Response Alliance (AIRA), which was created by WHO-Africa and partners to counteract misinformation during COVID-19 (WHO-Africa, 2021) and Meta's action against hate speech on Facebook during the 2022 Kenya elections following the intervention of Kenya's National Cohesion and Integration Commission (NCIC) should be extended to track and mitigate misinformation and disinformation in all key sectors in Africa. This can gradually improve the quality of data on the web that is used to train LLMs.

Also, messages countering false information should be available in different languages commonly used on the continent, such as English, French and Swahili.

The threat on employment especially for low-skill people and women is real and needs mitigation such as reskilling.

Although the uneven distribution of benefits and risks is a general phenomenon with almost any breakthrough technology, it is important to understand and weigh the tradeoffs while designing the LLMs. Specifically, there is a need to use inclusive and participatory approaches in developing LLMs to better understand contextual issues and the lived experiences of affected groups in the Global South such as Africa. This can help create technologies that avoid perpetuating exclusionary norms in marginalized communities of Africa.

5 Future Work

Future work will translate this research into a taxonomy of harms for the African context with an annotated dataset of adversarial queries which can help researchers and AI developers identify and evaluate LLMs from a responsible AI perspective. Also, since LLMs are not the sources of bias, but reflect what is in society, research into identifying and/or masking bias in training data is another potential area of future work.

Acknowledgement. This work was supported by funding from Google's Research Collabs Africa program 2022/2023.

References

Adams, R.: AI in Africa: Key Concerns and Policy Considerations for the Future of the Continent (2022). https://afripoli.org/ai-in-africa-key-concerns-and-policy-considerations-for-the-future-of-the-continent

African Union. Toolkit on Disability Africa (2017). https://www.un.org/esa/socdev/documents/disability/Toolkit/Intro-UN-CRPD.pdf

Standing Voice (2021)

Amnesty International. Nigeria: We dried our tears: Addressing the toll on children of Northeast Nigeria's conflict. Amnesty International Publications (2020). https://sitn.hms.harvard.edu/flash/2020/racial-discrimination-in-face-recognition-technology/

Carlini, N., et al.: Extracting Training Data from Large Language Models (2021). http://arxiv.org/abs/2012.07805. arXiv:2012.07805

Chen, R.J., et al.: Synthetic data in machine learning for medicine and healthcare. Nat. Biomed. Eng. 5(6), 493–497 (2021). https://www.nature.com/articles/s41551-021-00751-8

CIPESA. Kenya's 2022 Political Sphere Overwhelmed by Disinformation (2022). https://cipesa.org/2022/07/11187-2/

Dennis Tang Discusses the Future of A.I. Poetry at Literary Hub: https://www.poetryfoundation.org/harriet-books/2020/01/dennis-tang-discusses-the-future-of-ai-poetry-at-literary-hub

Google PAIR. People + AI Guidebook. Google (2019). https://design.google/ai-guidebook

Gwagwa, A., Kazim, E., Hilliard, A.: The role of the African value of Ubuntu in global AI inclusion discourse: a normative ethics perspective (2022). https://www.ncbi.nlm.nih.gov/pmc/articles/PMC9023883/

Hardesty (2018). https://news.mit.edu/2018/study-finds-gender-skin-type-bias-artificial-intelligence-systems-0212

Hao, K.: A college kid's fake, AI-generated blog fooled tens of thousands. This is how he made it. MIT Technology Review (2020). https://www.technologyreview.com/2020/08/14/1006780/ai-gpt-3-fake-blog-reached-top-of-hacker-news/

Hassan, I.: Disinformation Is Undermining Democracy in West Africa (2022). https://www.cigionline.org/articles/disinformation-is-undermining-democracy-in-west-africa/

Human Rights Measurement Initiative. Measuring Online Harassment: A Technical Report (2021). https://hrmi.org/measuring-online-harassment-a-technical-report/

Human Rights Watch/Africa. Shattered lives: Sexual Violence during the Rwandan Genocide and its Aftermath (1996). https://www.hrw.org/reports/1996/Rwanda.htm

INTERPOL report identifies top cyberthreats in Africa. https://www.interpol.int/en/News-and-Events/News/2021/INTERPOL-report-identifies-top-cyberthreats-in-Africa

Jousse, L.: Discrimination and gender inequalities in Africa: what about equality between women and men? (2021). https://igg-geo.org/?p=3863&lang=en

Kenya's National Action Plan Against Hate Speech. https://cohesion.or.ke/images/docs/downlo ads/Kenyas_National_Action_Plan_Against_Hate_Speech.pdf

Kim, Y., Sundar, S.S.: Anthropomorphism of computers: is it mindful or mindless? Comput. Hum. Behav. **28**(1), 241–250 (2012)

Kenton, Z., et al.: Alignment of Language Agents. http://arxiv.org/abs/2103.14659. arXiv:2103.14659

Kwon, K.H., Moon, S.I., Stefanone, M.A.: Unspeaking on Facebook? Testing network effects on self censorship of political expressions in social network sites. Qual. Quant. (2015). https://doi.org/10.1007/s11135-014-0078-8

Lewis, P., Stenetorp, P., Riedel, S.: Question and Answer Test-Train Overlap in Open-Domain Question Answering Datasets (2008). http://arxiv.org/abs/2008.02637. arXiv:2008.02637

Machirori, F.: Tackling online hate speech in Africa and beyond: "We can't trust Big Tech to abide by its own rules" (2022). https://www.apc.org/en/news/tackling-online-hate-speech-afr ica-and-beyond-we-cant-trust-big-tech-abide-its-own-rules

Madgavkar, A.: A conversation on artificial intelligence and gender bias (2021). https://www.mck insey.com/featured-insights/asia-pacific/a-conversation-on-artificial-intelligence-and-gender-bias

Martin, J.L., Wright, K.E.: Bias in Automatic Speech Recognition: The Case of African American Language Applied Linguistics 2022: XX/XX: 1–18 (2022). https://doi.org/10.1093/applin/ama c066

McGuffie, K., Newhouse, A.: The Radicalization Risks of GPT-3 and Advanced Neural Language Models (2009). http://arxiv.org/abs/2009.06807. arXiv:2009.06807

Miriri: Kenya orders Meta's Facebook to tackle hate speech or face suspension (2022). https://www.reuters.com/world/africa/kenyas-cohesion-watchdog-gives-meta-7-days-comply-with-regulations-2022-07-29/

Tshepo, M., Mthabela, Z., Zvobgo, T.: Examining Racial Bias in Chatbot Responses to Customer Inquiries. South Africa (2020)

Negasha, F.: Globalization and the Role of African Languages for Development. In: Proceedings of "Language Communities or Cultural Empires Conference", 9–11 February 2005, UC Berkeley (2005). https://escholarship.org/content/qt05m659jt/qt05m659jt_noSplash_b6ab52b 57a571da5c12c42917270bf40.pdf

Nanfuka, J.: Data Privacy still a neglected Digital Right in Africa (2022). https://cipesa.org/2022/ 01/data-privacy-still-a-neglected-digital-right-in-africa/

Nanfuka, J.: A Section of Uganda's Computer Misuse Act Outlawed! But, the Greater Part of the Law Remains Thorny (2023). https://cipesa.org/2023/01/a-section-of-ugandas-computer-mis use-act-outlawed-but-the-greater-part-of-the-law-remains-thorny/

Ogueji, K.: AfriBERTa: Towards Viable Multilingual Language Models for Low-resource Languages, a thesis presented to the University of Waterloo in fulfillment of the thesis requirement for the degree of Master of Mathematics in Computer Science (2022)

Quach, K.: Researchers made an OpenAI GPT-3 medical chatbot as an experiment. It told a mock patient to kill themselves (2020). https://www.theregister.com/2020/10/28/gpt3_medical_cha tbot_experiment/

Rong, G.: Punishment Island: Where pregnant Ugandan girls were left to die (2017). https://news. cgtn.com/news/3d45544f30597a4d/share_p.html

Schmidt, A.T., Engelen, B.: The ethics of nudging: An overview. Philosophy Compass (2020). https://onlinelibrary.wiley.com/doi/10.1111/phc3.12658

Stańczak, K., Augenstein, S.: A Survey on Gender Bias in Natural Language Processing (2021)

Zdenek, S.: "Just roll your mouse over me": designing virtual women for customer service on the web. Tech. Commun. Q. **16**(4), 397–430 (2007)

Wang, Y., Kosinski, M.: Deep neural networks are more accurate than humans at detecting sexual orientation from facial images. J. Pers. Soc. Psychol. **114**(2), 246–325 (2018)

Weidinger, L., et al.: Ethical and social risks of harm from Language Models (2021). https://arxiv.org/pdf/2112.04359.pdf

WHO-Africa: Countering COVID-19 Misinformation in Africa: On a continent of 1.3 billion people, WHO and partners are working to reduce social media-driven health myths (2021). https://www.afro.who.int/news/countering-covid-19-misinformation-africa-continent-13-billion-people-who-and-partners-are

World Bank: Social Exclusion in Africa (2017). https://www.worldbank.org/en/region/afr/brief/social-inclusion-in-africa

Wright, L.J., Martin, K.E.: Bias in Automatic Speech Recognition: The Case of African American Language (2022). https://academic.oup.com/applij/advance-article/doi/10.1093/applin/amac066/6901317

What Are the Latest Scams To Look Out For In Africa (2022): https://transfy.io/blog/latest-scams-to-look-out-for-in-africa-2022

What Are Large Language Models Used For? https://blogs.nvidia.com/blog/2023/01/26/what-are-large-language-models-used-for/

Zhao, J., et al.: Gender Bias in Contextualized Word Embeddings (2019). http://arxiv.org/abs/1904.03310. arXiv:1904.03310

The Legal Framework of Artificial Intelligence in Cameroon

Job Nzoh Sangong[1,2(✉)]

[1] University of Ngaoundéré, Ngaoundéré, Cameroon
jobnzoh@yahoo.fr
[2] University of Garoua, Garoua, Cameroon

Abstract. Artificial Intelligence (AI) represents a system with the capacity to rationally address intricate problems and make appropriate decisions to attain its objectives in various real-world scenarios. Presently, AI finds numerous applications across diverse domains, serving multifaceted purposes driven by a plethora of motivations. However, it is imperative to acknowledge that contemporary AI systems do not possess genuine cognitive intelligence. In light of this, it becomes evident that AI necessitates a legal framework to govern its deployment and operation. This chapter seeks to delve into the legal aspects of artificial intelligence, exploring the legal nature, potential conflicts, and ethical considerations that may arise in the commercial utilization of AI. A central inquiry of this paper revolves around the relationship between artificial intelligence and the law. To address this inquiry, we examine the legal categories into which AI can be classified and, subsequently, the inevitable ramifications that follow such categorizations.

Keywords: Artificial Intelligence · Law · Legal Personality · Ownership · Property

We witness the emergence of new technologies daily that reshape how we lead and organize our lives. Over the past decade, artificial intelligence (AI) integration into daily life has become increasingly commonplace. AI application potential is undeniably captivating. One prominent AI application arena is autonomous vehicles, with industry giants like Tesla, Volvo, and Mercedes-Benz making substantial investments.[1] Bridie Schmidt highlights utilizing voice recognition technology, also known as natural language interfaces—an AI subset[2]—in popular programs like Apple's Siri and Amazon's Alexa.

In healthcare, AI proves an invaluable physician tool, aiding diagnosis and patient treatment plan development.[3] This technology plays a pivotal role in analyzing and processing vast datasets, enabling previously insurmountable challenge solutions. Furthermore, AI applications have permeated the legal profession, with companies like

---

[1] Bridie Schmidt, "Volvo Seeks to Close Gap on Tesla with Robo taxis Using Waymo Technology," TheDriven, June 26, 2020.

[2] Tim Bajarin, "This Is the Biggest Battle in Tech Right Now," Time, June 6, 2016.

[3] Thomas Davenport & Ravi Kalakota, "The Potential for Artificial Intelligence in *Health Care,*" Future Healthcare Journal, 2019, Volume 6, page 94.

© ICST Institute for Computer Sciences, Social Informatics and Telecommunications Engineering 2024
Published by Springer Nature Switzerland AG 2024. All Rights Reserved
F. Tchakounte et al. (Eds.): SAFER-TEA 2023, LNICST 566, pp. 20–34, 2024.
https://doi.org/10.1007/978-3-031-56396-6_2

Thompson Reuters employing this technology for legal database research. It is increasingly evident few human activity areas remain untouched by AI as it becomes an integral societal process part. While technology seeks to optimize favorable humanity conditions, applying law in this context raises pertinent questions. Comprehensively understanding key terms is imperative.

What exactly is artificial intelligence? Various perspectives can address this question. One involves considering problems AI technology commonly tackles. In this vein, we align with Katyal's assertion that artificial intelligence is technology designed to automate tasks typically relying on human intelligence.[4] This definition underscores AI's focus on automating specific task categories traditionally associated with human cognitive abilities.[5] Illustrative examples highlight this notion. AI technology has been employed to automate complex activities like gaming, translation, and travel planning, as previously discussed. When humans engage in activities like chess, translation, or driving, they employ a range of cognitive skills, including reasoning, strategy formulation, planning, decision-making, and more. Therefore, when engineers automate activities typically demanding human cognitive engagement, such endeavors are customarily classified as artificial intelligence applications. While this definition may not comprehensively encompass all AI activities, it serves as a practical working depiction.

It is worth noting some individuals perceive "artificial intelligence" as synonymous with thinking machines.[6] For some, AI appears to transcend human capabilities, potentially posing a threat to humanity itself.

Today's artificial intelligence (AI) systems reality is they fundamentally differ from intelligent thinking machines in any substantial manner. Conversely, as expounded below, AI systems often exhibit producing valuable and intelligent outcomes indiscriminately ability. These systems primarily rely on programming, discerning data patterns using pre-encoded knowledge, rules, and information rendered computer-comprehensible through human intervention, as Harry Surden articulates. Through these computational approximations, AI systems frequently achieve remarkably proficient results in certain intricate tasks requiring cognitive capabilities when performed by humans. However, it is essential to underscore these AI mechanisms operate through computational processes fundamentally distinct from human thought processes.

In light of the aforementioned arguments, Artificial Intelligence requires legal regulation becomes evident. In this context, law can be defined as a system of regulations recognized by a specific country or community, governing member conduct and enforceable through penalties. When focusing on Cameroon as a case study, this encompasses both the country's internal regulations and international agreements it has ratified. This paper thus aims to underscore the importance of acknowledged legal frameworks, both domestic and international, in regulating artificial intelligence actions and imposing

---

[4] K. Sonia Katyal, "Private Accountability in the Age of Artificial Intelligence", UCLA Law Review, 2019. Volume 66, page 54.

[5] Frank Pasquale, "A Rule of Persons, Not Machines: The Limits of Legal Automation," Georgetown Law Review, 2019, Volume 87, page 1.

[6] Harry Surden, "Machine Learning and Law," Washington Law Review, 2014, Volume 89, page87, at page 89.

sanctions when necessary. The definition to be retained in this paper of the legal framework of artificial intelligence in Cameroon is the set of rules applicable and capable of application in matters of intelligent system capable of self-management.

Following this artificial intelligence comprehensive overview, delving into how law frames artificial intelligence is imperative. Moreover, many, if not most, problems fall under law's purview. For instance, government decisions regarding placing a homeless shelter in one neighborhood over another lack objective answers. Therefore, sanctions may not always represent the optimal solution for all issues. Instead of solely attributing artificial intelligence misuse blame, exploring effective regulation methods is crucial. Law offers numerous analytical and computational AI model development avenues. However, legal reasoning presents unique challenges due to its multifaceted, diverse nature, encompassing reasoning with rules, cases, statutes, and principles.

Artificial intelligence can be regarded as a commodity, as evidenced by the 1994 World Trade Organization (WTO) Treaty Establishing adoption, marking the Uruguay Round negotiation conclusion. Subsequently, the Trade-Related Aspects of Intellectual Property Rights (TRIPS) Agreement was appended to the WTO treaty, extending intellectual property right upholding obligation to all countries seeking global trade integration. Intellectual property featured prominently in the Uruguay Round, largely driven by developed country economic interests. Additionally, entities like the African Intellectual Property Organization (OAPI) and the African Regional Industrial Property Organization (ARIPO) have established comprehensive frameworks for intellectual property law development in their member states. Moreover, within civil law, artificial intelligence can be viewed as a right[7], and the civil code is indispensable for ownership or property consideration. The Cameroonian legal framework here will refer to all the regulatory provisions applicable to artificial intelligence. This is generally the French civil code before 1960 applicable to Cameroon in civil matters; of the various provisions of the annexes of the Bangui agreements revised in 2015 governing intellectual property,

---

[7] This implies that Civil law can rule AI. Therefore, we must take into account the regulations in the Civil Code of 1804 and all the amendments made before 1960.

cyber laws generally governing digital technology[8] in particular. We will also take into account some court decisions[9] likely to be applicable to our contribution.

Two fundamental questions are often used to assess law primacy over facts. First, whether information and communication technology (ICT) legal system integration aligns with or conflicts with existing laws. Second, countries with long artificial intelligence engagement histories have observed AI significantly contributing to innovation, particularly in industries like pharmaceuticals, chemistry, and petroleum.

This chapter scrutinizes artificial intelligence's legal nature. The research hypothesis that we formulate in the face of this legal problem is that the nature of artificial intelligence in Cameroon is possibly dual through a certain nature and a possible nature.

Over a period, some scholars regarded artificial intelligence as a right, but recent perspectives have adopted a different viewpoint. The objective is establishing AI as a legal entity with personality. Regardless of legal characterization, implications remain the same: protective regulation necessity for artificial intelligence in both contexts. This paper explores legal facets, conflicts, and ethical considerations arising from artificial intelligence commercial applications. It is imperative to reflect on whether we have diligently considered associated potential costs and risks with this advanced commercial technology. While extensive literature on this subject exists, it is noteworthy most authors originate from European backgrounds. This subject requires greater dissemination so artificial intelligence is recognized as an important topic in Africa, especially Cameroon, deserving more substantial attention. Furthermore, given manifold artificial intelligence-derived benefits, logically inquiring how the legal framework accommodates its existence in Cameroon and various other African countries is logical. This paper's central query revolves around the interplay between artificial intelligence and law. In response,

---

[8] Law No. 2010/21 of December 21, 2010 governing electronic commerce in Cameroon, http://www.legicam.org; Law No. 2010/013 of December 21, 2010 governing electronic communications in Cameroon, http://www.legicam.org; Law No. 2010/012 of December 21, 2010 relating to cybersecurity and cybercrime. Law N° 2010/013 of December 21, 2010 governing electronic communications in Cameroon, http://www.legicam.org; Framework law N° 2011/012 of May 6, 2011 on consumer protection, http://www.minpostel.gov.cm; Decree N° 2012/1318/PM of May 22, 2012 setting the conditions and procedures for granting authorization to exercise electronic certification activity, www.minpostel.gov.cm; Decree N° 2012/1640/PM of June 14, 2012 setting the conditions for interconnection, access to electronic communications networks open to the public and sharing of infrastructure, www.minpostel.gov.cm Decree No. 2013/0399 /PM of February 27, 2013 establishing the terms of protection of consumers of electronic communication services http://www.legicam.org. Law N° 2015/018 of December 21, 2015 governing commercial activity in Cameroon. http://www.legicam.org At the sub-regional level, Directive N° 09/08/UEAC/133/CM/18 harmonizing the legal regimes for electronic activities in the CEMAC member states and Regulation N°2 /08/UEAC/13/CM/18 relating to the harmonization of regulations and regulatory policies for electronic communications within the CEMAC member states which entered into force on December 19, 2008, establishes the regulatory framework relating to the protection of data to be transposed in the different CEMAC member states including Cameroon. Without forgetting Book V of the AUDCG relating to the computerization of the trade and property credit register.

[9] In particular case in "Leading Judgments on Intellectual Property Rights Members of the African Intellectual Property Organization (1997–2018)," edited by Max Lambert Ndéma Elongué and Joseph Fometeu, published in 2023.

one can assert distinct legal categories exist wherein artificial intelligence can be situated (Sect. 1). Subsequently, thorough resulting implication examination becomes indispensable (Sect. 2).

1 The Existence of Legal Categories Accommodating AI

In the realm of law, there are two fundamental categories: persons and rights. It is crucial to ascertain whether artificial intelligence (AI) can be classified as either a person or a right. This distinction forms the *summa divisio* of legal categorization. It is argued that while AI can unquestionably be categorized as a right, the classification of AI as a person remains uncertain, albeit conceivable.

1.1 The Certainty of AI as a Right

Traditionally, private law delineates between two kind of rights: real rights and personal rights. Real rights pertain to rights over objects and must be respected by all. Conversely, personal rights constitute rights enforceable against specific persons. A pertinent question arises regarding how artificial intelligence fits within the framework of real rights, considering that AI systems can generate tangible or intangible outputs.

The term "property" encompasses both physical objects such as furniture and buildings, in addition to ownership rights held by individuals. Legally, it refers to rights an individual may possess in relation to objects or entities with economic value, including artificial intelligence creations. These objects are subject to property rights concerning digital technologies.[10] Property law, a branch of private law, delineates the types of objects subject to property rights, the acquisition, transfer, and termination of these rights, the rights and duties of property holders, and the obligations of other individuals toward property holders.

Unchanged since 1804, Article 544 of the Civil Code provides a legal definition of ownership as the inherent right "to enjoy and dispose of things in the most absolute manner", provided such use does not violate laws or regulations. Property rights exhibit multiple dimensions, including entitlement to unimpeded enjoyment of tangible assets, authority to transfer these property rights, or the privilege to receive specified monetary compensation. Delineating the property concept necessitates meticulously examining these attributes and their applicability to artificial intelligence, illuminating the various property rights classifications and the potential inclusion of AI within these categories.

Some property rights entail a duty of non-interference, while others involve corresponding obligations. Additionally, some property rights align with neither duties nor obligations. Consequently, a uniform definition encompassing all property rights remains elusive. This definitional flexibility proves particularly advantageous when considering integrating AI into the property rights realm. Therefore, recognizing a spectrum of property rights proves imperative, admitting that not all constitute real rights.

---

[10] Article 544 of the Civil Code.

Essentially, AI may include entitlements such as the right to unimpeded enjoyment of tangible assets, ability to transfer property rights, or prerogative to receive predetermined monetary amounts.[11]

This section explores several pertinent questions. First, it examines whether property rights inherently involve interactions between individuals or primarily concern rights over objects. This concept applies to AI, as prevailing legal theory posits that property rights do not exclusively concern objects. This theory becomes significant when contemplating AI with legal personality. Second, it analyzes whether intangible entities can constitute objects of property rights, since AI-generated outcomes may be tangible or intangible. This analysis suggests the emergence of property rights with varying attributes. When AI produces tangible outputs, property rights may arise, establishing relationships between individuals and physical entities. These property rights align with societal obligations of non-interference regarding the property. AI advent does not significantly impact these considerations. However, with certain intangible outputs, direct relationships emerge between individuals, as evidenced in contractual obligations including debts. Notably, AI can constitute the object of contracts. In these instances, the ownership right applies not to a person but the obligation imposed on that person, resulting in another form of property right—a right against the duty-bound individual. This concept lays the foundation for regarding AI as a property holder. Finally, it explores property rights unbound to duties or obligations, revealing a third category—unilateral property rights—where no corresponding duty or obligation exists. Examples include rights of rescission or recovering erroneous payments when recipients are unaware of errors. This concept suggests AI could fall within these three categories.

Hohfeld[12] argued that rights in rem essentially comprise individual rights enforceable against multiple individuals. Under this view, property rights in rem do not inherently concern objects but rather relationships between individuals. This theory underscores that all legal rights reflect actual interpersonal relationships, rendering all property rights fundamentally relations between people.

Contrary to the precedent view of rights in rem always involving interactions between individuals, Penner contends that property rights constitute relationships between individuals and entities or objects. Penner[13] distinguishes between individuals and objects, recognizing that only individuals can possess rights to things. He explicitly rejects the prevailing notion that property rights invariably represent interpersonal relationships.[14] Per Penner, all society members have a duty not to interfere with things they do not own. This non-interference duty applies regardless of whether entity rights are known. Penner's approach challenges the idea that real rights primarily involve direct connections between right-holders and duty-bearers.[15] He proposes recognizing the concept of "duty in rem," denoting "a duty not to interfere with others' property, or some state

---

[11] Boris Barraud, "Humanisme et intelligence artificielle: Théorie des droits de l'homme numérique," L'Harmattan, 2022, page 24.

[12] W Hohfeld, "Fundamental Legal Conceptions as Applied in Judicial Reasoning," Yale Law Journal, 1917, Volume 26, page 710.

[13] J Penner, "*The Idea of Property in Law*," Oxford University Press, 2000, Oxford.

[14] *Ibid*, p. 25.

[15] *Ibid*, p. 25.

to which all others are equally entitled." Regardless of theoretical perspective, AI can integrate into this discussion. Consequently, Civil Code Article 544 could apply to AI, accommodating its unique absolute, exclusive and perpetual characteristics. AI owners can enjoy various natural and cultural returns, in addition to AI-generated income. Moreover, AI can create intellectual property, including patents, trademarks, industrial designs, and more. AI can also receive protections through trade names, copyrights, and unfair competition regulations. These aspects will undergo analysis in the subsequent section.

In conclusion, to this first section, we believe that artificial intelligence can fulfill the three attributes of property, namely exclusive use, peaceful enjoyment and voluntary disposition. It can be placed in the category of furniture or immovable by destination depending on the affection that we make of it. Moreover, the terms of enjoyment can be individual or collective like any type of property.

Importantly, those seeking an alternative AI perspective could conceive of a different AI legal status. Absent legal precedent, this position remains prospective. Some authors advocate recognizing AI as a legal person, introducing another dimension to the discourse.

1.2   The Uncertainty of AI as a Person

As artificial intelligence (AI) systems continue advancing and playing more significant societal roles, two distinct rationales exist for considering AI legal personhood recognition. First, it ensures accountability when things go awry, addressing potential accountability gaps arising from AI systems' speed, autonomy, and opacity, as Chesterman notes. Second, it provides a framework for rewarding successful AI. A growing body of literature explores intellectual property ownership issues regarding AI-created works.

The underlying debate centers on whether AI personhood stems from instrumental or intrinsic rationales. This paper section begins by addressing the immediate challenge of determining whether some AI legal personality form could fill liability voids or benefit legal systems. Based on historical precedents related to corporations and other artificial legal entities, most legal systems could likely grant AI systems some personality form. More intriguing questions involve whether they should do so and what specific attributes this personality might entail.[16]

Legal personality represents a foundational concept in soft law, prospective law, or law generally. Determining who can act and be subject to rights and duties constitutes a fundamental precursor to nearly every legal issue. In practice, most worldwide legal systems recognize two legal person types: natural and juridical. Natural persons gain recognition by virtue of their humanity.[17] Granting AI legal personality aims to ensure that someone can enjoy AI benefits. An expanding body of research examines AI system-related intellectual property ownership perspectives, debating whether personality is

---

[16] Boris Barraud, "Humanisme et intelligence artificielle: Théorie des droits de l'homme numérique," L'Harmattan, 2022, page 334.

[17] This assumes, of course, that there is agreement on the definition of "human" and terms like "birth" and "death". Refer to the work of N Naffine, "Who Are Law's Persons? From Cheshire Cats to Responsible Subjects," Modern Law Review, 2003, Volume 66, pages 346.

conferred for instrumental or genuine reasons. This paper section starts by tackling the immediate challenge of whether some legal personality form could address liability gaps or benefit adopting legal systems.[18]

Scholars and legal reform bodies have already proposed attributing some AI legal personality form to address liability issues. For instance, driverless car situations, where automated driving system behaviors may not be human-controlled or owner-predictable, necessitate considering automated driving system entity legal personality. Some scholars have further suggested establishing procedures for prosecuting AI "criminals," with "punishment" provisions involving reprogramming or, in extreme cases, destruction.[19]

Various theories have been proposed explaining corporate personality concepts, also potentially applicable to AI. The aggregate theory, often called the contractarian or sym-bolist theory, posits that corporations constitute legal devices enabling groups of individuals to collectively reflect their organization in legal interactions with other parties. However, this theory may have limited AI system applicability.[20]

The different personalist and corporate theories, despite distinct historical antecedents, ultimately converge on a common premise: corporations acquire legal personality through deliberate legal system endowment.[21] This concept resonates with an 1819 American Supreme Court observation characterizing a corporation as "an artificial being, invisible, intangible, and existing only in contemplation of law." Legal personality conferment serves specific policy objectives, like promoting entrepreneurial endeavors or enhancing legal system cohesion and stability, often by ensuring entity perpetual existence. Consequently, these theories exhibit flexible characters amenable to extension for Artificial Intelligence (AI) system inclusion.

Historically, legal personality was explicitly granted through charters or legislative acts, but this formal process gradually evolved into a mere procedural formality by the twentieth century.[22] These positivist perspectives closely align with legislative and judicial practices regarding legal personality recognition and hold potential for its expansion to AI systems.

The realist theory, favored by many scholars, posits that societies comprise objectively real entities existing independently before legal systems attribute personality to them. Under this view, societies may have members but act independently, with actions not directly attributable to members. The realist theory resonates more with theorists and sociologists than legislators and judges, suggesting that legal personality is not merely granted but earned.[23]

---

[18] André Akam Akam and Voudwe Barkreo, "Droit des sociétés commerciales OHAHA," L'Harmattan, 2017, page 18.

[19] Refer to the work of G. Hallevy, "Liability for Crimes Involving Artificial Intelligence Systems," Springer 2015; Y. Hu, "Robot Criminals" University of Michigan Journal of Law Reform, 2019, Volume 52, page 487.

[20] N. Banteka, *Artificially Intelligent Persons,* Houston Law Review, 2020 Volume 58.

[21] Refer to the work of Boris Barraud, "Humanisme et intelligence artificielle: Théorie des droits de l'homme numérique," L'Harmattan, 2022, page 274.

[22] G. Dari-Mattiacci and others, "The Emergence of the Corporate Form," Journal of Law, Economics, and Organization, 2017, Volume 33, page 193.

[23] S.M. Watson, "The Corporate Legal Person," Journal of Corporate Law Studies, 2019, Volume 19, page 137.

This section allows us to retain the conclusion that the consideration of artificial intelligence as a person remains conditioned by the choice of the legislator. In addition, its humanization or the violations of fundamental rights likely to result will depend on the different choices of the Cameroonian legislator.

Ultimately, the personality question is binary—either recognized or not. However, personality legal status specifics remain unclear. Whether an AI system truly deserves legal person recognition or the extent to which a state's AI rights and duties granting would achieve recognition still represents legislative choice matters. Essentially, each legislator will determine what AI represents. Despite AI's potential dual legal status nature, with property recognition appearing more certain than personhood, individual legislator decisions remain pending. Nevertheless, this potential AI dual nature holds significant consequences warranting further exploration.

2   The Presence of Protective Rules for AI

We are on the brink of the age of artificial intelligence (AI). AI is already ubiquitous, appearing in various contexts, from medical diagnosis and driving directions to stock trading and social networking, and even in law enforcement. As William Gibson aptly put it, "The future is already here, but it remains unpredictable." Therefore, it is likely that AI will have a profound impact on all economic, social, and political sectors, although the full extent of this impact remains uncertain.[24] When contemplating AI, it is crucial to heed the observation of another visionary, Roy Amara, who suggested that we should focus more on the long-term impacts rather than underestimating them and placing too much emphasis on short-term effects.

In light of the legal categorizations discussed earlier, it is essential to consider the rules that may apply to AI depending on its classification. To avoid confusion and account for the specific rules associated with each classification, we will examine conceivable rules for AI as property and foreseeable rules for AI as a legal person.

2.1   The Conceivable Rules Applied to AI as Property

Treating AI as property enables protecting it against infringement like other property forms. Common tangible property rules can also apply to AI. However, exploring intellectual property rule applicability to AI proves vital.

As AI technology investment surges, companies increasingly seek and enforce AI invention patents. Worldwide, AI-related patent applications are rising, with many patents already granted. For instance, the United States Patent and Trademark Office (USPTO) has granted thousands of AI technology patents. USPTO's 2019 publication of new patent eligibility guidelines likely contributed to increased AI patent grant rates.[25]

---

[24] James X. Dempsey, "Artificial Intelligence: An Introduction to the Legal, Policy and Ethical Issues," Berkeley Center for Law & Technology, August 10, 2020, page 13.

[25] Mark Nowotarski's article titled "AI Patents Make a Comeback at USPTO, Finance Patents Are Still Struggling," IP Watchdog, March 26, 2019.

Intellectual property rights enforcement efforts are also gaining momentum in the jurisdiction of the African Intellectual Property Organization (OAPI).[26] Judicial authorities within OAPI member states are gradually shaping intellectual property litigation through interpreting key concepts enshrined in the Bangui Agreement and annexes. Notably, these interpretations have clarified definitions related to likelihood of confusion, intellectual work, originality, novelty, trade names, counterfeiting, seizure, and unfair competition—areas applicable to AI.

The Bangui Agreement constitutes the uniform IP law applicable to all OAPI member states, effectively becoming each state's national IP law. The Agreement established the OAPI office, centralizing procedures and allowing applications submitted to OAPI to be deemed nationally filed in all member states. This centralization streamlines IP protection processes and ensures uniformity across member states.

AI could potentially qualify for patent protection if meeting certain legal criteria defined in Article 2(1) of the Bangui Agreement on the Recognition of African Registration (ABR-2015). Under this article, an invention is patentable if it is new, involves an inventive step, and is industrially applicable. Additionally, an invention can relate to a product, process, or use. All three criteria must be satisfied for a patent grant.[27] AI has the potential to meet these criteria. For instance, an invention is considered new if not anticipated by prior art, as established by Article 3 of Annex 1 of ABR-1999.

Moreover, AI-generated inventions may also be eligible for trademark registration. Trademark protection hinges on avoiding likelihood of confusion. Article 6(3) of Annex III to ABR-2015 prohibits reproducing, using, or affixing a trademark if likely creating public confusion. This article stipulates that likelihood of confusion must exist for these prohibitions to apply. Article 3(b) contains the same condition, prohibiting registering a trademark resembling an earlier mark to the extent of misleading or confusing.[28] AI-generated trademarks could potentially receive protection under these rules.

---

[26] The African Intellectual Property Organization (OAPI) is an intergovernmental international organization specializing in the field of intellectual property (IP). OAPI was officially established on September 13, 1962, operating under the initial Libreville Agreement, which was later revised and renamed the Bangui Agreement. The organization's headquarters are situated in Yaoundé, Cameroon. OAPI comprises a total of 17 member states, including Benin, Burkina Faso, Cameroon, Central African Republic, Chad, Comoros, Congo, Côte d'Ivoire, Equatorial Guinea, Gabon, Guinea, Guinea-Bissau, Mali, Mauritania, Niger, Senegal, and Togo.

[27] To further exploration of this topic, you can refer to the following sources: J. Schmidt-Szalewski and J.-L. Pierre, "*Droit de la propriété industrielle,*" 4th edition. Paris: Litec, 2007, page 37 and onwards.

[28] To further explore this topic, you may want to refer to the case of "Bosnalijek Pharmaceutical and Chemical Industry Co. v. Sanofi-Aventis SA," as outlined in Decision No. 157 dated April 26, 2012, by the OAPI High Commission of Appeal. Detailed information about this case can be found in the book "Leading Judgments on Intellectual Property Rights Members of the African Intellectual Property Organization (1997–2018)," edited by Max Lambert Ndéma Elongué and Joseph Fometeu, published in 2023, particularly on pages 38 and 39.

In contrast, U.S. law raises open questions about many AI patent validities. Courts have ruled abstract ideas ineligible for patent protection unless transformed into patent-eligible applications through an "inventive concept."[29] An inventive concept can arise from non-conventional and non-generic known element arrangements. However, using a computer to execute an abstract idea remains insufficient for patent eligibility.[30] The Mayo Collaborative Servs. v. Prometheus Labs., Inc. case reaffirmed that laws of nature or physical phenomena are unpatentable, even if their discovery leads to revolutionary improvements in diagnosis or care.[31]

The protection of artificial intelligence as an asset makes it possible to boost and consolidate the three characteristics of property resulting from the definition of article 544 of the civil code. It also makes it possible to recognize the protection resulting from copyright, patents, name, competition or that relating to goodwill in particular.

In copyright law, long-established precedent deems computer programs copyrightable but not the algorithms used in them. A separate question emerges regarding whether intellectual property protections should extend to AI-created works. This perspective necessitates granting AI legal personality, with implications potentially extending to recognizing AI creativity.

2.2 The Foreseeable Rules Applied to AI as a Person

Granting AI legal personality raises questions about what rights and obligations should be attributed to AI entities. This issue mirrors ongoing struggles for equal rights among various natural person groups, including women, ethnic/religious minorities, and other disadvantaged populations.[32]

One approach to AI legal personality could involve granting rights without accompanying obligations. This approach was used[33], for instance, in recognizing legal personhood for nature, as seen in Ecuadorian legislation.[34] Critics might argue such "personality" merely constitutes a legal construct addressing standing issues, allowing human

---

[29] Indeed, the cases you mentioned, "Alice Corp. v. CLS Bank Int'l, 134 S. Ct. 2347 (2014)" and "Electric Power Group, LLC v. Alstom S.A., 830 F.3d 1350 (Fed. Cir. 2016)," are notable decisions in the realm of patent law, particularly regarding the eligibility of software and business method patents. In Europe, Article 52 of the European Patent Convention establishes a similar principle. It stipulates that "schemes, rules, and methods for performing mental acts, playing games or doing business, and programs for computers" are not considered to be inventions eligible for patent protection.

[30] Content Extraction & Transmission LLC v. Wells Fargo Bank, N.A., 776 F.3d 1343, 1347–48 (Fed. Cir. 2014).

[31] Ariosa Diagnostics, Inc. v. Sequenom, 788 F.3d 1371 (Fed. Cir. 2015).

[32] JJ Bryson, ME Diamantis and TD Grant, "Of, for, and by the People: The Legal Lacuna of Synthetic Persons," Artificial Intelligence and Law, 2017, Volume 25, page280.

[33] Constitution of the Republic of Ecuador, articles 71–74.

[34] C Rodgers, "A New Approach to Protecting Ecosystems," Environmental Law Review, 2017, Volume19, page 266. New Zealand has established trustees to represent the interests of environmental entities granted legal personality.

individuals to act on a non-human rights holder's behalf.[35] However, this approach may not align with reasons for considering AI systems as legal persons.[36]

The concept of legal personality is fundamental to law, with terms like "person," "legal person," "natural person," "subject," "legal personality," and "legal capacity" regularly employed. Notably, these categories did not emerge from a single legal system but evolved over centuries through conceptual developments.

The term "persona" was used in various ancient Roman writings but initially lacked specific legal meaning. For example, Gaius mentioned "persona" as encompassing all human beings, whether free or enslaved.[37] Over time, "persona" evolved to mean "part," "role," "function," or "image." Not until the 16th century did legal scholars begin associating "persona" with universities and their elements. By then, "persona" had become central to legally analyzing the relationship between a human physical being and human legal subject.

In an information society context, a compelling argument exists for expanding private property entities beyond human individuals. Denying such entities' existence or potential legal status is becoming increasingly untenable. Artificial intelligence possesses characteristics potentially qualifying it as a new civil relations subject.

Currently, extensive discussion surrounds whether AI could qualify as a legal relationship subject. Researchers like Kleinberg[38] have recognized algorithms' extraordinary promise in addressing issues like discrimination. Thus, extending legal personality to AI, robots, algorithms, and other phenomena possessing certain legal relations participation-enabling characteristics seems plausible.

In intellectual property, patents can be viewed as exclusive invention rights. These inventions can comprise products or processes offering novel ways of performing actions or solving technical problems.[39] Patent holders can exclude others from making, selling, or using the patented invention for a limited period. AI-enabled systems are capable of performing functions and even generating inventions typically resulting from human cognitive processes. As Liza Vertinsky suggests, these machines can produce potentially patentable inventions.

The European Parliamentary Committee has acknowledged AI systems could potentially surpass human intelligence in various functions. However, AI systems' high autonomy level raises questions about how these entities control and manage their actions. Due to their significant autonomy enabling operation with minimal human intervention, protecting patent rights is essential when discussing AI systems.

AI-enabled systems can generate "discoveries during early research stages based on their capabilities". However, obtaining patents for such discoveries presents challenges, especially in satisfying patentability criteria. Patents require inventions to be

---

[35] See "Liability for Artificial Intelligence and Other Emerging Digital Technologies," EU Expert Group on Liability and New Technologies 2019, page 38.

[36] S. Chesterman, "Artificial intelligence and the limits of legal personality," Cambridge University Press for the British Institute of International and Comparative Law. June 26, 2023.

[37] Saveliev & Kofanova, 1997.

[38] Swapnil Tripathi and Chandni Ghatak, "Artificial Intelligence and Intellectual Property Law" Christ University Law Journal, 2018, Volume 7, N° 1, page 83.

[39] World Intellectual Property Organization (WIPO), "Patents,".

novel, involve an inventive step, and be industrially applicable.[40] Achieving novelty and inventive steps with AI-generated inventions can be particularly challenging.

Determining novelty is complicated for AI systems, as they can access prior art but may lack capacity to evaluate invention genuine novelty.[41] Similarly, establishing an inventive step can prove challenging if AI systems operate based on pre-defined objectives rather than demonstrating human-like creative judgment. The technology requires further advancement to equip AI systems with judgment call abilities in novel situations, currently a significant hurdle.

Furthermore, upon examining computer program patentability cases, it becomes evident that courts have denied patents to programs primarily due to their mechanical nature rather than degree of inventiveness.[42] This holds great importance given that AI fundamentally relies on computer programs crafted for specific functions, albeit with variations introduced by human inventors. The next section will elucidate the human versus AI inventor distinction, further underscoring AI-generated program patent grant challenges.

In contrast, the United States Copyright Office has explicitly stated it "will not register works produced by a machine or mere mechanical process that operates randomly or automatically without any creative input or intervention from a human author."[43] Determining the requisite creative input or human intervention extent to render machine output copyright eligible remains a case-by-case matter. Several other countries take a more expansive approach, extending copyright protection to machine-generated output.[44]

A separate yet relevant question involves owned intellectual property (IP) work created by a machine.[45] Numerous countries' copyright statutes unambiguously specify the computer-generated work author as "the person by whom the necessary arrangements for the creation of the work are undertaken."

However, countries like India have eliminated the rigid prerequisite that only computer programs coupled with new hardware qualify as patent eligible. In instances where an AI-enabled system generates software applicable to generic machines, practical utility is achieved, potentially spanning multiple industries. This satisfies the industrial applicability prerequisite for patentability. Generally, the current legal framework and guidelines require streamlining to facilitate AI-related invention patent grants.

Like no one, artificial intelligence can benefit from different personality rights, depending on the content that the legislator has given it.

In conclusion, AI presents multifaceted global legal landscape challenges, a circumstance not unique to Cameroon. The core issue revolves around what legal status can be

---

[40] The Patents Act, § 2(I), 1970 (India); The Patents Act, § 2(ja), 1970 (India); The Patents Act, § 2(ac), 1970 (India).

[41] Swapnil Tripathi and Chandni Ghatak, "Artificial Intelligence and Intellectual Property Law" Christ University Law Journal 2018, Volume 7, No. 1, page 88.

[42] Bilsk v. Kappos, 561 U.S. 593 (2010).

[43] U.S. Copyright Office, "The Compendium of U.S. Copyright Office Practices," Chapter 300, § 313.2 (revised September 29, 2017).

[44] Robert C. Denicola, "Ex Machina: Copyright Protections for Computer-Generated Works," Rutgers University Law Review 2016, Volume 69, pages 251–282.

[45] Andres Guadamuz, "Artificial intelligence and copyright", WIPO Magazine, October 2017.

attributed to AI entities. While AI legal personality conferral likelihood is growing, such recognition may be reserved for "strong" AI or superintelligence, characterized by self-awareness and the ability to make decisions based on personal experience. Additionally, it is presupposed that superintelligence will possess its own subjective experiences.

Attributing artificial intelligence subjectivity enabling legal relationship engagement does not inherently contravene established conventions acknowledging legal fictions' presence within the legal domain. Recognizing artificial intelligence legal personality will introduce a new legal entity, necessitating specialized statutes tailored to its unique characteristics. This acknowledgment will also encompass recognizing specific rights, including property rights and entitlements to AI-generated intellectual property. Property regulations could contemplate endowing artificial intelligence with distinct property rights, empowering AI entities to assume corresponding obligation responsibility, thereby streamlining dispute resolution.

Pending full-fledged artificial intelligence rights conferral resolution, specific assets can be entrusted to AI entities on a trust basis. In such scenarios, a distinct 'robot-agent' entity emerges, vested with executing particular business functions on the owner's behalf capability. Such arrangements can limit owner liability regarding obligations stemming from assets placed in trust.

Regarding creative works generated by artificial intelligence, it is conceivable to recognize intellectual property rights for AI-exclusive outcomes devoid of human intervention, thus acknowledging AI as an 'electronic personality.' Such recognition would apply in cases where AI is solely responsible for work creation.

However, as previously emphasized, AI's ultimate legal status will hinge on legislative decisions. Consequently, this paper raises fundamental AI legal nature questions. Any determinations made must carefully consider corporate and public policy implications, in addition to ethical considerations. It is paramount to bear in mind that life constitutes an inherently open, intricate, and unpredictable system. Regarding AI, the novel analogy underscores pausing to ponder not only whether we can create such thinking machines, but also whether we should.

Indicative References

Alekseev, S. (1981). *General theory of law*. Moscow: Legal Literature;

N. Banteka, *'Artificially Intelligent Persons'* (2020) 58 HousLR (forthcoming);

B. Barraud, (2022) *Humanisme et intelligence artificielle: Théorie des droits de l'homme numérique*, L'Harmattan;

Baranov, O. (2017). "The Internet of Things and Artificial Intelligence: Origins of the Problem of Legal Regulation". In *IT Law: Problems and Prospects for Development in Ukraine*. Lviv: National University of Lviv Polytechnic;

Borysova, V., Spasybo-Fateyeva, I., & Yarotsky V. (2007). *Civil law of Ukraine*. Kyiv: Yurinkom Inter. Bridy, A. (2016). "The Evolution of authorship: work made by code". *Columbia Journal of Law & Arts*, 39, 395–401;

Čerka, P., Grigienė, J. & Sirbikytėb G. (2017). "Is it possible to grant legal personality to artificial intelligence software systems?" *Computer Law & Security Review*, 33 (5), 685–699;

A. Chavanne and J.-J. Burst (1990) *Droit de la propriété industrielle*, 3rd edition, Paris: Dalloz;

S. Chesterman, 'Artificial Intelligence and the Problem of Autonomy' (2020) 1 Notre Dame *Journal of Emerging Technologies* 210;

S. Chesterman, 'Through a Glass, Darkly: Artificial Intelligence and the Problem of Opacity' (2021) *AJCL* (forthcoming);

Duarenus, F. (1554). "Epistola ad Andream Guillartum de ratione docendi, discendique Morkhat, P. (2018). "Intelligent robot as the author of a work or invention". *Legislation and law*, 8, 172–177;

M.L. Ndéma Elongué and J. Fometeu, (2023) *Leading Judgments on Intellectual Property Rights Members of the African Intellectual Property Organization (1997–2018)* OMPI;

Nekit, K., Kolodin, D. & Fedorov, V. (2020). "Personal data protection and liability for damage in the field of the Internet of things". *Juridical Tribune*, 10(1), 80–93;

J. Raynard, E. Py and P. Trefigny (2016) *Droit de la propriété industrielle.* Paris: LexisNexis;

Pearlman, R. (2018). "Recognizing artificial intelligence (AI) as authors and inventors under U.S. Intellectual Property Law". *Richmond Journal of Law & Technology*, 24(2), i-38;

Resource-Constrained Networks and Cybersecurity

A Gamification Architecture to Enhance Phishing Awareness

Jean Emmanuel Ntsama[1,4](✉) ⬤, Claude Fachkha[2] ⬤, Philippe Brice Owomo[3] ⬤, and Adrian Chickagwe Focho[3] ⬤

[1] Department of Mathematics and Computer Science, Faculty of Science, University of Ngaoundéré, Ngaoundéré, Cameroon
`j.ntsama@cycomai.com`
[2] College of Engineering and IT, University of Dubai, Dubai, UAE
`cfachkha@ud.ac.ae`
[3] Higher Technical Teachers Training College, Department of Computer Engineering, University of Bamenda, Bamenda, Cameroon
`{philowono,adrian.sigipes}@minesecdrh.cm`
[4] Cybersecurity With Computational and Artificial Intelligence Group (CyComAI), Yaoundé, Cameroon

Abstract. The development of emerging technologies, such as the Internet of Things and Artificial Intelligence, has provided a spectrum of online and remote solutions in various fields. However, the proliferation of targeted cyberattacks (e.g., phishing) against such technologies has made our assets and data relatively vulnerable to adversaries and hackers. Considering the higher number of victims, it is necessary to evaluate technical solutions that limit the development of a critical mass of people who can participate in collective resistance to such a phenomenon. Raising awareness is, undoubtedly, a way to prevent as many people as possible from falling prey. Given the changes in the different educational theories, we must seek the best way to sensitize cyberspace users to their varied profiles and needs. This study develops an educational gamification architecture that can ensure commitment, motivation, and consideration of a learner's profile. Subsequently, the problem of the best didactic means is posed with openness to the integration of artificial intelligence, the choice of the type of gamification, and the technologies that can contribute to ensuring that everyone is competent to enable each person to escape from traps of phishing, regardless of age or level of mastery of digital tools, or education. The proposed approach was evaluated according to its robustness and flexibility. The rest of the work consists of integrating the conversational aspect through chatbots.

Keywords: cyberspace · architecture · victimization · competence · gamification · phishing

© ICST Institute for Computer Sciences, Social Informatics and Telecommunications Engineering 2024
Published by Springer Nature Switzerland AG 2024. All Rights Reserved
F. Tchakounte et al. (Eds.): SAFER-TEA 2023, LNICST 566, pp. 37–57, 2024.
https://doi.org/10.1007/978-3-031-56396-6_3

1 Introduction

COVID-19 has helped to demonstrate the urgency of linking many structures, organizations, and countries to technological and scientific revolutions. It is in this wake that the rush observed towards digitalization is located without a real preparation for this mutation in most cases. Prodigious developments in the Internet of Things (IoT) and innovative technologies such as Artificial Intelligence (AI) are increasingly having an undeniable impact on teaching methods. Access to the common space of communication represented by cyberspace is not without its pitfalls. Said spaces are currently experiencing the proliferation of criminals of another kind. While taking advantage of ignorance or naivety, some users of cyberspace, on the fringes of lawful activities, perform increasingly sophisticated criminal actions by multiplying cyberattacks [1]. The cybercrimes encountered include infiltrations, malicious applications for ransoming systems and networks, theft of sensitive information, system paralysis, and financial embezzlement.

In Cameroon, a study conducted in 2021 by Ntsama et al. [2], revealed that crimes related to embezzlement of money were the most frequent, representing a portion of 70.51%. In addition to the technical detection and control solutions [3–5] which have not eradicated yet the phenomenon, it is necessary to use awareness-raising solutions, whose merit reduces victimization and prepares a critical mass for collective resistance to the phenomenon that is taking on a worrying scale. It is not surprising to agree with the report of the National Agency for Information and Communication Technologies (ANTIC) that severe losses were recorded, e.g., 12.2 billion CFA francs [6] loss for the Cameroonian economy in 2019.

Digitization with the race towards increasingly high-performance digital terminals exposes people to risk, but also augurs great prospects in solutions that offer everyone the possibility of learning or raising awareness of the situation without restriction. The problem of the best didactic offer to ensure user awareness remains.

Currently, techno-pedagogy offers scripting as a means of improving the transmission of content [7]. Gamification, on the other hand, introduces playful elements into a non-playful learning environment to increase motivation, create emulation, and captivate learners [8, 9, 10]. The use of automatic learning techniques [11] can bring the didactic approach closer to the learner's experience. Emphasis is on the level of awareness and skill development to enable learners to avoid easy prey. Furthermore, as cyberspace is not a domain reserved for a few elites, the gamification tools and architectures available often target specific segments of the population: class craft [12]. Cybermuna [13], PAP [14], and cyber awareness/girl scout at home [15]. In addition, these proposals have limits on aspects concerning the target of awareness, functionalities, and the didactic approach that considers the level of psychological development [16, 17]. At the same time, we observed the failure to consider the profile and needs of the learner [18], as well as the time taken to show competence through scenarios. Raising awareness using easily accessible tools must begin early. However, the thorny problem of the best didactic means allows awareness to even lead to real learning to escape the increasingly sophisticated traps of cyber criminals.

The work carried out enables the target to escape the increasingly sophisticated traps of criminals who threaten the digital economy and contributes as follows:

- Modeling an architecture of educational gamification which is either contained or user-centered;
- Putting together innovative didactic and pedagogic approaches to facilitate awareness for any user;
- Combining robustness and flexibility in the use of technologies;
- Enhancing the learning process through awareness, evaluation, and remediation.

The rest of the paper is organized as follows: Sect. 2 provides an overview on the background, with a review of educational theories and on existing gamification solutions in cybersecurity. In Sect. 3, we propose an architecture that evokes the methodology, the global view of the system, the exploited gamification, its general structure, its navigation scheme, its system operation, and the modeling of score evaluation. We propose in Sect. 4, a prototype in which we evaluate the described architecture of the system. Finally, Sect. 5 provides a conclusion and perspectives.

2 Background

2.1 Educational Theories

Many advances have been made in educational theories. We have observed a succession of numerous didactic approaches.

Behaviorism, in which appropriate stimuli lead to possible results as a proof of possible assimilation [19]. Behaviorists will be inclined to use exercisers, quizzes, educational games, and/or animations when designing and carrying out distance training. However, this theory seems too poor to be sustainable [20]. Figure 1 represents behaviorism theory.

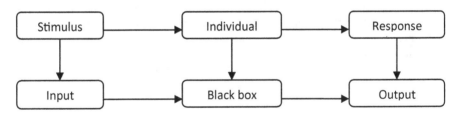

Fig. 1. Functional diagram of behaviorism

Cognitivism believes that the learning process cannot be limited to conditional recording. It is necessary to resort to strategies to manage memory [21]. Strategies depend on different types of knowledge to be developed, namely declarative, procedural, and conditional knowledge [37]. Constructivism, which admits that knowledge is acquired through construction. This model promotes not only the introduction of tools that offer great autonomy to students to progress at their own pace but also the development of computer-assisted problems [22]. Socio-constructivism, through which knowledge is acquired by construction and social interactions [23]. In addition, while giving a child a learning environment in which he offers the best of himself, the teacher's choices tend to encourage group work [24].

Connectivism, which, through the development of networks, has favored the prolif-eration of learning platforms, such as e-learning, distance education, and gamification [25, 36]. Many theories have militated in favor of the place of the game in the learning process. The said process should remain playful and engaging.

We can thus distinguish between the following: 1) serious games, where we must learn through a game to improve the learning experience of the target; and 2) gamification, which uses elements taken from the game in a non-gaming context to entertain the teach-ing/learning process [26, 27], as well as the development of interactions, engagement, and motivation [28]. Educational theories are summarized in Fig. 2.

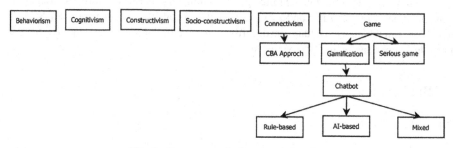

Fig. 2. Taxonomy of educational theories

Nowadays, apart from the face-to-face learning mode, e-learning, there is also dis-tance education that complements the face-to-face mode through the virtual class. Its contribution establishes skills developed in face-to-face part-time class with the stigmas of the context of COVID 19, through lessons, exercises, and revisions. However, distance education does not provide the possibility of making the teaching or learning process fun by introducing elements drawn from the context of the game to increase motivation, commitment, and emulation, such as points, progress bars, leadership boards, awards and avatars or images. To be close to the reality of the learner by a method of proximity pedagogy, it is necessary to consider his profile. In addition, the orientation towards digitalization of teaching was further explored. The boom observed in the use of digital terminals is part of the race for digitalization and, at the same time, offers a point of vulnerability. At the same time, these terminals can facilitate access to an awareness solution, regardless of the situation and profile.

2.2 Current Contributions in the Fields of Gamification and Cybersecurity

Many authors have developed gamified systems for one domain or another with a pre-determined target. The same has been done in the field of cybersecurity. The aim is to sensitize users of cyberspace about cybersecurity, and how to escape from attacks.

Through a web application, some have contributed to improvement of learner's knowledge of phishing through the practice of phishing (PAP) approach [14]. This app-roach is an animated website implementing a structural gamified system, with sound and animation for attractiveness, but also through its menus (basic knowledge, avoid phish-ing, useful tips, explore more about phishing), screenshots, boards, and games based on

MCQs segmented according to the profile associates, game elements such as points and scores. However, this game is not segmented into ages levels of the child's psychological development. There is also a lack of diagnostic assessments to verify prerequisites; the interactive side is very little perceptible outside the game. Lack of a progressive measurement of the evolution of learning and lack of ranking of the best to activate intrinsic motivation.

The Classcraft website is not dedicated to cybercrime; however, only secondary education is targeted. There is no extension to other levels of learner's psychological development (mental age). The way of thinking can be dependent of the target psychological age [12].

The Cybermuna website is committed to the protection of young people online through the training of students under 21-year-old, teachers, and parents using an interactive web application. This site carries out a diagnostic assessment of knowledge, targeting QUIZ of students: from 8 to 16 years old and under 21 years old. Teachers like parents are targeted by the same QUIZ. The user chooses one of the above profiles for learning. Online resources are downloadable, and the score is given at the end of QUIZ [11]. Note that it is not only students, parents, and teachers who require cybersecurity training. There are also uneducated people who also suffer from the effects of cyber criminality with the development of social engineering tricks in cyberspace. In this solution, it is not possible to clearly visualize the step-by-step progress of learners during the learning process. Such a deficiency can result in a lack of intrinsic motivation and emulation. Moreover, this proposal was not sufficiently interactive. However, learner progress cannot be measured as the learning process evolves. The score was given only at the end of QUIZ.

The site girl scout objective is to train young girls in cybersecurity by helping them deal with any attack by ransomware, phishing, passwords, game security, and video call security. It includes a menu of access to PDF resources, video courses of procedures, and the possible registration for a diploma as intrinsic motivation [15]. However, the need for cybersecurity training goes beyond the scope of young girls alone, even if this solution meets the need. Learner's progress is not implemented. We are not rewarded for the progress made: extrinsic motivation. Intrinsic motivation was found to be weak. We do not perceive progressive evolution through any passage from one level to another. Absence of diagnostic and formative evaluation to appreciate skills acquired by the target.

Recent research on "Cybersecurity Educational Games: Theoretical Framework," where the development of games for cybersecurity is to help individuals and organizations strengthen their defense against cybercrime [2, 29]. The finding is that the effectiveness of the existing games is low. This article aims to guide the design and testing of more effective cybersecurity educational games by developing a theoretical framework with independents variable as follows:

- Game characteristics: What contributes to the usefulness, interactivity, playfulness, or attractiveness of a game;
- Game context: Factors determining how a game is used, target audience, skills involved, history;
- Learning theory used: behaviorism, cognitivism, humanism, socio-constructivism;

- User characteristics: gender, age, computer experience, knowledge, perception.

Dependent variables with five characteristics: information, content, strategic knowledge, desire to learn, time spent, and behavior change.

This proposal does not consider satisfaction, emotion, immersion, and the level of the learner at the beginning of learning, which constitute important aspects of the evaluation of the solution.

In its first version, the PASEA platform (Practices against Social Engineering Attacks), was an implementation of an architecture of an educational gamification platform for cybercrimes through phishing [30]. The acquisition and improvement of learner's performance require the introduction of gamification elements [8, 9, 10]. However, the contribution of chatbots would have allowed this platform to adapt to the situation and specificity of a particular user and, therefore, to his profile. Missing Artificial Intelligence (AI) assets would have made it possible to adapt the training offered to users [2, 12, 23].

All these contributions show that either many online platforms reveal their limits in terms of target audience, functionalities, or didactic theories underlying the pedagogical approach adopted, which may not integrate the development of real skills. Either the integration of aspects of the subject's level of psychological development or ease of access in the context of the high cost of connections. Align the training offer increasingly with the needs or profile of the user. The time taken to show competency also needs to be considered.

The major objective is to provide an intelligent, adaptive, accessible, and flexible gamification architecture. It offers all guarantees of successful awareness raising and the development of proven and recognized skills. This is how we can prepare a critical population mass capable of accessing cyberspace without the risk of falling prey to cybercriminals. It is important that the architecture of awareness gamification adapts and aligns with the daily situation and non-static needs of cyberspace users. Any awareness strategy should be based on the target profile.

The use of automatic learning techniques can make it possible to bring the didactic approach closer to the learner's experience [11, 12, 31]. Companies must emphasize the level of awareness and their competence to act in a professional context to avoid being easy prey. Moreover, since cyberspace is not a domain reserved for a few elites, young people would benefit from starting awareness very early with easily accessible tools to protect themselves and thus create a critical mass ready for collective resistance to the phenomenon. However, the thorny problem of the best didactic means and robust architecture in an awareness platform to even lead to real learning to escape the increasingly sophisticated traps of cybercriminals.

3 Architectural Proposal

3.1 Methodology

To carry out this work, we followed the diagram shown in Fig. 3:

Existing studies allow us to investigate the existing to carry out an analysis of the needs and possible functionalities of the future system [31], to identify the strengths and

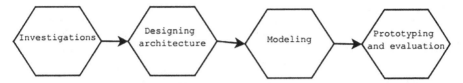

Fig. 3. Scheme of the methodology

weaknesses of existing gamification platforms in cybersecurity, and to identify future users and their expectations.

The choice of architecture allows starting from the limits of the existing one to proceed to the choice of the type and relevant elements of gamification.

Architecture modeling to proceed with the development of the system architecture.

Implementation and deployment of a prototype and evaluation, host a prototype online.

3.2 System Overview

This system aims to raise learner's awareness of cybercrime related to phishing, fake news, existing detection/fighting solutions against phishing, system/network security, and data security (Fig. 4).

Each aspect of raising awareness is based on the acquisition of resources, competent actions, and evaluation/remediation. After a lightened learning process, because of the different targets, the evaluation puts the learner in a situation that encourages him to exercise the skill. This approach does not fail to maintain a learner's interest and commitment. This is found in the gamification of the elements drawn from the game, such as points, scores, progress bars, and leaderboards. It is also relevant to add elements of artificial intelligence to this environment to get closer to the learner's profile, simulate scenarios, or adopt a virtual teacher as shown in Fig. 4a or Fig. 4b.

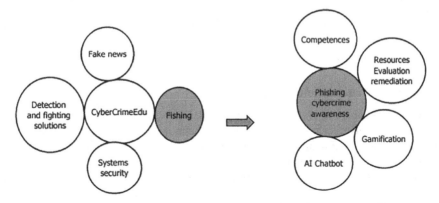

Fig. 4. (a) System overview diagram. (b) Phishing Cybercrime awareness diagram

3.3 Gamification Exploited

In this section, we presents choices made for the proposed system. It is the general structure of the modeled platform.

For Abdoul Basit et al., gamification has five stages: identifying the target audience and context, defining learning objectives, structuring the experience, identifying resources, and applying gamification elements [29].

According to Kapp (2012), there are two types of gamifications. Structural gamification or game elements are chosen to avoid altering the content [32]. Only the structure of the elements around the learning content resembles a game.

Content-centric and user-centric gamification. The content is adapted to the user and may look like a game, but not completely become one.

However, gamification can be mixed, that is, sometimes structural and sometimes centered on the needs of a user profile.

Our segmentation of users is based on their level of maturity and varied needs. The psychological age of a child can be a brake on rationalism and the representation he has on things and on his environment [33].

Existing works summarize stages of psychological development from child to adolescent based on logical, cognitive, and language levels, from 0 to 18 years old [34, 36]. This division fits well with the requirements of school careers. However, potential victims have varied profiles. It would be interesting to break down an awareness model that considers the diversity of profiles.

We will consider this architecture as an educational gamification at three levels (child, adolescent, and adult): under 13, under 21, and over 20. They will be educated or not, parents, and teachers. An evaluation or consideration of the learner's level on the basic notions related to digital technology and cyber security practices to limit victimization through phishing attacks with social engineering technics. The nature of the assessments was MCQ or QUIZ. Intrinsic and extrinsic motivations depend on the level at which the evaluation is carried out. We must measure progress made by individual or a group, and therefore, the evolution of the player or target trough formative evaluation. A learner's score should lead to conclusive summative assessment. At the same time, the level of acquired competence of a target is compared to other players at the end of the game.

In this case, the target can be anyone who could access cyberspace. The main objective is to let anyone acquire competencies to enable him avoid being easy prey faced to sophisticated traps of cybercriminals.

3.4 General Structure of the Application

The starting point for any user is registration and then logging in as an administrator or user. In administrator mode, you can perform administrative tasks, such as creating courses, levels, recording tutorials, evaluations, answers to prepare remediation, and the scoring guide. In addition, learners can connect to the course and the level corresponding to the user profile, learn there, or be evaluated. A successful evaluation advances, whereas an unsatisfactory evaluation requires remediation before returning to the previous level.

It is important to remember that you can exit at any level and the context is saved for the next connection, or the user is not required to start over at the beginning as shown in Fig. 5.

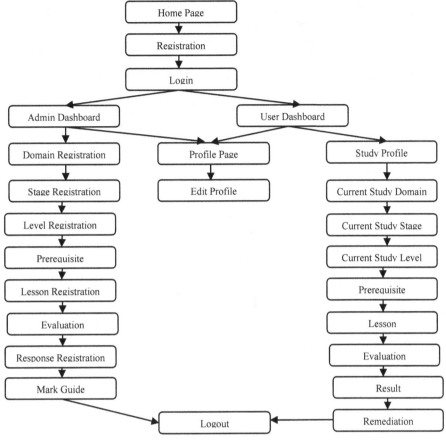

Fig. 5. Application structure

3.5 Navigation Scheme

The connection of any user to this platform with login parameters requires prior registration. They can exit the application at the desired time and return to continue or resume to improve their performance. The user can access the awareness tutorial and be assessed, and if the assessment is not favorable, proceed with remediation.

For navigation at this site, the user connects by declaring his level of Digital Tools Mastery (DTM), informs about his age, picture, e-mail, pseudonym (Pseudo), and password. The system verifies that this nickname exists for the same age and returns a Boolean value. If it exists, the context saved in the last connection is retrieved. Otherwise, depending on age, one is redirected to the appropriate stage of application.

Each user creates an account to connect to the system. A profile of a user is information concerning this user (Pseudo, avatar/picture, age, image, password, mastery of Digital Tools). Awareness is about the same specific theme as cybersecurity. All three stages are based on it, from the lower level to the higher one. Each stage has four levels. Level 1: Cybersecurity and social engineering, Level 2: means and stages of social engineering attacks, Level 3: aim of attack, Level 4: Types of attacks and safe practices. When a learner stops, his context is saved.

A learner starts at a stage related to his profile, psychological development level, and Digital Tools Mastery level. He can also continue where he stopped.

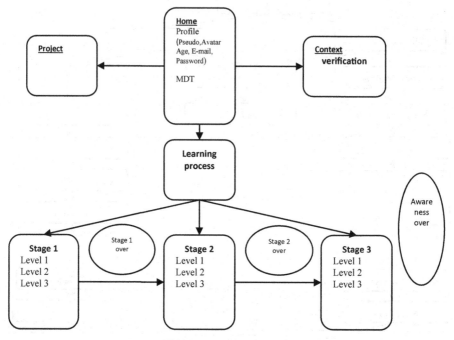

Fig. 6. Navigation scheme

The user is redirected to an appropriate stage depending on the age and level of digital proficiency. There are three stages adaptable according to the secondary school course: the cycle of observation, orientation, and the cycle corresponding to Lower sixth and Upper sixth. Considering the need to form a critical mass of persons from different background accessing cyberspace and exposed to the same risk of cyber criminality, we distinguish three stages: beginner, mastery, and expert. The same theme was developed with increasing levels of requirements. The model in connection with profiles has three stages, and each stage is divided into four levels. Each level deals with a specific theme. We have Level one (cybersecurity and social engineering), level two is about means and steps of a social engineering attack, Level three (The aim of an attack) and Level 4 (types of attacks and security practices). There are three levels of Mastery of Digital Tools (MDT): beginner (B), Intermediate (I) and Expert (E). Figure 6 and Fig. 7 give details in how it is implemented in the system.

3.6 Modeling of System Operation

The system comprises the three stages described above, and each of the stages comprises four levels or levels: Level K, $K \in \{1,2,3,4\}$.

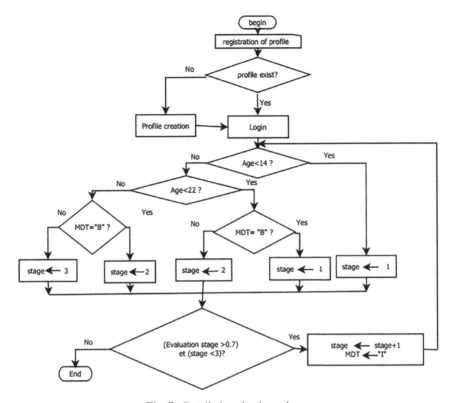

Fig. 7. Detailed navigation scheme

For any K, Level K verifies the prerequisites, learning, evaluation, and remediation if the evaluation is unfavorable.

To move from one stage to the next, the learner must be competent with a score greater than or equal to 70% at the last level of the previous stage.

The positive evaluation at Level 4 (Eval4 > 0.7) of stage N, N ∈ {1,2} makes it possible to move on to the next stage N + 1. Figure 8 shows the operation algorithm.

3.7 Moving From One Level to Another

To move from one level of a stage to the next level of the same or another stage, the learner must be competent with a score greater than or equal to 0.7 at the previous level in a reasonable time. If he is not competent, the remediation mechanism brings him back to the previous level. Each stage has four levels (level p with p ∈ {1,2,3,4}.

At each level, we assess prerequisites, learning, formative and summative assessment, and remediation can occur at a score < 0.7.

The transition from Level p, p ∈ {1,2,3} to Level (p + 1) is only possible if the score is greater than or equal to 0.7; otherwise, we go through remediation and return to Level p as shown in Fig. 9.

```
Function profile (pseudo, age, avatar, Email, password):
boolean
Begin
  if (profile=yes) //exist
  {
      St=   StContext;   LevelK=   Levelcontext;   State=
  stadecontext; //profileContext
  } else {
      If(age < 14)
          {
              St=1; LevelK=1;
          }
      elseif (Age<22)
          {
              If (MDT=B)
                  {
                      St=1;
                  }
              else
                  {
                      St=2;
                  }
          }
      else{
          if (MDT=B)
              {
                  St=2
              }
          else
              {
                  St=3
              }
      }//orientation of a learner

While (St<=3)
{
  LevelK= 1;

  While (LevelK<=4)
      {
          If (Evalk>0.7)
              {
                  LevelK= next (Level K);
                  print (Level Over);
              }

          Else
              {
                  Remediate LevelK; LevelK= LevelK;
              }
      }
}

Print (Over stage);

St=St+1;

Endwhile

Print (Game over); Print (score); Print (score board);

End
Print (Game over); Print (score); Print (score board);
End
```

Fig. 8. Operation algorithm

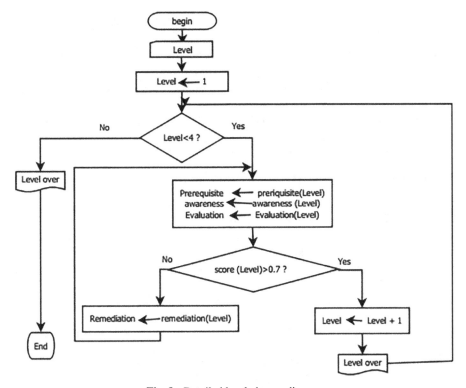

Fig. 9. Detailed level change diagram

3.8 Mathematical Modeling of Score Evaluation

Let N_{ij}^p be the score of the player p in stage i at level j, where i $\in$ {1,2,3}, j $\in$ {1,2,3,4} and p > 0.

Given u, v, w real numbers, Q_{ijk} is a question k in the set of m questions of evaluation in stage i and level j. R_{ijk}^p is marks awarded after responding to question k. for any player p, R_{ijk}^p is initialize with 0. During evaluation, $R_{ijk}^p = u$ for true answer, $R_{ijk}^p = v$ for false answer and $R_{ijk}^p = w$ when there is no answer.

We have matrix $N(N_{ij}^p)$ of scores of the different levels of a player or learner p according to stage i and level j. It is a n*m matrix with n = 3 et m = 4. $N_{ij}^p = \frac{1}{ku}\sum_{k=1}^{k=m} R_{ijk}^p$, to express the percentage of competency.

Given stage k $\in$ {1,2,3}, the stage score is $Sc_{i.}^p = \frac{1}{4}\sum_{j=1}^{j=4} N_{ij}^p$.

We obtain matrix $S(Sc_{i.}^p)$ of scores from different stages of a given player p. Sc is a row matrix $(Sc_{i.}^p)$, i $\in$ {1,2,3}. Let $(Sc_{1.}^p, Sc_{2.}^p, Sc_{3.}^p)$ be for any given player p.

At the end of the game, the player is evaluated through his arithmetic mean of scores of his different stages: average $(Sc_{i.}^p)$. However, some players started at Stage 2 or 3 without going through Stage 1.

We define M (0.75, 0.75, 0) a constant matrix and a column vector μ, which, for each learner, associates three default scores of a given player p in the three stages $S_D^p = M*(\varphi)^t$ with $\varphi = (\varphi_i)$, $i \in \{1,2,3\}$:

- If $Sc_{i.}^p = 0$; $i \in \{1,2\}$, $\varphi_i = 1$ for a given player p. Else $\varphi_i = 0$.
- In the conditions of age and digital proficiency allowing starting at stage 2, $(\varphi) = (1, 0, 0)$;
- In the conditions of age and digital proficiency allowing starting at stage 3, $(\varphi) = (1, 1, 0)$;
- In the rest of the cases, $(\varphi) = (0, 0, 0)$.

Final average score: $F^P = \frac{1}{3}\left(S_D^p + \sum_{i=1}^{i=3}(S_{i..}^p)\right)$.

4   System Prototype and Evaluation

The described architecture made it possible to implement an online awareness platform cyberssecurityawareness.com.

4.1   Used Tools

For our databases, we chose the MONGO DB. In this application, NoSQL is favored over SQL. This method is suitable for high-speed parallel activities. The number of accesses is unlimited. The SQL-pending trap has been avoided.

JavaScript, as opposed to other languages, uses fewer hardware resources to execute the tasks. A computational load occurs on the server side. Most browsers support said language, and there is an adaptation of the display. A script was provided to switch to another language.

We used cacoo.com to represent the Logical Data Model and WinDesign for UML diagrams.

Front-end server, we use ReackJS, and NodeJS for the back end to insure adaptability.

4.2   Conceptual Data Model (CDM)

To provide an abstract representation of the reality of the application, we propose the Conceptual Data Model below (Fig. 10). It presents entities involves in collection of data and their properties, such as user model, study profile model, domain model (awareness domain), evaluation profile model, user privilege model, rang model, stage model, level model, question model. Each learning (tutorial model) is linked to a level and a level is that of a stage. The evaluation of learning consisted of questions and answers to ensure remediation.

4.3   Use Case Diagram

The diagram in Fig. 11 highlights the possible actions of the administrator or the user in the system. The administrator can create an awareness domain, learning stages, and stage levels. For a given stage, he is called upon to create tutorials with their prerequisites

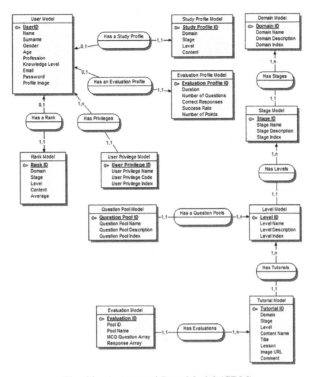

Fig. 10. Conceptual Data Model (CDM)

as well as evaluations by recording the questions and answers. The user is called upon to register, connect, start/continue learning the prerequisites for the assessment, and simply choose to self-assess.

4.4 User Activity Diagram

Figure 12 presents the interactions between the system and the user. The scheme presents the responses of the system to the user, the expectations of the system, and the actions to be carried out.

4.5 User State Diagram

Figure 13 shows the different states of the proposed application. Users visiting the platform must complete a registration form. After registration, he was able to connect and see his profile. In this profile, he begins or continues the awareness process.

4.6 Presentation of Interfaces

Those interfaces allow one to choose whether to register or log as an user or an administrator (Fig. 14).

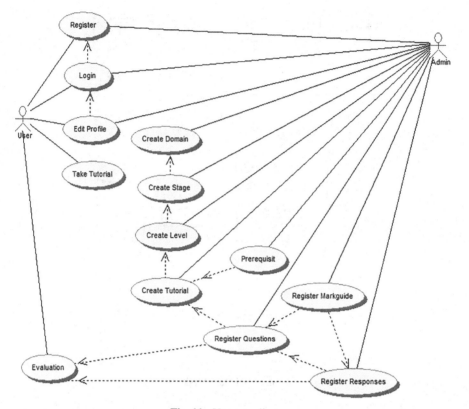

Fig. 11. Use case diagram

4.7 Evaluation of the Solution and Discussion

In this section, we highlight the benefits of the proposed architecture through evaluation. The prototype exists online through the link www.cyberssecurityawareness.com.

The assessment was based on the objective criteria. We based our study on the following criteria: the robustness and flexibility of the solution, and didactic and pedagogical innovation in improving the target's experience. Robustness refers to the capacity of the system to remain operational and resilient to possible limitations and pedagogical innovation refers to question old pedagogic practices versus those proposed in this architecture and check if they can generalize or give better results in a long-term perspective.

The robustness and flexibility of the architecture

Architecture

The adopted architecture makes a clear distinction between the front and back ends, which guarantees flexibility. Therefore, the same data can be used in several applications. In addition, the platform is scalable with reusable modules, the possible addition of sub-applications, and functionalities without taking the application offline or "hot update". In the development process, the separation allows a better division of labor between the front-end developer and the back-end developer.

Portability

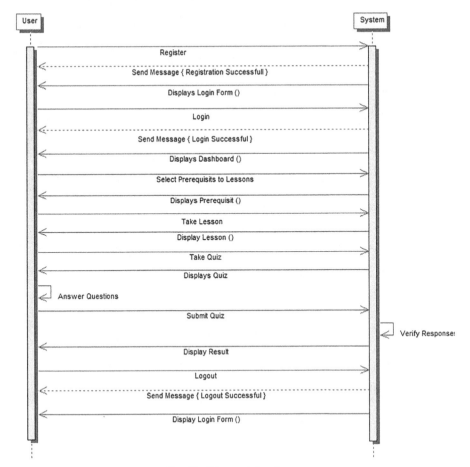

Fig. 12. User activity diagram

It is ensured by deploying the platform on desktops, laptops, tablets, and smartphones. The end user does not need more resources.

Technologies

Front-end and back-end are all developed in JavaScript so that the end-user will benefit from the advantages of the speed of this coding language. In addition, JavaScript uses fewer hardware resources to perform tasks. A computational load occurs on the server side. Most browsers support said programming language, and there is an adaptation of the display. A script was provided to switch to another language (translation). For the Data Base, MONGO DB is used. In this case, we favored NoSQL over SQL because it is suitable for high-speed parallel activities. The number of accesses is unlimited. The pitfall of SQL waiting for any update of any resource in use is avoided.

Didactic and pedagogical innovation in improving the target's experience.

Didactics considers two essential questions: the content taught and the way of teaching.

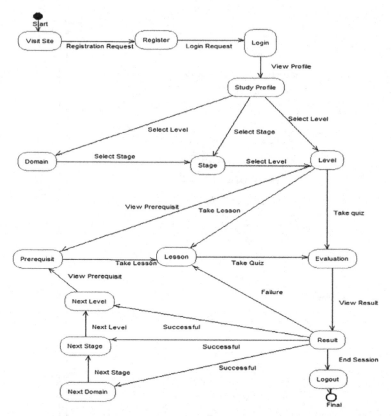

Fig. 13. User activity diagram.

Digitalization of Teaching Methods

It is at this stage that educational theories come into play. Gamification immerses the learner in a virtual environment with digital tools. The teacher can be virtual and the learner's geographic position is not an obstacle.

Gamification

Our gamification is mixed and considers both content and users. It is adaptive, according to the learner's profile. The principle of the Flipped Classroom pedagogy was applied. The user can first learn the subject before tackling it. We were flexible in remediating the questions that the learner did not find, and for a score below 70 percent. We use motivation, emulation, commitment, evaluation, remediation, and self-evaluation through the introduction of game elements such as points, score bars (individual or team), leader boards, and avatars, among others in the teaching-learning process. Evaluation is very important in the teaching-learning process, and it is necessary to always be aware of the initial state, the progress made during the learning process, and the efforts to enhance the learning process. Simultaneously, both individual and collective work must be valued. Pedagogical approaches are accessible to all, with the aim of enabling real learning to develop competence. At the same time, effective consideration of the psychological

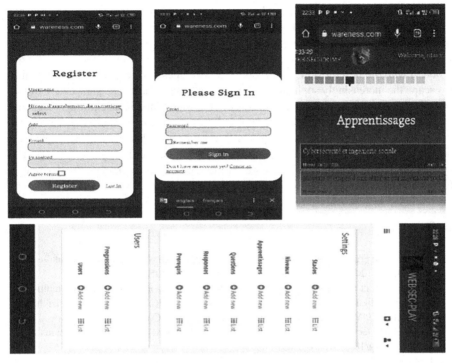

Fig. 14. Prototype Interfaces

development levels, profiles, and needs of users is important to improve their experience at the end. The provision in this model of the didactic tool, allows an awareness capable of leading to real learning and escape the increasingly sophisticated traps of cybercriminals. In the other hand, create a critical mass for collective resistance to the phenomenon.

Innovative Tool

The educational community has a flexible tool that can be adapted to the curricula, languages, and disciplines. In distance education, which is in progress at the Ministry of Secondary Education, this platform, in addition to content and exercises, provides evaluation, which is an important part of any teaching-learning activity. Moreover, making learning fun brings commitment, motivation, and emulation without which we observe a disinterest in the target. However, this work should rely a little more on staging audio animations to reach most children under 13. This approach has more facilities to meet their representation of things and environment.

5   Conclusion

The choice of an appropriate gamification architecture and the use of automatic learning techniques can make it possible to bring the didactic approach closer to the learner and his experience. Companies must emphasize their level of awareness and competence to act in a professional context to avoid being easy prey. Moreover, since cyberspace is not a domain reserved for a few elites, young people would benefit from starting awareness very early with easily accessible tools to protect themselves and thus create a critical mass ready for collective resistance to the phenomenon. However, there is a thorny problem with the best didactic means allowing awareness, which leads to real learning to escape the increasingly sophisticated traps of cybercriminals. The perspective of this work is to integrate the conversational model of artificial intelligence through Chatbots to make our gamification more adaptive, as in [29, 35], and to carry out tests on a sample of hundreds of individuals simultaneously. The architecture described in this paper does not consider emotions of the learner, his level of confidence during assessments. The system cannot manage cumulative scores at the same level which meet the desire of a learner to better perform. Those limitations are kept for future work.

References

1. Datta, P.: The promise and challenges of the fourth industrial revolution (4IR). J. Inf. Technol. Teach. Cases (2022). https://doi.org/10.1177/20438869211056938
2. Ntsama, J.E., et al.: Determinants of cybercrime victimization: experiences and multi-stage recommendations from a survey in Cameroon. In: Saeed, R.A., Bakari, A.D., Sheikh, Y.H. (eds.) AFRICOMM 2022. Lecture Notes of the Institute for Computer Sciences, Social Informatics and Telecommunications Engineering, vol. 499, pp. 317–337. Springer, Cham (2023). https://doi.org/10.1007/978-3-031-34896-9_19
3. Benavides, E., Fuertes, W., Sanchez, S., Sanchez, M.: Classification of phishing attack solutions by employing deep learning techniques: a systematic literature review. In: Rocha, Á., Pereira, R.P. (eds.) Developments and advances in defense and security. SIST, vol. 152, pp. 51–64. Springer, Singapore (2020). https://doi.org/10.1007/978-981-13-9155-2_5
4. Shie, E.W.S.: Critical analysis of current research aimed at improving detection of phishing attacks. Selected Computing Research Papers, p. 45 (2020)
5. Ho, H.T.N., Luong, H.T.: Research trends in cybercrime victimization during 2010–2020: a bibliometric analysis. SN Soc Sci 2, 4 (2022). https://doi.org/10.1007/s43545-021-00305-4
6. Andzongo, S.: Au Cameroun, la cybercriminalité fait perdre 12,2 milliards de FCFA à l'économie en 2021 (2021). https://www.investiraucameroun.com/gestion-publique/0703-17600-au-cameroun-la-cybercriminalite-fait-perdre-12-2-milliards-de-fcfa-a-l-conomie-en-2021-antic. Accessed 19 Aug 2022
7. Piaget, J., et al.: la formation du symbole chez l'enfant: initiation, jeu et rêve, image et représentation, Harmattan, 310 p (1978)
8. Schell, J.: The Art of Game Design: A Book of Lenses. CRC Press, Boca Raton (2008)
9. Seaborn, K., Fels, D.I.: Gamification in theory and action: a survey. Int. J. Hum.-Comput. Stud. 74, 14–31 (2015). https://doi.org/10.1016/J.IJHCS.2014.09.006s
10. Yue, N.: Computer multimedia assisted English vocabulary teaching courseware. Int. J. Emerg. Technol. Learn. 12(12), 67–78 (2017). https://doi.org/10.3991/ijet.v12i12.7955
11. Arakpogun, E.O., Elsahn, Z., Olan, F., Elsahn, F.: Artificial intelligence in Africa: challenges and opportunities. In: Hamdan, A., Hassanien, A.E., Razzaque, A., Alareeni, B. (eds.) The Fourth Industrial Revolution: Implementation of Artificial Intelligence for Growing Business Success. SCI, vol. 935, pp. 375–388. Springer, Cham (2021). https://doi.org/10.1007/978-3-030-62796-6_22
12. Sanchez, E., Young, S., Jouneau-Sion, C.: Classcraft: de la gamification à la ludicisation (2019). https://www.classcraft.com

13. Bebga, C.H.: Cybermuna (2019). www.cybermuna.com
14. Kanmogne, W.L.: Increasing user knowledge on email phishing scams in cyberspaces: a gamified system, Master thesis, Department of Mathematics and Computer Science, University of Ngaoundere (2019)
15. Palo, A.: Cyberawareness/girlscout at home (2019). www.girlscouts.org
16. Piaget, J., et al.: Psychologie de l'enfant, PUF, 310 p (1976)
17. Xyspas, C.: les stades du développement affectif selon Piaget, Harmattan, 169 p (2001)
18. Monterrat, B., et al.: Modèle de joueur pour la ludification adaptative d'une plateforme d'apprentissage, Agadir, Marocco, pp. 348–359 (2015)
19. Raynal, F., Rieunier, A., Postic, M.: Pédagogie: Dictionnaire des concepts clés: Apprentissages, formation, psychologie cognitive ESF (1997)
20. El Bouhdidi, J.: Une Architecture Intelligente Orientée objectifs basée sur les Ontologies et les Systèmes Multi-agents pour la Génération des Parcours d'Apprentissage Personnalisés (Doctorat, Université abdelmalek essaadi) (2013)
21. Da Costa, J.: BPMN 2.0 pour la modélisation et l'implémentation de dispositifs pédagogiques orientés processus, Doctoral dissertation, University of Geneva (2014)
22. Zainuddin, Z., et al.: The impact of gamification on learning and instruction: a systematic review of empirical evidence, Faculty of Education, The University of Hong Kong, Pokfulam Road, Hong Kong (2020)
23. Doise, W., Mugny, G.: Le développement social de l'intelligence (Vol. 1). InterEditions, Paris (1981)
24. Chekour, M., Laafou, M., Janati-Idrissi, R.: L'évolution des théories de l'apprentissage à l'ère du numérique. École Normale Supérieure de Tétouan, Maroc, researchgate **8**, 1–6 (2019)
25. Duplàa, E., Talaat, N.: Connectivisme et formation en ligne. Distances et savoirs **9**(4), 541–564 (2012)
26. Krause, M., Mogalle, M., Pohl, H., et Williams, J.J.: A playful game changer: Fostering student retention in online education with social gamification. Dans Proceedings of the Second (2015) ACM Conference on Learning@ Scale, pp. 95–102. ACM (2015)
27. Dichev, C., Dicheva, D.: Gamifying education: what is known, what is believed and what remains uncertain: a critical review. Int. J. Educ. Technol. High. Educ. **14**(9), 1–36 (2017). https://doi.org/10.1186/s41239-017-0042-5
28. Jayalath, J., Esichaikul, V.: Gamification to enhance motivation and engagement in blended eLearning for technical and vocational education and training. Technol. Knowl. Learn. (2020). https://doi.org/10.1007/s10758-020-09466-2
29. Hwang, Helser, S.: Jeux éducatifs sur la cybersécurité: cadre théorique (2021)
30. Ntsama, J.E.: Approche de Gamification educative pour la cyber-arnaque, memoire de Master, faculte de sciences, Universite de Ngaoundere (2021)
31. Böckle, M., Micheel, I., Bick, M., Novak, J.: A design framework for adaptative gamification application. In: Proceeding of the 51th Hawaii International Conference on System Sciences (2018)
32. Kapp, K.M.: The Gamification of Learning and Instruction: Game-Based Methods and Strategies for Training and Education. Wiley, Hoboken (2012)
33. Piaget, J.: Le langage et la pensée chez l'enfant: Etudes sur la logique de l'enfant. Neuvième édition, Delachaux et Niestle, Neuchâtel – Paris (1923)
34. Wallon, H.: L'évolution Psychologique de l'enfant, Librarie Armand Colin, Paris (1947)
35. Bezzina, S., et al.: leveraging gamification in education through artificial intelligence, University of Malta (MALTA) (2022). ORCID: 0000-0002-8689-3318
36. Meloupou, J.P.: Manuel de psychologie du developpement de l'enfantet de l'adolescent, Ed. Harmatan, P. 17 (2017)
37. Legault, B.: L'apport de la psychologie cognitive, Montréal, Les Editions Logiques, 474p (1992)

Improvement of Cloud-Assisted Identity-Based Anonymous Authentication and Key Agreement Protocol for Secure WBAN

Sidoine Djimnaibeye[1,2]([⊠]), Aminata Ngom[1], Igor Tchappi[4],
Borgou Mahamat Hassan[3], and Amro Najjar[4]

[1] Laboratoire LACGAA, Université Cheikh Anta Diop de Dakar, Dakar, Senegal
[2] Laboratoire LARTIC, Institut National Supérieur de Sciences et Techniques
d'Abéché, Abeche, Tchad
dthekplus@gmail.com
[3] Ecole National Supérieur des Technologie de l'Information et de Communication,
N'Djamena, Tchad
[4] Luxembourg Institute of Science and Technology, Luxembourg, Luxembourg
amro.najjar@uni.lu

Abstract. Kumar and Chand propose an Identity-based Anonymous Authentication and Key Agreement (IBAAKA) protocol for Wireless Body Area Network in the cloud-based environment, which achieves mutual authentication and user anonymity and can resist known attacks. However, Rakeei and Moazami show that their scheme is subject to a traceability attack. As a result of this attack, the scheme does not allow secure authentication because an adversary can successfully perform a man-in-the-middle attack and exchange a session key with the victim sensor. To provide security resilience against this attack, this paper proposes an improvement to the IBAAKA protocol. We also present the resilience of the proposed scheme against various security attacks, as well as ensuring secure mutual authentication and anonymity.

Keywords: E-healthcare · Anonymity · Authentication and Key Agreement (AKA) · Wireless Body Area Network (WBAN) · Elliptic Curve Cryptography (ECC)

1 Introduction

A wireless body area network (WBAN) connects independent sensors in clothing, on a person's body or under their skin. The network typically covers the entire human body and the nodes are connected by a wireless communication channel.

WBAN has many promising applications in remote health monitoring, home care, medicine, multimedia, sports, etc. In healthcare, a patient can be equipped with a wireless body network consisting of sensors that continuously measure

© ICST Institute for Computer Sciences, Social Informatics and Telecommunications Engineering 2024
Published by Springer Nature Switzerland AG 2024. All Rights Reserved
F. Tchakounte et al. (Eds.): SAFER-TEA 2023, LNICST 566, pp. 58–70, 2024.
https://doi.org/10.1007/978-3-031-56396-6_4

specific biological functions. The system analyses the sensor data in real time, provides advice and feedback to the user and can generate alerts based on the user's condition and activity level. In addition, all recorded information can be transmitted via the Internet to medical servers and seamlessly integrated into the patient's electronic medical record. The main concern with wireless communication channels for health monitoring is the privacy and security of patient information and data exchange [1].

In 2011, a mutual authenticated protocol was proposed by Debiao et al. [2] that allows user/Server session key agreement. They claim that their scheme also provides known session key security, perfect forward secrecy, impersonation without key compromise, unknown key sharing and key control. On the contrary, the analysis of Gouthan et al. [3] showed that their scheme has several security limitations, such as the problem of many connected users, privileged insider attack, impersonation attack, etc. And they proposed mutual remote authentication based on anonymous identity with a key agreement protocol over Elliptic Curve Cryptography using smart cards. The proposed scheme retains the advantages of Debiao's scheme while providing important security features such as identity protection, anonymity, and secure session keys. In 2017, Zhan et al. [4] found that Goutham et al.'s scheme [3] had some security flaws, such as incomplete anonymity and no provision for private key update. And They then proposed a new anonymous AKA protocol for a client-server environment.

A lightweight peer-to-peer AKA protocol for WBAN based on ECC are presented by Li et al. [5]. The vulnerability of the protocol was demonstrated. Sowjanya et al. [6] proposed an improved lightweight end-to-end authentication protocol based on ECC to overcome the security flaws of Li et al.'s scheme.

Fog computing connects a network node, consisting of low-resource devices, to cloud servers. Patonico et al. [7] proposed a identity-based mutually AKA protocol for this architecture, in which the peer device and the fog can establish secure communication without leaking their identities.

After revealing several weaknesses in the identity-based key establishment protocol of Mohammadali and al. [8] published in 2018, Mahmood and al. [9] have subsequently improved the protocol and have also shown that the improved protocol achieves not only anonymity but also untraceability. In 2020, Moghadam et al. [10] proposed an efficient AKA scheme in WBAN. Unfortunately, Kwon et al. showed that Moghadam et al.'s scheme [11] cannot prevent insider attacks and does not guarantee perfect secrecy. To address these weaknesses, they proposed a lightweight and secure mutual authentication protocol for Wireless Sensors Networks that guarantees perfect secrecy and mutual authentication.

In the same year, Kumar and Chand [12] presented an identity-based anonymous authentication and key agreement (IBAAKA) protocol. They claim under the random oracle model (ROM) and computational diffie-hellman (CDH) assumption, the proposed IBAAKA protocol is provably secured. however, Rakeei and Moazami [13] prove that their scheme can not resist to the CS masquerading attack. After this attack, the intruder can perform a man-in-the-middle attack and can exchange a session key with the target node.

The paper's main contribution can be summarized as follows.

1. An Improvement of identity-based anonymous authentication and key agreement (IBAAKA) protocol for WBAN.
2. Security analysis of the improved version of IBAAKA protocol.
3. Comparisons to security features, comparative computation and communication costs analysis of the improved version with IBAAKA protocol.

The organization of this paper is described as follows: Sect. 2 presentes Rakkeei and Moazamin's cryptanalysis of Kumar and Chand's scheme [13] and then an improvement of the same protocol is proposed in Sect. 3. Security and performance of the proposed protocol are analyzed in Sects. 4 and 5, respectively. Finally, we draw a conclusion.

2   Cryptanalysis of IBAAKA Protocol

2.1   Notations

See Table 1.

Table 1. Nomenclature

LN	Leaf node
CS	Cloud server
NM	Network manager
q	A large prime number
G_1	An additive cyclic group
G_2	A multiplicative cyclic group
P	Generator of G_1
s_0	Master key of NM
P_0	Public key of NM
l	Length of q
$H_i\ (i = 1, 2, \cdots, 5)$	Secure hash functions
TCS	Timestamp of CS
TLN	Timestamp of LN

2.2   IBAAKA Protocol

In the architecture of cloud enabled WBAN (See Fig. 1) presented by Kumar and Chand's scheme [12], there are five entities participating in the scheme with the following roles:

Network manager: NM registers the leaf node, root node, destination node and cloud server as a trusted third party and provides them secret keys corresponding to their identities.

Leaf Node: LN is a resource-constraint wearable/ implanted sensor that has limited storage space, battery life, and computation power.

Cloud servers: It is a computational rich and storage device that stores Protected Health Information. CS must register before connecting to a leaf node.

Target node: TN is a server that provides medical services to the patient.

Root node: It is an intermediate node between the leaf node and the target node

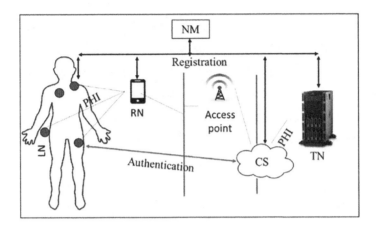

Fig. 1. Architecture of cloud-enabled WBAN

Kumar and Chand's scheme consists of setup, registration, and authentication phases:

Setup Phase. NM chooses a random l-bit large prime number q, an additive group G_1 and a multiplicative group G_2 of order of q. Let P be the generator of G_1. Let five hash functions:

$$H_1 : \{0,1\}^I \times G_1 \to Z_q^*$$

$$H_2 : \{0,1\}^{2I} \times G_1^2 \to Z_q^*$$

$$H_3 : G_2 \to \{0,1\}^{I+t} \times G_1^2 \times Z_q^*$$

$$H_4 : \{0,1\}^{2I+t} \times G_1^2 \to Z_q^*$$

$$H_5 : \{0,1\}^{2I} \times G_1^3 \to Z_q^*$$

NM chooses a master key $s_0 \in Z_q^*$ and sets the public key $P_0 = s_0 P$. It keeps s_0 secret and publishes in the public parameter $(k, q, P, P_0, G_1, G_2, H_1, H_2, H_3, H_4, H_5)$

Registration Phase
See Tables 2 and 3.

Table 2. Cloud server registration

CS Registration	
CS	MN
selects ID_{CS} $\rightarrow \{ID_{CS}\}$	
	checks ID_{CS}
	chooses a random integer:
$\{R_{CS}, s_{CS}\} \leftarrow$	$r_{CS} \in Z_q^*$
	computes the private key:
	$R_{CS} = r_{CS}P,$
	$s_{CS} = r_{CS} + s_0 H_1(ID_{CS}\|R_{CS})$
stores	
$\{R_{CS}, s_{CS}\}$	

Table 3. Leaf node registration

LN Registration	
LN	MN
selects ID_{LN} $\rightarrow \{ID_{LN}\}$	
	checks ID_{CS}
	chooses a random integer:
$\{R_{LN}, s_{LN}\} \leftarrow$	$r_{LN} \in Z_q^*$
	computes the private key:
	$R_{LN} = r_{LN}P,$
	$s_{LN} = r_{LN} + s_0 H_1(ID_{LN}\|R_{LN})$
pre-store	
$\{R_{LN}, s_{LN}\}$	
in LN'storage	

Mutual Authentication Phase

Step 1. LN Picks $x \in Z_q^*$ and computes $X = xP$, $g_{LN} = x(R_{CS} + H_1(ID_{CS}\|R_{CS})P_0)$. It picks the current timestamp T_{LN}, $k = s_{LN} + xH_2(ID_{LN}\|R_{LN}\|T_{LN}\|X)$ and encrypts $W = H_3(g_{LN}) \oplus (ID_{LN}\|R_{LN}\|T_{LN}\|k)$. LN sends (W, X) to CS

Step 2. On receiving (W, X), CS computes key $g_{CS} = s_{CS}X$, extracts ID_{LN} on decrypting W using the key g_{CS} as $(ID_{LN}\|R_{LN}\|T_{LN}\|k) = W \oplus H_3(g_{LN})$.

It checks T_{LN} and computes $h = H_2(ID_{LN}||R_{LN}||T_{LN}||X)$. aborted if $kP? = (R_{LN} + H_1(ID_{LN}||R_{LN})P_0) + hX$. After CS Picks $y \in Z_q^*$ and T_{CS}, It computes $Y = yP$, $t = H_4(T_{CS}||ID_{LN}||ID_{CS}||Y||X)$, $key_{CS} = ytX$ and $SK_{CS} = H_5(key_{CS}||ID_{LN}||ID_{CS}||Y||X)$. CS sends (t, T_{CS}, Y) to LN.

Step 3. LN checks T_{CS}. aborted if $t? = H_4(T_{CS}||ID_{LN}||ID_{CS}||Y||X)$. LN Computes $key_{LN} = xtY$ and session key $SK_{CS} = H_5(key_{LN}||ID_{LN}|| ID_{CS}||Y||X)$

Table 4. Authentication phase

Leaf Node LN		Cloud Server CS
Picks $x \in Z_q^*$, $X = xP$		
$g_{LN} = x(R_{CS} + H_1(ID_{CS}||R_{CS})P_0)$		
picks current timestamp T_{LN}	$\rightarrow \{W, X\}$	
$k = s_{LN} + xH_2(ID_{LN}||R_{LN}||T_{LN}||X)$		
$W = H_3(g_{LN}) \oplus (ID_{LN}||R_{LN}||T_{LN}||k)$		
		$g_{CS} = s_{CS}X$
		$(ID_{LN}||R_{LN}||T_{LN}||k) = W \oplus H_3(g_{LN})$
		checks T_{LN}
		$h = H_2(ID_{LN}||R_{LN}||T_{LN}||X)$
		aborted if
	$\{t, T_{CS}, Y\} \leftarrow$	$kP? = (R_{LN} + H_1(ID_{LN}||R_{LN})P_0) + hX$
		Picks $y \in Z_q^*$, $Y = yP$
		picks current timestamp T_{CS}
		$t = H_4(T_{CS}||ID_{LN}||ID_{CS}||Y||X)$
		$key_{CS} = ytX$
		$SK_{CS} = H_5(key_{CS}||ID_{LN}||ID_{CS}||Y||X)$
checks T_{CS}		
aborted if		
$t? = H_4(T_{CS}||ID_{LN}||ID_{CS}||Y||X)$		
$key_{LN} = xtY$		
$SK_{CS} = H_5(key_{LN}||ID_{LN}||ID_{CS}||Y||X)$		

They claim the proposed IBAAKA scheme is provably secure, as well as complete the required security properties and achieves User anonymity and untraceability, LN Impersonation attack, perfect forward secrecy etc. However, Rakkeei and Moazamin demonstrate that their scheme is vulnerable to the man in the middle attack (Table 4).

2.3   Rakkeei and Moazamin's Cryptanalysis

In this section, we present Rakkeei and Moazamin's cryptanalysis of Kumar and Chand's scheme [13]. They show how to trace LN in polynomial time and how an attacker can launch a CS impersonation attack and share a session key with the victim LN Table 5.

Traceability Attack: The protocol proposed by Kumar and Chand can be subject to a traceability attack if the attacker finds out the LN's ID_{LN}. Let CS_A (Adversary's Cloud Server) establishes an authentication session with LN. So, it knows ID_{LN}. Assuming that CS_A has the full control of the transmitted messages in the channel, they show that CS_A can easily trace any session initiated by LN.

- LN sends login message (W, X) to legal CS.
- In response, CS authenticates LN and sends a login response (t, T_{CS}, Y) towards LN.
- CS_A intercepts (t, T_{CS}, Y) and checks the correctness of $t = H_4(T_{CS}||ID_{LN}||ID_{CS}||Y||X)$. If the equation holds, it means that LN is successfully traced.

CS impersonation attack: The procedure is as follows:

- Let LN be traced successfully by CS_A, it picks $y_A \in Z_q^*$ and a new timestamp T_{CS_A} and computes $Y_A = y_A P$ and $t_A = H_4(T_{CS_A}||ID_{LN}||ID_{CS_A}||Y_A||X)$ where X is an intercepted value from login message. CS_A sends (t_A, T_{CS_A}, Y_A) to LN. Further, CS_A computes the shared session key $SK_{CS_A} = H_5(y_A t_A X||ID_{LN}||ID_{CS}||Y_A||X)$.
- LN receives (t_A, T_{CS_A}, Y_A) and verifies $t_A = H_4(T_{CS_A}||ID_{LN}||ID_{CS_A}||Y_A||X)$. Now, it sets the shared session key with impersonated CS_A as $SK_{CS_A} = H_5(x t_A Y_A||ID_{LN}||ID_{CS}||Y_A||X)$

CS_A is authenticated for LN and both shared the same session key SK_{CS_A}

Table 5. Rakkeei and Moazamin's cryptanalysis

Leaf Node LN	Adversary's Cloud Server CS_A	Cloud Server CS
Picks $x \in Z_q^*$, $X = xP$		
$g_{LN} = x(R_{CS} + H_1(ID_{CS}||R_{CS})P_0)$		
picks current timestamp T_{LN}	$\rightarrow \{W, X\} \rightarrow$	
$k = s_{LN} + x H_2(ID_{LN}||R_{LN}||T_{LN}||X)$		
$W = H_3(g_{LN}) \oplus (ID_{LN}||R_{LN}||T_{LN}||k)$		
		$g_{CS} = s_{CS} X$
	$\{t, T_{CS}, Y\} \leftarrow$	$(ID_{LN}||R_{LN}||T_{LN}||k) = W \oplus H_3(g_{LN})$
	$t' = H_4(T_{CS}||ID_{LN}||ID_{CS}||Y||X)$	chekcs T_{LN}
	if t' equals to t	$h = H_2(ID_{LN}||R_{LN}||T_{LN}||X)$
	LN is traced successfully	aborted if
	Picks $y_A \in Z_q^*$ and T_{CS_A}	$kP? = (R_{LN} + H_1(ID_{LN}||R_{LN})P_0) + hX$
	computes $Y_A = y_A P$	Picks $y \in Z_q^*$, $Y = yP$
	$t_A = H_4(T_{CS_A}||ID_{LN}||ID_{CS_A}||Y_A||X)$	picks current timestamp T_{CS}
	$\leftarrow \{t_A, T_{CS_A}, Y_A\}$	$t = H_4(T_{CS}||ID_{LN}||ID_{CS}||Y||X)$
		$key_{CS} = yt X$
		$SK_{CS} = H_5(key_{CS}||ID_{LN}||ID_{CS}||Y||X)$
checks T_{CS_A}		
aborted if		
$t_A? = H_4(T_{CS_A}||ID_{LN}||ID_{CS}||Y_A||X)$		
$key_{LN_A} = x t_A Y_A$		
$SK_{CS_A} = H_5(key_{LN_A}||ID_{LN}||ID_{CS}||Y_A||X)$		

3   Improvement of IBAAKA Scheme

The Rakkeei and Moazamin's analysis shows that the Kumar and Chand's scheme cannot resist cloud server spoofing attacks and does not provide perfect forward secrecy. In order to solve this problem and provide better security, in this section, we propose an improved authentication scheme based on Kumar and Chand's scheme that inherits and expands the merits of the original scheme.

Like Kumar and Chand's scheme, the improvement scheme has three phases: setup phase, registration phase and authentication phase. The improvements only apply to the authentication phase. We chose new hash functions:

$$H'_3 : G_2 \rightarrow \{0,1\}^I \times Z^*_q$$

$$H : G^2_2 \rightarrow Z^*_q$$

. Once registered with MN, LN and CS receive respectively $\{R_{LN}, s_{LN}\}$ and $\{R_{CS}, s_{CS}\}$.

Step 1. LN selects $x \in Z^*_q$ and computes $X = xP$ and $g_{LN} = x(R_{CS} + H_1(ID_{CS}||R_{CS})P_0)$. It picks the current timestamp T_{LN} and computes $K_{LN} = s_{LN} + xH_2(ID_{LN}||R_{LN}||T_{LN}||X)$. After it encrypts :
$W_{LN} = H_3(g_{LN}) \oplus (ID_{LN}||R_{LN}||T_{LN}||K_{LN})$. LN sends (W_{LN}, X) to CS

Step 2. On receiving (W_{LN}, X), CS computes key :
$g'_{LN} = s_{CS}X = xP(r_{CS} + s_0H_1(ID_{CS}||R_{CS}) = x(R_{CS} + H_1(ID_{CS}||R_{CS})P_0)$
It can extract $ID'_{LN}, R'_{LN}, T'_{LN}, K'_{LN}$ on decrypting W_{LN} using key g'_{LN} :
$(ID'_{LN}||R'_{LN}||T'_{LN}||K'_{LN}) = W \oplus H_3(g'_{LN})$.
It checks T'_{LN} and computes $h = H_2(ID'_{LN}||R'_{LN}||T'_{LN}||X)$. aborted if $K'_{LN}P? = (R'_{LN} + H_1(ID'_{LN}||R'_{LN})P_0) + hX$. Else LN is authenticated by CS and $(ID_{LN} = ID'_{LN})$ and $(R_{LN} = R'_{LN})$. After CS Picks $y \in Z^*_q$ and T_{CS}, It computes $Y = yP$, $g_{CS} = y(R_{LN} + H_1(ID_{LN}||R_{LN})P_0)$, $K_{CS} = s_{CS} + yH_2(ID_{LN}||R_{LN}||T_{CS})$, $W_{CS} = H'_3(g_{CS}) \oplus (T_{CS}||K_{CS})$ and $SK = H(g_{LN} + g_{CS})$. CS sends (W_{CS}, Y) to LN.

Step 3. On receiving (W_{CS}, Y), LS computes key $g'_{CS} = s_{LN}Y$, extracts T_{CS} and K_{CS} on decrypting W_{CS} using the key g'_{CS} as $(T'_{CS}||K'_{CS}) = W \oplus H'_3(g'_{CS})$. It checks T'_{CS} and computes $h' = H_2(ID_{LN}||R_{LN}||T'_{CS})$. aborted if $K'_{CS}P? = (R_{CS} + H_1(ID_{LN}||R_{LN})P_0) + h'Y$. Now, LN computes session key as $SK = H(g_{LN} + g_{CS})$ (Table 6).

Table 6. Improvement Authentication phase

Leaf Node (LN)	Cloud Server (CS)
Picks $x \in Z_q^*$, $X = xP$	
$g_{LN} = x(R_{CS} + H_1(ID_{CS}\|R_{CS})P_0)$	
picks current timestamp T_{LN} $\rightarrow \{W_{LN}, X\}$	
$K_{LN} = s_{LN} + xH_2(ID_{LN}\|R_{LN}\|T_{LN}\|X)$	
$W_{LN} = H_3(g_{LN}) \oplus (ID_{LN}\|R_{LN}\|T_{LN}\|K_{LN})$	
	$g'_{LN} = s_{CS}X$
	$(ID'_{LN}\|R'_{LN}\|T'_{LN}\|K'_{LN}) = W \oplus H_3(g'_{LN})$
	chekcs T'_{LN}
	$h = H_2(ID'_{LN}\|R'_{LN}\|T'_{LN}\|X)$
	aborted if
	$K'_{LN}P! = (R'_{LN} + H_1(ID'_{LN}\|R'_{LN})P_0) + hX$
	Else LN is authenticated by CS
$\{W_{CS}, Y\} \leftarrow$	$(ID_{LN} = ID'_{LN})$ and $(R_{LN} = R'_{LN})$
	Picks $y \in Z_q^*$, $Y = yP$
	$g_{CS} = y(R_{LN} + H_1(ID_{LN}\|R_{LN})P_0)$
	picks current timestamp T_{CS}
	$K_{CS} = s_{CS} + yH_2(ID_{LN}\|R_{LN}\|T_{CS})$
	$W_{CS} = H'_3(g_{CS}) \oplus (T_{CS}\|K_{CS})$
	where
	$SK = H(g_{LN} + g_{CS})$
$g'_{CS} = s_{LN}Y$	
$(T'_{CS}\|K'_{CS}) = W_{CS} \oplus H_3(g'_{CS})$	
checks T'_{CS}	
$h' = H_2(ID_{LN}\|R_{LN}\|T'_{CS})$	
aborted if	
$K'_{CS}P! = (R_{CS} + H_1(ID_{CS}\|R_{CS})P_0) + h'Y$	
Else CS is authenticated by LN	
$SK = H(g_{LN} + g_{CS})$	

4   Security Analysis

In this section, we present resistance of the proposed scheme against various security attacks as well as ensure secure mutual authentication and anonymity.

Proposition 1. *The proposed protocol can resist to the LN impersonation attack.*

Proof. To impersonate a legal LN, an adversary who intercepts the login request message $\{W_{LN}, X\}$ from LN or generates a valid login request, could initiate a connection to the CS. If he/she forwards to the CS, it returns $\{W_{CS}, Y\}$ to him/her. To compute xY and g_{CS}, the adversary will need respectively x and s_{LN}. However, without the correct x and S_{LN}, the adversary will not be able to compute the valid session key.

Proposition 2. *The proposed protocol can resist to the CS masquerading attack.*

Proof. To pretend to be the CS to the LN, the adversary who receives $\{W_{LN}, X\}$, he/she cannot compute valide g_{LN} without knowing the CS'secret element s_{CS}. However, without the correct g_{LN}, the adversary will not be able to decrypt W_{LN} and to compute W_{CS}.

Proposition 3. *The proposed protocol can resist to the replay attack*

Proof. The proposed scheme resists replay attacks because authentication requests W_{LN} and W_{CS} includes respectively current timestamps T_{LN} and T_{CS} which are masquered respectively by the g_{LN} and g_{CS}.

Proposition 4. *The proposed protocol preserves user anonymity and unlinkability*

Proof. Suppose that adversary intercepts public authentication messages $\{W_{LN}, X\}$ and $\{W_{CS}, Y\}$, he/she cannot guess or get ID_{LN} from W_{LN} which is masked as $W_{LN} = H_3(g_{LN}) \oplus (ID_{LN} \| R_{LN} \| T_{LN} \| K_{LN})$. Adversary cannot link messages requests to user cause x and y are randoms numbers which change value respectively of $\{W_{LN}, X\}$ and $\{W_{CS}, Y\}$ every time during communication. Hence anonymity and unlinkability is preserved.

Proposition 5. *The proposed protocol achieves mutual authentification*

Proof. The cloud server authenticates LN by verifying if $K'_{LN}P$ equals to $(R'_{LN} + H_1(ID'_{LN} \| R'_{LN})P_0) + hX$. And, the CS authenticates by LN by verifying if $K'_{CS}P$ equals to $(R'_{CS} + H_1(ID'_{CS} \| R'_{CS})P_0) + h'Y$

Proposition 6. *Perfect forward secrecy is ensured by the proposed protocol*

Proof. if any long term secret of either the LN s_{LN} or server s_{CS} or all are compromised, it never supports in recovering any earlier session key because there is no significant correlation among the session key. The two ephemeral random secrets elements x and y, involved in the computation of the session key, i.e. $SK = H_3(g_{LN} + g_{CS})$, which are conventional to be different each time. Therefore, under the CDH assumption, the improved scheme provides forward perfect secrecy

Proposition 7. *The proposed protocol ensures session key indepency*

Proof. The key independency property is guaranteed by:

- the hash function properties,
- the session's ephemeral random secrets elements x and y

Proposition 8. *The proposed protocol can resist to the session state reveal attack*

Proof. The knowledge of ephemeral secret keys does not give the attacker the possibility of forging the session key. In our protocole, to compute the session key $SK = H(g_{LN} + g_{CS})$, the adversary need the cloud server's long-term secrecy s_{CS} and LN's long-term secrecy s_{LN} to compute respectively g_{CS} and g_{LN}. Without g_{CS} and g_{LN}, he/she connot compute SK. Therefore, The proposed protocol can resist to the session state reveal attack.

Proposition 9. *The proposed protocol can resist to the man in middle attack*

Proof. The proposed protocol can resist both to the LN impersonation attack and to the CS masquerading attack (Table 7).

Table 7. Summary of security analysis

Property/Feature	IBAAKA [12]	Our
LN impersonation attack	✓	✓
CS masquerading attack	✗	✓
Replay attack	✓	✓
User anonymity	✗	✓
Untraceability	✗	✓
mutual authentification	✓	✓
Session key indepency	✓	✓
Perfect forward secrecy	✗	✓
Session sate reveal attack	✓	✓
Man in the middle attack	✗	✓

5   Comparative Analysis

Kumar and Chand anlysed in tables the performance of the proposed IBAAKA scheme for WBAN and compares it with Liu et al. [14], He et al. [15], Wang et

Table 8. Computation costs analysis

Operations	Notation
Modular multiplication	T_M
ECC-based multiplication	T_{SM}

Scheme	Computation cost	
	Leaf Node	Cloud Server
IBAAKA [12]	$2T_M + 3T_{SM}$	$5T_{SM}$
Our	$T_M + 6T_{SM}$	$T_M + 6T_{SM}$

Elements	length(in bits)
$|G_1|$	1024
$|G_2|$	512
$|Z_q|$	160
$|ID|$	16
$|T|$	16

Table 9. Communication costs analysis

Scheme	Communication cost	length(in bits)
IBAAKA [12]	$1|ID| + 2|T| + |3G_1| + 2|Z_q|$	3440
Our	$1|ID| + 2|T| + |3G_1| + 2|Z_q|$	3440

al. [16], Jia et al. [17], Sowjanya et al. [6], and Nikooghadam et al. [18] schemes, in terms of computational (Table 8) and communication costs (Table 9). Considering the improvements of IBAAKA scheme, we update these tables in this section.

Conclusion

In this paper, we have improved the authentication phase of the IBAAKA protocol. Under the ROM and CDH assumptions, the protocol achieves all the security properties. Further work should focus on designing a new lattice-based anonymous authenticated key agreement protocol for secure WBAN.

References

1. Shamir, A.: Identity-based cryptosystems and signature schemes. In: Blakley, G.R., Chaum, D. (eds.) CRYPTO 1984. LNCS, vol. 196, pp. 47–53. Springer, Heidelberg (1985). https://doi.org/10.1007/3-540-39568-7_5
2. Debiao, H., Jianhua, C., Jin, H.: An ID-based client authentication with key agreement protocol for mobile client-server environment on ECC with provable security. Inf. Fusion **13**(3), 223–230 (2012)
3. Goutham, R.A., Lee, G.-J., Yoo, K.-Y.: An anonymous ID-based remote mutual authentication with key agreement protocol on ECC using smart cards. In: Proceedings of the 30th Annual ACM Symposium on Applied Computing, SAC 2015, pp. 169–174. Association for Computing Machinery, New York (2015)
4. Zhang, W., Lin, D., Zhang, H., Chen, C., Zhou, X.: A lightweight anonymous mutual authentication with key agreement protocol on ECC. In: 2017 IEEE Trustcom/BigDataSE/ICESS, pp. 170–176 (2017)
5. Li, X., Peng, J., Kumari, S., Wu, F., Karuppiah, M., Choo, K.-K.R.: An enhanced 1-round authentication protocol for wireless body area networks with user anonymity. Comput. Electr. Eng. **61**, 238–249 (2017)
6. Dasgupta, M., Sowjanya, K., Ray, S.: An elliptic curve cryptography based enhanced anonymous authentication protocol for wearable health monitoring system. Int. J. Inf. Secur. **19**, 129–146 (2020)
7. Braeken, A., Patonico, S., Steenhaut, K.: Identity-based and anonymous key agreement protocol for fog computing resistant in the Canetti-Krawczyk security model. Wireless Netw. **29**(3), 1017–1029 (2019)
8. Mohammadali, A., Haghighi, M.S., Tadayon, M.H., Mohammadi-Nodooshan, A.: A novel identity-based key establishment method for advanced metering infrastructure in smart grid. IEEE Trans. Smart Grid **9**(4), 2834–2842 (2018)

9. Mahmood, K., Arshad, J., Chaudhry, S.A., Kumari, S.: An enhanced anonymous identity-based key agreement protocol for smart grid advanced metering infrastructure. Int. J. Commun. Syst. **32**(16), e4137 (2019)
10. Moghadam, M.F., Nikooghadam, M., Jabban, M.A.B.A., Alishahi, M., Mortazavi, L., Mohajerzadeh, A.: An efficient authentication and key agreement scheme based on ECDH for wireless sensor network. IEEE Access **8**, 73182–73192 (2020)
11. Kwon, D.K., Yu, S.J., Lee, J.Y., Son, S.H., Park, Y.H.: WSN-SLAP: secure and lightweight mutual authentication protocol for wireless sensor networks. Sensors **21**(3), 936 (2021)
12. Kumar, M., Chand, S.: A lightweight cloud-assisted identity-based anonymous authentication and key agreement protocol for secure wireless body area network. IEEE Syst. J. **15**, 1–8 (2020)
13. Rakeei, M.A., Moazami, F.: Cryptanalysis of an anonymous authentication and key agreement protocol for secure wireless body area network. Cryptology ePrint Archive, Report 2020/1465 (2020). https://eprint.iacr.org/2020/1465
14. Liu, J., Zhang, Z., Chen, X., Kwak, K.S.: Certificateless remote anonymous authentication schemes for wirelessbody area networks. IEEE Trans. Parallel Distrib. Syst. **25**(2), 332–342 (2014)
15. He, D., Zeadally, S., Kumar, N., Lee, J.: Anonymous authentication for wireless body area networks with provable security. IEEE Syst. J. **11**(4), 2590–2601 (2017)
16. Wang, C., Zhang, Y.: New authentication scheme for wireless body area networks using the bilinear pairing. J. Med. Syst. **39**, 1–8 (2015)
17. Jia, X., He, D., Kumar, N., Choo, K.R.: A provably secure and efficient identity-based anonymous authentication scheme for mobile edge computing. IEEE Syst. J. **14**(1), 560–571 (2020)
18. Nikooghadam, M., Amintoosi, H.: A secure and robust elliptic curve cryptography-based mutual authentication scheme for session initiation protocol. Secur. Priv. **3**(1), e92 (2020)

DIDOR: A Decentralized Identifier Based Onion Routing Protocol

Saha Fobougong Pierre$^{(\boxtimes)}$ and Mohamed Mejri

Department of computer science and software engineering, Laval University, 2325, rue de l'université, Québec, QC G1V 0A6, Canada
`{pisaf1,momej}@ulaval.ca`

Abstract. We propose a new communication protocol, called DIDOR, that provides strong anonymity and is based on a decentralized identifier (DID). The proposed protocol benefits from the persistence, anonymity, and resolvability properties of the DID and integrates a forward secrecy algorithm such as Ephemeral Diffie-Hellman. It is designed to protect the anonymity of communication between parties by combining DID properties and onion routing techniques. The chosen forward secrecy algorithm establishes a shared secret between the sender and the different nodes and strengthens security. The shared secret is then used at each onion layer to encrypt the message. Likewise, DID allows us to offer a protocol that overcomes some of the weaknesses of using digital certificates. Given the prior existence of the decentralized identity management system, our protocol requires less computation at each node, maintains low communication overhead and latency, and does not require directory servers on which most existing protocols rely. We finally analyze the security of our protocol and demonstrate how it can withstand the denial of service attack on DID documents. Overall, this protocol represents a promising approach to providing secure and anonymous communication in a wide range of applications.

Keywords: Anonymity · Onion routing · Decentralized Identifier (DID)

1 Introduction

The right to privacy is protected by many international conventions and laws, but it is often challenged in practice. Companies often collect users' data without consent or use it for purposes other than those for which it was collected. Governments use various surveillance methods to track citizens' activities, often without their consent and without proper scrutiny of surveillance powers. These are some reasons why the need for anonymous communication takes on its full meaning. Internet users want to communicate with confidence, without running the risk that their identities or their messages will be read by third parties.

In response to this concern, several anonymous communication protocols have emerged. The majority of these protocols are based on the onion routing technique [1]; which consists of wrapping the message between various communication nodes in successive layers of encryption. This ensures that each node can

© ICST Institute for Computer Sciences, Social Informatics and Telecommunications Engineering 2024
Published by Springer Nature Switzerland AG 2024. All Rights Reserved
F. Tchakounte et al. (Eds.): SAFER-TEA 2023, LNICST 566, pp. 71–85, 2024.
https://doi.org/10.1007/978-3-031-56396-6_5

remove exactly one layer from the onion: the one for which it has the encryption key. Encryption layers are designed to only reveal the identities of neighboring nodes. The nodes located between the source and the destination therefore only serve as relays.

Based on the above approach, several onion routing design have been proposed [2–8], as well as uses [9–12]. Starting from the Tor protocol, described in [1], each proposed protocol aims to improve an aspect of the previous one. These improvements have led, among others, to the use of telescoping [4] and forward secrecy [7] to solve the problem of possible compromise of a node's private key; the use of identity-based encryption [3] respectively to solve the scalability problem known to the classic single-pass model and that of the use of certificates issued by certificate authority, as well as the problems of performance improvement [8,13].

In practice, existing protocols must rely on the node's identifier. These identifiers are usually taken from the digital certificates defined to guarantee the execution of the TLS protocol. Therefore, the trust is based on confidence in certificate authority. The use of Decentralized Identifier (DID) [14] eliminates the need for a certification authority, thus resolving the problems resulting from its use, as identified by [3,7]. The user can persist his unique identifier (the DID) while being the only entity capable of modifying the associate encryption keys [15]. In the same vein, he can easily delegate the use of this identifier while maintaining control [14]. Ultimately, the user remains the entity controlling his data and is able to prove this ability to control it at any time.

In this paper, we take advantage of the properties (decentralization, anonymity, resolvability, persistence, privacy) natively guaranteed by the DID to propose an onion routing protocol that is secure in the sense of [16]. This protocol uses the Ephemeral Diffie-Hellman algorithm for generating symmetric keys and guaranteeing forward secrecy [17]. The need for forward secrecy lies in preventing an attacker who compromises the node's private key from gaining access to old messages, although this is more difficult in DIDOR.

1.1   Contributions

We propose DIDOR, a decentralized identifier-based onion routing protocol. We take advantage of DID properties and the associated DID document to enhance the symmetric key generation, key management and eliminate the use of digital certificates. Using DID as a pseudonym also helps to guarantee a minimum of privacy.

Provided the prior existence of a decentralized identity management system, we begin by proposing a modification of DID document's structure. This modification aims at allowing each node to add its Diffie-Hellman public parameters. Since each node fully controls the authenticity of the DID document, other nodes have the certainty of exchanging with the appropriate node at all times. Key rotation or pre-rotation properties also allow each node to change its private keys without changing the DID; thus guaranteeing its persistence. Similarly, the symmetric key generated by the Diffie-Hellman algorithm can be modified at any time; thus guaranteeing forward secrecy.

1.2 Outline

In Sect. 2, we present some onion routing work from the literature; as well as an overview of decentralized identity.

In Sect. 3, we present our DIDOR protocol. This presentation revolves around its setup, the cryptographic keys generation and use, and the circuit construction.

Section 4 deals with the security of DIDOR. We show how DIDOR satisfies some security properties and analyze its security based on [3,16] security requirements.

Finally, In Sect. 5, a comparison is made between DIDOR and TOR; which shows that given the prior existence of a decentralized identity management system, our protocol guarantees better security and performance.

2 Background

2.1 Onion Routing

According to Syverson et al. [18] the onion network mainly pursues two objectives: firstly to guarantee strong private communication through public networks and secondly to guarantee the anonymity of the nodes that communicate. An adversary observing the network traffic should not be able to understand it or identify the parties involved. In some cases, even the recipient of the message may not know who the sender is. These objectives are somewhat greatly satisfied by the combination of symmetric and asymmetric encryption techniques. However, several questions remain. How to improve network scalability? how to improve the overall performance of the network (latency, traffic volume, congestion, etc.)? How to improve node and service anonymity? And many others.

In [4], Dingledine et al. discussed the design and implementation of Tor, an anonymous network that allows users to browse the internet without revealing their IP addresses. They identify several problems related to the use of the initial version of Tor (single-pass circuit construction), including the need to balance circuit rotation frequency with efficiency and security concerns, as well as the need to provide anonymity for servers through the use of rendez-vous points and hidden services. To improve Tor's security and guarantee forward secrecy (proven by [19]), [4] proposes an incremental approach to circuit construction in which the source node negotiates a specific session key (incrementally) with each node on the circuit. However, the need for improving throughput and delay remains. Constructing a path of n nodes requires the exchange of $\theta(n^2)$ messages instead of $\theta(n)$ in a single-pass approach [2,20]. To improve the latency, [6] proposes Shortor, which uses multi-hop overlay routing. ShorTor improves latency by adding an extra hop between two relays in the Tor network. ShorTor is particularly effective at reducing the time it takes for data to travel between the slowest relays in the network, which benefits a small but significant number of Tor users. Dingledine et al. [4] also highlighted the fact that Tor does not guarantee unconditional anonymity and that Tor's circuit-level encryption does not protect against traffic confirmation attacks.

Observing that the majority of anonymous communication networks do not guarantee unconditional anonymity, [3] proposes Pairing-Based Onion Routing (PB-OR). It is based on identity-based encryption infrastructure and it uses pseudonyms generated by users to provide unconditional anonymity, and preserve privacy during key agreement and message exchange. PB-OR ensures that only the user who initiates the communication knows the complete circuit path, while each node in the circuit only knows its two adjacent nodes. However, there are some limitations to this approach, including the need for a trusted Public Key Generator (PKG) and potential vulnerabilities if multiple malicious PKGs are present in the network. Additionally, while the proposed protocol provides strong anonymity, it may not be suitable for applications that require strong authentication or accountability. We solved this issue by the user-centric control of keys provided by DID. PB-OR circuit construction is improved by Kate and Goldberg [20] with compact message formats that significantly compress the circuit construction messages. To strengthen sender, recipient, and relationship anonymity, [21] propose an approach based on multiple encryption wrapping and relay nodes. The sender is concealed within an anonymity set created using a cyclic circuit known as a ring, which facilitates one-way cover traffic. Subsequently, the message departs from a random location within the ring and, guided by a sender-selected random path, reaches the intended destination while employing a dummy inertia segment of the route for additional concealment.

Like Tor, many other onion communication networks are based on Public Key Infrastructure (PKI) for providing certificates used to identify the nodes. However, the main problem with PKI-based onion routing protocols is the need for certificates to be issued by trusted third parties, which can introduce additional overhead and complexity. Additionally, PKI-based systems may be vulnerable to attacks that compromise the security of the certificate authority or the certificates themselves. To address these shortcomings, [2,3] propose an onion routing protocol that uses identity-based encryption. Our DIDOR protocol also is not based on PKI and is therefore considered certificateless.

Although there are very few works exploiting blockchain in implementing onion routing, [9] proposed a framework that integrates artificial intelligence (AI) and blockchain to improve the reliability and security of onion routing in machine-to-machine (M2M) communications. The AI algorithm is run on the edge server to classify traffic as malicious or non-malicious before routing it on the onion's network. Each onion router (OR) node is connected to a blockchain node that stores and verifies the message request's verify token (VF) and time to live (TTL). This integration of blockchain technology ensures that the data is secure and reliable by maintaining data integrity.

Concerning onion routing security, [16] proposes a definition of security based on three pillars: correctness, integrity, and onion security. These are respectively ensure that: 1- the messages are delivered correctly and that the protocol does not leak information about users or their messages; 2- the messages are delivered without modification and that they come from the expected sender; 3- the intermediate nodes cannot link incoming and outgoing messages, and that users cannot be identified based on their traffic patterns. They demonstrate that a protocol satisfying these requirements is IND-CCA2 secure. In view of the difficulty of guaranteeing and demonstrating the guarantee of the last pillar, [3] shows that an onion routing protocol can also be considered secure if it is IND-CPA secure.

2.2 Decentralized Identifier

A decentralized Identifier (DID) is are a new type of identifier supported by W3C and Decentralized Identity Foundation (DIF) that enables verifiable, decentralized digital identity [22]. In concrete terms, it's a URI (Uniform Resource Identifier) that enables content-based addressing instead of the location-based addressing (URL) commonly used on the Internet. Its design goals are summarized into Decentralization, control, privacy, security, proof-based, discoverability, interoperability, portability, simplicity and extensibility [22]. Typically, DID usual architecture is organized as shown in Fig. 1. DID and DID Document are recorded in a verifiable data registry which is often a distributed ledger.

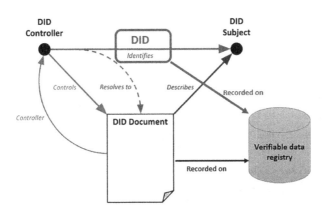

Fig. 1. DID architecture (adapted from [22])

The DID is cryptographically bounded to the subject it identifies, which enables the latter to maintain control of its identity as long as it keeps its private key secure [14,22]. As specified by the DIF: "DIDs enable an entity to provide cryptographic proof of control of the identifier, usually through a demonstration that the DID Controller knows some secret value, such as a private key". In its usage, each DID is associated with a DID document (see Fig. 2), which is obtained by resolving it. The resolution process [23] is simply the mechanism for obtaining the relevant information from the DID, such as the public key, evidence and other metadata. In its structure, the DID is composed of the *did* keyword, followed by the DID method (e.g. *didor*) used to perform the resolution and a unique reference (identifier) that identifies the targeted resource [22]. The DID method also specifies how DID documents are created, updated or deleted. Since, each DID document can contain public cryptographic material, and other useful information, we take advantage of this capability by adding the parameters of the Diffie-Hellman algorithm and the hash of the pre-rotate key in order to satisfy the objectives of the DIDOR protocol. An example of the result of this modification is shown in Fig. 2. We present our approach in the following sections.

3   Protocol Description

In this section, we describe our protocol. We begin with notation (Sect. 3.1) and setup phase (Sect. 3.2), followed by keys generation (Sect. 3.3) and circuit building (Sect. 3.4).

3.1   Notation

The different notations used in the presentation of our protocol, and their meanings, are given in Table 1.

Table 1. Protocol notation

Term	Definition
S, D	Source and Destination
DID_x	DID of the node x
m	A message to be exchanged
S_{SY}	Symmetric key used in communication between nodes S and Y
pk_{SX}	Public key generated by the node S during communication with nodes X
pk_X	Public key of the node X
sk_X	Secret key of the node X
$\{M\}_k$	Encryption of the message M with the key k
$\{M\}_{k^{-1}}$	Decryption of the message M with the key k
$\mathcal{H}(X)$	Cryptographic hash function $\mathcal{H}$ applied to X

3.2   Setup Phase

The setup phase consists of each node wishing to participate in the DIDOR protocol to publish their DID document on the distributed ledger. The DID Document must contain at least three keys: *pubkey*, *hashnextkey*, and *keyDH*.

A sample structure of such a document is shown in Fig. 2. The structure of this document conforms to the W3C standard. The first two keys are used to operationalize the decentralized identity management system. *pubkey* is used at all times to authenticate the DID document and guarantee that the user always maintains control of his DID. *hashnextkey* is mainly used to set up the mechanism for pre-rotating the keys; this is to improve the overall security of the decentralized management system (see Sect. 4.3). *hashnextkey* represents the hash value of the next key that will be used in case of key rotation. On the other hand, *keyDH* is essential for generating the symmetric key that will be used between the source and the node associated with the DID. It is one of the parameters for setting up key generation by the Diffie-Hellman protocol. This key is of a limited lifetime in order to maintain forward secrecy.

The sender randomly obtains the set of DIDs for the nodes in the circuit to be built. This can be done by querying the distributed ledger. It must have as many DIDs as there are nodes participating in the circuit construction.

```
{ "@context":"https://www.w3.org/ns/did/v1"
  "id": "did:didor: pqrstuvwxyz0987654321",
  "verificationMethod": [{
      "id": "did:didor: pqrstuvwxyz0987654321#pubkey",
      "type": "Ed25519VerificationKey2018",
      "publicKeyBase58": " H3C2AVvLMv6gmMNam3uVAjZpfkc",
      "controller": "did:didor: pqrstuvwxyz0987654321"
    },
    { "id": "did:didor: pqrstuvwxyz0987654321#hashnextkey",
      "type": "Ed25519VerificationKey2018",
      "publicKeyBase58": " VCpo2LMLhn6iWku8MKvSLg2ZAoC-n",
      "controller": "did:didor: pqrstuvwxyz0987654321"
    },
    {
      "id": "did:didor:pqrstuvwxyz0987654321#keyDH",
      "type": "EcdsaSecp256k1VerificationKey2019",
      "controller": "did:didor:pqrstuvwxyz0987654321",
      "expires": "2017-02-08T16:02:20Z",
      "publicKeyJwk": {
        "kty": "EC",
        "crv": "secp256k1",
        "kid": "1",
        "x":"7_lyUM2Wp3wX2HK3mUAGrfuqTIGzqzH1bRv1Po-X1pA",
        "y":"iz1G4a5D16oeWKsx46KCC2Ls7Uq_e331fDBYa8uaj10",
        "key_ops": ["deriveKey"]
      }}],
  "authentication":[
  "id": "did:didor: pqrstuvwxyz0987654321#pubkey",
  ],
  "JWS": "eyJiNciOiJFZERTQSJ9…22pbV143Z32CA9MkFHk0cY3obF8cdDRw"
}
```

Fig. 2. Sample of DID document structure

3.3 Keys Generation Phase

The generation of symmetric keys to be used between S and various circuit nodes begins with the DIDs resolution [23] of the concerned nodes. If the node X is part of the circuit to be built by S, the generation of the keys is as follows:

1. S resolved DID_X to get the public DH parameters specified by X in its DID Document.
2. S chooses his private key sk_S.
3. S generates its public key pk_S and the symmetric key S_{SX} which will be used as a session key with X.
4. During the circuit construction, in the portion of the message between S and X, S shall indicate pk_S.
5. Upon receipt of the message from S, X extract the public parameter pk_S and use its private key sk_X to generate S_{SX}.

3.4 Circuit Construction

The circuit construction between S and D follows these steps:

1. S randomly chooses from the distributed ledger, n nodes identified by their DID $(DID_1, \ldots, DID_n)$. The resulting circuit will therefore be:
   $DID_S \rightleftharpoons DID_1 \rightleftharpoons \ldots \rightleftharpoons DID_n \rightleftharpoons DID_D$.
2. After resolving each DID_i, $(i = 1 \ldots n)$ and DID_D, S generates the keys (pk_{S1}, S_{S1}), $\ldots$, (pk_{Sn}, S_{Sn}) and (pk_{SD}, S_{SD}).
3. Based on these different keys, the circuit for sending message m from S to D is as follows:
   $DID_1, pk_{s1}, \{DID_2, pk_{s2}, \{DID_3, pk_{s3}, \{DID_4, pk_{s4}, \ldots DID_n, pk_{sn}, \{DID_D, pk_{SD}, \{DID_S, m\}_{S_{SD}}\}_{S_{Sn}} \ldots\}_{s_{s3}}\}_{S_{S2}}\}_{S_{s1}}$
   A specific case of circuit construction with two nodes between S and D is presented in Fig. 3.
4. At the reception of the onion by a node DID_i, it uses the DH algorithm to generate the symmetric key known by S. It can thus decrypt it corresponding onion layer to find therein the DID of the next node of the circuit to which it must route the traffic. It, therefore, forwards the DID and the encrypted message to the next node. The process ends when node D receives message m.
5. Once the message is received, the destination node acknowledges receipt. The acknowledgment is transmitted from node to node to the source node. It can be envisaged that if the source node does not receive an acknowledgment after a certain period of time, it can build a new circuit with a new set of nodes chosen randomly and not appearing among the previously chosen nodes.

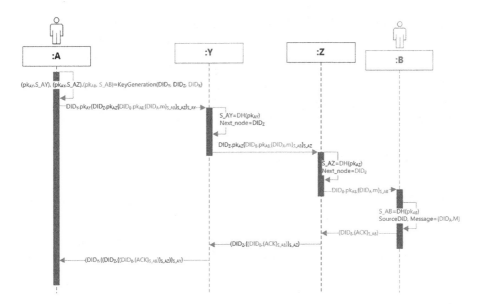

Fig. 3. Circuit construction with two intermediate nodes.

4 Security Analysis

4.1 Node Anonymity

As defined by [24], the "Anonymity of a subject from an attacker's perspective means that the attacker cannot sufficiently identify the subject within a set of subjects, the anonymity set". According to this, we find that our protocol provides anonymity at the level of each node of the circuit. Indeed, an adversary who compromises a node of the circuit has access only to the DIDs of the neighboring nodes. However, the DID is used as a pseudonym. It does not reveal any information to trace the node. It should be noted that for a specific node in the circuit, its anonymity set is equivalent to the set of nodes using the DIDOR protocol. It is almost impossible for an adversary to associate incoming traffic from a node in the circuit to a specific node in the network. However, there remains the possibility for an adversary to compromise the source and the destination nodes simultaneously and discover that these two nodes are communicating with each other. The latter possibility, however, remains highly unlikely. Unlike other onion routing implementations, in which nodes use their real identity during key agreement, DIDOR uses the DID as a pseudonym. As long as the DID remains a pseudonym, no element of identity is revealed and anonymity remains preserved.

4.2 Node Authentication

Given that one of the central elements of the DIDOR is the exploitation of the properties guaranteed by the DID, it is important that the DID be authenticated by the source which builds the circuit. Each node publishes the DID document, making it available for others to access and verify. The publication can happen on a distributed ledger, a trusted registry, or any other mechanism specified by the chosen DID method. When a source node wants to authenticate each randomly selected node, it retrieves its associated DID document by resolving its DID, using *didor* methods. To verify the authenticity of the DID and its document, the following steps are typically followed:

- S resolves the DID and obtains the corresponding DID document from which it extracts the public key (*pubkey*);
- It calculates a digest of the signed portion of the DID document;
- Using the retrieved public key, S decrypts the signature and compares it to the calculated digest. If the signature is valid and matches the calculated digest, the verification is successful and the selected node is authenticated.

Following this process, the source node can be confident that the DID document has not been tampered with and that it was indeed signed by the private key holder bound to the DID.

4.3   Denial-of-Service and Node Control

If an adversary managed to gain access to the private key associated with the DID of a network node, he could simply rotate it by publishing a new DID document. He could therefore cause a denial of service or even easily control a part of the DIDOR network. Conventional key rotation is not sufficient since if the adversary controls the terminal, he can still access the rotated key. We propose to modify the structure of the DID document in order to set up the keys pre-rotation as described by [25]. Pre-rotation consists of adding the current public key (*pubkey*) and the hash (*hashnextkey*) of the next public key to the DID document. Formally, it looks like this:

$DIDDOC_1$ $=$ $\{pk_1, \mathcal{H}(pk_2), pk_{DH}\}_{sk_1}$ $\circlearrowleft$ $DIDDOC_2$ $=$ $\{pk_2, \mathcal{H}(pk_3), pk_{DH}\}_{sk_2}$
$\circlearrowleft DIDDOC_3 = \{pk_2, \mathcal{H}(pk_3), pk_{DH}\}_{sk_2} \dots$

Where $\circlearrowleft$ indicates the pre-rotation event.

The pre-rotated key is escrow. This is so that if the user suspects a compromise of his terminal, he can retrieve the next key from escrow and rotate it. The different versions of the DID document ($DIDDOC_1$, $DIDDOC_2$, ...) are thus chained such as to remain linked to the DID. When the first DID document is created, it is signed with the private key corresponding to the public key in it. When the key needs to be rotated, the new document is signed with the pre-rotated private key. The DID is also derived from the public key. It is thus possible to check at any time that the hash of the current public key corresponds to the hash found in the previous version of the DID document.

4.4   Onion Security Requirements

In this section, we analyze our protocol under the prism of Onion's routing security definition proposed by [3,16].

Onion-Correctness. This is defined by [16] as: "condition that if an onion is formed correctly and then the correct routers process it in the correct order, then the correct message is received by the last router". Given that a node can only peel off a layer of onion intended for it and that according to the construction of the onion coming out of the source node, no node can peel off a layer intended for it before the nodes which precede it in the circuit, the decryption can only be done in the order defined by the protocol. Moreover, by respecting the protocol through the decryption of each onion at the level of the indicated node, the receiving node last decrypts the onion containing the message. It, therefore, appears trivially that our protocol satisfies the requirement of correctness.

Onion-Integrity. This is defined by [3] as: "if onions longer than some upper limit on the length can be recognized by routers". By fixing the maximum size of the circuit at n nodes and under the assumption that the messages exchanged between the source and destination nodes are of fixed size on the DIDOR network, it also appears trivial that routers will quickly recognized an onion with more than n layers of encryption. To do this, the node which receives it will only have to evaluate the size of the message.

Key Secrecy. As stated by [3], this requirement states that "an attacker controlling all but one honest node in a circuit should not be able to recover the secret key shared between the user and the honest node". The keys shared between the source and the different nodes are generated individually based on Elliptic Curve Diffie-Hellman Ephemeral (ECDHE) protocol. Even if an attacker controls all the nodes except an honest node H, he would have to find the shared key S_{SH} (or to find the private key of the honest node sk_H or of the source sk_S) knowing their public keys. Which would consist of the attacker solving the Computational Diffie-Hellman Problem (CDHP). As long as we consider this problem difficult to solve, it is obvious that the adversary has very little chance of discovering the session key shared between the source and the other node.

Forward Secrecy. Since we are implementing Ephemeral Diffie-Hellman, even if an attacker gains access to the private keys of one party, they will only be able to derive the shared secret for the current circuit. The session keys for past sessions, which were derived using ephemeral keys that are no longer available, remain secure. This ensures that the confidentiality of past communications is preserved even in the event of future key compromises. Moreover, the use of pre-rotation of keys guarantees that in the event of the DID private key compromise, the adversary will only be able to manipulate the DID Document as long as the associated private key has not been rotated. All this allows our protocol to guarantee forward secrecy.

Cryptographic Unlinkability. [3] has shown that this property can be guaranteed as long as the asymmetric encryption algorithm used to build the circuit is IND-CPA (Indistinguishability under Chosen-Plaintext Attack). DIDOR does not specify any symmetric encryption algorithm and one can choose any of them. Particularly, if the chosen symmetric encryption algorithm is secure against IND-CPA attacks (such as AES), then our protocol satisfies the cryptographic indistinguishability requirement. This is easily demonstrated by replaying the indistinguishability game proposed by [3]. Indeed, the pseudonyms used by [3] simply correspond to the DID in our protocol and are of fixed size. Moreover, session key security already proven for DIDOR.

Circuit Position Secrecy. Although our above-defined protocol is simple, it does not guarantee this property. However, It can be easily modified by relying on the approach proposed by [16]. This involves padding the message such that onion size's at each node substantially remain the same, making it harder for a node to determine its position in the circuit based on the size of the received onion. In the case of a circuit with three intermediates nodes X, Y, and Z, the onions passed by each node to the next would look like this.

$$A : DID_X.pk_{AX}.\{DID_Y.pk_{AY}.\{DID_Z.pk_{AZ}.\{DID_B.pk_{AB}.\{DID_A.M\}_{S_{AB}} \}_{S_{AZ}}\}_{S_{AY}})\}_{S_{AX}}, (R_A)$$

$$X : DID_Y.pk_{AY}.\{DID_Z.pk_{AZ}.\{DID_B.pk_{AB}.\{DID_A.M\}_{S_{AB}}\}_{S_{AZ}}\}_{S_{AY}}, (\{(R_A)\}_{S_{AX-1}}, R_X)$$

$$Y : DID_Z.pk_{AZ}.\{DID_B.pk_{AB}.\{DID_A.M\}_{S_{AB}}\}_{S_{AZ}}, (\{(\{(R_A)\}_{S_{AX-1}}, R_X) \}_{S_{AY-1}}, R_Y)$$

$$Z : DID_B.pk_{AB}.\{DID_A.M\}_{S_{AB}}, (\{(\{(\{(R_A)\}_{S_{AX-1}}, R_X)\}_{S_{AY-1}}, R_Y)\}_{S_{AZ-1}}, R_Z)$$

Each node i generates a random value R_i such that $|R_i| = |DID_i|$ and use it to pad the message. Both parts of the message are decrypted at each node and each node adds its random value before transmission to the next node.

5   Comparaison and Discussion

Table 2 compares DIDOR to Tor protocol.

Since DIDOR is Certificateless, it avoids the need for certificate verifications that are required in PKI settings like Tor. Each node uses a pseudonym which is publicly available on the distributed ledger. The number of messages exchanged by DIDOR is of the linear order $\theta(n)$ compared to the quadratic order of Tor $\theta(n^2)$ [2,3]. Indeed, the source node performs only n DID resolutions followed by sending the message. In the worst-case scenario, one could consider that the authentication of the nodes by the source is done by a challenge-response mechanism. Even then, message exchanges would remain linear.

Like Tor, our protocol uses DH for session key generation. However, we do not need to implement the telescoping [4] or use the RSA protocol for key exchange. Resolving the DID both authenticates the node and obtains its public key. This

Table 2. Tor Vs DIDOR

Criteria	Tor	DIDOR
Modifying the circuit on the fly	×	√
No use of certificate	×	√
No RSA Encryption required	×	√
No prior connection between nodes (TLS session)	×	√
No interaction in circuit construction	×	√
No identity renewal in case of suspected compromise	×	√
Self control of node identity	×	√
No use of Directory Server	×	√
Self-specification of node status (active/inactive)	×	√
IND-CPA security level	×	√
Number of messages exchanged	$\theta(n^2)$	$\theta(n)$

saves the source node from performing n RSA encryptions and 2n exponentiations, and the intermediate nodes from performing one RSA decryption and two exponentiations.

Another important aspect DIDOR protocol concerns the elimination Key Generator Center and taking forward secrecy into account. Indeed, each node of our protocol can change its keys by itself, provided that it respects the pre-established timeframe. In addition, the fact that each node can self-rotate its keys prevents the adversary from accessing old messages in case the active key is compromised.

6   Conclusion and Future Work

Observing the emergence of decentralized identity and its privacy-preserving properties, we have proposed an onion routing protocol that relies on decentralized identity. Our protocol does not use certificates and guarantees the same security properties offered by some existing onion routing protocols while avoiding some of their pitfalls. It is inspired by the protocols proposed by [2, 3, 16, 20] and with few slight adaptations, could be universally composable (UC) secure. By design, our protocol allows the user to rotate their keys whenever they wish. This helps ensure forward secrecy. The pre-rotation mechanism makes it harder for an attacker to take control of the network and therefore prevents denials of service targeting DID documents. Compared to the Tor protocol, we theoretically find that our protocol solves several known problems. These include the exchange of large volumes of messages, the significant encryption and decryption time resulting from the use of RSA, or even the use of a Key Generation Center (KGC).

However, the concrete implementation of DIDOR relies on the prior existence of a decentralized identity management system. This is why in our future research, we plan to implement this protocol in a practical way in order to evaluate its performance and compare it to that of existing protocols. It will also be interesting to consider algorithms other than Diffie-Hellman.

References

1. Reed, M., Syverson, P., Goldschlag, D.: Anonymous connections and onion routing. IEEE J. Sel. Areas Commun. **16**(4), 482–494 (1998)
2. Catalano, D., Fiore, D., Gennaro, R.: A certificateless approach to onion routing. Int. J. Inf. Secur. **16**, 327–343 (2017)
3. Kate, A., Zaverucha, G.M., Goldberg, I.: Pairing-based onion routing with improved forward secrecy. ACM Trans. Inf. Syst. Secur. (TISSEC) **13**(4), 1–32 (2010)
4. Dingledine, R., Mathewson, N., Murdoch, S., Syverson, P.: Tor: the second-generation onion router (2014 DRAFT v1). Cl. Cam. Ac, UK (2014)
5. Kuhn, C., Hofheinz, D., Rupp, A., Strufe, T.: Onion routing with replies. In: Tibouchi, M., Wang, H. (eds.) ASIACRYPT 2021, Part II. LNCS, vol. 13091, pp. 573–604. Springer, Cham (2021). https://doi.org/10.1007/978-3-030-92075-3_20
6. Hogan, K., Servan-Schreiber, S., Newman, Z., Weintraub, B., Nita-Rotaru, C., Devadas, S.: ShorTor: improving tor network latency via multi-hop overlay routing. In: 2022 IEEE Symposium on Security and Privacy (SP), pp. 1933–1952. IEEE (2022)
7. Øverlier, L., Syverson, P.: Improving efficiency and simplicity of Tor circuit establishment and hidden services. In: Borisov, N., Golle, P. (eds.) PET 2007. LNCS, vol. 4776, pp. 134–152. Springer, Heidelberg (2007). https://doi.org/10.1007/978-3-540-75551-7_9
8. Chen, C., Asoni, D.E., Barrera, D., Danezis, G., Perrig, A.: HORNET: high-speed onion routing at the network layer. In: Proceedings of the 22nd ACM SIGSAC Conference on Computer and Communications Security, pp. 1441–1454 (2016). https://doi.org/10.48550/arXiv.1507.05724
9. Gupta, R., Jadav, N.K., Mankodiya, H., Alshehri, M.D., Tanwar, S., Sharma, R.: Blockchain and onion-routing-based secure message exchange system for edge-enabled IIoT. IEEE Trans. Industr. Inf. **19**(2), 1965–1976 (2022)
10. Sakai, K., Sun, M.T., Ku, W.S., Wu, J., Alanazi, F.S.: Performance and security analyses of onion-based anonymous routing for delay tolerant networks. IEEE Trans. Mob. Comput. **16**(12), 3473–3487 (2017)
11. Haghighi, M.S., Aziminejad, Z.: Highly anonymous mobility-tolerant location-based onion routing for VANETs. IEEE Internet Things J. **7**(4), 2582–2590 (2019)
12. Kita, K., Koizumi, Y., Hasegawa, T., Ascigil, O., Psaras, I.: Producer anonymity based on onion routing in named data networking. IEEE Trans. Netw. Serv. Manage. **18**(2), 2420–2436 (2020)
13. Wardana, H.K., Handianto, L.F., Yohanes, B.W.: The onion routing performance using shadow-plugin-TOR. In: 2017 4th International Conference on Electrical Engineering, Computer Science and Informatics (EECSI), pp. 1–5. IEEE (2017)
14. Preukschat, A., Reed, D.: Self-Sovereign Identity: Decentralized Digital Identity and Verifiable Credentials. Manning Publications Co. (2021)
15. Alangot, B., et al.: Decentralized identity authentication with auditability and privacy. Algorithms **16**(1), 4 (2022)

16. Camenisch, J., Lysyanskaya, A.: A formal treatment of onion routing. In: Shoup, V. (ed.) CRYPTO 2005. LNCS, vol. 3621, pp. 169–187. Springer, Heidelberg (2005). https://doi.org/10.1007/11535218_11
17. Diffie, W., van Oorschot, P.C., Wiener, M.J.: Authentication and authenticated key exchanges. Des. Codes Crypt. **2**(2), 107–125 (1992)
18. Syverson, P., Tsudik, G., Reed, M., Landwehr, C.: Towards an analysis of onion routing security. In: Federrath, H. (ed.) Designing Privacy Enhancing Technologies. LNCS, vol. 2009, pp. 96–114. Springer, Heidelberg (2001). https://doi.org/10.1007/3-540-44702-4_6
19. Goldberg, I.: On the security of the Tor authentication protocol. In: Danezis, G., Golle, P. (eds.) PET 2006. LNCS, vol. 4258, pp. 316–331. Springer, Heidelberg (2006). https://doi.org/10.1007/11957454_18
20. Kate, A., Goldberg, I.: Using sphinx to improve onion routing circuit construction. In: Sion, R. (ed.) FC 2010. LNCS, vol. 6052, pp. 359–366. Springer, Heidelberg (2010). https://doi.org/10.1007/978-3-642-14577-3_30
21. Buccafurri, F., De Angelis, V., Idone, M.F., Labrini, C.: WIP: an onion-based routing protocol strengthening anonymity. In: 2021 IEEE 22nd International Symposium on a World of Wireless, Mobile and Multimedia Networks (WoWMoM), pp. 231–235. IEEE (2021)
22. W3C: Decentralized Identifiers (DIDs) v1.0: Core architecture, data model, and representations. https://w3c.github.io/did-core/. Accessed 23 May 2023
23. W3C: Decentralized Identifier Resolution (DID Resolution) v0.3 Resolution of Decentralized Identifiers (DIDs). https://w3c-ccg.github.io/did-resolution/. Accessed 23 May 2023
24. Pfitzmann, A. Hansen, M.: A terminology for talking about privacy by data minimization: anonymity, unlinkability, undetectability, unobservability, pseudonymity, and identity management (2010)
25. Smith, S.M.: Key event receipt infrastructure (KERI). arXiv preprint arXiv:1907.02143 (2019)

Feature Analysis and Classification of Collusive Android App-Pairs Using DBSCAN Clustering Algorithm

Roger Yiran Mawoh[1,3]([✉]), Franklin Tchakounte[2,3], Joan Beri Ali[1], and Claude Fachkha[4]

[1] Department of Computer Science, Faculty of Science, University of Buea, Buea, Cameroon
mawohry3030@gmail.com
[2] Department of Mathematics and Computer Science, Faculty of Science, University of Ngaoundéré, Ngaoundéré, Cameroon
[3] Cybersecurity with Computational and Artificial Intelligence Research Group, Faculty of Science, University of Ngaoundéré, Ngaoundéré, Cameroon
[4] College of Engineering and IT, University of Dubai, Dubai, UAE

Abstract. In this study, we tackle the issue of application collusion, which involves multiple apps working together to achieve malicious goals that they couldn't achieve individually. The current security model of Android, which focuses on permissions, doesn't effectively address this threat because it only mitigates risks associated with individual apps. To address this limitation, we carried out an extensive analysis of features to identify the key Android permissions utilized by colluding app-pairs. We propose an approach to classify collusive app-pairs using the DBSCAN clustering algorithm. Our results provide valuable insights into the relationship between specific Android permission sets and the malicious activities performed by colluding app-pairs. We identified 12 permissions as the most important features contributing to the classification of collusive app-pairs. We also identified 4 distinct clusters of colluding Android app-pairs.

Keywords: App collusion · Android App-pairs · Clustering · DBSCAN

1 Introduction

Due to the high prevalence of Android applications, they have become prime targets for malware attacks. According to Statista's statistics [10], there were 26.61 million instances of Android malware in March 2018. As of March 2020, there were more than 482,000 new Android malware samples developed each month. According to G Data security specialists, more than 1.3 million new malware samples were found each month in 2020 [6]. In fact, they found that new versions of such malicious software were published at an average rate of 1.3 s.

© ICST Institute for Computer Sciences, Social Informatics and Telecommunications Engineering 2024
Published by Springer Nature Switzerland AG 2024. All Rights Reserved
F. Tchakounte et al. (Eds.): SAFER-TEA 2023, LNICST 566, pp. 86–96, 2024.
https://doi.org/10.1007/978-3-031-56396-6_6

A potential future threat in the realm of malware development, as reported in various studies [3,9], is the concept of app collusion. App collusion is the situation where multiple apps collaborate to perform malicious activities, often created by the same developer. The fact that each cooperating piece of malware simply needs to ask for a tiny number of permissions raises serious security concerns, making it appear harmless when analyzed as a standalone app [3,9]. There is a significant motivation for malware authors to create colluding malware, as it allows them to bypass detection mechanisms.

Android app collusion has been the focus of extensive research in recent years. Several models have been developed by both academia and industry to analyze and detect collusion. However, most of these approaches primarily focus on detecting app collusion by classifying a group of applications as either benign or colluding. As a result, there is a need for solutions that allow end-users and security analysts to gain a deeper understanding of the code structure and behavior of colluding apps. In this article, we introduce a methodology for analyzing a dataset of pairs of colluding Android apps, aiming to address three key research questions:

- Research Question-1: Do colluding Android app-pairs use a specific set of Android permissions to carry out suspicious activities?
- Research Question-2: Can a condensed list of Android permissions be built for effective collusive app pair classification?
- Research Question-3: What are the various categories of colluding Android malware?

We collected a dataset of colluding Android app-pairs and used various data analysis techniques such as correlation analysis, variance threshold, clustering, and classification to answer these research questions. Our findings offer insights into the relationship between specific Android permission sets and malicious activities performed by colluding Android app-pairs. We also identify the most important features that contribute to the classification of collusive Android app-pairs and construct a reduced Android permission set for efficient classification. Finally, we group similar types of colluding Android malware together based on their permission sets.

2   Related Works

The literature has examined colluding Android app-pairs using a range of techniques, including static analysis, dynamic analysis, and machine learning. However, most of these studies do not consider the relationship between specific Android permissions and the malicious activities performed by colluding app-pairs. In this section, we review the key research conducted in this field and highlight the gaps that our work aims to fill.

Casolare et al. (2021) present a novel approach for distinguishing trustworthy applications from those exhibiting malicious behavior due to app collusion [4].

Their approach involves analyzing the audio signal generated by converting an application into an audio file.

In another study, Casolare et al. (2020) introduce a model-checking-based technique to identify collusion attacks between multiple apps. Additionally, they provide a heuristic feature to cut down on the number of apps that need to be examined and locate the collusion [5].

Bhandari et al. (2016) propose an automaton framework that detects intent-based collusion at the component level and is scalable to application sizing [1].

Machine learning approaches have also been employed to detect colluding Android app-pairs. Md Faiz et al. (2018) propose techniques to detect collusive app-pairs based on a set of crucial parameters and using machine learning classifiers [8]. In another study, Md Faiz et al. (2019) describe a new and easy method for utilizing machine learning classifiers to find app-pairs that are colluding. They use a two-stage classification model in their technique, which has shown success in detecting collusive app-pairs [7].

While these studies have made valuable contributions to the identification of colluding Android app-pairs, this work differs in that we focus on analyzing colluding Android app-pairs to identify the key Android permissions utilized by them. We propose an approach to classify collusive app-pairs using the DBSCAN clustering algorithm. Our results provide valuable insights into the relationship between specific Android permission sets and the malicious activities performed by colluding app-pairs. We identified 12 permissions as the most important features contributing to the classification of collusive app-pairs. We also identified 4 distinct clusters of colluding Android app-pairs.

3 Methodology

In the methodology section, we elaborate on our approach for clustering colluding applications. The proposed Methodology is shown in Fig. 1. We begin by extracting the permissions utilized by colluding Android app-pairs. From these permissions, we extract numerical features that represent them. Once we have obtained the features, we use them as a dataset for analysis to identify the most frequently used permissions by colluding with Android app-pairs. Subsequently, we employ feature reduction techniques to identify the most significant permissions for classifying colluding Android app-pairs. Finally, we apply clustering techniques to group colluding Android app-pairs into clusters.

- Step 1: To collect the input dataset, we begin with the data collection phase to acquire the necessary data for our analysis. At this stage, we take into consideration a dataset of .apk files consisting of colluding Android app-pairs. The permissions used by Android applications are then extracted from the original Android documentation[1] using a Python code developed by the authors for automated retrieval of Android permissions. Subsequently, we extract the required permissions from each .apk file using Apktool[2] and a Python code developed by the authors. The obtained results are exported to a CSV file.

Each row in the CSV file contains the permissions associated with each colluding app pair in our dataset. The presence of a permission in an app-pair is denoted by '1', and the absence is denoted by '0'.

- Step 2: Feature Engineering, After extracting the features, we analyze our dataset using frequency analysis to identify the most commonly used permissions by colluding Android app-pairs. Permissions that have a frequency of zero, indicating no usage in the entire dataset, are discarded. This process results in a reduced set of permissions. Once we have obtained the reduced set of permissions, we conduct correlation analysis to determine the most frequently used combinations of permissions by colluding Android app-pairs.
- Step 3: Feature Reduction, The cvs file was then analyzed using Variance Threshold to determine a reduced set of permissions that can be used to classify colluding Android app-pairs.
- Step 4: After obtaining a reduced set of permissions, we apply the elbow method and silhouette method to the dataset, using the reduced number of permissions, to determine the optimal number of *eps* for our dataset. We then use this value as the *eps* value in the DBSCAN algorithm, with a *minPts* value of 8, to cluster our dataset.

The DBSCAN, a density-based clustering algorithm, can manage noise and outliers without requiring a predetermined number of clusters. The DBSCAN algorithm works by finding the core points that have at least *minPts* neighbors within a radius of *eps* and expanding the clusters from the core points by adding the reachable points that are within *eps* distance from any core point. The points that are not reachable by any core point are considered noise and are excluded from the clusters.

4 Experimental Results

In this section, we elaborate on the dataset and feature extraction, the engineering methods applied to the dataset, the clustering techniques used to identify types of colluding Android malware, and the various classification algorithms used to create an effective system for classifying colluding Android malware.

4.1 Dataset and Feature Extraction

In this study, our dataset consists of 241 colluding Android app-pairs collected from [2].

In order to develop a classification model for malware classification systems, we collected features through static and/or dynamic analysis of Android applications. Any malware classification system must include the feature vector. Using the Apktool[3] reverse engineering program, Android applications were disassembled for this study. Files like AndroidManifest.xml, library files, assets, and more can be found in an app that has been disassembled. The list of Android permissions that are utilized by an application is declared in the AndroidManifest.xml

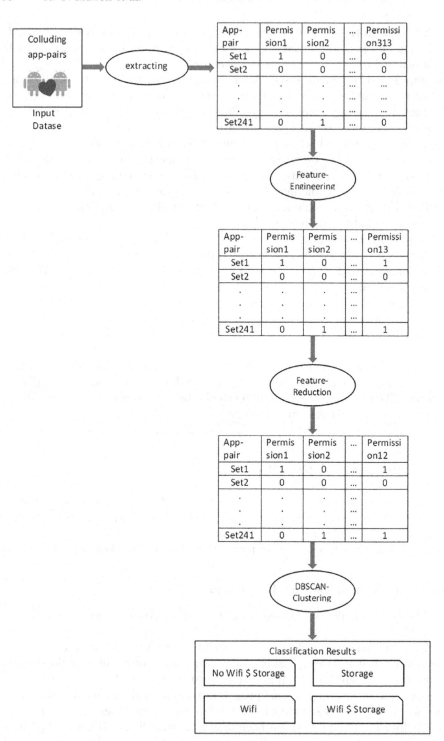

Fig. 1. Flow diagram of obtaining relevant features and clustering colluding app-pairs

file. We took the original Android documentation's comprehensive list of all permissions[4] and added it to our database. The list consists of 313 permissions and their respective API levels, spanning between API Levels 1 to 33. Such a list has deprecated permissions that are not compatible with the latest Android version, such as PERSISTENT_ACTIVITY and GET_TASKS. Additionally, all app-pairs from the malware dataset were decompiled using Apktool. In order to create the feature vector, that has a list of the permissions leveraged by each app pair, the parsers then went through the AndroidManifest.xml of each application. In Eq. (1), where X stands for a permission matrix, this procedure is encapsulated. Each column in an app-pair a_i indicates the permissions that the relevant applications in that app-pair have sought, and each row corresponds to an app-pair a_i.

$$X_{241,313} = \begin{pmatrix} a_{1,1} & a_{1,2} & \cdots & a_{1,313} \\ a_{2,1} & a_{2,2} & \cdots & a_{2,313} \\ \vdots & \vdots & \ddots & \vdots \\ a_{241,1} & a_{241,2} & \cdots & a_{241,313} \end{pmatrix} \tag{1}$$

where, for every app pair a_i

$$x_{i,j} = \begin{cases} 1 & \text{if } j^{t^h} \text{ permission exists.} \\ 0 & \text{else.} \end{cases} \tag{2}$$

4.2   Feature Engineering

After extracting features from applications, we involve feature engineering and develop models for classification. Examining the feature vector gave insightful information about how Android permissions are used. Out of a total of 300 permissions, there were no colluding app-pairs. Further analysis revealed that some app-pairs were using deprecated permissions such as READ_HISTORY_BOOKMARKS, GET_TASKS, which are no longer supported in newer versions of Android.

In Fig. 2, we can visualize the frequency of permissions in the dataset. The most frequently used permission in colluding app-pairs was INTERNET, as these apps attempt to send sensitive data to third-party servers. The next two widely used permissions were READ_EXTERNAL_STORAGE, READ_HISTORY_BOOKMARKS, and WRITE_EXTERNAL_STORAGE.

When describing the degree of relationship lineage between two variables, a correlation grid is employed. As per our findings, the top Android permissions by collaborating app pairings are correlated in Fig. 3. The correlations that exhibited the highest values were between CHANGE_WIFI_STATE & ACCESS_WIFI_STATE and WRITE_EXTERNAL_STORAGE & READ_EXTERNAL_STORAGE, which have a correlation of 1.00 and 0.99. This is followed by GET_TASKS & ACCESS_WIFI_STATE, GET_TASKS & CHANGE_WIFI_STATE, GET_TASKS & GET_ACCOUNTS, GET_TASKS & RECORD_AUDIO with correlations of 0.065 and GET_TASKS

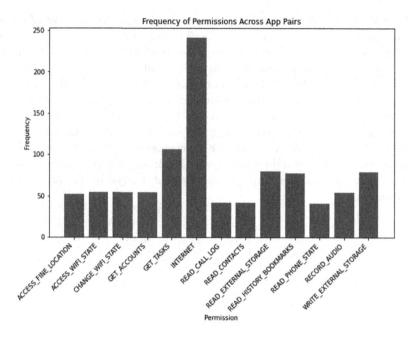

Fig. 2. The permissions' frequency in colluding app-pairs.

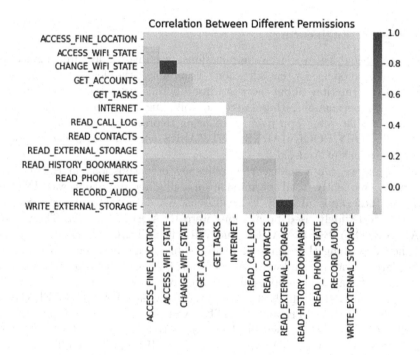

Fig. 3. Permissions utilized by complicit app-pairs are correlated in a matrix.

& ACCESS_FINE_LOCATION, READ_PHONE_STATE & WRITE_EXTER-NAL_STORAGE with correlations of 0.043 and 0.013 respectively.

4.3 Feature Reduction

Since each system that is defined by an Android permission has only one identifier (total of 313), as such, the feature vector contains 313 characteristics as well. The construction of a classification model using so many features, however, might be computationally costly, take longer to train and test, be less interpretable, and be more susceptible to the dimensionality curse. To address these issues, we used feature reduction techniques such as variance threshold for feature subset selection.

We performed feature reduction using Variance Threshold to reduce the number of features from 313 to 12. The Variance Threshold method removes all features whose variance does not meet a certain threshold. We set the threshold to 0.1 and removed all features with a variance lower than this value. The remaining 12 features were selected as the most important features for our analysis. Because the vast majority (301) of permissions have zero variance, they have no bearing on classification. GET_TASKS, READ_EXTERNAL_STORAGE, WRITE_EXTERNAL_STORAGE, and READ_HISTORY_BOOKMARKS have the highest variance of 0.247, 0.222, 0.221 and 0.219 respectively. Table 1 displays all 12 permissions of Android, listed according to their variance in descending order.

Table 1. Significant Permission Ranking

Android Permission	Ranking
GET_TASKS	8
READ_EXTERNAL_STORAGE	7
WRITE_EXTERNAL_STORAGE	6
READ_HISTORY_BOOKMARKS	5
RECORD_AUDIO, GET_ACCOUNTS, CHANGE_WIFI_STATE, ACCESS_WIFI_STATE	4
ACCESS_FINE_LOCATION	3
READ_CALL_LOG, READ_CONTACTS, READ_PHONE_STATE	2
READ_PHONE_STATE	1

4.4 Clustering

We used both the elbow method and silhouette score to find the best (optimal) count of clusters in our dataset. Figure 4(a) depicts an "elbow" point at k = 3,

where the SSE began to level off. We selected k = 3 as our optimal number of
clusters based on this plot. As shown in Fig. 2(b), the silhouette score plot also
showed a peak at k = 3 with a score of 0.5. Therefore, we decided to use k = 3
as our optimal number of clusters.

We then used DBSCAN clustering with an *eps* value of 3 and *min_sample*
value of 8. We obtained 4 clusters from this. We then analyzed each cluster for
similarities by observing patterns of permission usage. We named the clusters
based on these patterns. Table 2 illustrates our findings.

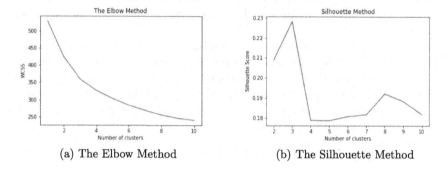

(a) The Elbow Method   (b) The Silhouette Method

Fig. 4. Elbow and Silhouette Method

Table 2. Permission usage by colluding app-pairs

Cluster	Number of App-pairs	Observed Pattern in Permission Usage	Name
0	126	no access to ACCESS_WIFI_STATE, CHANGE_WIFI_STATE, READ_EXTERNAL_STORAGE, and WRITE_EXTERNAL_STORAGE	No Wifi and Storage Access
1	61	access READ_EXTERNAL_STORAGE, and WRITE_EXTERNAL_STORAGE	Storage Access
2	36	access to ACCESS_WIFI_STATE, and CHANGE_WIFI_STATE	Wifi Access
3	18	access to ACCESS_WIFI_STATE, CHANGE_WIFI_STATE, READ_EXTERNAL_STORAGE, and WRITE_EXTERNAL_STORAGE	Wifi and Storage Access

5 Conclusion

In this study, we have provided a thorough feature analysis to pinpoint the important Android permissions used by colluding Android app-pairs and proposed a collusive app pair classification approach using the DBSCAN clustering algorithm. Our results provide insights into the relationship between specific Android permission sets and malicious activities performed by colluding Android app-pairs. We have identified 4 distinct clusters of colluding Android app-pairs and shown that 12 permissions are the most important features that contribute to the classification of collusive Android app-pairs. Our approach could be used to study app collusion in real-world scenarios and extended to other platforms or domains. However, there are some limitations and challenges of our approach that need to be addressed in future work. For example, our approach relies on static analysis of permissions and does not consider dynamic behavior or user interactions. Future work could explore how to integrate dynamic analysis or user feedback into our approach to improve its accuracy and effectiveness.

References

1. Bhandari, S., Laxmi, V., Zemmari, A., Gaur, M.S.: Intersection automata based model for android application collusion. In: 2016 IEEE 30th International Conference on Advanced Information Networking and Applications (AINA), pp. 901–908 (2016). https://doi.org/10.1109/AINA.2016.92
2. Blasco, J., Chen, T.M.: Automated generation of colluding apps for experimental research. J. Comput. Virol. Hacking Tech. **14**, 127–138 (2018)
3. Bosu, A., Liu, F., Yao, D.D., Wang, G.: Collusive data leak and more: large-scale threat analysis of inter-app communications. In: Proceedings of the 2017 ACM on Asia Conference on Computer and Communications Security, ASIA CCS 2017, pp. 71–85. Association for Computing Machinery, New York (2017). https://doi.org/10.1145/3052973.3053004
4. Casolare, R., Giacomo, U.D., Martinelli, F., Mercaldo, F., Santone, A.: Android collusion detection by means of audio signal analysis with machine learning techniques. Procedia Comput. Sci. **192**, 2340–2346 (2021). https://doi.org/10.1016/j.procs.2021.08.224. https://www.sciencedirect.com/science/article/pii/S1877050921017208, knowledge-Based and Intelligent Information & Engineering Systems: Proceedings of the 25th International Conference KES2021
5. Casolare, R., Martinelli, F., Mercaldo, F., Nardone, V., Santone, A.: Colluding android apps detection via model checking. In: Barolli, L., Amato, F., Moscato, F., Enokido, T., Takizawa, M. (eds.) WAINA 2020. AISC, vol. 1150, pp. 776–786. Springer, Cham (2020). https://doi.org/10.1007/978-3-030-44038-1_71
6. Defense, G.D.C.: G data mobile security report: Conflict in Ukraine causes decline in malicious android apps (2022). https://www.gdata-software.com/news/2022/08/37506-g-data-mobile-security-report-conflict-in-ukraine-causes-decline-in-malicious-android-apps
7. Faiz, M.F.I., Hussain, M.A., Marchang, N.: Machine learning based app-collusion detection in smartphones. In: 2019 IEEE 23rd International Symposium on Consumer Technologies (ISCT), pp. 134–137 (2019). https://doi.org/10.1109/ISCE.2019.8901022

8. Iqbal Faiz, M.F., Hussain, M.A., Marchang, N.: Detection of collusive app-pairs using machine learning. In: 2018 IEEE International Conference on Consumer Electronics - Asia (ICCE-Asia), pp. 206–212 (2018). https://doi.org/10.1109/ICCE-ASIA.2018.8552106

9. Liu, F., Cai, H., Wang, G., Yao, D., Elish, K.O., Ryder, B.G.: MR-Droid: a scalable and prioritized analysis of inter-app communication risks. In: 2017 IEEE Security and Privacy Workshops (SPW), pp. 189–198 (2017). https://doi.org/10.1109/SPW.2017.12

10. Statista: Global android malware volume 2020 (2022). https://www.statista.com/statistics/680705/global-android-malware-volume/

Feature Engineering Considerations in IoT: A Case Study

Jean-Marie Kuate Fotso[1,5](✉) (iD), Ismael Abbo[2] (iD), Franklin Tchakounté[2] (iD), William Shu[3] (iD), and Claude Fachkha[4] (iD)

[1] Department of Mathematics and Computer Science, Faculty of Science, Doctoral Training Unit "Mathematics, Computer Science, and Applications", University of Ngaoundéré, P.O. Box 454, Ngaoundéré, Cameroon
jm.kuate@cycomai.com

[2] Department of Mathematics and Computer Science, Faculty of Science, University of Ngaoundéré, P.O. Box 454, Ngaoundéré, Cameroon

[3] University of Buea, P.O. Box 63, Buea, Cameroon

[4] College of Engineering and IT (CEIT), University of Dubai, Dubai, UAE

[5] Information, Communication Technologies and Artificial Intelligence Commission, National Committee for Development of Technologies, Ministry of Scientific Research and Innovation, P.O. Box 1457, Yaoundé, Cameroon

Abstract. Since the emergence and integration of the Internet of Things, homes have become increasingly intelligent and communicative. These connected homes require special control and security from conception, as they can expose people through confidential data sharing and system attacks. To cope with this, Intrusion Detection Systems remain the best solution, despite the need for improvement and adaptation, since these technologies frequently monitor enormous volumes of data flow with unnecessary and duplicated capabilities, this has a detrimental effect on how well they work. Current work on the Internet of Things shows a real willingness on the part of researchers to propose lightweight, accurate IDS-IoTs with reduced functionality. This study aims to provide an overview of the design of a security solution, by experimenting with Feature Engineering extraction and selection techniques. As such, the PCA, IG, ANOVA, LDA and RFE algorithms were evaluated on the TON_IoT dataset. The features obtained for each technique were evaluated through the Random Forest model using indicators, such as ROC, Accuracy, selection time for each algorithm, and training time for each group of features obtained. Each algorithm was trained and evaluated using differ param-eters to detect optimal thresholds of 1, 15 and 20. We obtained an accuracy of 98.18% for RFE with a training time of 74.8 s, and the PCA algorithm gave us the best feature acquisition time 2.8 s.

Keywords: IoT · Smart home · Feature Engineering · Intrusion Detection System · Malware

© ICST Institute for Computer Sciences, Social Informatics and Telecommunications Engineering 2024
Published by Springer Nature Switzerland AG 2024. All Rights Reserved
F. Tchakounte et al. (Eds.): SAFER-TEA 2023, LNICST 566, pp. 97–107, 2024.
https://doi.org/10.1007/978-3-031-56396-6_7

1 Introduction

Over the past decade, the development of digital technology has played a significant role through the concept of connected objects, which has encouraged its adoption in several parallel fields, including: smart agriculture, smart cities, energy management and health (Bedir et al. 2023; Ikram et al. 2019). Through this successful integration, statisticians projected that approximately 24.6 billion objects will be connected in 2025 compare to 12 and 8.8 billion in 2019 and 2010, respectively, with a large number being smart homes and smart buildings. However, researchers are concerned about the security of connected homes because of the information generated about smart home environment and user privacy (Shahbaz et al. 2023; Elvira et al. 2022). Given their popularity and reputation, security architectures are being researched to propose viable security solutions, most of which focus on blockchain with smart contracts, and the security of the communication protocols used (Wi-Fi or Bluetooth), that enable remote viewing via smartphones and web applications (Shahbaz et al. 2023; Sujit et al. 2023; Krishan and Rajendra 2022). Intrusion detection systems (IDS) are the ideal solution for combating attacks proportional to their scale (Arnaud et al. 2023). Broadly, they are designed to handle the following tasks: data pre-processing, functionality engineering, classification, and performance evaluation. To avoid bias in the process, attention must be paid to each task, and to the type of feature engineering addressed (Muhammad et al. 2020; Xin-Ning et al. 2022).

In (Mohanad et al. 2021; Hanli et al. 2020; Quoc-Dung et al. 2020), several feature reduction techniques, including datasets UNSW-NB15, TON_IoT and CSE-CIC-IDS2018 proved that there is no clear FE: Principal Component Analysis (PCA), Auto-Encoder (AE), Linear Discriminant Analysis (LDA), or Deep Feed Forward (DFF), Convolutional Neural Networks (CNN), Neural Networks (NN), Decision Tree (DT), Logistic Regression (LR), Naïve Bayes (NB) model that can obtain the best scores for all datasets with an optimal IDS at feature threshold between 15 and 20. Although LDA can reduce model performance, the authors are required to perform further work on the search for reference features. The fact that PCA is considered by some authors as a technique that could lead to perfect detection, has led some researchers to experiment with it to construct lightweight neural networks (Sharipuddin et al. 2020; Ruijie et al. 2022). Some studies present the LDA feature extraction method as a promising technique when linked with deep learning techniques, even when experimenting with lower dimensions compared to other dimensionality techniques, and could reach 98.34% accuracy with Deep Feed Forward (DFF) (Mohanad et al. 2021). TON_IoT is recent and comes in a variety of files formats (CSV, pcap, TXT, blg and log), and has already been the subject of several studies with the general aim of designing cybersecurity tools (Nour et al. 2021). Various categories of TON_IoT data such as IoT (Internet of Thing)/IIoT (Industrial Internet of Thing), network datasets, Linux and Windows datasets have been analyzed as new IoT datasets applicable to cybersecurity, with some of these analyses exploiting machine learning techniques (Tim et al. 2021; Abdullah et al. 2020; Nour and Sheri 2021). The major limitation of some works, despite their performance compared to traditional IDS with a performance of 0.99%, lies in the quality of old data, but most work on attacks such as Distributed Denial-Of-Service (DDOS) (Pushparaj and Deepak 2021). In addition, some Internet of Things IDSs from databases such as DARPA, KDD CUP99,

DEFCON, CAIDA, LBNL, CDX, Kyoto, Twente, UMASS, ISCX2012, ADFA, UNSW-NB15 and CIC-IDS-2017, are considered obsolete today, as they do not present the real aspect of the IoT ecosystem, which is heterogeneous, although they have experimented with Feature Selection techniques and applied Machine Learning methods (Ankit and Ritika 2021; Sanjay et al. 2021). Model performance and input data definition are the two essential roles of feature engineering in the management of classification problems with low- and high-dimensional data. This cyclical process has four stages: brainstorming, creating features, running models, and measuring performance. Through the link created between the data and machine learning models, this process enables the selection of the most relevant variables from the raw data and the elimination of redundancies (Shenggang et al. 2023; Mohammed and Ali 2022).

1.1 Description of Feature Engineering Techniques

There are several algorithms for feature engineering, but their choice is guided by how features are extracted or selected of features (Fig. 1).

Feature Extraction allows the automatic building of new features from raw data. It lets one reduce a large number of observations to a manageable set that can be modeled directly via predictive algorithms. Unsupervised clustering and principal component analysis are two techniques that can be applied (Dhiaa et al. 2023).

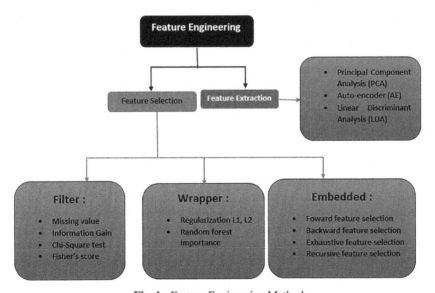

Fig. 1. Feature Engineering Method

Feature Selection, unlike Feature Extraction, removes data attributes that are useless or redundant in the context of the problem to be solved; it automatically selects the subset that is most useful. Thus, algorithms can use methods such as correlation or other Feature Importance (FI) methods to rank and select features (Xiangyu and Yanhui 2023).

Another, more advanced technique is to create and evaluate models automatically until the most appropriate model for prediction is found. The choice of features was validated through classification performance. Today, deep learning is a recommended tool for this purpose, with settings of metrics such as batch size, epochs, and activation functions (Bambang and Riri 2020).

1.2 Comparison with Related Works

Resource management of IoT systems is a topic of current concern, which should allow researchers to deploy IoT security solutions adapted to the design, strategy, and protocols of IoT operating systems. Our study, in relation to existing work, is particularly focused on the desire to produce lightweight solutions, which can be a greedy resource (memory, processor, energy) and has very good performance metrics. We base our experiment on the TON_IoT data, which is a large, recent database, because many studies offer so-called IoT solutions but with data that today does not reflect the reality of the IoT network (Pushparaj and Deepak 2021). On the other hand, some works exploiting this same dataset do not refer to resources, which are one of the most important criteria of Tiny Machine Learning (TinyML) (Mohanad et al. 2021). Our study of the two large groups of feature engineering and several algorithms allows us to better position ourselves for many other studies that present limited experimentation in terms of learning techniques (Ruijie et al. 2022).

2 Methodology

The methodology of this study is centered around the evaluation of feature engineering techniques on the TON_IoT dataset to detect their particularities in the design of IoT vulnerability detection solutions.

The first, data pre-processing formalizes the data in readiness for training. There in, duplicates and certain unnecessary identifiers, such as timestamps, are removed, and problems with missing resolved. That way, managing the data size and the definition of functionalities are eased. The second step, functionality engineering exploited the classes of feature extraction and feature selection techniques. The techniques in each class were tested against an experimentally defined threshold (Fig. 2). The third step, classification used the Random Forest model for automatic learning, and to train different algorithms obtained for feature extraction and selection. The last prediction step evaluates the efficiency of our algorithms in the dataset. In this study, the execution times to extract or select features (time_select) and those to train the Random Forest model to classify the dataset are evaluated.

2.1 Algorithms Description

The algorithms for feature selection and feature extraction are given as follows (Saurabh and Neelam 2012; Pushparaj and Deepak 2021):

- **Principal Component Analysis (PCA)** is an algorithm specific to feature reduction. It was used prior to classification in machine learning to improve the performance of the chosen model through information synthesis and compression. Although it can be normalized, it can only measure linear links. In this study, we exploit this to find the most significant features in TON_IoT.
- **Information Gain (IG)** is an algorithm used for feature selection to evaluate the Gain of each variable within the context of the target variable. Thus, it minimizes entropy and divides the dataset into groups for efficient classification. It is used to decide the order of attributes in the nodes of the decision tree.
- **ANOVA:** This statistical test shows whether the difference between the mean values is statistically significant. In this study, attack and normal groups were compared.
- **Linear Discriminant Analysis (LDA):** This technique explains and predicts class membership in a supervised classification scheme. It is used to create new features using the TON_IoT.
- **Recursive Feature Elimination (RFE)** is highly effective for problems linked to the selection of features in a training dataset that are relevant for predicting the target variable. We retained important features from the TON_IoT.

3 Experimentation and Discussion

3.1 Hardware Specification

For this experiment we used a laptop with the following specifications: RAM: 16 GB DDR4 2400 MHz Dual Channel, CPU: Intel i5 9th Gen @2.40 GHz, Model - DELL G3 15, Operating System: Windows 11 version 22H2.

3.2 Dataset

For this supervised learning, the dataset used was TON_IoT, a database available since 2019. These are the most recent iterations of heterogeneous IoT and Industrial IoT datasets from Industry 4.0. The dataset contains attacks such as reconnaissance activities, exploits, worms, DDoS, Backdoors, among others. The database also provides a statistical description of IoT data, from Linux, Windows, and network systems, as well as various connected objects on the network. Through observations made on the data, pre-processing has enabled the digitization of certain fields (such as weird_notice, weird_add, weird_name, protocol, source and destination IP addresses); presence of features with no logical importance on prediction such as timestamp; null or outlier data; and removal of attack type labels. Each feature is briefly described. The variable attack_cat of the float type used to specify the name of each category of the nine attacks contained in the dataset. The typology of the forty-eight features in this dataset is as follows:

- **Nominal:** scrip, dstip, proto, state, service, attack_cat
- **Integer:** spkts, swin, dwin, stcpb, dtcpb, smeansz, dmeansz, trans_depth, res_bdy_len, st_state_ttl, ct_flw_http_mthd, ct_ftp_cmd, dsport, sport, dbytes, sbytes, dttl, ct_srv_src, ct_srv_dst, ct_dst_ltm, ct_src_dport_ltm, ct_dst_sport_ltm, and ct_dst_src_ltm

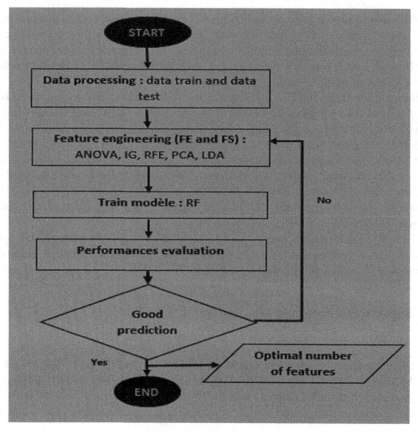

Fig. 2. Research methodology

- **Float:** Dloat, Sjit, dur, Sintpkt, Dintpkt, synack, sload, Djit, tcprtt, ackdat
- **Timestamp**: Stime, Ltime
- **Binary:** is_sm_ips_ports, label, is_ftp_login

3.3 Algorithm Settings

The algorithms used in this study were divided into two main groups, one for feature selection and the other for feature extraction. For each group, we attempted to identify parameters that could positively influence our study. For example, the number of features is fixed, whereas the percentage level of extraction is specified. Based on existing work and the specifics of our dataset, we evaluated performance on 30, 20, 15, 10 features for FS techniques and 1, 2, 8, 20 for extraction, where we retain the thresholds 01, 15, and 20 as those that should make it possible to produce satisfactory performances (Table 1).

3.4 Performance Measures

To ensure the quality of the work of the various FE techniques, they were trained and evaluated using several performance metrics, namely ROC AUC, Accuracy, selection time, and execution time, with the Random Forest model. After analyzing the various metrics, we stabilized the different parameters that would enable us to improve the performance. Thus, ANOVA, IG, RFE on the thresholds 30, 20, 15, 10 and according to the values of the metrics were optimal at 15. On the other hand, the Feature Extraction techniques APC and LDA experimented on the thresholds of 01, 2, 8, and 20 were optimal, respectively, for 20 and 01. The RFE method for this experiment revealed the best performance, with 98.18% accuracy then followed by LDA, IG, ANOVA, and PCA as shown Fig. 3. Table 1 below gives a formal overview of the results obtained using a machine learning techniques. Figure 4, on the other hand, shows an assessing each of the feature engineering methods (selection or extraction) on the two chosen performance metrics.

Table 1. Feature Engineering and their evaluation as applied to the Random Forest model (K = number of feature to select and N = number of component extracted)

Evaluation Model	FE Techniques	Number of features	Threshold	ROC AUC	Accuracy	Training time (s)	Selection time (s)
Random Forest (RF)	ALL features	41		0.797462	0.981259	2175.2	
	Selection Techniques (K)						
	ANOVA	30; 20;15;10	15	0.806285	0.978612	302.5	0.7
	IG	30; 20;15;10	15	0.810607	0.978728	293.3	359.5
	RFE	30; 20;15;10	15	0.814188	0.9818	74.8	4073.1
	Extraction Techniques (N)						
	PCA	2;8;20	20	0.779422	0.947068	203.5	2.8
	LDA	1	1	0.785526	0.980830	104.4	7.4

Although this first experiment is already appreciable, the particularity of IoT technology through Tiny Machine Learning requires further questioning regarding the lightweight state of the solution. Resource consumption has not been evaluated in this early stage of the project, but we have used parameters such as time to correlate with memory writing, rate usage of the processor, and energy consumption. Details are given in the graph or Fig. 4.

We can see from this curve that RFE has an extremely high selection time, but its training time is shorter than that of others. This suggests that it could be useful in designing lightweight solutions.

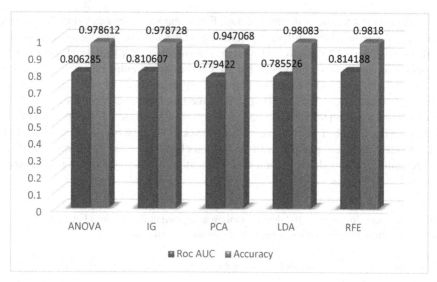

Fig. 3. Performance diagram

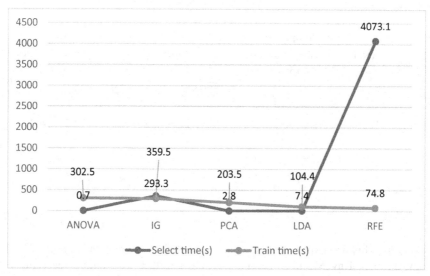

Fig. 4. Graphs of techniques vs selection times to extract or select feature and training time to classify datasets on the Random Forest model

3.5 Limitations

The first limitation of this work concerns resource consumption (memory occupancy, processor time, and battery life), which is an essential element in defining the lightweight state of a program and rejecting greedy programs that cannot be deployed on in embedded system. To date, we have been testing feature selection and extraction techniques with supervised learning techniques, but Deep Learning techniques have shown better results in certain studies. This experiment, conducted on a single dataset, can be extended to several to identify the particularities of FE work for the IoT.

4   Conclusion

The purpose of this paper is to determine how feature engineering can be exploited or guided in the definition of optimal lightweight intrusion detection systems for IoT. This study involved experimenting with feature engineering techniques on the TON_IoT dataset, which is a current dataset with most realities of the IoT ecosystem. We experimented with two types of Feature Engineering: feature extraction and selection. The precision of each FE technique was evaluated using Random Forest model. During this experiment, the extraction, selection, and prediction times were evaluated to identify the resource-hungry techniques. In general, future studies will focus on the identification of other parameters (resource consumption) to favor the design of an appropriate solution for embedded systems. This will involve extending this work to other datasets by inserting deep learning models. As TinyML is currently a dynamic and developing field that enables a cross-appraisal between hardware, software, and algorithms, it will enable future work to measure the resources (memory, processor, energy) consumed during selection, extraction, and classification, and to choose the most lightweight, high-performance, and cost-effective algorithm in terms of resources.

References

Abdullah, A., Nour, M., Zahir, T., Abdun, M., et al.: TON_IoT telemetry dataset: a new generation dataset of IoT and IIoT for data-driven intrusion detection systems. IEE Access **8**, 165130–165150 (2020)

Ankit, T., Ritika, L.: A survey on intrusion detection system: feature selection, model, performance measures, application perspective, challenges, and future research directions. Artif. Intell. Rev. (2021). https://doi.org/10.1007/s10462-021-10037-9

Arnaud, R., Eloïse, C., Mustapha, G., et al.: Study of network IDS in IoT devices. SN Comput. Sci. (2023). https://doi.org/10.1007/s42979-023-01849-3

Bambang, S., Riri, F.S.: Intrusion detection in IoT networks using deep learning algorithm (MDPI, Ed.). Information **11**(279), 2–11 (2020)

Bedir, T., Omer, K., Turgay, Ç.: System architecture design of iot-based smart cities. Appl. Sci. (2023). https://doi.org/10.3390/app13074173

Deng, C., Xiaofei, H., Jiawei, H.: Training linear discriminant analysis in linear time. In: IEEE 24th International Conference on Data Engineering (9963678). IEEE, 12 April 2008. https://doi.org/10.1109/ICDE.2008.4497429

Dhiaa, M., Meera, A., Fahd, A., et al.: Intrusion detection system using feature extraction with machine learning algorithms in IoT. MDPI **12**, 2–19 (2023)

Elvira, I., Laurie, H., Nripendra, R., Yogesh, D.: Security, privacy and risks within smart cities: literature review and development of a smart city interaction framework. Inf. Syst. Front., 393–414 (2022). https://doi.org/10.1007/s10796-020-10044-1

Fatima, H., Rasheed, H., Syed, A.H., Ekram, H.: Machine learning in IoT security:current solutions and future challenges. IEEE Commun. Surv. Tutor. (2020). https://doi.org/10.1109/COMST.2020.2986444

Hanli, Q., Jan, O.B., Huazhou, C.: A Machine learning based intrusion detection approach for industrial networks. In: 2020 IEEE International Conference on Industrial Technology (ICIT). IEEE, 06 April 2020. https://doi.org/10.1109/ICIT45562.2020.9067253

Ikram, U.D., Mohsen, G., Suihaidi, H., et al.: The internet of things: a review of enabled technologies and future challenges. IEEE Access **PP**(99), 1 (2019)

Krishan, G., Rajendra, K.: IoT and object identification enabled Smart Home Security System. Int. J. Mech. Eng. **07** (2022)

Lionel, S.: Number of Internet of Things (IoT) connected devices worldwide from 2019 to 2021, with forecasts from 2022 to 2030 (in billions), 22 November 2022. https://www.statista.com/statistics/1183457/iot-connected-devices-worldwide/. Accessed 26 Apr 2023

Mohammed, M., Ali, M.: Towards an explainable universal feature set for IoT intrusion detection. Sensors **22**, 2–18 (2022). https://doi.org/10.3390/s22155690

Mohanad, S., Siamak, L., Nour, M., et al.: Feature extraction for machine learning-based intrusion detection in IoT networks. Digital Communications and Networks (DCN) (2021)

Muhammad, S., Zhihong, T., Ali, K., et al.: IoT malicioustraffic identification usingwrapper-based feature selection mechanisms. Comput. Secur. **94** (2020). https://doi.org/10.1016/j.cose.2020.101863

Nour, A.: New distributed architecture for evaluating AI-based security systems at the edge: Network TON_IoT datasets (2021)

Nour, M.: The TON_IoT Datasets. Intelligent Security Group (ISG) (n.d.). https://research.unsw.edu.au/projects/toniot-datasets. Accessed 22 May 2023

Nour, M.: A new distributed architecture for evaluating AI-based security systems at the edge: network TON_IoT datasets. Sustain. Cities Soc. **72** (2021). https://doi.org/10.1016/j.scs.2021.102994

Nour, M., Sheri, F.: Data Analytics-Enabled Intrusion Detection: Evaluations of ToN_IoT Linux Datasets (2021)

Nour, M., Mohiuddin, A., Sherif, A.: Data analytics-enabled intrusion detection: evaluations of ToN_IoT linux datasets. In: 2020 IEEE 19th International Conference on Trust, Security and Privacy in Computing and Communications (TrustCom) (20425627), 09 February 2021. https://doi.org/10.1109/TrustCom50675.2020.00100

Pushparaj, N., Deepak, K.: Feature selection for intrusion detection system in Internet-of-Things (IoT). Korean Inst. Commun. Inf. Sci. **7**, 177–181 (2021)

Quoc-Dung, N., Huy-Trung, N., Van-Hoang, L., Doan-Hieu, N.: A survey of IoT malware and detection methods based on static features. Korean Inst. Commun. Inf. Sci. (KICS) **6**, 280–286 (2020)

Ruijie, Z., Guan, G., Zhi, X., Jie, Y.: A novel intrusion detection method based on lightweight neural network for internet of things. IEEE Internet Things J., 9960–9972 (2022). https://doi.org/10.1109/JIOT.2021.3119055

Sanjay, M., Sanjeev, S., Divya, B.: Tools and Techniques for Collection and Analysis of Internet-of-Things malware: a systematic state-of-art review. J. King Saud Univ. Comput. Inf. **34**, 9867–9888 (2021)

Saurabh, M., Neelam, S.: Intrusion detection using naive bayes classifier with feature reduction. **4**, 119–128 (2012). https://doi.org/10.1016/j.protcy.2012.05.017

Shahbaz, S., Sufian, H., Syed, A.S., et al.: Smart contract-based security architecture for collaborative services in municipal smart cities. J. Syst. Archit. **135**(102802) (2023)

Sharipuddin, Benni, P., Kurniabudi, Eko, A.W.: Features extraction on IoT intrusion detection system using principal components analysis (PCA). In: 2020 7th International Conference on Electrical Engineering, Computer Sciences and Informatics (EECSI), 12 November 2020. https://doi.org/10.23919/EECSI50503.2020.9251292

Shenggang, Z., Shujuan, J., Yue, Y.: A Software Defect Prediction Approach Based on Hybrid Feature Dimensionality Reduction. Hindawi (2023)

Sujit, R., Humaun, K., Tofail, A.: IoT based low-cost smart home automation and security system using wireless technology. Aust. J. Eng. Innov. Technol. (2663–7790), 101–112 (2023)

Taylor, P.: New Internet of Things (IoT) connections in 2025 compared to 2019 (in billions). New IoT connections in 2025 compared to 2019, 19 January 2023. https://www.statista.com/statistics/1101127/new-iot-connections-by-2025/. Accessed 06 Nov 2023

Tim, M., Irina, C., Erik, M., Nour, M., et al.: ToN_IoT: the role of heterogeneity and the need for standardization of features and attack types in IoT network intrusion data sets. IEEE Internet Things J. **9**, 485–496 (2021). https://doi.org/10.1109/JIOT.2021.3085194

Xiangyu, L., Yanhui, D.: Towards effective feature selection for IoT botnet attack detection using a genetic algorithm. Electronics **12**, 1260 (2023)

Xin-Ning, Y., Wen-Kang, G., Yin-Zhe, L., et al.: An automatic features extraction model of IDS for IOT. In: Proceedings of the 12th International Conference on Computer Engineering and Networks, October 2022. https://doi.org/10.1007/978-981-19-6901-0_132

Correlation Clustering Adapted for Cell Site Management of Mobile Networks in Developing Countries

Ado Adamou Abba Ari[1,2](✉) [iD], Yekoniya Ndjekiltemai[3] [iD],
Jocelyn Edinio Zacko Gbadouissa[2,3] [iD], Arouna Ndam Njoya[4] [iD],
Lyse Naomi Wamba Momo[5] [iD], Ousmane Thiare[6] [iD], Sondes Khemiri Kallel[1] [iD],
and Abdelhak Mourad Gueroui[1] [iD]

[1] DAVID Lab, Université Paris-Saclay, University of Versailles,
Saint-Quentin-en-Yvelines, France
adoadamou.abbaari@gmail.com
[2] LaRI Lab, University of Maroua, PO Box 814 Maroua, Cameroon
[3] African Institute for Mathematical Sciences (AIMS-Cameroon), Po Box 608 Limbé,
Cameroon
[4] Department of Computer Engineering, University Institute of Technology,
University of Ngaoundéré, Po Box 455 Ngaoundéré, Cameroon
[5] KU Leuven, Oude Markt 13 - bus 5005, 3000 Leuven, Belgium
[6] Department of Computer Science, Gaston Berger University of Saint-Louis,
Po Box 234 Saint-Louis, Senegal

Abstract. Any mobile network operator's primary concern is ensuring a better customer experience for their subscribers. For this reason, they need to ensure that their infrastructure is working correctly. However, managing telecommunication infrastructure, especially cellular base stations, has never been an obvious task in the African and Middle Eastern regions due to the landlocked nature and lack of access roads, especially in rural areas. Despite the many solutions developed by operators, ranging from monitoring tools to the deployment of technicians in the field, this still needs to be solved. Some operators prefer to entrust these cell sites to Managed Service Providers (MSPs) or Tower Companies (Tower-Cos) and concentrate on other services. To address this issue, we propose an adapted correlation clustering for cell site management, considering the operator's parameters and a site accessibility parameter. This approach makes it possible to determine the optimal number of cells to allocate to a technician to make his interventions efficient; this will minimize Operational Expenditure (OpEx) and cell downtime due to breakdowns and maximize the quality of service offered to customers.

Keywords: Cell Sites Management · Correlation Clustering · Task Allocation · Mobile Network Operator · Tower Company · Hierarchical Clustering

© ICST Institute for Computer Sciences, Social Informatics and Telecommunications Engineering 2024
Published by Springer Nature Switzerland AG 2024. All Rights Reserved
F. Tchakounte et al. (Eds.): SAFER-TEA 2023, LNICST 566, pp. 108–127, 2024.
https://doi.org/10.1007/978-3-031-56396-6_8

1   Introduction

The telecommunications market is booming, driven by very different needs and levels of development from one country to another [3]. Active mobile broadband subscriptions worldwide increased from 268 million in 2007 to 6.554 billion in 2021, which explained an average annual growth rate of 40% [19]. Mobile services subscribers accounted for 67% of the world population in 2019 and will reach 70% by 2025 [3,10,14]. This growth in subscribers leads directly to an increase in telecommunication sites for Mobile Operators. Considering only Africa, the total number of mobile telecommunication sites has reached 180,000. However, more than this increased number of telecom sites (towers) is needed since there are still six times more subscribers per tower in Africa compared to North America [6]. To effectively meet this challenge, mobile operators prefer to outsource tower management and focus on service delivery. Thus, the deployment and management of towers and cell sites are outsourced to Managed Service Providers (MSP) and Tower Management Companies (TowerCos). For better management, MSP and TowerCos developed Intelligent Site Asset Management solutions for remote monitoring of cell sites to improve the service delivery quality while minimizing related risks and costs. However, some maintenance cannot be done using the monitoring tool since it requires manual intervention, especially for failures related to the equipment, so the outsourced third-party company assign a set of cell sites to each field technician for daily maintenance and data collection activities [2,11].

Moreover, the rapid growth of the telecom industry is accompanied by an explosion of new offerings and services. Mobile operators are outsourcing tower management to focus on service delivery. To carry out the cell management task, MSPs and TowerCos have developed tools to monitor sites remotely to have a clear view of the towers and correct specific faults, called Network Management System (NMS). However, some failures cannot be managed remotely and require manual intervention. Thus, a set of sites is allocated to technicians to ensure maintenance and continuity of services. This section studies tower management strategies developed to meet the operator's expectations effectively.

A Network Management System (NMS) comprises hardware and software designed to monitor, maintain and optimize a network. It can be used to monitor a network's software and hardware components. It typically records data from remote points on a network for central reporting to a system administrator. It provides primary services such as network monitoring, device detection, device management, fault management, and performance analysis.

The Field Maintenance Engineer (FME) is responsible for maintaining the towers and ensuring their proper functioning. They compensate for the limitations of the NMS, which does not allow troubleshooting a failure requiring manual intervention. Our recent surveys on tower allocation strategy among FMEs reveal that this latter is based on three criteria: geographical location of towers, availability of logistics and priority of towers.

The first allocation criterion is the area where the sites are located; the maintenance of sites in urban areas is more accessible than those in rural areas due to the sites' density, proximity, and availability of road accesses. While in rural areas, the sites are sometimes located in areas that are difficult to access. Although the sites in urban areas are more remunerative, the availability of logistics makes them prior for rural sites that often serve as relays with the backbone network-finally, high-priority sites require more attention.

Despite the strategies of outsourcing and allocation of technicians to a pool of sites, it has always been difficult for TowerCos to meet its Service Level Agreement (SLA) and reach its Key Performance Indicator (KPI) target; this is because many cell sites are located in hard-to-reach areas, especially in remote rural areas, making it very costly and time-consuming for a technician to travel to these sites.

In this paper, we intend to investigate an effective scheduling strategy for technicians and the optimal number of cell sites to allocate to these latter. Our contribution is to go beyond the tower management strategies discussed in the literature review and provide an efficient clustering of towers to facilitate the management by the technician. We consider this problem as that of grouping objects based on their similarities.

The rest of the paper is organized as follows: Sect. 2 presents a brief review of the concepts related to cell sites management; in Sect. 3, we present some mathematical backgrounds as well as the clustering theory; in Sect. 4, we present our feature engineering process; the proposed clustering models are presented in Sect. 5; Sect. 6 presents the performance evaluation and discussion; and the conclusion and perspectives for our future works are presented in Sect. 7.

2   Related Work

Clustering in mobile networks is not new; several works have been done in this field with significant results. In [21], Guang et al. presented a hierarchical clustering algorithm (SC-HCA) for interference management in ultra-dense small-cell networks. To achieve their goal, the authors designed a new function called the suitability function and two new matrices called connection matrix and clustering suitability matrix. A series of system-level simulations verified the effectiveness of the proposed SC-HCA. These simulations show that the proposed approach improves the system throughput compared to other schemes. In [22], Hans-Martin et al. proposed a dynamic cell clustering in cellular multi-hop networks. The idea is to balance the different cells by dynamically creating clusters of cells. To achieve this, the authors first performed an evaluation based on a graph-theoretical network model and then, in a second step, implemented the decentralized approach in NS-2. After simulations, their findings show that numerical optimization yields the best results.

One of the most popular clustering algorithms is K-means. Several studies based on this algorithm have been carried out in many domains, including telecommunication [11], image processing [18], marketing [16], etc., and have proven the effectiveness of this clustering method. In [11], Gbadoubissa et al. used the k-means clustering algorithm to allocate field technicians to a pool of cell sites. To mitigate the sensitivity of k-means to initialization, the authors proposed an initialization method based on the geometry of a sphere. The authors conducted a series of experiments with a sample of thousands of cell towers from OpenCellID by considering three (03) main parameters, including latitude, longitude, and range which is the approximate area in which the cell could be located. The results showed that K-means with geometric initialization outperformed both classical and K-means++.

In [18], Siddheswar et al. proposed a method for determining the number of clusters in K-Means classification and application to the segmentation of color images. The challenge in this work lies in the parameter k, which is the number of clusters; it has to be predefined. Siddheswar et al. presented a simple validity measure based on intra-cluster and inter-cluster distance measures that allows to determine the number of clusters automatically. The basic procedure is to produce all the segmented images for 2 clusters up to $Kmax$ clusters, where $Kmax$ represents an upper bound on the number of clusters. Then the validity measure is calculated to determine the best clustering by finding the minimum value of the measure. The proposed method has been tested on synthetic images and natural images. The results show that the proposed validity measure for these two types of images works well, producing a minimum value for the expected number of clusters. In [15], an estimation of road traffic congestion from cellular handoff information using cell-based neural networks and K-means clustering was proposed by Hongsakham et al. The authors proposed two approaches; the first experimental approach used the K-means clustering algorithm, and the second used a multilayer neural network with a backpropagation algorithm. The results of these approaches show that both methods give consistent results, but the results obtained by the neural network approach were further accurate.

A single-pass streaming algorithm was used for max-agree, while multipass streaming algorithms were also considered. The proposed method outperformed the results of Chierichetti et al. in their work [7]. Similarly, Ty Rico et al. introduced interactive correlation clustering with existential cluster constraints in their research [1]. The authors presented a new feedback approach for interactive clustering, where users provide existential constraints on cluster features. They argued that existential cluster constraints are a natural form of feedback that doesn't require users to inspect individual data points. Instead, users use their mental model of what the output clustering should look like to define the clusters.

In the same vein, interactive correlation clustering with existential cluster constraints was proposed by Rico et al. in [1]. In this work, the authors introduced a new feedback paradigm for interactive clustering in which users provide existential constraints on cluster features. They advocated existential cluster constraints as a natural form of feedback that does not require users to inspect many individual data points but rather to use their mental model of what the output clustering should look like to define the clustering constraints. They introduced an inference algorithm to incorporate existential clustering constraints into the correlation clustering framework. The output of this method shows that their proposed inference method improves efficiency over must-link and cannot-link constraints. On the other hand, some related clustering algorithms have also been shown to be effective.

Chihli et al. proposed the hierarchical self-organizing segmentation model (HSOS) in [16], a market segmentation method based on a hierarchical self-organizing map for multimedia on-demand markets. This model uses a visualized two-dimensional hierarchical map better to explain the market segmentation process to a real-world decision-maker. To evaluate this model, 227 final data were collected through personal interviews with residents of Taipei, the only city in Taiwan to have deployed a MOD system. The experimental results show that using HSOS allows a better understanding of visualizing market segmentation results than traditional hierarchical clustering approaches and growing hierarchical self-organizing map [9]. In [12], Gbadoubissa et al. proposed a heuristic clustering based on hypergraph theory, called HyperGraph Clustering (HGC), that aims to optimize the energy of the sensor nodes. This algorithm comprises three phases: initialization, cluster generation and cluster formation. The evaluation of this algorithm showed that this clustering method consumed less energy during the cluster formation and cluster head selection phase. The results showed that HGC outperformed the compared protocols regarding the number of active nodes, residual energy, and total network consumption in different scenarios.

3   Correlation Clustering and Its Mathematical Background

Clustering or cluster analysis is an unsupervised learning technique that gathers unlabeled datasets based on similarity. Closer objects remain in the same cluster. Many clustering algorithms are distinct from each other by their identification strategy. The choice of technique to apply depends on the nature and structure of the data.

The correlation clustering was introduced by Bansal et al. [4] in 2004. It is a method that allows to divide the data into an optimal number of clusters according to the similarity between the data points without defining the number of clusters beforehand (see Algorithm 1). This method has two main objectives, minimizing the disagreements or maximizing the agreements between the data partitions. We seek to minimize the disagreements between the different clusters for our case study inspires the method we propose [8], in their paper, Demaine et al. present an $O(logn)$ approximation algorithm that uses linear programming and region-growing techniques for minimizing disagreements. The region-growing technique consists of progressively enlarging a region around its starting point.

Definition 1. *A ball $B(u,r)$ of radius r around a node u is the set of nodes N such that $x_{uv} \leqslant r$, as well as the subgraph induced by these nodes and the $\frac{r-x_{uv}}{x_{vw}}$ edges (u,w) with only one endpoint $v \in B(u,r)$*

Algorithm 1. Round algorithm

1: Radomly pick a node $u \in G$
2: Initialize $r = 0$
3: Increase r by $min\{(d_{uv} - r) > 0 : v \notin B(u,r)\}$ includes another edge. Repeat until $Cut(B(u,r)) \leqslant c * ln(n+1) * Vol(B(u,r))$.
4: Output the set of nodes in $B(u,r)$ as one cluster of C.
5: Remove the nodes and incident edges of $B(u,r)$ from G
6: Repeat the above steps until G is empty.

Definition 2. *The cut of a set S is the weight of the positive edges with exactly one endpoint in S.*

$$Cut(S) = \sum_{|(v,w) \cap S|=1, (v,w) \in E^+} c_{vw}$$

The cut of a ball is $Cut(S)$ where $S = \{v | v \in B(u,r)\}$.

Definition 3. *The volume of a set S is the weighted distance of edges (u,v) such that $u, v \in S$.*

$$Vol(S) = \sum_{(v,w) \subset S, (v,w) \in E^+} c_{vw} x_{vw}$$

The volume of the ball $B(u,r)$ includes a fractional weighted distance of the positive edges leaving $B(u,r)$. If $(u,v) \in E^+$ is a cut positive edge of $B(u,r)$ with $v \in B(u,r)$ and $w \notin B(u,r)$ then (v,w) contributes weight of $c_{vw}(r - x_{uv})$ to the volume of $B(u,r)$. Let I be the initial volume of the ball, so the volume of $B(u,0)$ is I.

Considering the above definitions, the authors present the algorithm for rounding a fractional solution to an integral solution. Let F be the volume of the graph G. Assume that the weight of the positive mistakes made by the fractional solution is F. Let the initial volume $I = F/n$ and c be a constant.

Definition 4. *Let $u(\varphi_1, \lambda_1)$ and $v(\varphi_2, \lambda_2)$ be two points defined by their geographical coordinates in radians and let denote by $\theta = \frac{d}{r}$, the central angle between any two points on a sphere, where r is the radius of the sphere and d the distance between u and v along a great circle of the sphere. The haversine formula allows the haversine of θ (denoted $hav(\theta)$) to be computed directly from the coordinates of u and v as shown in Eq. 1.*

$$hav(\theta) = hav(\varphi_2 - \varphi_1) + \cos(\varphi_1)\cos(\varphi_2)hav(\lambda_2 - \lambda_1), \tag{1}$$

$$hav(\theta) = \sin^2\left(\frac{\theta}{2}\right) = \frac{1 - \cos(\theta)}{2}. \tag{2}$$

Now, to solve for the distance d, apply the archaversine (inverse haversine) to $h = hav(\theta)$ or use the *arcsin* (inverse sine) function (Eq. 3):

$$d = 2r \times \arcsin\sqrt{\sin^2\left(\frac{\varphi_2 - \varphi_1}{2}\right) + \cos(\varphi_1)\cos(\varphi_2)\sin^2\left(\frac{\lambda_2 - \lambda_1}{2}\right)} \tag{3}$$

4   Features Engineering

4.1   Data Origins

The data collected for the analysis are from opencellID, the world's largest collaborative community project that collects GPS locations of cell towers, used free of charge, for various commercial and private purposes [17]. In the context of this work, we limited our choice to cell sites in Cameroon. The data collected consist of 29307 observations with 14 columns, indicating respectively the number of cells and the features describing each cell. Table 2 gives a detailed description of the features. Before the clustering process, it is essential to apply domain knowledge to transform these raw data into features, better representing the underlying problem and improving model accuracy on unseen data. The feature engineering allowed keeping five (05) features and creating four (04) more features for the clustering purpose (see Table 1).

Table 1. List of features used in the allocation strategy

Notations	Features	Description
x_1	mcc	Mobile Country Code
x_2	net	Mobile Network Code
x_3	area	Location Area Code (LAC)
x_4	lon	Approx longitude
x_5	lat	Approx latitude
x_6	road	Nearest road to the cell site
x_7	zone	Rural or Urban zone
x_8	traffic	Traffic load of the cell site
x_9	priority	Priority of the cell site

4.2   Feature Based on Geographical Location of Towers

Managing cell sites in developing countries remains challenging for Mobile Network Operators. Some towers are found in hard-to-reach areas, especially those in rural areas. Most of the sites in rural zones are off-grid (not connected to the electricity grid). Thus, they are powered by diesel generators and solar panels [5]. The average revenues of a rural cell site can be ten times lower than those of an urban site, but its network infrastructure's construction and maintenance costs are higher [13]. The maintenance of sites in urban areas is less burdensome than those in rural areas, mainly due to their accessibility.

In this work, the geographic locations of cell sites constitute a relevant factor that will be exploited during the allocation process. The geographic coordinates of each cell site are used for deriving the town or village where they are located

Table 2. Description of features

Features	Description
radio	The generation of broadband cellular network technology. It can be GSM, UMTS, CDMA or LTE
mcc	Mobile Country Code, mcc Cameroon=624
net	Mobile Network Code
area	Location Area Code (LAC)
cell	Cell tower code (CID)
unit	Primary Scrambling Code (PSC) for UMTS networks. Physical Cell ID (PCI) for LTE networks. An empty value for GSM and CDMA networks.
lon	Approx longitude of the cell tower
lat	Approx latitude of the cell tower
range	Approximate area within which the cell could be. (radius in meters)
samples	Number of measures processed to get this data
changeable	Defines if the coordinates of the cell tower are exact or approximate. 1 = The location is determined by processing samples 0 = The location was obtained directly from the telecommunications company.
created	The first time when the cell tower was seen and added to the OpenCellID database. (UNIX timestamp)
updated	The last time when the cell tower was seen and updated. (UNIX timestamp)
averageSignal	Average signal strength from all assigned measurements for the cell

through the reverse *geocoding*. Reverse *geocoding* transforms a geographic coordinate (latitude, longitude) into a city/village name or human-readable address. The city/village name enables determining whether the cell site is in an urban or rural zone.

4.3 Feature Based on the Nearest Road

The quality of the roads leading to each site must be considered while assigning these sites to the technicians for maintenance. We generate a new feature that takes into account the road, based on existing features from Table 2 in ??. We collected a road dataset from OpenStreetMap [20] and extracted information on Cameroon roads, ports, airports, waterways, bridges, obstacles, and railways. We are interested in the feature that describes the different categories of roads (1: Highway, 2: Primary Road, 3: Secondary Road, etc.). Each nearest road to a cell site is determined based on the ck-dimensional tree algorithm, a customized version of the k-dimensional tree.

Let's denote P_r the finite collection of roads such that $P_r = \{r_1, r_2, r_3, ..., r_n\}$ and N the finite set of cell sites such that $N = \{s_1, s_2, s_3, ..., s_n\}$. Each road r_j is a set defined as $r_j = \{p_1, p_2, \ldots, p_l\}$, with $p_k = (x_4^k, x_5^k)$, and each cell site is defined as $s_i = (x_4^i, x_5^i)$. We want to determine the nearest road r_j to s_i such that Eq. 4 is satisfied.

$$\forall s_i \in N, \text{ find } k_0, \text{ such that } w_{ik_0} = \min_j \left\{ \min_{p_k \in r_j} \{w_{ik}\} \right\} \tag{4}$$

The nearest road r_j is determined using the ck-dimensional tree described by Algorithm 2. For each road r_j, this algorithm finds its closest point $p_{k_0}^j$ to the cell site s_i based on the haversine distance given by Eq. 5. Then, the road r_{j_0} having the closest point among the $p_{k_0}^j$ is selected as the nearest to s_i.

Algorithm 2. ck-dimensional tree

    Input: s_i, $P_r = \{r_1, r_2, r_3, ..., r_n\}$
    Output: $p_{k_0} \in r_j$
1: $tmp = \infty$
2: **for** $r_j \in P_r$ **do**
3:    **for** $k = 1 : l$ **do**
4:       **if** $tmp > w_{ik}$ **then**
5:          $tmp = w_{ik}$
6:       **end if**
7:    **end for**
8: **end for**

4.4   Feature Based on the Priority of Towers

As part of their cell site management strategy, some tower companies set priorities for each site depending on various parameters for maintenance purposes. These priorities are technical, government, VIP, business, and standard sites. Technical important sites carry other sites and serve as relays with the backbone network. Government or VIP-related sites cover locations of high public authorities and MNO managers. Business sites include all sites that generate significant revenue for the operator. They are usually high-traffic sites or sites that cover VIP users. The remaining sites are considered of normal priority.

Our allocation strategy considers the traffic volume of the cell site to set the priorities. We group the cell sites into three classes: C_1, C_2, and C_3. The class C_1 encompasses technical important and government/VIP sites. Class C_2 is for business sites, and class C_3 groups the normal sites. We define two thresholds λ_1 and λ_2 of the traffic volume, with $\lambda_1 > \lambda_2$. Algorithm 3 assigns the priorities as follows: Any site from C_1, C_2 or C_3, with a traffic volume $x_8 \geq \lambda_1$ is of priority 1. A site s_i is said of priority 2, if it is of class C_1, C_2 or C_3 with a traffic volume $\lambda_2 \leq x_8^i < \lambda_1$. If x_8 is lower than λ_2, then the cell site has the priority 3 if it belongs to C_3. Otherwise, the cell site has a priority of 4. Cell sites with the highest-priority value should be maintained first.

Algorithm 3. Towers priorities

   Input: $N = \{s_1, s_2, s_3, ..., s_n\}$
   Output: priority of s_i
1: **if** $x_8^i \geq \lambda_1$ **then**
2:   $x_9^i \leftarrow 1$
3: **else if** $(\lambda_2 \leq x_8^i < \lambda_1)$ **then**
4:   $x_9^i \leftarrow 2$
5: **else**
6:   **if** $(x_8^i < \lambda_2)$ **then**
7:     **if** $s_i \in C_3$ **then**
8:       $x_i \leftarrow 3$
9:     **else**
10:       $x_i \leftarrow 4$
11:     **end if**
12:   **end if**
13:
14: **end if**

---

5   Proposed Clustering Models

5.1   Problem Formulation

The mobile cellular network can be represented by an undirected and weighted graph $G = (N, E)$, which consists of a finite, non-empty set of vertices N, representing the centre of cells and a set of edges E. Each edge is a set $e\{u, v\}$ of centre of cells and W the set of weight such that $w(u, v) = w_{e\{u,v\}} \in W$, the weight of the edge $e\{u, v\}$. In the next section, we propose a two-level clustering model, where we first rely on hierarchical clustering to group cells hierarchically by mcc, mnc and then by lac. We then propose an adapted correlation clustering to the previous clustering, which will be based on the distance between cells and their proximity to the road (Fig. 1).

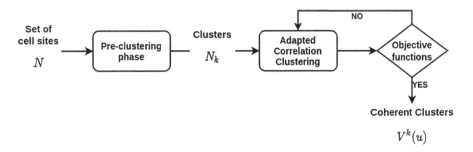

Fig. 1. Flow chart of the proposed clustering method

Definition 5. *Let* $N = \left\{ s_i = (x_1^i, x_2^i, \ldots, x_8^i); \ i = 1, \ldots, n \right\}$ *be the set of nodes (or cell sites) and* R *the radius of the earth. Then, the weight* w_{ij} *of edge* $e\{s_i, s_j\}$ *is given by*

$$w_{ij} = 2R \arcsin \sqrt{\sin^2\left(\frac{x_4^j - x_4^i}{2}\right) + \cos(x_4^i)\cos(x_4^j)\sin^2\left(\frac{x_5^j - x_5^i}{2}\right)} \qquad (5)$$

5.2   Pre-clustering Phase

We propose a heuristic to group the cell towers based on their country, mobile operator, and location area codes. The hierarchy of this clustering is such that at the first level, the cells are grouped according to their *mcc*, which is the code of the country where the cell is located. At the second level, the cells belonging to the same *mcc* are grouped according to the *mnc*, the operator's code. Finally, at the base of the hierarchy, the cells are grouped by the Location Area Code (LAC), the unique number assigned to each location area within a mobile network. Let us recall the features x_1, x_2, x_3, successively the country code, mobile operator code and location area code (as shown in Table 1). Given any two nodes $(s_i, s_j) \in N$, the pseudocode of the proposed hierarchical clustering is presented in Algorithm 4. At the end of this clustering, we get k clusters N_k as illustrated in Fig. 2.

Algorithm 4. Pre-clustering phase

    Input: $N = \{s_i; \ i = 1, \ldots, n \}$
    Output: N_k clusters
1: **for** $s_i \in N$ **do**
2:    **for** $s_j \in N$ and $s_j \neq s_i$ **do**
3:       **if** $x_1^i == x_1^j$ and $x_2^i == x_2^j$ and $x_3^i == x_3^j$ **then**
4:          Add s_j to cluster N_i
5:       **end if**
6:    **end for**
7: **end for**

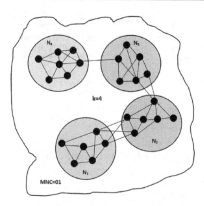

Fig. 2. Clusters obtained after pre-clustering

5.3   Adapted Correlation Clustering

We based on concepts from the correlation clustering to design the following model. We consider a weighted graph $G_w = (N, E, W)$, where each edge's weight is a positive integer. This algorithm exploits the features x_4, x_5, and x_6. We also exploit the weight $w_{ij} \in W$ of an edge $e(s_i, s_j)$ as described in Definition 4 and Definition 5.

Definition 6. *Let N_k be the k clusters obtained from the pre-clustering phase such that $N = \bigcup_k N_k$, $G_w^k = (N_k, E, W)$ be a weighted graph of N_k, and $P_r = \{r_l; \ l = 1, \dots, m\}$ the set of primary roads. We call the cluster or neighbourhood of s_i in N_k, the set $V^k(s_i)$ (or V_i^k) defined by Eq. 6*

$$V_i^k = \left\{ s_j \in N_k : w_{ij} < \varepsilon_1 \ \ and \ \ w_{jl_i^k} < \varepsilon_2 \right\}, \forall s_i \in N_k, \tag{6}$$

where $w_{jl_i^k}$ denotes the weight between the node s_j and the closest road $r_{l_i^k}$ to the cluster V_i^k.

5.4   Clustering Objectives

The proposed clustering model is subject to optimization constraints: Minimizing the intra-cluster criteria and maximizing the inter-cluster criteria. The intra-cluster criteria refer to the measure of the similarity within a cluster. We quantify it as the sum of weights w_{ij} of edges between sites s_i and s_j of a neighbourhood V_i^k, mathematically described by Eq. 7, and also as the sum of weights between nodes s_j and the nearest road to V_i^k (see Eq. 8). Thus, the objective is to minimize these quantities. Minimizing the intra-cluster values is equivalent to choosing the optimal values of parameters ε_1 and ε_2.

$$\min_{V_i^k} \left(\sum_{s_j \in V_i^k} w_{ij} \right), \quad \forall s_i \in N_k \tag{7}$$

$$\min_{V_i^k} \left(\sum_{s_j \in V_i^k} w_{jl_i^k} \right), \quad \forall r_l \in P_r \tag{8}$$

The inter-cluster criteria measure the dissimilarity between neighbourhoods V_i^k and V_j^k. With this measure, we aim to maximize the minimum weights (see Eq. 9) between any two points $s_{i_0} \in V_i^k$ and $s_{j_0} \in V_j^k$ belonging to different clusters.

$$\max_{N^k} \left(\min_{s_{i_0} \in V_i^k, s_{j_0} \in V_j^k} w_{i_0 j_0} \right) \tag{9}$$

6   Performance Analysis

6.1   Data Preprocessing and Exploratory Data Analysis (EDA)

The data preprocessing reveals no missing values, which facilitates the analysis. However, during the features engineering, the reverse geocoding reveals that some cells are located in the boundaries of a city in the border country. A cross-check was performed using the country map to align these cells to the appropriate location. Furthermore, among the new features created in Sect. 4, we have one (01) categorical feature, the "zone" feature (see Table 1). We handle this categorical feature such that an urban area cell site has the value $zone = 1$, and the one in a rural area has $zone = 0$.

We performed a univariate analysis for more insight into categorical variables (see Fig. 3). This analysis provides information on the distribution of cells by operator and by region. In our dataset, we count four different mobile operators distinguished from each other by their MNC (Mobile Network Code). Thus the operator whose MNC = 02 is the one that has the highest number of cells is followed by the operator MNC = 02. The operators MNC = 04 and MNC = 05 have a negligible number of cells. Moreover, more than 80% of the cells are located in urban areas and less than 20% in rural areas.

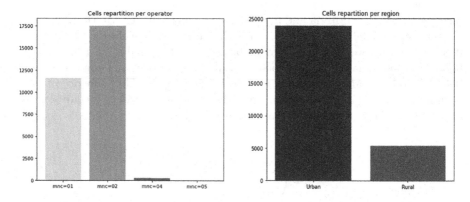

Fig. 3. Univariate analysis for categorical features.

Table 3 shows a descriptive statistic regarding the new numerical variables. These statistics tell us that, on average, the cells are 697 m from the road, with the closest site being 0.3 m from the road while the site furthest from the road is about 147 km from the road. The standard deviation 2.72 reveals that the cells are more spread out and mostly away from the road than the average distance. As for traffic generated, rescaling the values between 0 and 1 gives us a good distribution of traffic between cells.

Table 3. Descriptive statistics for numerical variables

Features	count	mean	std	min	25%	50%	75%	max
dist_road	29307	0.696519	2.722165	0.000383	0.073349	0.268806	0.727264	146.794307
traffic	29307	0.499116	0.291025	0.000001	0.243662	0.499628	0.753635	0.999923
priority	29307	0.000000	0.000000	0.000000	0.000000	0.000000	0.000000	0.000000

For an in-depth analysis, we perform a univariate analysis of the numerical new features. The boxplots shown in Fig. 4 are respectively for the variables distance to the road (dist_road) and traffic distribution between cells (road). We have many outliers from the boxplot of dist_road, which justifies the standard deviation value; many sites are very far from the road. While from the traffic boxplot, we note no outliers as the values have been normalized, the minimum traffic is 0, and the maximum traffic is 1.

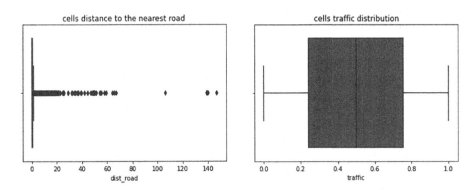

Fig. 4. Univariate analysis for numerical features.

To better explore our data, we perform a bivariate analysis, including the distance of cells to the road as a function of regions and the distribution of traffic as a function of regions. Figure 5 shows the violin plot of the *dist_road* and the traffic by region, respectively. Although the maximum distance of the cell to the nearest road in the urban area is up to 50 km, the violin plot reveals that most of the cells very far from the road are located in the rural area, with a maximum distance of up to 146 km. In comparison, the violin plot of the traffic distribution by region shows a balanced distribution of traffic between rural and urban areas.

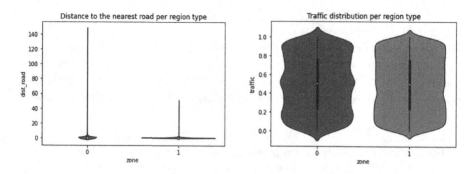

Fig. 5. Bivariate analysis for numerical features.

Finally, using multivariate analysis, we are interested in the relationship between the new features we have created. Figure 6 is a pair plot explaining the correlation between our new variables. It consolidates the previous analyses, including the cells farthest from the road, mainly those in rural areas. Then, although the traffic values are normalized, the pair plot tells us that urban traffic is higher than in rural areas (Table 4).

6.2   Performance Metrics

To evaluate the performance of the adapted correlation clustering, we used the *Silhouette coefficient*, which is a popular metric used to evaluate clustering algorithms; it combines both cohesion and separation. It is defined for each sample and is composed of two scores: a, the mean distance between a sample and all other points in the same class and b, the mean distance between a sample and all other points in the next nearest cluster. Hence, the silhouette coefficient for a given point (p) is given by

$$sc_p = \frac{b_p - a_p}{\max_{1 \leq i \leq n}(a_i, b_i)}.$$

A global measure of clustering quality can be obtained by calculating the average silhouette of all points, and its value varies between -1 for bad clustering and 1 for the best clustering.

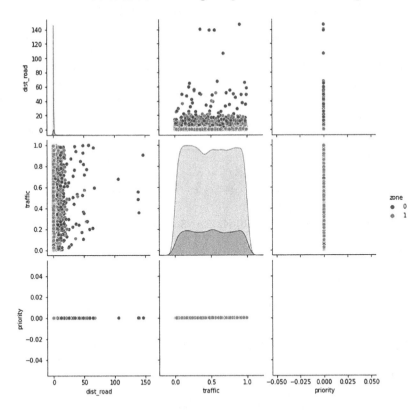

Fig. 6. Multivariate analysis of new features.

Table 4. Silhouette coefficient for different k values

k parameter	2	3	4	5	6	7	8	9	10	11
Silhouette coef	0.7781	0.7450	0.8169	0.8317	0.8409	0.8489	0.8441	0.7938	0.8110	0.8126

Table 5. Silhouette coefficient for eps = 0.5 and different minPts values

minPts parameter	2	3	4	5	6	7	8	9
Silhouette coef	0.2864	0.3352	0.3527	0.3548	0.3545	0.3545	0.3545	0.3545

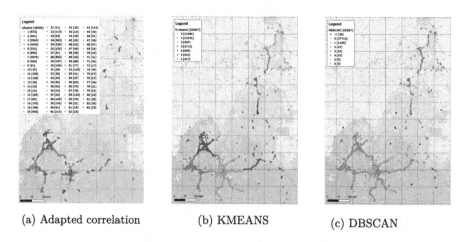

(a) Adapted correlation   (b) KMEANS   (c) DBSCAN

Fig. 7. Clustering algorithm result

6.3   Results and Discussion

The adapted correlation clustering was implemented and tested, focusing on our clustering objectives described in Sect. 5.4. We performed several simulations with different values of the parameters ε_1 and ε_2, and we observed that the clustering results depend on these parameters. The larger the values of the parameters, the more we have large clusters with a reduced number of clusters but with a fair clustering coefficient. It is thus necessary to make a judicious choice of these parameters. For $\varepsilon_1 = 10$ and a minimal cluster size $= 21$, we obtain an excellent clustering with 82 compact clusters as shown in Fig. 7a. The evaluation was based on the Silhouette coefficient described in Sect. 6.2, and we obtained a score of 0.978878. However, it should be noted that this setting gave 911 outliers which are very distant cells that do not meet the parameters criteria. Dealing with the outliers may require increasing the parameters' values, but the wrong parameters can lead to a lousy clustering coefficient. The number of clusters obtained is logical and very close to the actual context for allocation to FME for maintenance operations.

To evaluate the performance of our proposed method, we implemented two other clustering algorithms, K-MEANS and DBSCAN.

K-means is a classical unsupervised learning algorithm that aims to partition data into k clusters so that data points in the same cluster are similar and data points in different clusters are further apart. The user must define the k parameter. In our simulation, the parameter k was chosen based on the Elbow curve and the different silhouette coefficients, and the one that gives the best score is $k = 7$, with a score of 0.8489. The different clusters are shown in Fig. 7b. Although K-means produces a coherent cluster with an acceptable score, it is limited by the interpretable features that are only limited to geocoordinates. It is also unbalanced with two clusters that contain more than 70% of the data to be clustered, which does not make it the best algorithm for our study case.

The Density-Based Spatial Clustering of Applications with Noise (DBSCAN) is an unsupervised learning algorithm that requires two (02) parameters: eps: specifies how close points should be to each other to be considered a part of a cluster. $minPts$: the minimum number of points required to form a cluster.

The efficient choice of these parameters is based on domain knowledge. In our case, we estimate a minimum distance of 5 km between the cell sites and a minimum of 6 sites to be considered a cluster. Nevertheless, these values showed the limit of DBSCAN, which finds only one cluster for the whole dataset. So we used the default value recommended by sci-kit-learn, which is $eps = 0.5$, and we used the Silhouette coefficient to evaluate for different values of $minPts$, the result is given on the Table 5, we observe convergence at $minPts = 6$ with a fair 0.3545 Silhouette coefficient. Considering the best score with $minPts = 5$, we implemented it with the default value of $eps = 0.5$, and we obtained 7 clusters and 20 outliers, as shown in Fig. 7c.

7 Conclusion and Future Work

In this work, we introduced a method for optimal partitioning of cell sites. The proposed method is a two-level clustering, the first based on operator parameters and the second on two defined clustering objectives that allow dynamically allocating the cells in clusters based on their similarity. The evaluation of our method using the Silhouette coefficient metric shows that the algorithms outperform the classical clustering algorithms, k means and DBSCAN, on both metric and accurate context matching. Furthermore, the inclusion of current operator data and the new features we created make our method ready to be used to help operators, MSPs, TowerCo's and any other third party involved in cell site management in the telecom sector to reduce their operating costs by efficiently assigning cell sites to their technicians for maintenance purposes. Future work will mainly include the introduction of a self-learning algorithm to facilitate the selection of the best ε_1 and ε_2 parameters, as many domain knowledge-based tests have been used so far.

Acknowledgement. We thank the editor and the anonymous reviewers for their valuable remarks that helped us improve the paper's content and presentation. Moreover, the author is grateful for the facilities the AIMS-Cameroon Research Center provides and its kind hospitality.

Conflict of Interest statement. On behalf of all authors, the corresponding author states that there is no conflict of interest.

References

1. Angell, R., Monath, N., Yadav, N., McCallum, A.: Interactive correlation clustering with existential cluster constraints. In: International Conference on Machine Learning, pp. 703–716. PMLR (2022)

2. Ari, A.A.A., Djedouboum, A.C., Gueroui, M., Thiare, O., Mohamadou, A., Aliouat, Z.: A three-tier architecture of large-scale wireless sensor networks for big data collection. Appl. Sci. **10**(15), 5382 (2020)
3. Ari, A.A.A., Gueroui, A., Titouna, C., Thiare, O., Aliouat, Z.: Resource allocation scheme for 5G C-RAN: a swarm intelligence based approach. Comput. Netw. **165**, 106957 (2019)
4. Bansal, N., Blum, A., Chawla, S.: Correlation clustering. Machine learning **56**(1), 89–113 (2004)
5. BearingPoint: Electricite et telecom en afrique: la convergence? (2017). https://www.agenceecofin.com/. Accessed 18 Sept 2021
6. Brickner, T.: Closing Africa's infrastructure gap with sustainability at the heart of Helios towers. shorturl.at/dkMS2 (2020). Accessed 12 May 2021
7. Chierichetti, F., Dalvi, N., Kumar, R.: Correlation clustering in mapreduce. In: Proceedings of the 20th ACM SIGKDD International Conference on Knowledge Discovery and Data Mining, pp. 641–650 (2014)
8. Demaine, E.D., Emanuel, D., Fiat, A., Immorlica, N.: Correlation clustering in general weighted graphs. Theoret. Comput. Sci. **361**(2), 172–187 (2006). https://doi.org/10.1016/j.tcs.2006.05.008. https://www.sciencedirect.com/science/article/pii/S0304397506003227, approximation and Online Algorithms
9. Dittenbach, M., Merkl, D., Rauber, A.: The growing hierarchical self-organizing map. In: Proceedings of the IEEE-INNS-ENNS International Joint Conference on Neural Networks, IJCNN 2000, Neural Computing: New Challenges and Perspectives for the New Millennium, vol. 6, pp. 15–19 (2000). https://doi.org/10.1109/IJCNN.2000.859366
10. Djedouboum, A.C., Ari, A.A.A., Gueroui, A.M., Mohamadou, A., Thiare, O., Aliouat, Z.: A framework of modeling large-scale wireless sensor networks for big data collection. Symmetry **12**(7), 1113 (2020)
11. Gbadoubissa, J.E.Z., Ari, A.A.A., Gueroui, A.M.: Efficient k-means based clustering scheme for mobile networks cell sites management. J. King Saud Univ. Comput. Inf. Sci. **32**(9), 1063–1070 (2020). https://doi.org/10.1016/j.jksuci.2018.10.015. https://www.sciencedirect.com/science/article/pii/S131915781830778X
12. Gbadouissa, J.E.Z., Ari, A.A.A., Titouna, C., Gueroui, A.M., Thiare, O.: HGC: hypergraph based clustering scheme for power aware wireless sensor networks. Future Gener. Comput. Syst. **105**, 175–183 (2020). https://doi.org/10.1016/j.future.2019.11.043. https://www.sciencedirect.com/science/article/pii/S0167739X1932240X
13. GSMA: GSMA Connected Society, Closing the Coverage Gap. GSM Association (2019)
14. GSMA: The mobile economy 2020. GSM Association, 1 edn. (2020)
15. Hongsakham, W., Pattara-atikom, W., Peachavanish, R.: Estimating road traffic congestion from cellular handoff information using cell-based neural networks and k-means clustering. In: 2008 5th International Conference on Electrical Engineering/Electronics, Computer, Telecommunications and Information Technology, vol. 1, pp. 13–16 (2008). https://doi.org/10.1109/ECTICON.2008.4600361
16. Hung, C., Tsai, C.F.: Market segmentation based on hierarchical self-organizing map for markets of multimedia on demand. Expert Syst. Appl. **34**, 780–787 (2008). https://doi.org/10.1016/j.eswa.2006.10.012
17. OpenCelliD: What is opencellid? https://opencellid.org/#zoom=16&lat=37.77889&lon=-122.41942. Accessed 20 June 2021

18. Ray, S., Turi, R.: Determination of number of clusters in k-means clustering and application in colour image segmentation. In: Proceedings of the 4th International Conference on Advances in Pattern Recognition and Digital Techniques (ICAPRDT 1999) 1, August 2000

19. Satista: Number of active mobile broadband subscriptions worldwide from 2007 to 2021 (2021). https://www.statista.com/statistics/273016/number-of-mobile-broadband-subscriptions-worldwide-since-2007/. Accessed 28 Aug 2022

20. WFPGeoNode: Metadata: Cameroon road network (main roads). https://geonode.wfp.org/layers/geonode:cmr_trs_roads_osm/metadata_detail. Accessed 04 Apr 2021

21. Yang, G., Esmailpour, A., Nasser, N., Chen, G., Liu, Q., Bai, P.: A hierarchical clustering algorithm for interference management in ultra-dense small cell networks. IEEE Access **PP**, 1 (2020). https://doi.org/10.1109/ACCESS.2020.2989502

22. Zimmermann, H.m., Seitz, A., Halfmann, R.: Dynamic cell clustering in cellular multi-hop networks. In: 2006 10th IEEE Singapore International Conference on Communication Systems, pp. 1–5 (2006). https://doi.org/10.1109/ICCS.2006.301458

A Lightweight Authenticated Key Agreement Scheme for Resource-Constrained Devices Based on Implicit Certificates and Finite Graphs

Mounirah Djam-Doudou[1], Ado Adamou Abba Ari[1,2,3]($\boxtimes$),
Hortense Boudjou Tchapgnouo[1], Abdelhak Mourad Gueroui[3],
Alidou Mohamadou[1], Nabila Labraoui[4], and Ousmane Thiare[5]

[1] Department of Computer Science, University of Maroua, PO Box 46,
Maroua, Cameroon
[2] CREATIVE, Institute of Fine Arts and Innovation, University of Garoua,
PO Box 346, Garoua, Cameroon
[3] DAVID Lab, Université Paris-Saclay, University of Versailles,
Saint-Quentin-en-Yvelines, France
adoa-damou.abba-ari@uvsq.fr
[4] Department of Computer Science, University Abou Bekr Belkaid Tlemcen,
PO Box 230, 13000 Chetouane, Tlemcen, Algeria
[5] Department of Computer Science, Gaston Berger University of Saint-Louis,
PO Box 234, Saint-Louis, Senegal

Abstract. In this paper, we discuss the issue of secure communication among devices with limited resources. We introduce a key agreement protocol that utilizes implicit certificates with elliptic curves specifically designed for devices with limited capacity. We establish a certification chain within a finite graph to depict the connection among nodes within the identical group and propose a workload distribution strategy across all cluster nodes. Additionally, we present a trust scheme that enables nodes to generate implicit certificates on an elliptic curve and securely create keys with their counterparts. The group leader acts as the root CA and constructs a hierarchical structure within the finite graph, establishing a certification chain in an organized manner with an intermediate certificate authority (ICA) at every level. This chain is utilized by nodes for generating and sharing implicit certificates, from which symmetric keys for communication between nodes are derived. We then implement the solution using TelosB sensors in the TOSSIM simulator with an AVL Tree. We evaluate the security and resilience of our proposed scheme through informal analysis and a formal model. The informal analysis demonstrates the robustness of our scheme in achieving key security objectives, while the formal analysis using the extended Canetti-Krawczyk (eCK) model confirms its security and efficiency. Furthermore, we compare the performance of our scheme with other related schemes, highlighting its effectiveness for resource-constrained devices.

© ICST Institute for Computer Sciences, Social Informatics and Telecommunications Engineering 2024
Published by Springer Nature Switzerland AG 2024. All Rights Reserved
F. Tchakounte et al. (Eds.): SAFER-TEA 2023, LNICST 566, pp. 128–155, 2024.
https://doi.org/10.1007/978-3-031-56396-6_9

Keywords: Authenticated Key Exchange · AVL Tree · Elliptic Curve · Implicit certificate · Lightweight Cryptography · Security Model

1 Introduction

1.1 Background

A wireless sensor network is a set of sensors deployed randomly in a geographical area to monitor a physical phenomenon and collect data autonomously [5,8,18]. In such a network, the nodes communicate via radio links. They collect information and transmit it, directly or in collaboration with other nodes, to a collection point (base station or sink). Secure communication in devices with limited resources is a significant challenge, and cryptography is one of the solutions used to address this issue [19,38]. We distinguish two primary categories of cryptographic solutions: asymmetric cryptography and symmetric cryptography. Computationally efficient, symmetrical cryptography also uses smaller keys. However, for communication to occur, the key used for decryption and encryption by the parties involved should be the same. Distributing this key to the entities is a critical operation, especially as the overall number of nodes in the network grows. On the other hand, asymmetric cryptography requires longer keys and more complex computations [6,46].

These needs are not a significant issue in systems that do not have resource limitations. However, for resource-poor devices (energy, memory, computational power) [1,14,23,33,42,43], the use of traditional cryptographic key management protocols based on asymmetric cryptosystems becomes challenging in this scenario. This is because, in order to provide sufficiently robust security, these protocols necessitate the use of lengthy keys [15,37].

However, elliptic curve cryptography is well suited to resource-poor devices, as it can provide comparable security with a shorter key. What's more, its efficiency can be enhanced through mathematical techniques [36].

The key exchange protocols made famous by the Diffe-Hellman (DH) key exchange protocol refer to cryptographic protocols that enable two parties with no shared secret information to establish a secret key through public communication [12]. However, the lack of authentication between the communicating parties has led to the birth of new authenticated key exchange (AKE) protocols to granulate the authenticity of the parties and allow them to compute a shared key. This work extended from the proposed protocol in [14], which focuses on resource-constrained devices, is part of this dynamic, which is the subject of much research in both security models and protocols.

1.2 Authors' Contributions

This paper focuses on the issue of security in communication between devices with limited resources. We present a protocol for establishing pairwise keys between nodes in the same group. Our approach is to use a finite graph constructed by the group leader on the basis of criteria that can be used to obtain an ordering relationship between the parties. The leader of the group serves as the root CA for their respective group, while the leaders of each level within the hierarchy act as intermediate CAs for the sub-trees under their control. A trust model is thus established and the root CA initiates the establishment of implicit certificates on an elliptical curve for each node in its network. Certificates are issued and signed in a hierarchical manner from the leader to the lowest node in the tree. To communicate, nodes exchange their certificates and then derive session keys to exchange information with confidence. An simulation of the protocol with TelosB sensors in the TOSSIM simulator using AVL Tree demonstrates the robustness of the protocol, which we evaluated against three other widely recognized protocols. Our contribution can be summarized as follows:

1. Formulating the organization of a cluster as a communication problem in finite graph;
2. The creation of a certification chain on a finite graph as a support for implicit certificate construction on an elliptic curve by nodes of the same group;
3. Formulating a quasi-fairness distribution of resource consumption (memory, computation) in the whole group
4. A method for key agreement between two nodes based on implicit certificates;
5. A simulation of the proposed system in a concrete environment to show its feasibility followed by a comparison with other well known protocols.

1.3   Organization of the Paper

The rest of the paper is organized as follows: Sect. 2 presents a brief review of the essential concepts used in the work; In Sect. 3, we present previous work in the field then in Sect. 4, we make an exhaustive presentation of the protocol; Followed by a formal analysis of its security in the Sect. 5. We then present a concrete implementation of the protocol in Sect. 6. The comparison with other schemes follows in Sect. 7 and the conclusion is the subject of Sect. 8.

2   Preliminaries

2.1   Fundamental Assumptions

Let $\mathbb{G}$ a multiplicative cyclic group of prime order q, generated by $g \in \mathbb{G}$ and $\mathbb{G}^*$ the set of non-identity elements in $\mathbb{G}$.

The discrete logarithm function is defined by Eq. 1

$$DLOG : \mathbb{G} \to \mathbb{Z}_p$$
$$Y \to x/Y = g^x \tag{1}$$

The computational Diffe-Hellman function is defined by Eq. 2

$$CDH : \mathbb{G}^2 \quad \to \mathbb{Z}_p$$
$$(X, Y) \to g^{DLOG(X).DLOG(Y)} \tag{2}$$

The decisional Diffie-Hellman function is defined by Eq. 3

$$DDH : \mathbb{G}^3 \quad \to \mathbb{Z}_p$$
$$(Y, X, Z) \to \begin{cases} 1, \; where \; CDH(Y, X) = Z, \\ 0, \qquad\qquad\quad otherwise. \end{cases} \tag{3}$$

Definition 1. *Given an algorithm S, probability that given $X \xleftarrow{\$} \mathbb{G}^*$ returns correctly $DLOG(X)$ is called the advantage of S for discrete logarithm solving problem denoted, $Adv^{DLOG}(S)$.*

Definition 2. *Given an algorithm S, given as input*
$(X; Y) \xleftarrow{\$} (\mathbb{G}^*)^2$ and oracle access to $DDH(.;.;.)$, the probability that, S correctly returns $CDH(X; Y)$ is called the advantage of S for solving the Gap Diffie-Hellman (GDH) problem denoted, $Adv^{GDH}(S)$.

Theorem 1. *If there is no efficient adversary capable of solving the GDH problem with nontrivial probability, then $\mathbb{G}$ fulfills the GDH hypothesis.*

2.2 Elliptic Curve

Elliptic curve cryptography appears to be an alternative to asymmetric cryptography algorithms such as RSA for which it offers the same quality of security, while using shorter keys than the others. This is a set of techniques for securing data while consuming a minimum of resources. [20,32]. The small size of its keys means lower memory and power consumption and faster computation, making it a suitable candidate for resource-constrained devices.

2.3 Mathematical Considerations

A finite field $\mathbb{F}$ is a field with a finite number of elements. The number of elements is the order of the field, noted q, which can be represented by the power of a prime number $q = p^n$, where p is a prime number, called the characteristic of the field, and $n \in \mathbb{Z}_+$. So, if p is a prime number then $\mathbb{F}_p$ given in Eq. 4 is a finite field.

$$\mathbb{F}_p = \mathbb{Z}/p\mathbb{Z} = \mathbb{Z}(mod\,p) \tag{4}$$

Definition 3. *Let $\mathbb{K}$ be a field. An elliptic curve on $\mathbb{K}$ is the collection of solutions in $\mathbb{K}^2$ of a cubic equation called Weierstrass normal form defined by Eq. 5.*

$$E : y^2 + a_1 xy + a_3 y = x^3 + a_2 x^2 + a_4 x + a_6 \tag{5}$$

where $N_i \in \mathbb{K}$ are coefficients in $\mathbb{K}$

Definition 4. *The Weierstrass equation of an elliptic curve can be simplified, if the curve is defined on a prime finite field* $\mathbb{F}p$ *whose characteristic is different from values 2 and 3. We then obtain the following simplified Weierstrass Eq. 6.*

$$y^2 = x^3 + ax + b \tag{6}$$

where $a, b \in \mathbb{F}_p$ *with the discriminant of the curve* $\triangle$ *given in Eq. 7.*

$$\triangle = 16(4a^3 + 27b^2) \neq 0 \tag{7}$$

This form of curve is the most used in the literature and the one we also use for our work.

The security level of ECC depends strongly on the difficulty of solving the discrete logarithm problem (see Eq. 1) on elliptic curves, that is, given an elliptic curve E defined over a field $\mathbb{F}p$ with P and Q two point of $E(\mathbb{F}p)$ it is difficult to determine an integer n such that $Q = nP$.

There are many encryption systems based on ECC [12,13,17], but no matter which encryption system is used. Guessing the secret always comes down to solving the discrete logarithm problem.

2.4   Security Models

A security model is an approach that specifies what constitutes a security failure and the adverse behaviors against which it is protected. We distinguish different models that have been adopted in numerous studies [4,7,9,11,21,24,40] among which Canetti-Krawczyk (CK) [11] and extended Canetti-Krawczyk (eCK) [24] are the most known and the most used. We present in more detail the eCK model which is the one we use to analyze the security of our protocol.

The parties considered in eCK model which focuses on the public key setting are probabilistic polynomial time machines, $\hat{P}_1, ..., \hat{P}_n$, interconnected with each other.

Axiom 1. *All parties share a common certification authority (CA) and a group G, from which their static public keys are chosen.*

Definition 5. *A key exchange is a protocol involving two parties (machines), and a session is an example of a protocol executed by one party.*

When a session is activated, a session state is created to contain specific parameters for the created session. Each session is activated with parameters $(\hat{P}_i, \hat{P}_j, \phi, \Phi, \tau)$.

Definition 6. *The set* $(\hat{P}_i, \hat{P}_j, \phi, \Phi, \tau)$ *is called session identifier who required to be unique at each party involved in the session.*

where :

- $\hat{P}_i$ initiate a session with peer $\hat{P}_j$ or respond to a session initiated at $\hat{P}_i$;

- ϕ the outgoing ephemeral key and Φ the incoming one;
- $\tau \in \{Initiator; Responder\}$ the role of $\hat{P}_i$ in the session.

Axiom 2. *Two sessions with initial identifier* $(\hat{P}_i, \hat{P}_j, \phi, \Phi, \tau)$ *and* $(\hat{P}_i, \hat{P}_j, \phi, \Phi, \tau\prime)$ *with* $\tau \neq \tau\prime$ *are said to be matching.*

Definition 7. *The adversary $\mathcal{M}$ is a probabilistic polynomial time machine that controls communications between the parties; The adversary $\mathcal{M}$ is able to control all communications between the parties by sending arbitrary messages to one party impersonating the other party, obtaining responses from one party and/or making decisions about their delivery.*

For the following we note a session identifier *sessionID*. The adversary $\mathcal{M}$ is given the following queries, aiming to model information leakages:

- *StaticKeyReveal:* this request provides the attacker with the static private key of the entity on which it is issued. It allows the capture of static key leakages;
- *SessionKeyReveal(sessionID):* this request provides the session key to the attacker if the sessionID session has already ended, otherwise the request is ignored;
- *StaticKeyReveal(party):* this request allows the attacker to obtain the static private key of the entity on which it is issued;
- *EstablishParty(party):* With this request, the adversary registers a static public key on behalf of a party. The party on which this request is issued is assumed to be fully controlled by the adversary;
- *EphemeralKeyReveal(sessionID):* this request allows the attacker to obtain the ephemeral key of the session identified by sessionID;
- *Test(sessionID):* when the test request is issued on a completed (not expired) session, a bit is randomly chosen, and depending on the chosen value, the adversary is provided with either the session key or a random value chosen under the distribution of session keys.

To satisfy the model, a session's ephemeral key must contain all session-specific information, and all computations performed to derive a party's session key must depend deterministically on the party's ephemeral key, the long-term secret key, and the communication received from the other party [24]. The protocol is appreciated through two paradigms which are session freshness and security which uses previous requests as follows:

Let *sessionID* be an AKE session performed by one party $\hat{P}_1$ with another party $\hat{P}_2$, and *sessionID* be the session corresponding to *sessionID*, eventually performed by $\hat{P}_2$.

Definition 8. *(Freshness) The session sessionID is said to be fresh if none of the following holds:*

1. *The adversary $\mathcal{M}$ issues a SessionKeyReveal query on sessionID or eventually on sessionID;*

2. *The adversary $\mathcal{M}$ issues an EphemeralKeyReveal query on sessionID and a StaticKeyReveal query on $\hat{P}_1$;*
3. *The adversary $\mathcal{M}$ makes a StaticKeyReveal query on $\hat{P}_2$ and an EphemeralKeyReveal query on sessionID which exist;*
4. *The adversary $\mathcal{M}$ makes a StaticKeyReaveal query on $\hat{P}_2$ before the completion of the sessionID session and the session with identifier sessionID does not exist.*

Without the last condition, if the session with identifier sessionID does not exist and $\hat{P}_2$ makes a StaticKeyReveal query on $\hat{P}_1$ the sessionID session is said to be strongly fresh.

Definition 9. *(Security) A protocol in which two honest parties conduct corresponding sessions and both calculate the same session key is considered secure (respectively strongly secure), if given a session key distribution, no polynomially constrained adversary can distinguish a fresh (respectively a strongly fresh) session key from a random value chosen from said distribution with a probability significantly superior to 1/2.*

In other words, the advantage of the adversary $\mathcal{M}$ in the AKE experiment with AKE protocol Π is defined as:

$$Adv_\Pi^{ake} = Pr[\mathcal{M} \ wins] - \frac{1}{2} \tag{8}$$

3   Related Works

In the field of secure key agreement protocols, a non negligible number of protocols have been proposed. In this section, we present some that have inspired our work.

The NAXOS protocol establishes a shared symmetric key between two parties, each of whom has a long-term private key, and who initially know the public key of all the other participants. In this protocol, it is presumed that the adversary can gain both the long-term private keys and the short-term data generated during a protocol session, which does not include the private key. The idea is that by mixing the long-term private key and the short-term ephemeral key in the hash function, the attacker would have enough material to build an attack [24]. NAXOS is secure in the eCK model but as we can see it does not care particularly about the distribution of resources (memory, calculation) between the parties.

The popular MQV authenticated protocol uses public key authentication and is designed to achieve a remarkable list of security properties [25]. It introduces implicit key authentication, which means that an adversary cannot learn anything from the session key agreed upon between two parties, provided that he does not have invasive access to any of the ephemeral or static keys of either party or to a session key derived from these private keys. Moreover the MQV protocol was not based on a formal security proof.

The HMQV protocol, which is an enhancement of MQV, offers the same performance and functionality as it [22]. It is based on a concept derived from the Schnorr identification scheme [39]. In the principle, two parties can compute the same signature; one party chooses the challenge and the other party solves it by knowing the private signature key.

In [47], the authors exploit the limitations of the MQV and HMQV protocols and propose a new family of implicitly authenticated protocols (OAKE) that prove resilience to component and exponent leakage under simple standard assumptions, without relying on the assumption of exponent knowledge. It preserves confidentiality and introduces the concept of the fairness property of the calculation.

As for the VOAKE protocol, it is presented as a variant of the OAKE family and exploits the NAXOS technique which it applies to the computation of the ephemeral public key taking into account the specified computation environment; its security is proven in the PACK model proposed by the same author [45].

The protocol outlined in [36] utilizes implicit certificates and elliptic curves, with a topology organized into clusters. The cluster-heads have special capabilities that maintain the static nature of this topology. Nodes establish shared keys by interchanging their implicit certificates, and these are then used to derivate the keys. Validity of the certificates requires signature from the cluster-head, acting as the root CA. This puts the responsibility of cryptographic operations entirely on the leader (CA), creating a protocol that depends on a fixed topology with a node at the center with significantly higher capacities than other cluster members. Furthermore, this protocol is not evaluated in a formal security model.

NETS [26] is an authenticated key exchange protocol that dispenses with the bifurcation lemma to provide simple and rigorous security over the HMQV and MQV protocols on which it is based. Its security is proven in the extended Canetti-Krawczyk (eCK) model under the random oracle assumption and the Diffe-Hellman gap (GDH) assumption [12].

We note that almost all the above protocols do not define concrete execution environments. Private keys are supposed to be assigned uniformly and randomly and only one party (CA) is responsible for verifying the public key and issuing the associated certificate. Each party learns the other's public key through the certificate each time a new session is initiated. This centralization of the workload on a single party (CA), in addition to the supposed trust in the unique verification of the certificate, poses a real security problem because it creates a centralization point. In a network of low-resource devices (e.g., sensor networks), intensive work on the leader node (CA) would lead to its premature death and thus the death of the network.

4   DEKM AKE Protocol

Low-resource devices such as sensors require lightweight cryptographic techniques that can be supported by sensor nodes without hindering their normal operation, all while using the least amount of resources possible. We are especially interested in the key establishment process for inter-node communication within a group (see Fig. 2). The interest is to distribute the workload on all the nodes of the group and not on a particular node in order to avoid a point of centralization (and thus vulnerability) while extending the life of the network. In this section, we present the formal definition of our protocol. We set up the system implementation environment and specify the information flow between devices, including the entire computation process in the protocol, the type of security breach that can be modeled by an adversarial query, and the type of information that can be revealed and by which query.

In the following, we will use the terminology summarized in Tab. 1.

Table 1. Notations

Notation	Description
X	Node ID
K	Network global key (for authentication)
rX	Secret random number (generated by node X)
R_X	Point value on the curve for the certificate required by node X
$Cert_X$	Implicit certificate for node X
$TrustChain_X$	Trust list for X
$HTrustChain_X$	Hash value for X trusted list
$CertChain_X$	X certificate chain
e	Certificate Hash value
s	The value used to compute the private key of the requester node
d_X	X private key
Q_X	X Public key
N_X	Random nonce generated by X
K_{XY}	Shared key between X and Y

We will also use the following expressions:

- A group of nodes (cluster) is denoted by CL;
- A group leader is designated by CH;
- A group member is noted Clm;
- The value of the RSSI signal of a node s_i coming from a node s_j; $i \neq j$; $s_i, s_j \in s$ is noted $VR(s_i, s_j)$;
- We note $VRm = \{VR(s_i, CH), VR(s_j, CH), .., VR(s_k, CH)\}s_i, s_j, ..., s_k \in s; i \neq j \neq ... \neq k$; the set of RSSI values from the nodes to the CH;
- $\{X, VR(s_X, CH)\}, s_X \in s$ an associative array composed of the identifier of node U and the value of its RSSI signal to the leader.
- $H_1 : \{0,1\}^* \to \mathbb{Z}_q$; $H_2 : \{0,1\}^* \to \{0,1\}^\lambda$, two hash function modeled as independent random oracles where λ is a constant.

Definition 10. *Let $G_r = (V, E)$ be a finite graph with $v > 1$ vertices, a generalized tree generated by $s = \{s_1, s_2, \ldots\ldots s_n\}, n \in \mathbb{N}$ a set of n sensors nodes of the same group;*
  As a generalized tree, G_r has the following properties.

- G_r *has no simple cycles.*
- G_r *is connected.*
- G_r *has no simple cycles and has $v - 1$ edges ($|E| = |V| - 1$)*
- G_r *has $v - 1$ edges.*
- G_r *is acyclic.*
- *if an edge is added that joins two nonadjacent vertices, exactly one cycle is formed.*
- G_r *is connected, unfortunately if an edge is deleted, the graph G_r becomes disconnected.*
- *Every pair of vertices is connected by exactly one path.*

Theorem 2. *All properties given in Definition 10 are equivalent.*

Definition 11. *We consider the relation $\leq$ (less or equal to) on VRm. We have:*

- *Reflexivity:*
  $\forall\, x \in VRm \;\Rightarrow\; x \leq x$
- *Transitivity:*
  $\forall\, x, y, z \in VRm \;\; x \leq y \,;\, y \leq z \;\Rightarrow\; x \leq z$
- *Antisymmetry:*
  $\forall\, x, y \in VRm \;\; x \leq y \,,\, y \leq x \;\Rightarrow\; x = y$

Theorem 3. *According to all properties given in Definition 11:, the relation $\leq$ (less or equal to) defines a total order relation on the set VRm in G_r.*

Therefore, VRm can be used by the CH to organize G_r into a hierarchical structure.

4.1   Protocol Description

A digital certificate is a document that attests that the associated public key is that of its legitimate owner. To be taken seriously, a certificate must be signed by a trusted third party, usually called a certification authority. Based on this principle, a chain of trust can be established in a hierarchical fashion between different certification authorities called intermediate authorities up to the root authority which has a self-signed certificate [28]. Figure 1 shows an illustration of the principle.

In an elliptic curve, the generator G is the first point chosen on the curve. The whole curve is an endless loop. The order n is the number of distinct points on the curve (the numbers of possible private keys). From a random private key k, which is multiplied by the generator point G, we obtain another point on the curve which is the public key K. As the generator point is always the same, for the same private key k we always obtain the same public key K. There is a direct link between k and K, but it can be calculated only in one direction (from k to K). The public key can be shared with everyone, without risk of revealing the private key. The public key can be calculated from the private key, but not the reverse, because the mathematical functions used are not invertible (discrete logarithm problem Eq. 1).

Before being deployed, each node is pre-loaded with elliptic curve parameters, along with a global key K, used to identify individual nodes in the network and a unique identifier X. After setting up the CL and identifying all CH leader, every $Clm \in s = \{s_1, s_2, \cdots, s_n\}$ send a join message $\{X, VR(s_X, CH)\}$ to CH. At the end, CH uses VRm to build a hierarchical structure he is the only one to know. In a CL, CH is the root CA.

At each level of the structure, the main Clm of the level is an intermediate certification authority (ICA) for the s_i nodes that depend on it, and so on. When a Clm wants to acquire or renew a certificate, it first creates it. Then, it forwards its certificate in a request to its local certification authority (ICA), which is its first node in the hierarchy. The local certification authority signs the certificate with its private key and sends the signed certificate back to the applicant. This certificate is returned with the certificate chain ($CertChainX$) that leads from the certification authority to the node to be addressed. In this way, cryptographic tasks are distributed over the entire network, rather than a single certification authority.

The process of implementing the chain of trust begins with the root certification authority (root CA), which initiates it. It begins by issuing its own certificate, from which it draws its key pair. Next, the Clm that lie just below the root CA in the hierarchical structure request certificates from the root CA. When they have done so, they start the exact same process for the s_i at the next step down, who in their turn apply for certificates, and so forth until they reach last level of the tree. The resulting chain is based on the same principle as RFC5280 [28]. At each level, the ICA (signing authority) sends back the certificate signed contained in $CertChain$.

At last, the CH return back to each node X of the cluster a message that contains its public key, $TrustChain_X$, and $HTrustChain_X$.

Static Public/Private Key Pair.

In the case of an implicit certificate that we use, the certificate is the public key of a subject reconstructed from some data [10,35]. To issue a certificate, the CH takes the following steps:

1. Outputs two big random numbers:

$$rCN1 \in [1, n-1] \cap \mathbb{N}$$
$$rCN2 \in [1, n-1] \cap \mathbb{N}$$

$$(9)$$

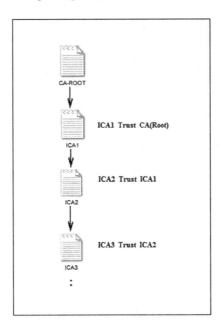

Fig. 1. Chain of certificates

2. Computes its certificate

$$Cert_{CA} = rCN1 + rCN2 \times G \tag{10}$$

3. Then it calculates

$$e = H_1(Cert_{CA}) \text{ and}$$
$$s = erCN1 + erCN2 \ (mod \ n) \tag{11}$$

4. Finally computes its own private key

$$d_{CA} = erCN1 + s \ (mod \ n)$$

and its own public key $\tag{12}$

$$Q_{CA} = d_{CA} \times G$$

Other nodes take the subsequent steps:

1. It output a random number

$$rX \in [1, n-1] \cap \mathbb{N}$$

then computes $\tag{13}$

$$R_X = rX \times G$$

2. It outputs a nonce N_X and calculates

$$MAC_K[RX, N_X, X, TrustChain_X] \tag{14}$$

3. The node then forwards X, $HTrustChain_X$, $TrustChain_X$, R_X and N_X with the MAC to its ICA
4. For each level, When a CA i receives a request message, it verifies the chain of trust and the requester's MAC. If the verification is successful, the CA generates a number $rCN_i \in [1, n-1] \cap \mathbb{N}$ and then computes the certificate.

$$Cert_X = R_X + rCN_i \times G \qquad (15)$$

5. Then, calculates s using $Cert_X$, rCN_i and its private key (d_{CN_i}),

$$e = H_1(Cert_X) \text{ and}$$
$$s = erCN_i + d_{CN_i} \pmod{n} \qquad (16)$$

6. CA returns to the requester node X, $CertChain_X$ and a nonce N_{CN_i}, and s

$$MAC_K[CertChain_X, N_{CN_i}, s, X] \qquad (17)$$

When the message is delivered, X reviews the MAC, $HTrustChain_X$ and $TrustChain_X$ from the root CA. If all is ok, X then calculates $e = H_1(Cert_X)$ using the identical function as its ICA
7. X then calculates its private key

$$d_X = erX + s \pmod{n}$$
and public key $\qquad (18)$
$$Q_X = d_X \times G$$

Ephemeral Public/Private Key Pair

The background idea is similar to that of the Bellare-Rogaway (BR) model [7] which seems to be equivalent to the Canetti-Krawczyk model, where no ephemeral reveals are allowed, except that here the recording of keys is not done honestly. Here no ephemeral keys are needed because public keys are not shared but calculated from some data when a session is set up.

Session Key

Consider the subsequent session identifiers: $(X, Y, \ , \ , Initiator)$, $(X, Y, \ , \ , Responder)$ and $TrustChain_X$, $TrustChain_Y$ the lists that contain the elements of the trust chains of the X and Y parties; $HTrustChain_X$ and $HTrustChain_Y$ the corresponding signatures linked to each trust lists, respectively generated using the root certification authority's private key.

When X wishes to reach Y, it first sends a request with a Nonce N_X, with $CertChain_X$, $TrustChain_X$ and $HTrustChain_X$. When Y receives the request message from X, it applies the root CA's public key to check the signature of $HTrustChain_X$.

If the signature verification is successful, Y will check its list against the one it received by executing the Eq. 19

$$\psi = TrustChain_X \cap TrustChain_Y \tag{19}$$

If $\psi \neq \{\varnothing\}$, it can then verify the certificate's authenticity by computing the initiator's public key using Eq. 20. In this way, in order to obtain the public key, it is also possible to ascertain the validity of the certificate chain. Since certificates are linked by chain signatures, the discovery of an invalid certificate in the sequence would automatically cause the calculation to fail.

$$
\begin{aligned}
Q_{X_i} &= d_{X_i}G \\
&= (e_i r X_i + s_i (mod\ n))G \\
&= (e_i r X_i + e_i r C N_{i-1} + d_{CN_{i-1}}(mod\ n))G \\
&= e_i(rX_iG + rCN_{i-1}G(mod\ n)) + d_{CN_{i-1}}G(mod\ n) \\
&= e_i(rX_iG + rCN_{i-1}G(mod\ n)) + (e_{i-1}rX_{i-1} + e_{i-1}rCN_{i-2} + d_{CN_{i-2}})G(mod\ n) \\
&= e_i(rX_iG + rCN_{i-1}G(mod\ n)) + e_{i-1}(rX_{i-1}G + rCN_{i-2}G(mod\ n)) + d_{CN_{i-2}}G(mod\ n) \\
&= e_i(rX_iG + rCN_{i-1}G(mod\ n)) + e_{i-1}(rX_{i-1}G + rCN_{i-2}G(mod\ n)) + \cdots \\
&\quad + (e_{i-m}rX_{i-m} + e_{i-m}rCN_{i-m-1} + d_{CN_{i-m-1}})G(mod\ n) \\
&= e_i(rX_iG + rCN_{i-1}G(mod\ n)) + e_{i-1}(rX_{i-1}G + rCN_{i-2}G(mod\ n)) + \cdots \\
&\quad + e_{i-m}(rX_{i-m}G + rCN_{i-m-1}G(mod\ n)) + d_{CN_{i-m-1}}G(mod\ n) \\
&= e_i(RX_i + rCN_{i-1}G(modn)) + e_{i-1}(RX_{i-1} + rCN_{i-2}G(mod\ n)) + \cdots \\
&\quad + e_{i-m}(RX_{i-m} + rCN_{i-m-1}G(mod\ n)) + d_{CA}G(mod\ n) \\
&= e_i Cert_{X_i} + e_{i-1}Cert_{X_{i-1}} + \cdots + e_{i-m}Cert_{X_{i-m}} + d_{CA}G \\
&= \sum_{j=0}^{m} e_{i-j}Cert_{X_{i-j}} + d_{CA}G, \quad m \in \mathbb{N} \\
&= \sum_{j=0}^{m} e_{i-j}Cert_{X_{i-j}} + Q_{CA}, \quad m \in \mathbb{N} \\
&= \sum_{j=0}^{m} H_1(Cert_{X_{i-j}})Cert_{X_{i-j}} + Q_{CA}, \quad m \in \mathbb{N}
\end{aligned}
$$

$$Q_{X_i} = \sum_{j=0}^{m} H_1(Cert_{X_{i-j}})Cert_{X_{i-j}} + Q_{CA}, \quad m \in \mathbb{N} \tag{20}$$

If the check is successful for the Y part, it then sends the same informations to X, which performs the same check in a similar manner. Each node is now able to compute the pairwise key, which is the result of its private key multiplied by the other node's public key. Therefore, Y coputes Eq. 21.

$$H_2(\sigma) = H_2(d_Y Q_X) = H_2(d_Y d_X G) \tag{21}$$

while X computes Eq. 22

$$H_2(\sigma) = H_2(d_X Q_Y) = H_2(d_X d_Y G) \tag{22}$$

Remark 1. Public key validation is of major importance for the security of key agreement protocols. Its omission can have serious consequences as proven with the HMQV and MQV protocols [30,31]. This validation prevents the potential leakage of private information [3]. It provides some assurance in calculations involving its private keys [30,31,44]. In this work, the validation of the public key does not require a particular treatment exclusively dedicated to it, since the calculation of the public key automatically leads to the validation of the latter which is an mandatory step in the implementation of the protocol.

5   Security of DEKM Protocol

In this section, we present a formal security proof of DEKM protocol under the Gap Diffe-Hellman (GDH) assumption and the random oracle assumption (RO).

Theorem 4. *For H_1 and H_2 modeled as random oracles, G a group where the GDH assumption holds, and G_r a finite graph organized according to a relation of order, the advantage of any adversary $\mathcal{M}$ to attack the AKE security of DEKM in the eCK model is negligible.*

Corollary 1. *The probability of any adversary's advantage in attacking the security of DEKM protocol in the eCK model is said to be negligible if it is less or equal than $\frac{1}{2}$.*

Proof of Theorem 4

Let $\mathcal{M}$ be any AKE adversary against DEKM and P_r the probability for an adversary to win DEKM. Observing that, the session key is computed as $K = H_2(\sigma)$ for some 3-tuple σ, the adversary $\mathcal{M}$ has only two ways to distinguish K from a random string:

- *Forging Attack. At some point the adversary $\mathcal{M}$ queries H_2 on the same 3-tuple σ;*
- *Key Replication Attack. The adversary $\mathcal{M}$ successfully forces the establishment of another session key computed for the same 3-tuple σ and identical to the session key of the test session.*

We now define the following events:

- *E_1: The adversary $\mathcal{M}$ wins the security experiment with probability $P_r = \frac{1}{2} + \varepsilon$, where ε is non-negligible;*
- *E_2: The adversary $\mathcal{M}$ asks random oracle H_2 with same 3-tuple σ of the test session;*
- *E_3: The test session has matching session.*

Since the σ entry determines the session key (with a corresponding session or a session equivalent to the test session) adversary $\mathcal{M}$ has no advantage to win if event E_3 does not occur. Our probability bounding process takes into account various combinations with it.

Case 1. Event $E_2 \wedge E_3$

Each of the distinct AKE sessions must have a distinct 3-tuple, and thus if the random oracles produce no collisions, the key replication attack is impossible because the equality of the session keys implies the strict equality of the corresponding 3-tuples (d_X, d_Y, G).

In this situation, the adversary must reproduce the elements of the 3-tuples. To do so, he must win the discrete logarithm challenge twice (the pairwise key being the product of the private keys of the games).

Let us note, however, that with Diffie-Hellman, in a cyclic group of prime modulus p, the adversary can perform an efficient computation of the discrete logarithm with the Pohlig-Hellman algorithm if the order of the group does not have large prime factors [34].

However, this is not the case here since the prime factors are important. For the test, the adversary being reasonably incapable of solving the discrete logarithm challenge twice, we deduce that his probability of success $P_r \approx 0$, we can conclude that P_r is negligible.

Case 2. event $E_1 \wedge E_3$

To establish a new pairwise key between the parties, the adversary must necessarily obtain the trust lists of each of the parties which serve as an entry point for the establishment of the keys (Eq. X). But these chains are known only to the leader. In order to succeed, the opponent must therefore have access to the leader.

So for a group of $n \geqslant 2$ nodes, the probability of falling on the leader (and thus of succeeding in the attack) is:

$$P_r = \frac{1}{n} = \frac{1}{2} + \varepsilon \Rightarrow \varepsilon = \frac{1}{n} - \frac{1}{2}$$

we have therefore   (23)

$$\lim_{n \to +\infty} \varepsilon = -\frac{1}{2} \Rightarrow \lim_{n \to +\infty} P_r = 0$$

In this case also, we can easily deduce that the probability P_r is negligible.

6 A Concrete Implementation of the DEKM Protocol

In order to show the realistic character of our proposal, we present in this section a concrete implementation of it with TelosB sensors with on TOSSIM simulator [41].

The simulation environment is completed by using the SHA1 algorithm for hashes and the group of seven nodes is organized as an AVL tree. The certification chain is built on an AVL tree organization as a support for the construction of implicit certificates on an elliptic curve that provides the cryptographic capabilities.

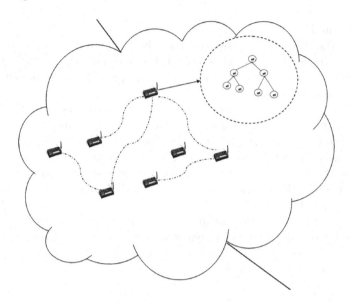

Fig. 2. View of a cluster

6.1 Overview of AVL Tree

Definition 12. *A binary tree is a finite set of vertices that can be empty or comprised of a vertex known as the root, along with two binary subtrees that are separate from each other and from the root. These subtrees are referred to as the left and right subtrees.*

Theorem 5. *A binary tree Abr is either the empty tree or a subset of the set $\mathbb{E}$ = $\{0,1\}^*$ such that*
   $\forall\ x,y\ \in \mathbb{E},\ xy\ \in Abr\ then\ x \in Abr$

Definition 13. *A balanced binary tree is defined as a binary tree in which the height of the left and right subtrees of any node does not differ by h, where h is generally equal to 1.*

Definition 14. *An AVL tree can bee seen as a balanced search tree. An AVL is also a binary tree with the properties given hereinafter.*

   Consider x, y and z as three nodes such that x is in the left subtree of y and z is in its right subtree. We have:

- $key(x) < key(y) \leq key(z)$
- The elements are kept in memory in the internal nodes.
- A symmetric path of the tree visits the keys in ascending order.
- For each internal node y, the heights of the left and right sub-trees are 1 apart at most (equilibrium factor noted here as bal).

   In another words, we have the following axioms:

Axiom 3. $\forall n \in Abr, if\, Abr \neq \{\emptyset\}$ *then* $|h(AbrR(n))\text{-}h(AbrL(n))| \leq 1$

Axiom 4. *if* $Abr = \{\varnothing\}$ *or* $Abr = (root, AbrL, AbrR)$ *then* $|h(AbrR)\text{-}h(AbrL)| \leq 1$
$bal(n) = bal(Abr(n)) = h(AbrR(n))\text{-}h(AbrL(n))$

Axiom 5. $\forall n \in Abr, if\, Abr \neq \{\emptyset\}$ *then* $bal(n) \in \{-1, 0, +1\}$

where AbrL, AbrR are respectively the left and right subtrees of Abr while also being AVL trees, $h(x)$ the height of an x tree and bal the balancing factor.

Algorithm 1. AVL tree pseudo code

1: Initiate the tree with left subtree and left subtree;
2: **for** (i *in* VRm) **do**
3:     Go to the appropriate leaf node to insert;
4:     Compare $VR(i, CH)$ with root Key of the current tree;
5:     **while** (leaf node is not reached) **do**
6:         **if** $(VR(i, CH) < rootKey)$ **then**
7:             insert $VR(i, CH)$ on the left subtree of current node;
8:         **end if**
9:         **if** $(VR(i, CH) > rootKey)$ **then**
10:            insert $VR(i, CH)$ on the right subtree of current node;
11:        **end if**
12:        **if** $(VR(i, CH) < VR(leaf, CH))$ **then**
13:            make i Node as the left Child of leaf Node;
14:        **else**
15:            make i Node as right Child of leaf Node;
16:        **end if**
17:        **if** (balanceFactor > 1) **then**
18:            **if** (new Node Key < left Child Key) **then**
19:                do right rotation;
20:            **else**, do left-right rotation;
21:            **end if**
22:        **end if**
23:        **if** (balanceFactor < −1) **then**
24:            **if** (new Node Key> right Child Key) **then**
25:                do left rotation;
26:            **else**
27:                do right-left rotation;
28:            **end if**
29:        **end if**
30:    **end while**
31: **end for**

6.2   Operating Mechanism

Certificate management relies on the AVL tree principle, where operations such as insertion, deletion and creation are of the order $O(logn)$, resulting in significant time savings.

The CH leader first produces his key pair and forwards it to a base station (BS). And then, with the RSSI signals VRm received from the nodes in its group, it builds the AVL tree. The CH organize the AVL tree according to Definition 11 and Theorem 3 (See Algorithm 31). He thus sets up a logical topology of which he is the only one to have full knowledge. The others will just be informed later of their position in the tree.

The CH is the certification authority (rootCA). The primary Clm of the level is an ICA for the s_i nodes of its subnetwork, at each level of the tree and so forth. Figure 3 summarizes the process of setting up implicit certificates.

Remark 2. An AVL tree is indeed a graph in the sense of Definition 10. Moreover, its hierarchical structure is based on the values of its keys (which are the values of the RSSI signals received from the cluster members) for which there is indeed an order relation (see Definition 11 and Theorem 3).

At the end, the certificates are set up and the result is like on Fig. 4

Key Agreement Process. For two parties U and V of the tree that want to establish a pairwise key, the process is the one explained in Sect. 4.1 and summarized by Fig. 5.

6.3   Results Obtained

For the simulation, in addition of TelosB (16-bit architecture, 8 MHz maximum CPU speed, 48 kB flash, 10 kB RAM) and the SHA1 algorithm running in TOSSIM simulator [16], we use some features of the CC2420 radio chip [5,41]. In addition SHA1 algorithm and to the TOSSIM simulator, which is used with TelosB (48 kB flash, and 10 kB RAM, a 16-bit architecture with a maximum CPU speed of 8 MHz) [16], we also utilize certain features of the CC2420 radio chip [5,41] for the simulation. The message size is 84 bytes and the structure is similar to the one in the Table 2.

The results presented in Fig. 6 are achieved by switching on and off all optimization options and Shamir's trick, and the measurements are made in terms of execution time and memory usage.

In most cases, the highest consumption of resources (key calculation, RAM, ROM) is registered at the ICA level. Minimum consumption is recorded at the requester level. Intermediate consumption is observed at the root certification authority level. This trend illustrates the distribution of the workload between all nodes, in contrast to a solution centered on the root certification authority, in which The certification authority is responsible for calculating and issuing certificates to all network nodes.

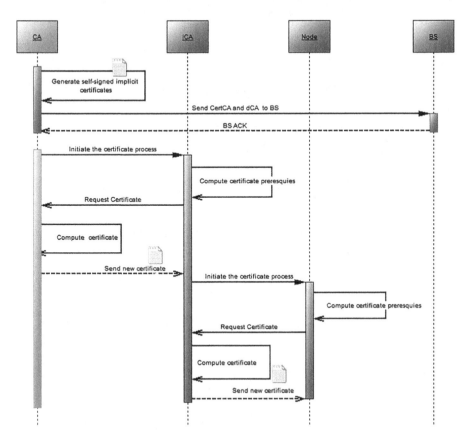

Fig. 3. Implicit certificate process

Table 2. Message Component

Component	size (bytes)
EC	44
Node ID	2
Random Nonce	4
MAC	10
$timeStamp$	6
$TrustChain$	4
$HTrustChain$	4
$CertChain$	6

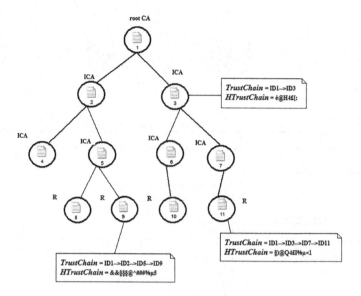

Fig. 4. Trust chain illustration

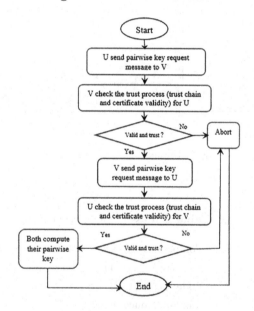

Fig. 5. Pairwise key establishment process

One might naturally question what occurs if one node is burdened with excessive work while another node receives significantly less. This is not a concern because nodes are distributed according to a balanced tree, which inherently ensures a degree of equitable distribution of workload. Additionally, as every node communicates directly with its ICA, the protocol minimizes the communication cost of generating a certificate and setting a key to just two direct message exchanges without an intermediary. In contrast, in a large network organized around a fixed CA, multiple relays must be established between nodes to forward requests and processes.

Simulation results show that by disabling optimization techniques, we get the smallest consumption of ROM and RAM. On the other hand, the activation of these technologies leads to a surplus of consumption. Disabling Shamir's Trick once gives a resource gain over activating all techniques. We also note that the working time directly measured on the node follows the same trend for all operations (see Table 3).

Regardless of the type of operation, the maximum size of RAM memory consumption is 4101 bytes in the worst case and 24944 bytes for ROM. Knowing that TelosB-type nodes provide up 10 KB of RAM and 48 KB of ROM [41], Based on the results, it can be inferred that the protocol is lightweight enough to be implemented on devices with limited resources.

Table 3. Execution Time

Operation (ms)	Disable all opt	Enable all opt	Without Shamir's trick
Initialization	2,33	12596	6524
Certificates request generation	99531	6729	6949
Certificates generation	201766	13558	13565
Certificates verification	9864	6728	6935
Keys computation	212745	13745	13758

6.4 Security Analysis

As the security of the protocol has already been proven in a formal model (see Sect. 5), we present here an informal security analysis of its present implementation for some security objectives.

1. *Authentication and Integrity.* Before deployment, which takes place in time T, all nodes are precharged with the K network key. Each message contains a MAC authenticated by K and a timestamp to preserve data integrity and freshness.
2. *Scalability.* When a new node would like to join the cluster, it first transmits a request to the CA. After successful verification, the CA rebuilds part or all of the tree according to the value of the newcomer's signal. The AVL tree build time, which is of order $(logn)$ [2], accelerates the reconfiguration process. The

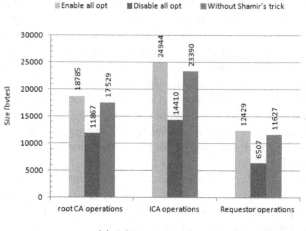

(a) ROM consumption

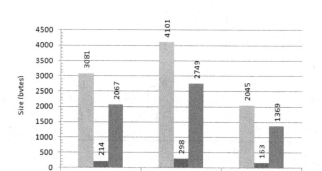

(b) RAM consumption

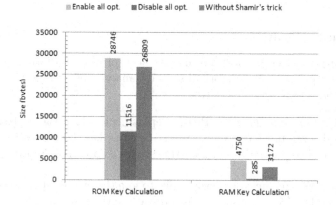

(c) Key calculation

Fig. 6. Simulation results

nodes concerned receive the new chain of trust and can obtain certificates from their ICA. The same process occurs when a node is withdrawn from the cluster. This also has the added advantage of updating the keys, which enhances security. As a result, new nodes can use their certificates to establish peer keys with their neighbors, ensuring both parties are authenticated in the same cluster, allowing the network to expand without issues.

3. *Confidentiality.* The use of pairwise keys guarantees implicit trust and legitimacy, further enhanced by the establishment of a chain of trust. The shared key is derived from two pre-computed values, ensuring security. After the deployment time T, all communication becomes encrypted. Each node stores only the secret key shared with its communicating nodes. In the event of a compromise, the tree is reconfigured and all shared keys with other nodes are updated.

4. *Non-repudiation.* The use of certificates ensures that no node can avoid responsibility. Certificate creation and key pair establishment require a valid chain of trust and its signature, both of which are issued exclusively by the CA using its private key. This ensures no unauthorized node can generate a certificate. However, a node that has been compromised may persist in trying to establish a pairwise key with its neighbors. Therefore, as in [36], we assume that the techniques presented in [19, 29] can be used to identify malicious nodes. When a node is identified as rogue, its ID is broadcast to all nodes in the network, its certificate is revoked, and its is blocked.

5. *Availability.* The ability of nodes to issue a secure key pair for communication ensures the guarantee. In addition, distributing the workload (such as key computation and memory usage) within the cluster can improve its lifespan, by eliminating the need to designate nodes with dedicated resources to play a lead role within the cluster.

7 Comparison with Other Schemes

7.1 Protocols Comparison

The comparison with some well-accepted AKE protocols in the random oracle model concerns the security model used, the number of hash computations, and the number of total exponentiations used in the key computation, all of which are well-known metrics of the domain [11, 26, 27, 45].

While DEKM uses no exponentiation in the calculation of the key, NAXOS+ [27] requires 5 exponentiations per party, NAXOS 4 [11], CMQV [31] and NETS 3 [26]. Regarding the hash operations, there are 2 operations for NAXOS and NAXOS+, 4 for CMQV, 2 for NETS and 2 for DEKM. In addition, all the protocols mentioned use an ephemeral key whose implementation requires calculations and memory, which is not the case for DEKM. Table 4 draws up a summary of the comparison.

Remark 3. To our knowledge, none of the mentioned protocols has a concrete implementation in a real operational environment. This is not the case of our proposal which presents an implementation in a realistic environment.

Table 4. Protocols Comparison

Protocol	Expo.	Security	Hash	Implementation
NAXOS+	5	eCK	2	✗
NAXOS	4	eCK	2	✗
CMQV	3	eCK	4	✗
NETS	3	eCK	2	✗
DEKM	0	eCK	2	✓

8 Conclusion

In this work, we have introduced a protocol for authenticated key establishment based on implicit certificates, designed specifically for low-resource devices.

This protocol offers robust protection while considering for the restricted capabilities of the devices. The scheme employs a certificate chain structure, allowing devices to derive symmetric elliptic keys based on implicit certificates. This structure is established on a finite graph, defining the certificate hierarchy. Each node within the structure stores its certificate, trust chain, and the signature of that trust chain. The decentralized nature of communication and computation operations across all nodes ensures independence from any node with specific properties. Furthermore, the protocol's security has been validated in the eCK security model, and a practical implementation has demonstrated its resilience and viability in a realistic setting. Looking ahead, we envision integrating the protocol into a comprehensive key management solution, encompassing routing, clustering, and energy-saving operations.

Acknowledgement. The authors would like to thank the anonymous reviewers as well as the editors for their valuable remarks. This enabled us to better improve the content and presentation of the paper.

Conflict of Interest statement. On behalf of all authors, the corresponding author states that there is no conflict of interest.

References

1. Abba Ari, A.A., et al.: Optimizing relay sensors in large-scale wireless sensor networks: a biologically inspired approach. Int. J. Eng. Res. Afr. **63**, 119–135 (2023)
2. Adelson-Velskij, G., Landis, E.: An algorithm for the organization of information. Doklady Akad. Nauk SSSR **146**, 263–266 (1962)
3. Antipa, A., Brown, D., Menezes, A., Struik, R., Vanstone, S.: Validation of elliptic curve public keys. In: Desmedt, Y.G. (ed.) PKC 2003. LNCS, vol. 2567, pp. 211–223. Springer, Heidelberg (2003). https://doi.org/10.1007/3-540-36288-6_16
4. Ari, A.A.A., Djam-Doudou, M., Njoya, A.N., Tchapgnouo, H.B., Thiare, O., Gueroui, A.M.: Towards a lightweight cryptographic key management system in IoT sensor networks. In: Woungang, I., Dhurandher, S.K. (eds.) WIDECOM 2023.

LNDECT, vol. 185, pp. 29–45. Springer, Cham (2024). https://doi.org/10.1007/978-3-031-47126-1_3

5. Ari, A.A.A., Yenke, B.O., Labraoui, N., Damakoa, I., Gueroui, A.: A power efficient cluster-based routing algorithm for wireless sensor networks: honeybees swarm intelligence based approach. J. Netw. Comput. Appl. **69**, 77–97 (2016)

6. Babaghayou, M., Labraoui, N., Ari, A.A.A., Lagraa, N., Ferrag, M.A.: Pseudonym change-based privacy-preserving schemes in vehicular ad-hoc networks: a survey. J. Inf. Secur. Appl. **55**, 102618 (2020)

7. Bellare, M., Rogaway, P.: Provably secure session key distribution– the three party case. In: Proceedings of 27th ACM Symposium on the Theory of Computing, October 1995. https://doi.org/10.1145/225058.225084

8. Benmansour, F.L., Labraoui, N.: A comprehensive review on swarm intelligence-based routing protocols in wireless multimedia sensor networks. Int. J. Wireless Inf. Networks **28**(2), 175–198 (2021)

9. Blake-Wilson, S., Johnson, D., Menezes, A.: Key Agreement Protocols and their Security Analysis, pp. 30–45, April 2006. https://doi.org/10.1007/BFb0024447

10. Campagna, M.: Sec 4: Elliptic curve Qu-vanstone implicit certificate scheme (ECQV). Standards for Efficient Cryptography, Version 1 (2013)

11. Canetti, R., Krawczyk, H.: Analysis of key-exchange protocols and their use for building secure channels. In: Pfitzmann, B. (ed.) EUROCRYPT 2001. LNCS, vol. 2045, pp. 453–474. Springer, Heidelberg (2001). https://doi.org/10.1007/3-540-44987-6_28

12. Diffie, W., Hellman, M.: New directions in cryptography. IEEE Trans. Inf. Theory **22**(6), 644–654 (1976). https://doi.org/10.1109/TIT.1976.1055638

13. Diffie, W., Hellman, M.: New Directions in Cryptography (1976), pp. 421–440, February 2021. https://doi.org/10.7551/mitpress/12274.003.0044

14. Djam-Doudou, M., et al.: A certificate-based pairwise key establishment protocol for IoT resource-constrained devices. In: Ngatched Nkouatchah, T.M., Woungang, I., Tapamo, J.R., Viriri, S. (eds.) Pan-African Artificial Intelligence and Smart Systems, vol. 459, pp. 3–18. Springer, Cham (2023). https://doi.org/10.1007/978-3-031-25271-6_1

15. Du, X., Xiao, Y., Ci, S., Guizani, M., Chen, H.H.: A routing-driven key management scheme for heterogeneous sensor networks. In: 2007 IEEE International Conference on Communications, pp. 3407–3412 (2007). https://doi.org/10.1109/ICC.2007.564

16. Eastlake, D., Jones, P.: US secure hash algorithm 1 (SHA-1), September 2001

17. Elgamal, T.: A public key cryptosystem and a signature scheme based on discrete logarithms. IEEE Trans. Inf. Theory **31**(4), 469–472 (1985). https://doi.org/10.1109/TIT.1985.1057074

18. Gbadouissa, J.E.Z., Ari, A.A.A., Titouna, C., Gueroui, A.M., Thiare, O.: HGC: hypergraph based clustering scheme for power aware wireless sensor networks. Futur. Gener. Comput. Syst. **105**, 175–183 (2020)

19. Jokhio, S.H., Jokhio, I.A., Kemp, A.H.: Node capture attack detection and defence in wireless sensor networks. IET Wirel. Sens. Syst. **2**(3), 161–169 (2012)

20. Koblitz, N.: Elliptic curve cryptosystems. Math. Comp. **48**, 243–264 (1987). https://doi.org/10.1090/S0025-5718-1987-0866109-5

21. Krawczyk, H.: HMQV: a high-performance secure Diffie-Hellman protocol. In: Shoup, V. (ed.) CRYPTO 2005. LNCS, vol. 3621, pp. 546–566. Springer, Heidelberg (2005). https://doi.org/10.1007/11535218_33

22. Krawczyk, H.: HMQV: a high-performance secure Diffie-Hellman protocol. Cryptology ePrint Archive, Paper 2005/176 (2005). https://eprint.iacr.org/2005/176

23. Kuila, P., Jana, P.K.: Energy efficient clustering and routing algorithms for wireless sensor networks: particle swarm optimization approach. Eng. Appl. Artif. Intelli. **33**, 127–140 (2014). https://doi.org/10.1016/j.engappai.2014.04.009. https://www.sciencedirect.com/science/article/pii/S0952197614000852
24. LaMacchia, B., Lauter, K., Mityagin, A.: Stronger security of authenticated key exchange. In: Susilo, W., Liu, J.K., Mu, Y. (eds.) ProvSec 2007. LNCS, vol. 4784, pp. 1–16. Springer, Heidelberg (2007). https://doi.org/10.1007/978-3-540-75670-5_1
25. Law, L., Menezes, A., Qu, M., Solinas, J., Vanstone, S.: An efficient protocol for authenticated key agreement. Des. Codes Cryptogr. **28**, 119–134 (1999). https://doi.org/10.1023/A:1022595222606
26. Lee, J., Park, C.: An efficient authenticated key exchange protocol with a tight security reduction. IACR Cryptology ePrint Archive 2008, 345, January 2008
27. Lee, J., Park, J.: Authenticated key exchange secure under the computational Diffie-Hellman assumption. IACR Cryptology ePrint Archive 2008, 344, January 2008
28. LTTng: The linux trace toolkit next generation (2020). http://lttng.org/
29. Lu, R., Li, X., Liang, X., Shen, X., Lin, X.: GRS: the green, reliability, and security of emerging machine to machine communications. IEEE Commun. Mag. **49**(4), 28–35 (2011). https://doi.org/10.1109/MCOM.2011.5741143
30. Menezes, A.: Another look at HMQV. J. Math. Cryptol. **1**(1), 47–64 (2007). https://doi.org/10.1515/JMC.2007.004
31. Menezes, A., Ustaoglu, B.: On the importance of public-key validation in the MQV and HMQV key agreement protocols. In: Barua, R., Lange, T. (eds.) INDOCRYPT 2006. LNCS, vol. 4329, pp. 133–147. Springer, Heidelberg (2006). https://doi.org/10.1007/11941378_11
32. Miller, V.S.: Use of elliptic curves in cryptography. In: Williams, H.C. (ed.) CRYPTO 1985. LNCS, vol. 218, pp. 417–426. Springer, Heidelberg (1986). https://doi.org/10.1007/3-540-39799-X_31
33. Njoya, A.N., et al.: Data prediction based encoder-decoder learning in wireless sensor networks. IEEE Access **10**, 109340–109356 (2022)
34. Pohlig, S., Hellman, M.: An improved algorithm for computing logarithms over GF(p) and its cryptographic significance (corresp.). IEEE Trans. Inf. Theory **24**(1), 106–110 (1978). https://doi.org/10.1109/TIT.1978.1055817
35. Poornima, A., Amberker, B.: Tree-based key management scheme for heterogeneous sensor networks. In: 2008 16th IEEE International Conference on Networks, pp. 1–6. IEEE (2008)
36. Porambage, P., Kumar, P., Schmitt, C., Gurtov, A., Ylianttila, M.: Certificate-based pairwise key establishment protocol for wireless sensor networks. In: 2013 IEEE 16th International Conference on Computational Science and Engineering, pp. 667–674. IEEE (2013)
37. Rivest, R.L., Shamir, A., Adleman, L.: A method for obtaining digital signatures and public-key cryptosystems. Commun. ACM **21**(2), 120–126 (1978). https://doi.org/10.1145/359340.359342
38. Saidi, H., Labraoui, N., Ari, A.A.A., Maglaras, L., Emati, J.H.M.: DSMAC: privacy-aware decentralized self-management of data access control based on blockchain for health data. IEEE Access, 1 (2022). https://doi.org/10.1109/ACCESS.2022.3207803
39. Schnorr, C.P.: Efficient identification and signatures for smart cards. In: Brassard, G. (ed.) CRYPTO 1989. LNCS, vol. 435, pp. 239–252. Springer, New York (1990). https://doi.org/10.1007/0-387-34805-0_22

40. Shoup, V.: On formal models for secure key exchange, October 2002
41. TELOSB: TELOSB datasheet. shorturl.at/krJNV (2022). Accessed 17 Feb 2022
42. Titouna, C., Aliouat, M., Gueroui, M.: FDS: fault detection scheme for wireless sensor networks. Wirel. Pers. Commun. **86** (2015). https://doi.org/10.1007/s11277-015-2944-7
43. Titouna, C., Ari, A.A.A., Moumen, H.: FDRA: fault detection and recovery algorithm for wireless sensor networks. In: Younas, M., Awan, I., Ghinea, G., Catalan Cid, M. (eds.) MobiWIS 2018. LNCS, vol. 10995, pp. 72–85. Springer, Cham (2018). https://doi.org/10.1007/978-3-319-97163-6_7
44. Ustaoglu, B.: Obtaining a secure and efficient key agreement protocol for (H)MQV and NAXOS. Des. Codes Cryptogr. **46**, 329–342 (2008). https://doi.org/10.1007/s10623-007-9159-1
45. Wen, W., Wang, L., Pan, J.: Unified security model of authenticated key exchange with specific adversarial capabilities. IET Inf. Secur. **10** (2015). https://doi.org/10.1049/iet-ifs.2014.0234
46. Xiao, Y., Rayi, V.K., Sun, B., Du, X., Hu, F., Galloway, M.: A survey of key management schemes in wireless sensor networks. Comput. Commun. **30**(11), 2314–2341 (2007). https://doi.org/10.1016/j.comcom.2007.04.009. https://www.sciencedirect.com/science/article/pii/S0140366407001752, special issue on security on wireless ad hoc and sensor networks
47. Yao, A., Zhao, Y.: OAKE: a new family of implicitly authenticated Diffie-Hellman protocols, pp. 1113–1128, November 2013. https://doi.org/10.1145/2508859.2516695

Emerging Artificial Intelligence Applications

Machine and Deep Learning Models for the Prediction of Performance and Speed Regulation Parameters of a Turbojet Engine Using Electric Power Transfer

Patrick Njionou Sadjang$^{(\boxtimes)}$ ⓘ and Nelson Issondj Banta Jr ⓘ

National Higher Polytechnic School, University of Douala, Douala, Cameroon
pnjionou@yahoo.fr

Abstract. In this paper, we focus our attention on "Machine Learning and Deep Learning Models for Prediction of Performance and Speed Regulation Parameters of a Turbojet Engine Using Electric Power Transfer Concept". The principal objective of the study is to implement and compare deep learning and machine learning models for the Prediction of Performance and Speed regulation Parameters of a Turbojet Engine Using the Electric Power Transfer Concept. The novelty of this work is the direct calculation of SFC and Net thrust without any sub-model with a good precision. The data for this study are from the CFM 56–3 turbojet engine equipped with a special EPT architecture. The work showed that the different models (Multi-Linear Regression, Random Forest, and Artificial Neural Networks) give reliable and precise results. Globally neural network model produces the most precise results (Except for LPTCN), and the Linear Regression model is the least precise. The ANN gives an Root Mean Square Error (RMSE) value between 0.19% and 7% of the range of the concerned variable, which is better than those observed in the literature. The results of this work could serve as the first tools for more optimal design and control of next-generation turbojets.

Keywords: Turbojet Engine · Machine Learning · Electric Power Transfer · Performance Modelling

Nomenclature

RMSE	Root Mean Square Error
CRME	Cotton Methyl Esther
CTME	Corn Methyl Esther
EPT	Electric Power Transfer

The authors thank Hossein Balaghi Enalou, and Serhiy Bozhko for making data available.

ⓒ ICST Institute for Computer Sciences, Social Informatics and Telecommunications Engineering 2024
Published by Springer Nature Switzerland AG 2024. All Rights Reserved
F. Tchakounte et al. (Eds.): SAFER-TEA 2023, LNICST 566, pp. 159–174, 2024.
https://doi.org/10.1007/978-3-031-56396-6_10

HPC	High Pressure Compressor
HPT	High Pressure Turbine
LPC	Low Pressure Compressor
LPT	Low Pressure Turbine
MEE	More Electric Engines
P3	High Pressure Compressor Outlet Pressure
T3	High Pressure Compressor Outlet Temperature
TET	Temperature Entry Turbine
ITB	Inter Turbine Burner

1   Introduction

Turbojet engines are propulsion systems that transform the chemical energy of a fuel into a reaction-generated thrust. They are essential elements in the aeronautical industry, where they are used for aircraft propulsion, and in the military industry, where they are used for missile propulsion. In the process of designing or optimizing the performance of a turbojet, modeling, and simulation occupy a prominent place. Thus, Gazzeta et al. [1] described and implemented a model to efficiently simulate the performance of turbines comprising between 01 and 03 shafts. The result achieves a compromise between real-time operating accuracy and calculation speed. Ali et al. [2] carried out experimental studies to study the performance of pollutant emissions by a turbojet engine running on various biofuels ((Corn Methyl Esther (CTME), Cotton Methyl Esther (CRME), and their mixtures). Marszałek N. [3], Ujam, A.J. et al., [4] Klein, D. et al. [8], and Jeffryes W. C. et al. [6] worked on the thermodynamic 0D modeling of a gas turbine engine, taking into account several operating conditions. This work has the advantage of emerging models that are easy to implement as part of the design or regulation of a gas turbine engine. However, these models remain very limited for high-precision applications. To integrate transient regime prediction, Kim et al. [7] and Klein et al. [8] produced a turbojet model with Matlab Simulink. This work gives consistent and acceptable results for the simulation and study of the performance of a turbojet. In parallel, Evans et al. [9] implemented a linear multivariate model for a twin-shaft turbofan, examining the correlation between fuel flow and turbine rotational speed. The advantage of this model is that it is very similar to a linearized thermodynamic model in terms of calculation time but offers slightly higher accuracy.

In recent decades, with the rapid progress of computing and data storage technologies, the use of knowledge-based methods and machine learning tools has increased considerably [10]. In the context of turbojet modeling, Nott et al. [11] used three artificial intelligence approaches (neural networks, Bayesian belief networks, and statistical expectation) to predict sensor failures in the SR-30 turbojet engine. Chira et al. [12] implemented a neural feedforward network for modeling the correlation between turbine shaft velocity and fuel flow. It shows that the complex operating dynamics of turbojet engines must be modeled using nonlinear s-models. Torella et al. [13], using two neural network architectures, will study the effects of the air supply system on the operating dynamics of the engine. Their results will make it possible to improve preventive maintenance techniques for this equipment. More recently, Mortda et al. [14] worked on predicting of turbojet performance using an artificial neural network, it was found that showed goo capability for disclosing turbojet behaviours and attained a satisfactory agreement with the analytical model. Mostafa et al. [17] worked on predicting the performance of a turbojet using artificial neural network. The data in this study come from the resolution of a physical model of the turbocharger, and the validation was done by assessing the satisfactory differences between the physical model and the neural model. The resulting model can be used to pre-specify turbojet design parameters more quickly.

The additional modules connected to the motors generally modify its operating dynamics, making it much more complex and often very difficult to understand with conventional models. This work aims to develop and compare deep learning and machine learning models for the Prediction of Performance and Speed regulation Parameters of a Turbojet Engine Using the Electric Power Transfer Concept. The results of this work could serve as the first tools for more optimal design and control of next-generation turbojets. The results of this work could serve as the first tools for more optimal design and control of next-generation turbojets car because it allows better engine management through effective prediction of engine regulation parameter taking in account the Electric Power Transfer system.

After this introduction we will present successively the system of study and data preprocessing methodology, the models used and the results obtained.

2 Presentation of the System and Data Preprocessing

This study aims to implement and compare deep learning and machine learning models for the Prediction of Performance and Speed regulation Parameters of a Turbojet Engine Using the Electric Power Transfer Concept. In this part we make a presentation of a Turbojet Engine Using the Electric Power Transfer Concept and we describe dataset and data preprocessing method used.

2.1 Presentation of the System

The data for this study are from the CFM 56–3 turbojet. It is a high-bypass ratio turbojet engine manufactured by CFM International. It equips many aircraft, such as some Boeing (civil and military) and Airbus. Figure 1 shows the general architecture of a turbofan engine.

Definition of the parameters given on Fig. 1

- H –ambient conditions,
- 0 –inlet conditions,
- 1 –Fan inlet conditions
- 1a –Low Pressure Compressor (LPC) inlet conditions,

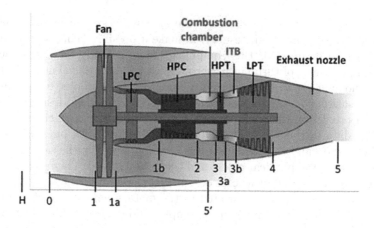

Fig. 1. General architecture of a turbofan engine [3].

- 1b – High Pressure Compressor (HPC) inlet conditions,
- 2 –chamber inlet conditions,
- 3 –High Pressure Turbine (HPT) inlet conditions,
- 3a – Inter Turbine Burner (ITB) inlet conditions,
- 3b –Low Pressure Turbine (LPT) inlet conditions,
- 4 –LPT outlet conditions,
- 5 – exhaust nozzle outle conditionst,
- 5'– cold nozzle outlet conditions.

In view of the future development of electric aircraft, More Electric Engines (MEE) are expected to be equipped with electric generators connected to each shaft for power off-take and supplying on-board electrical loads. The work of Kloos, V. et al. [15] shows that the implementation of an inter-shaft power transfer using an electrical route, i.e. Electric Power Transfer (EPT), in the MEE optimizes the performance of the engines and decouples the shaft speed. The studied engine is equipped with a special EPT architecture (Fig. 2) designed by Hossein S. and Balaghi E. B. [16] with the inter-component-volume (ICV) method.

This architecture makes it possible to considerably increase the performance of the turbojet engine during the cruising phases by reducing the specific fuel consummation and the marge surging.

2.2   Data Analysis and Preprocessing

Data Description. The data for this study were collected from the recent work of Hossein S. and Balaghi E. B. [16]. A recap of the laboratory test conditions is presented in Table 1. The speed regulation coefficients (LTPCN, LPCCN, HPCCN) are taken from experimental measurements, in various flight conditions (Altitude, Mach number, Ambient conditions, etc.) on the turbojet CFM 56–3

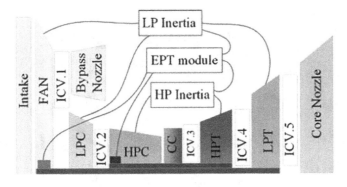

Fig. 2. Model architecture [15]

equipped with a special EPT architecture. Engine performance data (Net Thrust and SFC) are calculated from a zero-dimensional (0-D) model, which has provided reliable results. A total of 6655 points were collected

Table 1. Recap of the laboratory test conditions

Variables	Range
Altitude	0–7000 m
Mach Number	0–0.6
ISA Deviation	–10–50 C
EPT Power	100–2600 kW
Fuel Flow	0.0143–0.2160 kg/s
Inlet_Massflow	0.866–11.566 kg/s
Temperature Entry Turbine (TET)	784.84–2073.6 K
High Pressure Compressor Outlet Pressure (P3)	2.1–23.8 bar
High Pressure Compressor Outlet Temperature (T3)	445.38–889.86 K
Engine Power	1000–2500 kW

Data Analysis. The Fig. 3 is the pairplot between the different features, one can see that there is not multi-collinearity. There is no need in this step to proceed for example with a principal component analysis.

Data Preprocessing. The pretreatment here consisted mainly of a standardization operation. In Standardization scaling method the values are uniformly distributed around the mean with a unit standard deviation. It guarantees the same scale to all the variables. This allows the algorithms to converge faster

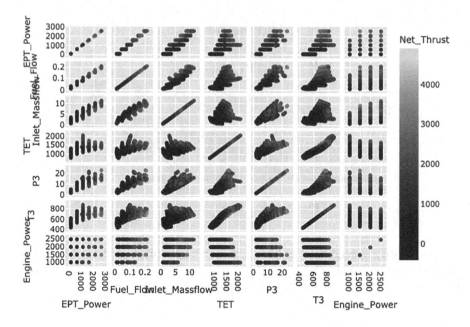

Fig. 3. Pairplot between the different features.

there by improving their adaptability. The formula for standardization is

$$X_i = \frac{X_i - \bar{X}_i}{\sigma(X_i)} \tag{1}$$

where X_i corresponds to one of the features (EPT Power, Fuel Flow, Inlet Mass-flow, TET, P3, T3 and Engine Power). Note that in our studies only the feature followed the step of standardization. The five targets variables (LPTCN, LPCCN, HPCCN, SFC and Net Thrust) remain the same. All these computations was performed using a Jupyter script with Scikit-Learn for the Linear regression and the Random Forest models and TensroFlow for the neural networks models. The architectures for each neural network will be describe when need arises.

2.3   Description of the Models

Multiple Linear Regression (MLR). Multiple linear regression (MLR), which is sometime called multiple regression for short, is a statistical technique that uses several explanatory variables to predict the outcome of a response variable. The goal of multiple linear regression is to model the linear relationship between the explanatory (independent) variables and response (dependent) variables. Multiple regression is a generalization of the least-squares interpolation technique because it involves more than one explanatory variable. They are formulated by the equation

$$Y = a_0 + a_1 U_1 + a_2 U_2 + \ldots + a_p U_p + \varepsilon.$$

Here U_1, U_2,...,U_p stand for the independent variables or features and Y is the dependant variable or target.

Random Forest (RF). The random forest algorithm is a classification algorithm that reduces the variance of predictions from a single decision tree, thus improving their performance. To realize that, it uses a bagging type approach to combine many decision trees. It is used widely in Classification and Regression problems. Random forests have the advantage of giving good results for large datasets, they are very simple to implement and have few parameters. The Random Forest Algorithm can handle the data set containing continuous variables, as in the case of regression, and categorical variables, as in the case of classification.

Artificial Neural Network (ANN). The architecture implemented in this paper, is a multi-layer feed-forward neural network (MFNN), which for some targets (LPTCN, LPCCN, HPCCN) consists of three layers (input layers with 7 neurons, hidden layers with 128 neurons and output layers with 1 neuron) and for other targets consists four layers (input layers with 7 neurons, two hidden layers with 256 neurons for each and an output layer with one neuron). The networks of the signal is transmitted using the activation function this depending on the hidden neurons layers. The activation functions for the input and the hidden layers are the rectified linear unit (ReLU) and for the output layer is the linear function. Note that the rectified linear unit is defined by

$$\text{ReLU}(x) = \begin{cases} x & \text{if} \quad x \geq 0 \\ 0 & \text{if} \quad x < 0 \end{cases}.$$

These networks ANN were trained for 2000 to 5000 epochs. In the input layer, the features (EPT Power, Fuel Flow, Inlet Massflow, TET, P3, T3 and Engine Power) are processed and in the output layer one of the five targets (LPTCN, LPCCN, HPCCN, SFC and Net Thrust) is calculated and compared to the training data set.

3 Outcomes and Comments

3.1 Prediction of the LPTCN

The representation of the features in terms of the seven features in Fig. 4 shows that none of the feature shows a good correlation with our target variable LPTCN.

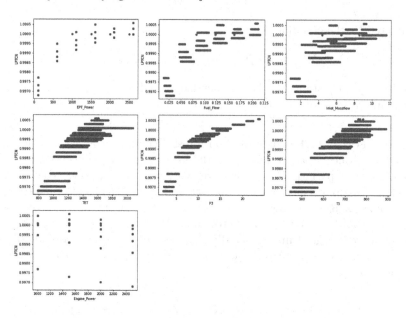

Fig. 4. Representation of the LPTCN in terms of the seven features

After the parameterization, training, and adjustment, the different models are used to predict the output variables. Figure 5 shows the regression plots of LPTCN for the linear regression, the random forest regression, and the neural network models. Table 2 presents the values of RMSE and R2 for the different models obtained.

Table 2. Summary results of the three models for LPTCN.

Methods	R^2 values	RMSE values
Linear regression	0.96480	200.417×10^{-6}
Random Forest	0.99994	8.31811×10^{-6}
Artificial Neural Network	0.94040	260.809×10^{-6}

This Table shows that the RMSE values are around 10–4 for the multi-linear regression model (5.26% of the range) and the neural network model (6.85% of the range) and around 10–6 for the random forest model (0.22% of the range). These values are acceptable, and the models obtained can be considered reliable. The analysis of the R2 shows that the model that best predicts the LPTCN (Non-dimensional corrected speed of Low Pressure Turbine) is the random forest model.

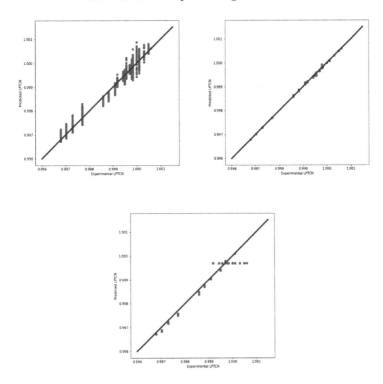

Fig. 5. Regression plot of the LPTCN for the linear regression

3.2   Prediction of LPCCN and HPCCN

The Non-dimensional corrected speed of the Low Pressure The Non-dimensional corrected speeds of the Low-Pressure Compressor (LPCCN) and High-Pressure Compressor (HPCCN) are very important parameters for managing the performance of a turbocharger. In this paragraph, the prediction results of these parameters are explained.

The representation of the features in terms of the seven features in Fig. 6 shows that none of the feature shows a good correlation with our target variable HPCCN.

The Figs. 8, 9 et 10 show the regression plots of HPCCN and LPCCN for the linear regression, random forest regression, and neural network models. Tables 3 and 4, respectively, show the values of RMSE and R2 for the different models obtained for HPCCN and LPCCN.

We note that the RMSE for the multi-linear regression model (2.60% of the range for HPCCN and 5.43% of the range for LPCCN), for the neural networks model (0.19% of the range for HPCCN and 0.21% of the range for LPCCN), and for the random forest model (0.39% of the range for HPCCN and 0.72% of the range for LPCCN) guarantee us a good reliability of the model. We can also observe that the neural network provides better results. The results of this

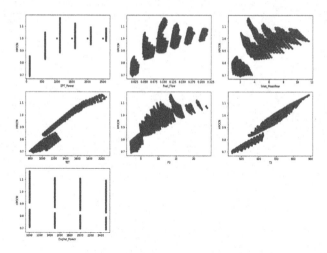

Fig. 6. Representation of the HPCCN in terms of the seven features

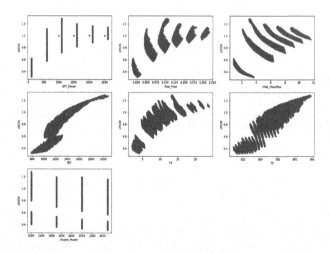

Fig. 7. Representation of the LPCCN in terms of the seven features

Table 3. Summary results of the three models for HPCCN.

Methods	R^2 values	RMSE values
Linear regression	0.98697	0.01237
Random Forest	0.99969	0.00188
Artificial Neural Network	0.99992	0.00092

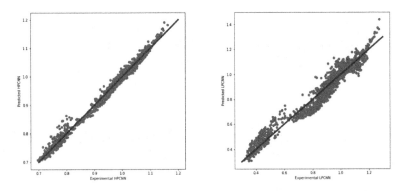

Fig. 8. Regression plot of HPCCN (Left) and LPCCN (right) for the linear regression

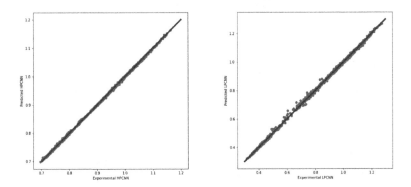

Fig. 9. Regression plot of HPCCN (Left) and LPCCN (right) for the Ranfom Forest

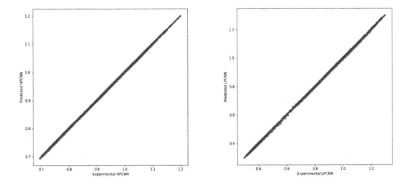

Fig. 10. Regression plot of HPCCN (Left) and LPCCN (right) for the neural network

Table 4. Summary results of the three models for LPCCN.

Methods	R^2 values	RMSE values
Linear regression	0.95576	0.05231
Random Forest	0.99922	0.00693
Artificial Neural Network	0.99993	0.00201

section and the previous mean that using this models would make possible to design very precise controllers with a lower response time.

3.3   Prediction of Performance

The representation of the features in terms of the seven features in Fig. 11 and Net Thrust 12 show that none of the feature shows a good correlation with our target variable SFC or Net Thrust.

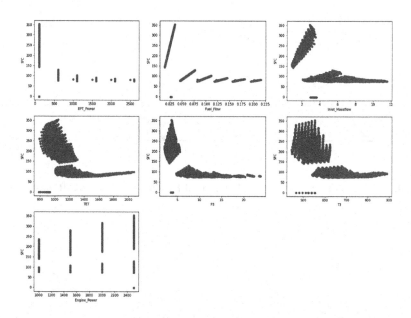

Fig. 11. Representation of the SFC in terms of the seven features

The Specific Fuel Consumption (SFC) and the Net Thrust are the main performance indicators used to evaluate turbojet engines. Figures 8, 9, and 10 show the regression plots of SFC and Net thrust for the linear regression, the random forest regression, and the neural network models. Tables 3 and 5 present, respectively, the values of RMSE and R2 for the different models obtained for SFC and Net thrust.

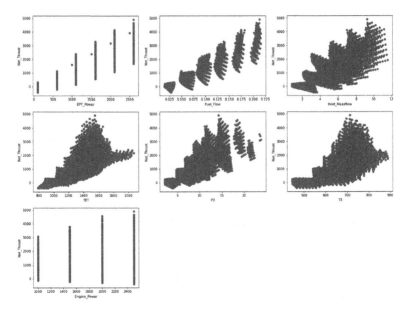

Fig. 12. Representation of the Net Thrust in terms of the seven features

The Figs. 13, 14 et 15 show the regression plot of SFC for the linear regression, the random forest regression and the neural network models. We can observe that the neural network provides better results.

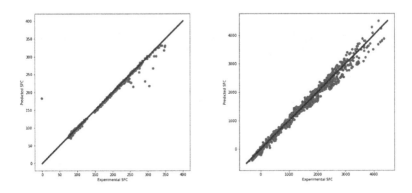

Fig. 13. Regression plot of SFC (left) and Net Thrust (right) for the linear regression

Tables 5 and 6 present, respectively, the values of RMSE and R2 for the different models obtained for SFC and Net thrust.

Here, the RMSE for the multi-linear regression model (1.86% of the range for HPCCN and 4.89% of the range for SFC), for the neural networks model (0.50% of the range for HPCCN and 1.00% of the range for LPCCN) and for the random

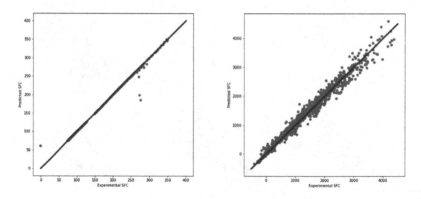

Fig. 14. Regression plot of SFC (left) and Net Thrust (right) for the Ranfom Forest

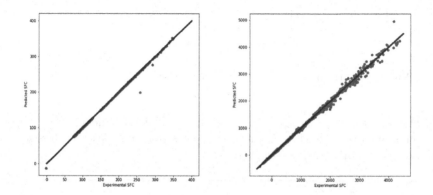

Fig. 15. Regression plot of SFC (left) and Net Thrust (right) for the neural network

Table 5. Summary results of the three models for SFC.

Methods	R^2 values	RMSE values
Linear regression	0.98854	6.59097
Random Forest	0.99638	3.70283
Artificial Neural Network	0.99917	1.77088

Table 6. Summary results of the three models for Net Thrust.

Methods	R^2 values	RMSE values
Linear regression	0.93175	259.702
Random Forest	0.98043	139.069
Artificial Neural Network	0.99713	53.2685

forest model (1.05% of the range for HPCCN and 2.62% of the range for LPCCN) gives us a good level of reliability of the model. We can also observe that the neural network provides better results. A comparison with another works like the work of Mortda et al. [14] shows similarities between prediction results, thus validating the quality of the results obtained showing the great efficiency of the artificial neural networks.

4   Conclusions

In this work, machine learning (Random Forest, Multilinear Regression) and deep learning (Artificial Neural Networks) techniques have been used with a data set from [16]. The inputs of the models were EPT power, Fuel Flow, Inlet Mass flow, TET, P3, T3 and Engine Power. The model could calculate the LPTCN, LPCCN, HPCCN, SFC and Net Thrust with very good precision and reliability for a wide range of input values. It was found that, except for the LPTCN, where the Random Forest model gives the better result, the Artificial Neural Networks provide better results for the other targets. The ANN gives an RMSE value between 0.19% and 7% of the range of the concerned variable, which is better than those observed in the literature. This work can be extended to model pollutants emissions and design after-treatment systems.

Declaration of interests. The authors declare that they have no known competing financial interests or personal relationships that could have appeared to influence the work reported in this paper.

References

1. Gazzetta, H.J., Cleverson, B., Joao, R.B., Jesuino, T.T.: Real-time gas turbine model for performance simulations. J. Aerosp. Technol. Manag. **9**(3), 346–356 (2017). https://doi.org/10.5028/jatm.v9i3.693
2. Ali, A.H.H., Ibrahim, M.N.: Performance and environmental impact of a turbojet engine fueled by blends of biodiesels. Int. J. Environ. Sci. Technol. **14**(6), 1–10 (2017). https://doi.org/10.1007/s13762-016-1228-4
3. Marszalek N.: The impact of thermodynamics parameters of turbofan engine with ITB on its performance. Combust. Engines **182**(3), 16–22 (2020). https://doi.org/10.19206/CE-2020-303
4. Ujam A.J.A., Ifeacho F., Cband Anakudo G., modeling performance characteristics of a turbojet engine. Int. J. Manuf. Mater. Mech. Eng. Res. **1**(1), 1–16 (2013)
5. Klein, D., Abeykoon, C.: Modelling of a turbojet gas turbine engine. In: host publication, pp. 198–204 (2015)
6. Jeffryes, W.C., Thomas, M.L., Jonathan, S.L.: Practical Techniques for Modeling Gas Turbine Engine Performance, NASA/TM-2016-219147, 26p. (2016)
7. Kim, S.K., Pilidis, P., Yin, J.: Gas turbine dynamic simulation using simulink, SAE Technical Papers, vol. 2000-01-3647 (2000). https://doi.org/10.4271/2000-01-3647
8. Klein, D., Abeykoon, C.: Modelling of a turbojet gas turbine engine. In: 2015 Internet Technologies and Applications, 6th IEEE International Conference on Internet Technologies & Applications, pp 198–204 (2015)

9. Evans, C., Chiras, N., Guillaume, P., Rees, D.: Multivariable modelling of gas turbine dynamics. In: ASME Proceedings the International Gas Turbine & Aeroengine Congress, New Orleans (LA), 4–7 June 2001

10. Speak, T.H., Sellick, R.J., Kloos, V., Jeschke, P.: Dual drive booster for a two-spool turbofan: performance effects and mechanical feasibility. J. Eng. Gas Turbines Power **138**(2), 022603–022609 (2015)

11. Nott, C., Ölçmen, S.M., Karr, C.L., Charles, L.K.: SR-30 turbojet engine real-time sensor health monitoring using neural networks, and Bayesian belief networks. Appl. Intell. **26**, 251–265 (2007). https://doi.org/10.1007/s10489-006-0017-z

12. Chiras, N., Evans, C., Rees, D.: Nonlinear gas turbine modeling using feedforward neural networks, ASME Turbo Expo 2002: Power for Land, Sea, and Air GT2002-30035, pp. 145–152 (2002). https://doi.org/10.1115/GT2002-30035

13. Randjelovic, D., Bengin, A., Torella, G., Mainiero, G.: A study of the turbomachine air system with error back propagation neural network. In: Conference: 8th International Conference on Defensive Technologies, Serbie., (2018)

14. Mohammed, M., Taher, M.K., Khudhair, S.: Prediction of turbojet performance by using artificial neural network. Mater. Today: Proc. **60**(2) (2021). https://doi.org/10.1016/j.matpr.2021.12.027

15. Kloos, V., Speak, T.H., Sellick, R.J., Jeschke, P.: Dual drive booster for a two-spool turbofan: high shaft power offtake capability for mea and hybrid aircraft concepts. J. Eng. Gas Turbines Power **140**(12), 121201–121210 (2018)

16. Hossein, B.E., Serhiy, B.: Electric power transfer concept for enhanced performance of the more electric engine. J. Eng. Gas Turbines Power **143**(9), 33p (2021). https://doi.org/10.1115/1.4050154

17. Mostafa, E., Ibrahim, A.S., Omar, S.E., Mohammed, W.: On using neural networks for turbofan aircraft performance analysis. In: Proceedings of NILES2022: 4th Novel Intelligent and Leading Emerging Sciences Conference (2022). https://doi.org/10.1109/NILES56402.2022.9942435

Advancing High-Resolution Weather Prediction Through Machine Learning and GNSS Techniques

Robert Galatiya Suya[1,2]([envelope])

[1] Faculty of Science and Engineering, University of Nottingham, Ningbo 315100, China
`rsuya@mubas.edu.cn`
[2] School of the Built Environment, Malawi University of Business and Applied Sciences, Private Bag 303, Blantyre 3, Malawi

Abstract. Accurate high-resolution weather prediction is essential for numerous applications, including agriculture and disaster management. However, traditional forecasting methods face challenges in achieving precise predictions. This study addresses the challenge of weather prediction by harnessing the fusion of machine learning and Global Navigation Satellite System (GNSS) techniques. Specifically, novel machine-learning models are developed to predict precipitable water vapour and temperature, critical variables affecting weather patterns. The models seamlessly combine GNSS and meteorological datasets from the Continuously Operating Reference Station (CORS) in Mzuzu City, Malawi, to estimate weather attributes with exceptional accuracy. Experimental results demonstrate that the proposed models achieve prediction accuracies, enabling the capture of subtle variations in precipitation and temperature contents. Among the developed models, a suitable candidate for weather forecasting is identified based on its superior performance. The development of this model represents a significant step towards the realization of a real-time weather prediction system capable of providing accurate and localized forecasts. Furthermore, by leveraging the power of machine learning and integrating GNSS data, this research addresses the challenge of achieving high-resolution weather prediction and contributes to overcoming the limitations of traditional forecasting methods.

Keywords: High-Resolution · Weather Prediction · Machine Learning · GNSS · Meteorological data

1 Introduction

Water vapour is an immensely significant constituent of the Earth's atmosphere, playing a pivotal role in the regulation of global climate and intricate weather patterns. As highlighted by Adams et al. [1], the accurate quantification of atmospheric water vapour poses a formidable challenge due to its pronounced variability in both temporal and spatial dimensions. To address this challenge, a diverse array of techniques has been

© ICST Institute for Computer Sciences, Social Informatics and Telecommunications Engineering 2024
Published by Springer Nature Switzerland AG 2024. All Rights Reserved
F. Tchakounte et al. (Eds.): SAFER-TEA 2023, LNICST 566, pp. 175–189, 2024.
https://doi.org/10.1007/978-3-031-56396-6_11

developed to gauge the presence of atmospheric water vapour in climate studies. Currently, a particularly promising avenue of such equipment involves the measurement of excess delay in radio signals that traverse the atmosphere. The Global Navigation Satellite System (GNSS), such as global positioning system (GPS), and Very Long Baseline Interferometry (VLBI) are widely used [2]. The former and latter rely on satellite-based and interferometric observations, respectively. For better performance, both the GPS and VLBI require homogenized in situ meteorological data [3].

Besides GPS and VLBI, several other techniques complement the sensing of atmospheric water vapour. Also known as weather balloons, radiosondes, provide valuable data on temperature, humidity, and atmospheric pressure, which are used to derive water vapor measurements. An example of the application of radiosondes can be found in, for example, Martin et al. [4]. Apart from radiosondes, Raman LIDAR (Light Detection and Ranging) systems are another piece of equipment that employs laser beams and Raman scattering to assess water vapor concentration. For instance, Martucci et al. [5] employed Raman Lidar to relate temperature and relative humidity based on the characteristics of clouds. Not only that, another instrument is microwave radiometry, which measures the thermal emissions of water vapor at different frequencies. As indicated in [6], microwave radiometry such as the Copernicus Imaging Microwave Radiometer (CIMR) mission is one of the systems used in studying climate in Polar Regions. Moreover, Sonic Obstacle Detection and Ranging or simply Sonic Detection and Ranging (SODAR) instruments are another remote sensing instrument that uses sound waves to measure humidity profiles [7, 8]. Other traditional instruments are hygrometers, which are designed specifically for humidity measurement.

In response to the escalating demand for atmospheric data, numerous endeavours have been undertaken to acquire meteorological parameters such as surface pressure and temperature. In GPS meteorology, these weather measurements are the required input data in the retrieval of precipitable water vapour (PWV, [9]). One commonly employed approach comprises the development of models for predicting meteorological parameters, for example, the Global Pressure and Temperature 3 (GPT3 [10]). In the GNSS community, the GPT3 is one of the extensively used numerical models for correcting atmospheric delays that affect the GNSS signals. While GPT3 can be applied globally, their general weakness is that they have a low resolution. In the quest of improving the resolution, regional models specific to particular areas are also available [11]. Despite the improvement in spatial resolution and accuracy, the regional models are area-constrained (i.e., cannot be applied universally). Another alternative for obtaining global-scale weather parameters is through numerical weather prediction (NWP) products [12]. An example of NWP products with multiple geospatial applications is the fifth-generation European Centre for Medium-Range Weather Forecasts reanalysis (ERA5, [13]). Compared to numerical models, NWP datasets offer meteorological variables with higher precision. Nevertheless, the reanalysis data from NWP have significant time delays, and cannot meet the requirements of instantaneous applications.

The advent of machine learning (ML) has opened up thrilling opportunities for extracting meaningful patterns and insights from the vast amount of available data. In GNSS meteorology, numerous ML algorithms are employed to address regression and classification challenges. The commonly used linear models in weather prediction include multi-linear regression [14], and support vector [15, 16]. In the case of classification-based ML models, random forests [17, 19], decision trees [19], and neural networks [20] are widely used. For more robust modelling, ensemble ML techniques have also been applied in GNSS meteorology and geospatial sciences. For example, Huang et al. [21] applied the gradient-boosting approach in the prediction of solar power. In precision agriculture, Mishra et al. [22] developed an adaptive boosting ML model for predicting crop yield using meteorological parameters. Weyn et al. [23] suggested a deep convolutional neural network for predicting near-surface temperatures. Furthermore, recurrent neural networks (RNN, [24]) and long short-term memory RNN [25], and convolutional RNN [26] models have been successfully employed to forecast temperature, humidity, wind speed, and precipitation. The studies reviewed here have shown the remarkable capabilities of the different ML models in addressing weather prediction problems. Despite such merits, it is worth mentioning that the choice of model depends on the scope and the nature of the input dataset.

In this paper, different machine learning algorithms are compared in order to identify the optimal model for predicting meteorological parameters. The meteorological parameters are estimated using GNSS techniques. Bias modeling is applied before inputting them into an ML model. The underlying objective is to develop a real-time weather prediction system capable of providing localized forecasts. The model utilises various datasets, resulting in the establishment of an ML model that addresses the multicollinearity among the input parameters. Moreover, all the biases affecting the satellite-based dataset are carefully modelled, before model preprocessing for ML, using GNSS data processing techniques. The outcome of the GNSS data processing is taken as input in the ML model. This paper is organised as follows. Section 2 describes the GNSS data processing approach used in this paper. Section 3 presents the ML model development including its architecture. Section 4 introduces the experimental tests conducted to test the proposed model. Section 5 summarises the concluding remarks.

2 GNSS Data Processing

In this section, the GNSS mathematical models for weather prediction are presented, highlighting their significance in capturing the complex dynamics of the Earth's atmosphere. The tropospheric delay and the precise data processing are described, including the modelling of the errors that affect GNSS signals.

2.1 Tropospheric Delay Modelling

As the GPS electromagnetic wave passes through the atmosphere, the gases affect the velocity of the wave. In the troposphere, the GPS signal is delayed, and the extent of the delay depends on atmospheric conditions such as humidity, pressure, and temperature. Accurate estimation and correction of the tropospheric delay are necessary for precise GPS positioning. This is fulfilled through a proper characterization of tropospheric delay with respect to the nature of the gases. The atmospheric gases can be wet or dry, and the atmospheric delay takes the same fashion. These delays are modelled using mapping functions in the zenith direction, and one example is the one proposed by Nell [27]. As such, the tropospheric delay is split into two components: zenith wet delay (ZWD) and zenith hydrostatic delay (ZHD). In consideration of the ZWD and ZHD, the tropospheric delay is also known as the zenith total delay (ZTD).

The ZHD can be estimated using the atmospheric pressure, latitude, and altitude of a particular location. According to Davis [28], the ZDH can be deduced as

$$\text{ZHD} = \frac{(2.27683157 \times 10^{-3})P_0}{(1 - 0.0026\cos 2\varphi - 0.00028h_0)} \tag{1}$$

where P_0, φ, and h_0 denote the pressure, latitude, and height of a certain geographical location, respectively. Accounting for the refractivity of the air along the signal path, the ZWD can be formulated as the integral of the product of specific humidity and that refractivity. The reason is that the air refractivity considers the effect of water vapour on the GPS signal. Hence, the integral of ZWD can be expressed as

$$\text{ZWD} = 10^{-6} \int_{h_0}^{\infty} \left(k_2' \frac{e}{T} Z_w^{-1} + k_3 \frac{e}{T^2} Z_w^{-1} \right) dh \tag{2}$$

where T denotes the temperature; e denotes the partial pressure of the water vapour; w denotes water vapour, such that Z denotes the constant of compressibility of w; k_2' and k_3 denote the constants of refractivity which are assigned $22.10\,K2\,hPa^{-1}$ and $373900\,K2\,hPa^{-1}$ respectively [29]. From Eq. (2), it can be concluded that T and e vary with the h of a particular station.

To express the relationship between the ZTD, ZWD, and ZHD, the Hopfield model [30] is employed as

$$\begin{cases} \text{ZWD} = 1552 \times 10^{-7} \frac{4810e_0}{T_0^2} H_{Wet} \\ \text{ZHD} = 1552 \times 10^{-7} \frac{P_0}{T_0} H_{Dry} \\ H_{Wet} = 11.000 \\ H_{Dry} = 40.136 + 14,872(T_0 - 27,316) \\ mw(E) = \left(\sin(E^2 + 2.25)^{1/2} \right)^{-1} \\ mh(E) = \left(\sin(E^2 + 6.25)^{1/2} \right)^{-1} \\ \text{ZTD} = \text{ZHD}mh(E) + \text{ZWD}mw(E) \end{cases} \tag{3}$$

where H_{Wet} and H_{Dry} denote the ZWD and ZHD, respectively; mw and mh denotes the mapping function for the wet and dry delay, respectively, and denote the height of the GPS satellite above the horizon as observed from the receiver position such as a weather station.

2.2 Precise Point Positioning

To estimate the tropospheric delay parameters described in Sect. 2.1 above, the precise point positioning (PPP) technique was employed. PPP is a GNSS algorithm that aims to provide highly accurate and precise positioning solutions using a single receiver.

Unlike differential positioning approaches that require base stations, the PPP enables stand-alone solutions without relying on any reference stations. Basically, in GPS data processing using the PPP technique, all the errors due to the satellites, propagation errors, and receivers (weather stations) are precisely modelled and corrected. These errors are illustrated in Fig. 1. In this figure, the satellite-based errors are the clocks, orbits, earth rotation, relativistic effects, satellite antenna offsets, satellite antenna variations, and phase wind-up effects. The propagation errors comprise the tropospheric delay, ionospheric delay, and multipath effects. The receiver-specific errors include the clocks, tidal effects, and antenna offsets and variations. The modelling implementation of these errors is adapted from Suya et al. [17], and is not repeated here. After proper modelling using least squares adjustment, the XYZ coordinates, ZTD, temperature, pressure, and relative humidity are estimated.

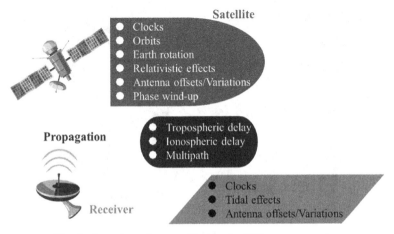

Fig. 1. Overview of errors affecting the GPS measurements.

3 ML Model Implementation

This section presents the meteorological dataset and the machine learning models employed to evaluate and predict weather patterns. Two distinct datasets are described before suggesting the ML models for potential weather prediction.

3.1 Meteorological Datasets

This paper combined meteorological and GNSS data in weather forecasting. Firstly, the meteorological parameters such as the ZTD, ZHD, ZWD, humidity, and temperature were computed using the GNSS data processing approach described in Sect. 2 above. This was achieved by using the GNSS datasets from the MZUZ Continuously Operating Reference Stations (CORS) in Malawi. MZUZ CORS is a geodetic station constructed through the Africa Array GPS Network project [33]. This CORS monument is one of the six stations at Latitude: $-11°\,25'\,30.36''$, Longitude: $34°\,00'\,21.24''$, and Elevation: 1261.24 m in Mzuzu City in the northern region of Malawi [9]. Specifically located at 1276.72 m above mean seal level, MZUZ CORS is mounted at the roof-top of a building. Figure 2 depicts the location of MZUZ CORS, highlighted in yellow on the map. Additionally, the actual location is illustrated through a satellite image and picture superimposed on the map. This station is equipped with TRIMBLE NETR8 geodetic receiver and TRM59800.00 antennae that can track GPS and GLONASS (Globalnaya Navigazionnaya Sputnikovaya Sistema or Global Navigation Satellite System) satellite signals.

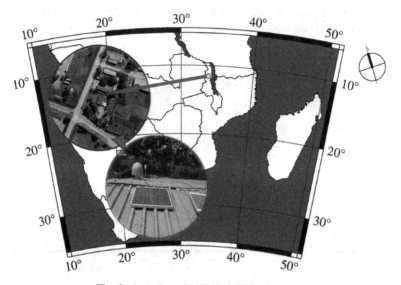

Fig. 2. Location of MZUZ CORS monument.

Due to intermittent data availability for this site, eleven years of data spanning from the day of the year (DOY) 236 in 2010 to 104 in 2021 was obtained for model development. For example, Fig. 3 shows the number of visible satellites at MZUZ station on DOY 001 in two different years, 2011 (left panel) and 2021 (right panel). From this figure, 11 and 10 GPS (denoted by G) satellites were visible, respectively. At the time of installation, only GPS satellites could be tracked at this station. Through instrument upgrades, the station can now observe both GPS and GLONASS (denoted by R) satellites. Figure 4 illustrates the combined visible number of satellites on DOY 001 in 2021. On this day, seven GLONASS satellites were visible, making a total of seventeen when combined with those of GPS.

In addition to the GNSS-derived data, a set of meteorological data was obtained from the European Centre for Medium-Range Weather Forecasts (ECMWF) including temperature, humidity, precipitation, soil moisture, and solar flux. For this set, the data window was from DOY 001 in 1982 to DOY 151 in 2023 (about forty-one years). By realising that complete data is necessary for accurately evaluating the performance of the ML learning model, the two datasets were combined to account for gaps in the GNSS

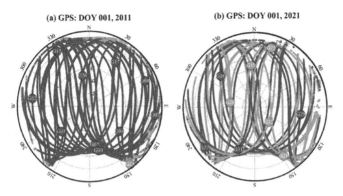

Fig. 3. GPS satellites on two different days at the MZUZ monument.

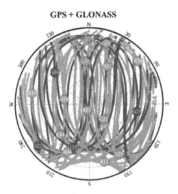

Fig. 4. GPS and GLONASS satellites on DOY 001 in 2021.

data. That is, the ECMWF and GNSS results were integrated and used for learning the models in order to have an accurate representation of the model. Thus, the datasets for learning the model included the year, DOY, geodetic latitude, geodetic longitude, soil moisture, temperature, precipitation, and humidity.

3.2 Machine Learning

To prepare a strong foundation for real-time weather prediction using GNSS in Malawi, six different ML algorithms were explored in this paper. The employed models are Multi-Layer Perceptron Regressor (MLPRegressor); ElasticNet regression; Gradient Boosting; Random Forest; Ridge regression, and Support Vector Regression. Out of these models, the Ridge and ElasticNet are the regularized regression methods, whereas the Gradient Boosting and Random Forest are the ensemble techniques [32]. The support vector regression is the support vector machine method, while the MLPRegressor is an artificial neural network type of model. The Ridge regression applies the Ridge regularization to reduce the magnitude of coefficients and prevent overemphasis on any particular feature.

The nature of data (presented in Sect. 3.1) in this paper is highly correlated, and for that reason, this model was applied because it is suitable for handling multicollinearity.

On the other hand, the ElasticNet was tested used to assess its characteristic nature of combining the Ridge and Lasso regularization techniques. Considering the nature of the data, this model was also convenient because of its ability to control the balance with alpha parameterization. Besides, the Random forest was used to simplify the handling of linearly-dependent measurements. Further details about this model can be found, for example, in 30. Hengl et al. [31]. As explained in Sect. 3.1, the data used in this paper is multi-dimensional. As such, the Support Vector technique was employed to test its property of effectively dealing with high-dimensional data and nonlinear relationships. In addition, the MLPRegressor was tested to assess its capability in treating measurement with complex relationships. The characteristics of these models are illustrated in Fig. 5.

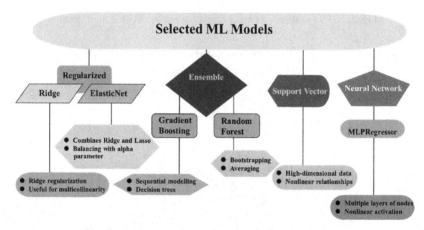

Fig. 5. Basic characteristics of the selected ML models.

4 Experimental Validation

In this section, the characteristics of meteorological parameters are highlighted with a focus on their intricate relations. The soil properties for the study are evaluated and related to precipitation. Then, the section discusses the relationship between precipitation and temperature before concluding with the model validation.

4.1 Characteristics of Meteorological Attributes

The two sets of data were used to learn the ML models depicted in Fig. 5. Soil moisture can influence convective processes in the atmosphere that are responsible for the formation of clouds and precipitation. Furthermore, the relationship between soil moisture and precipitation vary depending on spatial location. As indicated by Wei et al. [18], soil moisture and flux convergence can influence precipitation. Thus, the soil properties were considered in the model development. Figure 6 illustrates the time series for soil wetness at MZUZ CORS monument from 1982 to 2023. From this figure, it can be observed that the soil wetness generally fluctuates more than the root zone and profile over the entire period. This indicates a noticeable variation in the water content with soil layers over the study period.

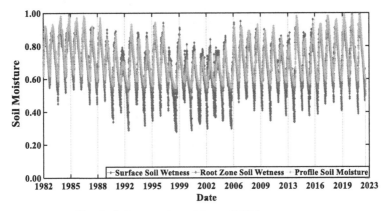

Fig. 6. Soil properties at Mzuzu CORS monument.

In addition to the soil moisture, it is worth noting that precipitation and temperature are intricately connected to the meteorological parameters. Temperature influences the moisture-holding capacity of the atmosphere, with higher temperatures attracting increased moisture that potentially leads to intense precipitation. Though insights about cloud and precipitation formation can be found, for example, in Gerard et al. [35] and Larkin et al. [36]. In the case of Mzuzu City, it is traditionally known as a city with low temperatures in Malawi. This can be evidenced by Fig. 7 which relates the precipitation and temperature for about forty-one years in Mzuzu City estimated using the GNSS and secondary data (Sect. 3.1). From the figure, it can be discerned that considerable precipitation varies between 0 and 33 mm. For demonstration purposes, Fig. 8 illustrates the estimated ZTD and visible number of satellites (NSAT) for the month of January in 2021. As can be seen, the ZTD generally varies between 215 and 230 mm. As for the NSAT, about seven GPS satellites could be tracked during this month. As for the temperature, Mzuzu experiences a moderate climate with an average temperature of about 19 °C.

From this figure, Mzuzu experienced considerably lower temperatures between 1982 and 1990 of about 8 °C. Such characteristics in historical time series data are pertinent in providing valuable information for predicting the future. Filling missing data using a machine learning model may not provide a true reflection of the environmental phenomena. Moreover, that framework within the dataset may present a limited predictive power, especially when there is no historical analogue [37]. Therefore, the different ML models were validated using this data in addition to other datasets.

4.2 ML Performance Comparison

The performance of various regression models was evaluated in predicting precipitation, employing the mean square error (MSE) as a measure of predictive accuracy.

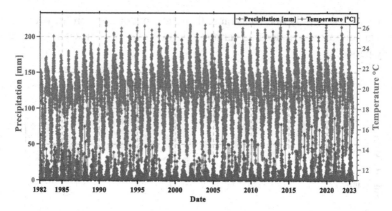

Fig. 7. Precipitation and temperature variation at Mzuzu CORS monument.

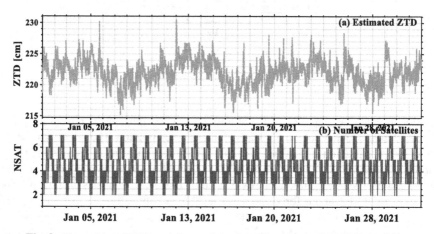

Fig. 8. The estimated ZTD and the number of satellites for the DOY 001-31, 2021.

Figure 9 compares the performance of different ML models in predicting precipitation. The models were evaluated using a testing session of 29 months and 30 days (2.38 years, from January 2021 to July 2023). Among the models examined (Fig. 5 and Fig. 9), the MLPRegressor achieved an MSE of 1.508, ElasticNet Regression yielded an MSE of 1.510, Gradient Boosting Regression demonstrated the lowest MSE of 1.318, Random Forest Regression obtained an MSE of 1.512, Support Vector Regression resulted in an MSE of 1.511, and Ridge Regression achieved an MSE of 1.346. Notably, the Gradient Boosting Regression model exhibited the most favorable performance, showcasing the lowest MSE value among the models evaluated. This implies that the Gradient Boosting Regression model provides the closest approximation to the observed precipitation values, thus demonstrating its potential as a reliable and accurate tool for precipitation prediction in the given context. However, further analysis and validation are warranted to confirm its suitability and robustness for broader applications in precipitation forecasting.

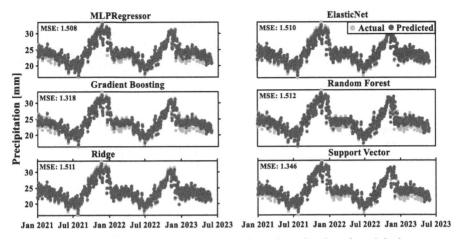

Fig. 9. Performance of different ML models on the estimation of precipitation.

In addition to precipitation, the performance of various regression models was also evaluated for temperature prediction using the mean square error (MSE) as an assessment metric. Using the same testing period Fig. 10 shows the performance of distinct ML techniques on the estimation of temperature. Among the models investigated, the MLPRegressor achieved the lowest MSE of 1.420, followed by Gradient Boosting Regression with an MSE of 1.485, Ridge Regression with an MSE of 1.517, Random Forest Regression with an MSE of 1.501, ElasticNet Regression with an MSE of 1.538, and Support Vector Regression with an MSE of 1.543. The numerical statistics are summarised in Table 1. Comparing these results, it is evident that the MLPRegressor exhibited the best performance, attaining the lowest MSE among the models assessed. This implies that the MLPRegressor provided the most accurate predictions, with a closer alignment between the predicted and actual temperature values. These findings highlight the potential of the MLPRegressor model for precise temperature estimation. However, further investigation and validation are recommended to confirm its suitability and reliability for broader applications in temperature forecasting.

In addition to the MSE metrics, we also calculated Pearson Correlation coefficients based on the results obtained from various ML models. Figures 11 and 12 illustrate the correlation coefficients for six ML models tested for precipitation and temperature prediction, respectively. The vertical and horizontal axes represent predicted and actual values, while the color bars in each figure visualise the discrepancies between predicted and actual values.

All six ML models used for predicting both precipitation and temperature achieved a Pearson correlation of approximately 0.92 (Table 1). For precipitation, the Gradient Boosting and Support Vector models showed slightly better correlations, around 0.93 (Fig. 11). Similarly, in temperature prediction, Gradient Boosting outperformed the other models with a correlation of about 0.93 (Fig. 12). This indicates a stronger positive correlation between actual and predicted values when using Gradient Boosting and Support Vector models for precipitation forecasting. Additionally, Gradient Boosting exhibits a more robust linear relationship in temperature prediction compared to the other

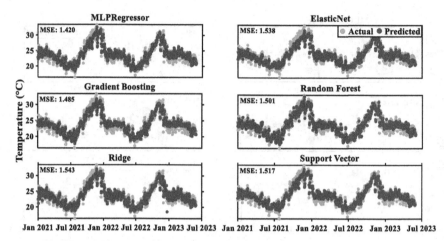

Fig. 10. Performance of different ML models on the estimation of temperature.

Table 1. Metrics achieved by different ML models.

SN	ML Models	Precipitation		Temperature	
		MSE (mm)	r	MSE (°C)	r
1	MLPRegressor	1.508	0.92	1.420	0.92
2	ElasticNet	1.510	0.92	1.538	0.92
3	Gradient Boosting	1.318	0.93	1.485	0.93
4	Random Forest	1.512	0.92	1.501	0.92
5	Ridge	1.511	0.92	1.543	0.92
6	Support Vector	1.346	0.93	1.517	0.92

models. Overall, these models demonstrate a strong positive linear relationship between actual and predicted parameters. This suggests that the precipitation and temperature prediction models accurately capture the underlying patterns and trends in Mzuzu City, increasing confidence in their predictive accuracy.

5 Conclusion and Outlook

This paper addressed the problem of high-resolution weather forecasting through the integration of GNSS and traditionally collected meteorological data. The underlying challenge was conducted using datasets for the MZUZ CORS monument. To assess the significance of data fusion, different ML algorithms were suggested and their performance was thoroughly established.

Among the evaluated models, the MLPRegressor demonstrated the best performance in terms of mean square error (MSE) for precipitation prediction. It achieved the lowest

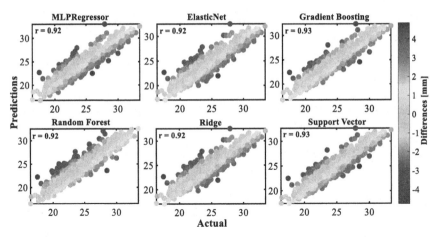

Fig. 11. Pearson correlation coefficients for precipitation for various ML models.

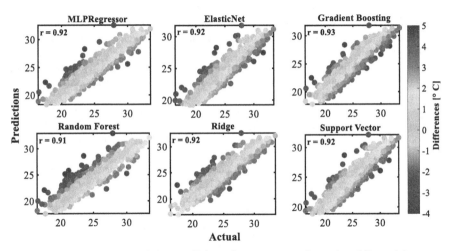

Fig. 12. Pearson correlation coefficients for temperature for various ML models.

MSE value, indicating a closer fit between the predicted and observed precipitation values. This suggests that the MLPRegressor model may be a suitable choice for accurate precipitation estimation. For temperature prediction, the MLPRegressor model again showcased superior performance by achieving the lowest MSE among the considered models. This implies that the MLPRegressor provides the most accurate temperature predictions, with a better alignment between the predicted and actual temperature values. Consequently, the MLPRegressor model holds the potential as a reliable tool for temperature estimation.

In summary, both for precipitation and temperature prediction, the MLPRegressor model consistently outperformed the other regression models based on the mean square error metric. This indicates its potential for accurate and precise estimation in both meteorological variables. However, further validation and analysis are necessary to confirm the robustness and suitability of the MLPRegressor model for broader applications in precipitation and temperature forecasting.

References

1. Adams, D.K., et al.: The Amazon dense GNSS meteorological network: a new approach for examining water vapor and deep convection interactions in the tropics. Bull. Am. Meteor. Soc. **96**(12), 2151–2165 (2015)
2. Alshawaf, F., Balidakis, K., Dick, G., Heise, S., Wickert, J.: Estimating trends in atmospheric water vapor and temperature time series over Germany. Atmos. Meas. Tech. **10**(9), 3117–3132 (2017)
3. Balidakis, K., et al.: Estimating integrated water vapor trends from VLBI, GPS, and numerical weather models: sensitivity to tropospheric parameterization. J. Geophys. Res. Atmos. **123**(12), 6356–6372 (2018)
4. Martin, A., Weissmann, M., Reitebuch, O., Rennie, M., Geiß, A., Cress, A.: Validation of Aeolus winds using radiosonde observations and numerical weather prediction model equivalents. Atmos. Meas. Tech. **14**(3), 2167–2183 (2021)
5. Martucci, G., et al.: Validation of temperature data from the RAman Lidar for Meteorological Observations (RALMO) at Payerne. An application to liquid cloud supersaturation. Atmos. Meas. Tech. Discuss **2020**, 1–32 (2020)
6. Kilic, L., et al.: Expected performances of the Copernicus Imaging Microwave Radiometer (CIMR) for an all-weather and high spatial resolution estimation of ocean and sea ice parameters. J. Geophys. Res. Oceans **123**(10), 7564–7580 (2018)
7. Yavuz, V., et al.: Analysing of atmospheric conditions and their effects on air quality in Istanbul using SODAR and CEILOMETER. Environ. Sci. Pollut. Res., 1–20 (2022)
8. Holmstrom, M., Liu, D., Vo, C.: Machine learning applied to weather forecasting. Meteorol. Appl. **10**, 1–5 (2016)
9. Suya, R.G., et al.: Applying Malawi continuously operating reference stations (CORS) in GNSS meteorology. South Afr. J. Geomatics **11**(2), 218–233 (2022)
10. Landskron, D., Böhm, J.: VMF3/GPT3: refined discrete and empirical troposphere mapping functions. J. Geodesy **92**(2018), 349–360 (2018)
11. Alves, D.B.M., Sapucci, L.F., Marques, H.A., de Souza, E.M., Gouveia, T.A.F., Magário, J.A.: Using a regional numerical weather prediction model for GNSS positioning over Brazil. GPS Solutions **20**, 677–685 (2016)
12. Di Napoli, C., Barnard, C., Prudhomme, C., Cloke, H.L., Pappenberger, F.: ERA5-HEAT: a global gridded historical dataset of human thermal comfort indices from climate reanalysis. Geosci. Data J. **8**(1), 2–10 (2021)
13. Muñoz-Sabater, J., et al.: ERA5-Land: a state-of-the-art global reanalysis dataset for land applications. Earth Syst. Sci. Data **13**(9), 4349–4383 (2021)
14. Anusha, N., Chaithanya, M.S., Reddy, G.J.: Weather prediction using multi linear regression algorithm. IOP Conf. Ser. Mater. Sci. Eng. **590**(1), 012034 (2019)
15. Nayak, M.A., Ghosh, S.: Prediction of extreme rainfall event using weather pattern recognition and support vector machine classifier. Theor. Appl. Climatol., 583–603 (2013)
16. Kavitha, S., Varuna, S., Ramya, R.: A comparative analysis on linear regression and support vector regression. In: 2016 Online International Conference on Green Engineering and Technologies (IC-GET), pp. 1–5. IEEE (2016)
17. Herman, G.R., Schumacher, R.S.: "Dendrology" in numerical weather prediction: what random forests and logistic regression tell us about forecasting extreme precipitation. Mon. Weather Rev. **146**(6), 1785–1812 (2018)

18. Danandeh Mehr, A., Tur, R., Çalışkan, C., Tas, E.: A novel fuzzy random forest model for meteorological drought classification and prediction in ungauged catchments. Pure Appl. Geophys. **177**, 5993–6006 (2020)
19. Geetha, A., Nasira, G.M.: Data mining for meteorological applications: decision trees for modeling rainfall prediction. In: 2014 IEEE International Conference on Computational Intelligence and Computing Research, pp. 1–4. IEEE (2014)
20. Liu, Y., et al.: Application of deep convolutional neural networks for detecting extreme weather in climate datasets. arXiv:1605.01156 (2016)
21. Huang, J., Perry, M.: A semi-empirical approach using gradient boosting and k-nearest neighbors regression for GEFCom2014 probabilistic solar power forecasting. Int. J. Forecast. **32**(3), 1081–1086 (2016)
22. Mishra, S., Mishra, D., Santra, G.H.: Adaptive boosting of weak regressors for forecasting of crop production considering climatic variability: an empirical assessment. J. King Saud Univ.-Comput. Inf. Sci. **32**(8), 949–964 (2020)
23. Weyn, J.A., Durran, D.R., Caruana, R.: Improving data-driven global weather prediction using deep convolutional neural networks on a cubed sphere. J. Adv. Model. Earth Syst. **12**(9), e2020MS002109 (2020)
24. Priatna, M.A., Djamal, E.C.: Precipitation prediction using recurrent neural networks and long short-term memory. Telkomnika (Telecommun. Comput. Electron. Control) **18**(5), 2525–2532 (2020)
25. Zaytar, M.A., El Amrani, C.: Sequence to sequence weather forecasting with long short-term memory recurrent neural networks. Int. J. Comput. Appl. **143**(11), 7–11 (2016)
26. Zhang, Z., Yuan, D.: Temperature forecasting via convolutional recurrent neural networks based on time-series data. Complexity **2020**, 1–8 (2020)
27. Niell, A.E.: Global mapping functions for the atmosphere delay at radio wavelengths. J. Geophys. Res. Solid Earth **101**(B2), 3227–3246 (1996)
28. Davis, J.L., Herring, T.A., Shapiro, I.I., Rogers, A.E.E., Elgered, G.: Geodesy by radio interferometry: effects of atmospheric modeling errors on estimates of baseline length. Radio Sci. **20**(6), 1593–1607 (1985)
29. Bevis, M., et al.: GPS meteorology: mapping Zenith wet delays onto precipitable water. J. Appl. Meteorol. (1988–2005), 379–386 (1994)
30. Hopfield, H.S.: Two-quartic tropospheric refractivity profile for correcting satellite data. J. Geophys. Res. **74**(18), 4487–4499 (1969)
31. Hengl, T., Nussbaum, M., Wright, M.N., Heuvelink, G.B., Gräler, B.: Random forest as a generic framework for predictive modeling of spatial and spatio-temporal variables. PeerJ **6**, e5518 (2018)
32. Acharjee, A., Finkers, R., Visser, R.G., Maliepaard, C.: Comparison of regularized regression methods for ~omics data. Metabolomics **3**(3), 1–9 (2013)
33. Nyblade, A.: Africa Array GPS Network - MZUZ-Mzuzu P.S., The GAGE Facility Operated by EarthScope Consortium, GPS/GNSS Observations Dataset (2010). https://doi.org/10.7283/T5GB225F
34. Wei, J., Su, H., Yang, Z.L.: Impact of moisture flux convergence and soil moisture on precipitation: a case study for the southern United States with implications for the globe. Clim. Dyn. **46**, 467–481 (2016)
35. Gerard, L., Piriou, J.M., Brožková, R., Geleyn, J.F., Banciu, D.: Cloud and precipitation parameterization in a Meso-Gamma-Scale operational weather prediction model. Mon. Weather Rev. **137**(11), 3960–3977 (2009)
36. Larkin, N.K., Harrison, D.E.: Global seasonal temperature and precipitation anomalies during El Niño autumn and winter. Geophys. Res. Lett. **32**(16) (2005)
37. Lobell, D.B., Cahill, K.N., Field, C.B.: Historical effects of temperature and precipitation on California crop yields. Clim. Change **81**(2), 187 (2007)

French-Fulfulde Textless and Cascading Speech Translation: Towards a Dual Architecture

Tala Metalom Diane Carole[1] ⓘ, Yenke Blaise Omer[2] ⓘ,
and Fendji Kedieng Ebongue Jean Louis[2(✉)] ⓘ

[1] Department of Mathematics and Computer Science, Faculty of Science, University of Ngaoundere, Ngaoundere, Cameroon
[2] Department of Computer Engineering, University Institute of Technology, University of Ngaoundere, Ngaoundere, Cameroon
lfendji@gmail.com

Abstract. Speech-to-Speech translation is attracting increasing attention from researchers due to its potential of easing the communication. It can be leveraged to develop voice user interfaces for important services, such as agriculture in low-literate communities where poorly resourced languages such as Fulfulde are used. If an earlier technique, such as cascading speech, requires textual data, a recent and textless one, such as direct speech-to-speech, only considers speech corpus, playing a crucial role in considering oral languages. In this work, a general app-roach for a dual architecture is proposed integrating direct speech-to-speech and speech-to-speech translation using automatic speech recognition, machine trans-lation, and text-to-speech translation. Beyond proposing an architecture, this paper focuses on an important step in cascading speech translation, namely automatic speech recognition (speech to text translation). Automatic speech recognition for the Fulfulde language, using the Kaldi toolkit, allowed obtaining an average Word Error Rate of 28.91% for S2T with the monophone acoustic model and a WER of 26.58% for S2T with the triphone acoustic model. The dataset used is based on agricultural words recorded by natives of northern Cameroon.

Keywords: Speech-to-Speech translation · machine translation · text-to-Speech · speech-to-text · textless speech-to-Speech translation · agriculture

1 Introduction

The development of rural areas is a problem throughout the world due to the low literacy level that prevents the local population from accessing relevant information or com-municating in general. Especially in some regions of Sub-Saharan Africa, the level of illiteracy can reach 68%, with the majority of the population engaged in activities such as trade, livestock breeding, fishing, and mainly agriculture, but with miserable production results. To improve local activities, a lot of initiatives have been launched, including the development of digital services. But the user interfaces of almost all proposed digital solutions are still textual. Consequently, the adoption of such solutions is still very low,

© ICST Institute for Computer Sciences, Social Informatics and Telecommunications Engineering 2024
Published by Springer Nature Switzerland AG 2024. All Rights Reserved
F. Tchakounte et al. (Eds.): SAFER-TEA 2023, LNICST 566, pp. 190–199, 2024.
https://doi.org/10.1007/978-3-031-56396-6_12

due to the low literacy level of potential end-users who only speak local languages that are most of the time only oral. For example, a local language spoken by a large number of communities in sub-Saharan Africa is Fulfulde. Not only do very few developers speak the language, but the fact that local populations speak the language but cannot read or write it makes it harder to adopt digital services that only use textual content. Therefore, there is a need to leverage speech processing techniques such as automatic speech recognition, machine translation, and speech synthesis, to develop voice user interfaces in local languages such as Fulfulde.

Fulfulde is considered a low-resourced language due to the small amount of available digital and usable data. In the field of agriculture, a few textual data can be found in material such as dictionaries. Additional work needs to be performed in partnership with linguists to enrich and create a usable data set that can be used for automatic speech recognition, text translation, and speech synthesis for this language. As transcription remains a challenging task, it can be skipped when using techniques such as direct speech-to-speech.

Actual solutions using textual or even interactive user interfaces, for instance, in French, can be transformed into interactive voice user interfaces in Fulfulde. To achieve this, two options are possible. The first option is to translate the French text into Fulfulde text and then run this through a text-to-speech system to get the corresponding Fulfulde speech. The second option is to take the French text as input to output the French speech, and then use this speech as input to the French to Fulfulde speech translation module without a transcription.

As research in the field of machine translation, text-to-speech translation, and speech-to-text translation for the Fulfulde language is making great progress, it is essential to make a comparison between both approaches for this language in order to determine the best course of action for future research in this field and for this language. To date, we have found no evidence of speech-to-speech translation involving the Fulfulde language. Whether it is a cascade or a direct translation, we have not seen any work in this language. In this paper, we propose an architecture that integrates the following modules.

1. Textless Speech to Speech (TS2S) for textless translation of French speech to the corresponding Fulfulde speech and vice versa;
2. Speech-to-Text (S2T) translation from Fulfulde speech to the corresponding Fulfulde text;
3. Machine translation (MT) for the translation of French texts into corresponding Fulfulde texts and vice versa;
4. Text-to-Speech (T2S) for the translation of Fulfulde texts into the corresponding Fulfulde speech.

Of these four modules, the S2T developed using the Kaldi toolkit has been presented in detail in this paper, while the other modules will be presented in future work. The word error rate (WER) using the TS2S translation will be evaluated, then using the cascade model from S2T through MT to T2S. The best WER obtained determines the best approach between TS2S and cascading speech-to-speech translation.

The remainder of this paper is structured as follows. In Sect. 2, we briefly review the literature. A presentation of the Fulfulde language will be given in Sect. 3, and the system architecture will be proposed in Sect. 4. In Sect. 5, we detail the Fulfulde automatic speech recognition system that we proposed and present, as well as discuss the results. The paper ends with a conclusion and the next steps of the work.

2 Literature Review

Many works have been carried out on speech-to-speech translation for Hindi [1, 2], Indian [3], Chinese to English [4, 5], German-English [6] and Spanish-English [7–9]. In their papers, some authors have developed sequence-to-sequence models and others have developed direct translation models. Automatic speech recognition is undergoing a particular evolution, and more and more researchers are focusing on this field. A comparative study of speech recognition papers for limited vocabularies has been carried out in [10], where the authors compare the error rates of systems designed taking into account the environment (noisy or not), the size of the dataset, the number of speakers making the recordings, the sampling frequency, and the toolkit used to design the recognition system. All this work is done for highly resourced languages, and for translation, the authors use either the cascade method including ASR, MT and speech synthesis or the direct method. We have not seen work on both approaches for the same translation.

We propose an architecture based on a dual approach combining direct speech-to-speech and cascading speech-to-speech for the translation of French into Fulfulde. This model will bring out two WERs that will ultimately enable us to say whether it is preferable to use the direct or cascading method for the translation of French speech into the Fulfulde language.

To design a system that meets the specific requirements of the Fulfulde language, it is necessary to know the particularities of this language.

3 The Fulfulde Language

Fulfulde is a language spoken in several African countries: Senegal, Sudan, Niger, Mauritania, Cameroon, and Mali [11]. Despite the similarities that exist between Fulfulde spoken in these different countries, there are notable differences even for Fulfulde spoken in the same country. Differences in word pronunciation and even in the way certain words are written. In this work, we focus on Fulfulde spoken in Cameroon. Among the 530 agricultural Fulfulde words recorded in the three northern regions where this language is spoken, we have curated the data set to select only reliable data. Today, very few researchers have conducted research on speech recognition, speech synthesis, and direct speech-to-speech translation for this language.

In the following, we propose an architecture based on the direct speech-to-speech translation without text model of the French language for the Fulfulde language and the cascading translation model of a French language voice for a Fulfulde language voice.

4 Proposed Architecture

The development of French interactive interfaces is a fast-growing field that continues to expand in the field of artificial intelligence. Making these interfaces interactive in Fulfulde involves developing a speech-to-speech translation system, as shown in Fig. 1.

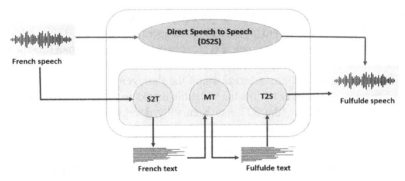

Fig. 1. Architecture of direct and cascading French speech to Fulfulde speech

The function of each module will be detailed in the next subsections; we remind the reader that in this architecture only the S2T module is achieved.

To enable developers who do not speak Fulfulde to use their French interactive interfaces to develop Fulfulde interactive interfaces, there are two options: direct or textless speech-to-speech translation given in Subsect. 4.1 and cascading speech-to-speech translation given in Subsect. 4.2.

4.1 Direct Speech-to-Speech Translation (DS2S)

In this case, the translation is carried out without the use of intermediate texts. French speech is passed to the direct speech-to-speech module, which returns Fulfulde speech. This module was covered in [12], the results have not been fully achieved, but research is continuing. As French and Fulfulde are written and unwritten languages, respectively, we use a six-layer encoder, a decoder to obtain the spectrogram, and a vocoder to return the target speech, as presented in [12].

4.2 Cascading Speech-to-Speech Translation (S2T - MT - T2S)

Send the French (or Fulfulde) speech to the Speech-to-Text module, which will output a French (or Fulfulde) text. The resulting text will be passed to the translation module (MT), which will return a Fulfulde (or French) text, and then send it to the T2S module for Fulfulde speech.

Speech-to-Text (S2T) Module. It corresponds to Fulfulde automatic speech recognition; this module is detailed in the next section, and the developed model is evaluated by giving the WER.

Machine Translation Module (MT). This module translates the French text into Fulfulde. It includes a bilingual French-Fulfulde corpus and a monolingual Fulfulde corpus. Translation involves statistical analysis, in which we estimate the probability $p(s|t)$ that the target text t in Fulfulde language corresponds to the source text s in the French language. $P(s|t)$ is determined using the translation model. The language model will also be used to calculate the probability $p(t)$ that the target text t is correct and fluent.

Text-to-Speech (T2S) Module. The translation of Fulfulde text into speech comprises two submodules: the word processor and the speech synthesizer. The word processor integrates functions to break down text into phonetic units (phonemes) and prosodic processing functions. The voice synthesizer uses acoustic analysis to establish differences between theoretical characteristics and the data generated during the learning phase. The vocal synthesizer returns the vocal file thanks to the Griffin vocoder.

Among these modules, the S2T has been fully developed and evaluated, and is presented in the following section.

5 Fulfulde Automatic Speech Recognition (S2T) with the Kaldi Toolkit

To perform automatic speech recognition for the Fulfulde language, we need a pronunciation dictionary for Fulfulde words, a speech and text database, and a Fulfulde vocabulary. The audio signal received passes through a cepstral parameter extraction module and the output result is passed to the input of a decoder which integrates a language model and an acoustic model to return the word with the highest probability of being pronounced. Figure 2 illustrates this principle.

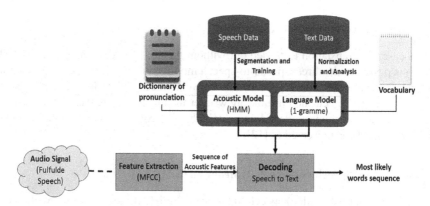

Fig. 2. Architecture of Fulfulde speech to text translation [10]

Kaldi is an open source speech recognition tool developed by Daniel Povey et al. [14], programmed in C++ and using script languages such as Python, Perl, Bash, and Awk. It can be installed on both Unix and Windows systems. Kaldi includes several C++ libraries that depend on the external libraries Open FST (Finite-State Transducer) and BLAS/LAPACK (Basic Linear Algebra Subroutines/Linear Algebra Package) [14, 15]. Open FST is used to achieve a higher recognition rate [16].

Speech recognition for the Fulfulde language using the Kaldi toolkit involves data preparation, extraction of cepstral parameters, language modeling, acoustic modeling, and decoding.

5.1 Data Preparation

530 agricultural words were collected. To reflect the specificities of the three regions of northern Cameroon, 81 words were selected. These words were passed through microphones using six recorders, including 2 men and 2 women from each region of northern Cameroon. The recording environment was non-noisy, the data were sampled at a frequency of 16000 kHz and took 1 h 30 min to record. 162 words (33.33%) belonged to the test database, and the remaining (324 words) to the training database. During these recordings, despite the fact that the environment was not noisy, the audio files nevertheless contained the echo of the microphone. The wav surfer software was used to remove the echo from the smartphones. Audacity, a free audio editing program, was used to cut the lyrics to remove silences. The audio files obtained after processing allowed us to obtain the transcription files for Table 1. All these files are created in the training and test databases.

Table 1. Some Kaldi Toolkit files.

File name	Description (Sample data)
Spk2gender	Information about the gender of recorders (Fadimatou F)
Wav.scp	Link each utterance to an audio file (…/basilic.wav)
Text	Contains all utterances and text (fadimatou_aloe_vera alovera)
Utt2spk	Links user IDs to recorders (fadimatou_aloe_vera fadimatou)
Corpus.txt	Contains all textual occurrences (ɓernde)

5.2 Extracting Cepstral Parameters

Once data preparation has been completed, the next step is data extraction. Parameters extraction with Kaldi involves the steps described in Fig. 3.

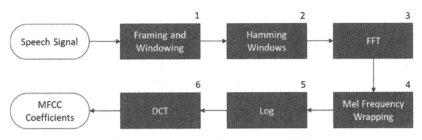

Fig. 3. Steps of extraction parameters [10]

It all starts with splitting the signal into several 20-ms windows. To reduce spectral distortion, small signals pass through the Hamming window. The frequency domain is obtained by discretizing the different windows using the fast Fourrier transformation (FFT). The human auditory system is reproduced by Mel Frequency Wrapping; then, logarithm (Log) is applied to obtain the compressed mel spectrum. Cepstral coefficients are obtained using the discrete cosine transform (DCT).

5.3 Language Modeling

We used the dictionary in Table 2 to translate the words from the data set into a sequence of phonemes. We have used 28 phonemes representing the letters of the Fulfulde alphabet, to which a sil phoneme was added for the silence that materializes the beginning and end of a word. The letters ɓ, ɗ and ŋ are pronounced like b, d and n respectively, but with an implosion.

Table 2. Fulfulde script and equivalent symbols used in S2T

a A	b B	ɓ ʼB	c C	d D	ɗ ʼD	e E
a A	b B	b B	tch tch	d D	d D	e E
f F	g G	h H	i I	ʝ	k K	l L
f F	gu GU	h H	i I	dz	k K	l L
m M	n N	ŋ	o O	p P	r R	s S
m M	n N	n	o O	p P	rr RR	ss SS
t T	ʃ	u U	w W	y Y	ýY	z Z
t T	c	ou OU	w W	j J	y Y	z Z

The dictionary in Table 2 was used to obtain the lexicon representing the pronunciation dictionary, part of which is given in Table 3.

Table 3. Partial Lexicon Used in Kaldi

Word	Phoneme sequence
ceede	Sil ʃ e e d e Sil
dankaliije	Sil d a ŋ k a l i i ʝ e Sil
kayarlaaje	Sil k a ý a r l a a ʝ e Sil
bantugo	Sil ɓ a n t u g o Sil
layol	Sil l a j o l Sil

5.4 Acoustic Modeling

The acoustic model used here is based on the Gaussian mixture model (GMM) and the subspace GMM (SGMM). The GMM corresponds to a collection of densities representing a hidden Markov model (HMM) hidden state machine. For SGMM, Kaldi follows the implementation described in [13]. Separate GMM classes were used to implement speaker adaptation and the maximum likelihood linear transform (MLLT) [14].

5.5 Decoding

The decoding algorithm used is based on weighted finite-state transducers (WFST). The decoding consists of decoding HCLG graphs involving the HMM model, context dependency, language models, and encode grammar. These graphs are built from simple finite state transducer (FST) graphs. The decoding time was approximately 0.12 h, measured on an Intel ® core TM i7 – 4610M CPU at 3.00 GHz.

5.6 Results

S2T was carried out with the n-gram language model trained on the textual corpus of words recorded by inhabitants of the northern Cameroon zone as described above. The detailed method used to build the data set is described in [12].

Initially, the experiment was carried out using an HMM-GMM monophone training, and the results (wer_LMW) of the tests as a function of language model weight (LMW) are presented in Table 4. Here, we show the number of words inserted, the number of words deleted, the number of words substituted, and the word error rate (WER).

Table 4. The WER % of the monophone model

Wer_LMW	Insert	Delete	substitute	WER (%)
Wer_7	3	3	38	32.64
Wer_8	3	3	38	30.56
Wer_9	3	3	38	30.56
Wer_10	2	3	37	29.17
Wer_11	2	3	37	29.17
Wer_12	1	3	37	28.47
Wer_13	1	4	35	27.78
Wer_14	0	4	35	27.08
Wer_15	0	4	35	27.08
Wer_16	0	4	36	27.78
Wer_17	0	4	36	27.78

On the same dataset, we performed the experiment using the SGMM Triphone training (Tri1) and the results are given in Table 5.

Table 5. The WER % of the triphone model

Wer_LMW	Insert	Delete	substitute	WER (%)
Wer_7	6	4	34	30.56
Wer_8	5	4	34	29.86
Wer_9	5	4	34	29.86
Wer_10	2	4	32	26.39
Wer_11	1	4	32	25.69
Wer_12	0	4	31	24.31
Wer_13	0	4	32	25.00
Wer_14	0	4	32	25.00
Wer_15	0	4	32	25.00
Wer_16	0	4	32	25.00
Wer_17	0	0	33	25.69

At the end of the tests, it emerged that the best WER was obtained for the experiment with the tri1 acoustic model, with a WER of 24.31. The highest error rate was obtained for the monophone model, with a WER of 32.64. The average error rate for the monophone was 28.91, compared to 26.58 for the triphone model. For a poorly resourced language not yet studied in this field, we can say that the WER is acceptable.

6 Conclusions and Perspectives

In this paper, we have proposed a global architecture for translating French speech into Fulfulde speech using two approaches. The first approach consists of not using intermediate texts, thanks to the DS2S module, and the second approach corresponds to cascading speech-to-speech translation, which starts with speech-to-text (S2T) module and ends with text-to-speech via machine translation module. The data set consists of words from the agricultural domain. The S2T module has been fully developed and has been proven by evaluating the word error rate. The WER deviates from 0 partly because the dataset is undersupplied, as the number of people who made word recordings is very insignificant. As a result, we do not find a maximum of vocal accents in the recordings. As Fulfulde audio data from the agricultural domain do not yet exist, the dataset we have built will be enriched day by day to improve speech recognition. The next step will be to implement the other modules and compare the results.

References

1. Bali, K., Sitaram, S., Cuendet, S., Medhi, I.: A Hindi speech recognizer for an agricultural video search application. In: Proceedings of the 3rd ACM Symposium on Computing for Development - ACM DEV 2013, Bangalore, India, p. 1. ACM Press (2013). https://doi.org/10.1145/2442882.2442889

2. Mrinalini, K., Vijayalakshmi, P.: Hindi-English speech-to-speech translation system for travel expressions. In: 2015 International Conference on Computation of Power, Energy, Information and Communication (ICCPEIC), Melmaruvathur, Chennai, India, pp. 0250–0255. IEEE, April 2015. https://doi.org/10.1109/ICCPEIC.2015.7259472

3. Vemula, V.V.B., Narne, P.K., Kudaravalli, M., Tharimela, P., Prahallad, K.: ANUVAADHAK: a two-way, Indian language speech-to-speech translation system for local travel information assistance. Int. J. Eng. Sci. Technol. **2** (2010)

4. Zong, C., Xu, B., Huang, T.: Interactive Chinese-to-English speech translation based on dialogue management. In: Proceedings of the ACL-02 Workshop on Speech-to-Speech Translation: Algorithms and Systems - Not Known, pp. 61–68. Association for Computational Linguistics (2002). https://doi.org/10.3115/1118656.1118665

5. Zhang, R., et al.: BSTC: a large-scale Chinese-English speech translation dataset. ArXiv210403575 Cs, April 2021. http://arxiv.org/abs/2104.03575. Accessed 11 Nov 2021

6. Beilharz, B., Sun, X., Karimova, S., Riezler, S.: LibriVoxDeEn: a corpus for German-to-English speech translation and German speech recognition. ArXiv191007924 Cs, March 2020. http://arxiv.org/abs/1910.07924. Accessed 17 Dec 2021

7. Jia, Y., et al.: Direct speech-to-speech translation with a sequence-to-sequence model. In: Interspeech 2019, ISCA, pp. 1123–1127, September 2019. https://doi.org/10.21437/Interspeech.2019-1951

8. Weiss, R.J., Chorowski, J., Jaitly, N., Wu, Y., Chen, Z.: Sequence-to-sequence models can directly translate foreign speech. ArXiv170308581 Cs Stat, June 2017. http://arxiv.org/abs/1703.08581. Accessed 15 Dec 2021

9. Lee, A., et al.: Direct speech-to-speech translation with discrete units, ArXiv210705604 Cs Eess, July 2021. http://arxiv.org/abs/2107.05604. Accessed 4 Mar 2022

10. Fendji, J.L., Tala Metalom, D.C., Yenke, B., Atemkeng, M.: Automatic speech recognition using limited vocabulary: a survey. Appl. Artif. Intell. **36**, 2947 (2022). https://doi.org/10.1080/08839514.2022.2095039

11. Christiane Seydou: La langue peule. https://llacan.cnrs.fr/expo/bonus-notices/litteraires/ecrite/langue-peule.html. Accessed 20 June 2023

12. Tala Metalom, D.C., Fendji Kedieng, E.J.L., Yenke, B.O.: Towards to a direct speech to speech for endangered languages in Africa. CARI DSCHANG Cameroon, October 2022. https://hal.science/hal-03711256

13. Povey, D., et al.: The subspace Gaussian mixture model—a structured model for speech recognition. Comput. Speech Lang. **25**(2), 404–439 (2011). https://doi.org/10.1016/j.csl.2010.06.003

14. Povey, D., et al.: The Kaldi speech recognition toolkit. In: IEEE Workshop on Automatic Speech Recognition & Understanding, p. 4 (2011)

15. Babu, L.B., George, A., Sreelakshmi, K.R., Mary, L.: Continuous speech recognition system for Malayalam language using Kaldi. In: 2018 International Conference on Emerging Trends and Innovations in Engineering And Technological Research (ICETIETR), Ernakulam, India, pp. 1–4 (2018). https://doi.org/10.1109/ICETIETR.2018.8529045

16. httpp://kaldi-asr.org: Kaldi ASR Org. https://kaldi-asr.org/doc

Assessment of Thermal Comfort Using PMV, aPMV, ePMV and TSV Indices in a Naturally Ventilated Building

Tsague Cathy[1(✉)], Medjo Astrid[2], Jean Seutche[1], and Tchinda Rene[2]

[1] Energy Systems, Electric and Electronic Laboratory, University of Yaoundé I, P.O BOX: 812, Yaoundé, Cameroon
cathytsague@yahoo.com
[2] Fotso Victor University Institute of Technology, University of Dschang, P.O BOX: 96, Dschang, Cameroon

Abstract. Thermal comfort significantly impacts human health and activity in offices, hospitals, and residential and commercial buildings. A study of thermal comfort was carried out in a naturally ventilated building in the city of Yaoundé. Thermal comfort indices such as the predicted mean vote (PMV), the adaptive predicted mean vote (aPMV), the extended predicted mean vote (ePMV) and the thermal sensation vote (TSV) were used for this study by considering two scenarios; the first in an ideal environment and the second in a real environment. Using the Humphrey model, we obtained a comfort temperature of 26.66 °C, corresponding to the operating temperature to the nearest 0.1. Whether in an ideal or real environment, the PMV index is unsuitable for studying thermal comfort in a naturally ventilated building. In an ideal environment, the aPMV index is the most appropriate for assessing thermal comfort, but in a real environment, the most appropriate index is the ePMV index.

Keywords: Assessment · Thermal comfort · Building · Natural ventilation

1 Introduction

The world's population is constantly growing. In 2017 there were approximately 6 billion inhabitants, and by 2100, there will be 10 billion [1]. An increase in population and the perpetual development of the world's countries imply an increase in tertiary and residential buildings, industries, and growth in the transport and agricultural sector. These sectors are the biggest energy consumers and, therefore, the biggest emitters of greenhouse gases. The building sector, particularly in Cameroon, consumes 40% of the total country's energy [2]. The building sector is responsible for a third of greenhouse gas emissions, so this sector strongly impacts climate change. In the tertiary sector, the largest energy consumers are office buildings [3]. Since the primary function of a building is to provide occupants with a comfortable and conducive indoor environment, the energy consumed in these buildings is used for air conditioning, heating, ventilation

© ICST Institute for Computer Sciences, Social Informatics and Telecommunications Engineering 2024
Published by Springer Nature Switzerland AG 2024. All Rights Reserved
F. Tchakounte et al. (Eds.): SAFER-TEA 2023, LNICST 566, pp. 200–215, 2024.
https://doi.org/10.1007/978-3-031-56396-6_13

and lighting, thus contributing to thermal comfort. According to Kemajou et al., audits carried out in artificially ventilated buildings in tropical Africa show that the proportion of electricity consumption due to air conditioning ranges from 40% to 80% of the building's total electricity consumption, making this area a key focus for energy-saving measures [4]. On the other hand, Kameni noted the lack of data on thermal comfort throughout the intertropical sub-Saharan region of Africa [5]. We need to determine the assessment parameters for thermal sensation in order to solve this problem. In this era of climate change and global warming, where all actions in buildings converge on energy performance, providing thermal comfort to building occupants while limiting energy consumption is quite difficult but must remain a major concern of all architects and other building designers in this 21st century. Thus, a database on thermal comfort and knowledge of the comfort temperature range is needed for the various parties involved in the design and construction of buildings – this will help to define guidelines for constructing more comfortable buildings in Cameroon [5]. This will help make indoor environments more comfortable and facilitate the regulation of energy consumption, thus influencing its sustainability [6].

Once the comfort range has been defined, it becomes fairly easy to reduce the energy consumption of air conditioners, as the comfort temperatures will be set. Given the high rate of urbanisation, the preponderance of economic activity and the importance of buildings in the cities of Yaoundé and Douala [4, 7] these have the site of many studies, including thermal comfort studies.

According to Tanadej, the concept of reducing energy consumption by maintaining an optimum indoor temperature, also known as the set temperature policy, has been implemented in several countries worldwide [8].

Given the importance of thermal comfort in both health and human activities, several studies have attempted to evaluate thermal comfort in various locations inc, including Hotels, houses [9], climatic chambers, offices [10] and schools [11]...) with people, dummies or empty rooms. According to the ISO 7730 standard, thermal comfort assessment is based on statistical predictions of thermal satisfaction. Thus, the analytical determination and interpretation of thermal comfort are made by calculating the PMV and PPD indices [12], the heat index [13], the universal thermal climate index [14] and local thermal comfort criteria. The thermal comfort approaches used are those of GIVONI [15], FANGER [12], GAGGE [16] and the adaptive approach pioneered by HUMPHREYS [6]. While the adaptive system uses in situ measurements and field surveys to assess comfort temperature, the GIVONI, FANGER and GAGGE approaches, in addition to surveys and in situ measurements, use the human body heat balance to determine comfort indices in a given environment.

Studies of thermal comfort began in the 20th century with the work of Gagge to solve the problem of stress in workers. Over time, several indices for assessing the state of comfort have been developed and used: calculation of the PMV and PPD in buildings with artificial ventilation, etc. [17, 18] calculation of ePMV and aPMV in naturally ventilated buildings, heat index, standards, experimental study of thermal comfort [9] (Figs. 1, 2, 3 and 4).

2   Materials and Methods

2.1   Materials

The equipment used was installed in a residential building with natural ventilation in the city of Yaoundé, the capital of Cameroon. The equipment used in the installations and the various parameters collected are shown in the diagrams below (see Fig. 5).

Fig. 1. Electronic box

Fig. 2. LCD screen

2.2   Methods

Thermal comfort, according to ASHRAE 55-66 of 1966 (American Society of Heating, Refrigerating and Air-conditioning Engineers) for a person, is defined here as <<that state of mind which expresses satisfaction with the thermal environment>>. Comfort is everything that constitutes well-being or everything that contributes to it. The body

Fig. 3. Anemometer

Fig. 4. Data logger

temperature, which is 37 °C, can only be maintained if it can constantly dissipate into the environment in which it finds itself [19]. According to [19] thermal comfort depends on the following:

- Ambient temperature;
- Air humidity;
- Wind speed;

Based on [20] to these three parameters that characterise thermal comfort, we must add:

- Clothing;
- Average radiant temperature;
- Metabolism.

A person's state of thermal comfort is influenced by their physical activity (metabolism), the quality of the clothing they wear, and environmental factors such as

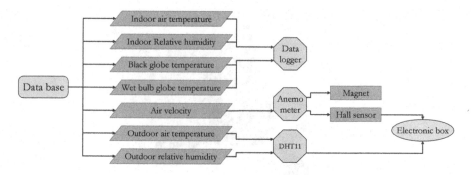

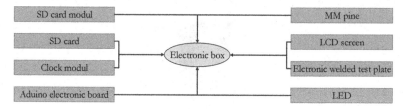

Fig. 5. Diagram of materials and parameters

ambient temperature, airspeed, relative humidity, mean radiant temperature, and partial water vapour pressure.

In buildings with artificial ventilation, thermal comfort is determined by calculating several indices using the GIVONI, FANGER and GAGGE approaches, in addition to in situ surveys and measurements and the human body heat balance. According to [21] the most widely used is Fanger's PMV model because it is combined with the theory of thermal regulation of the human body. The Predicted Mean Vote (PMV) is a parameter that indicates how occupants judge the indoor climate. PMV shows the degree of comfort of the environment. This index, established by Fanger on a sample of 1,300 people, measures the overall thermal sensation of the human body based on metabolism. It gives the average of the votes of a group of people expressing a voice by reference to a thermal sensation scale. This scale is directly related to Fanger's relatively complex comfort equation. The advantage of this index lies in the fact that it makes it possible to obtain a single comfort parameter (or, more precisely, thermal sensation) that considers all the main parameters influencing comfort (physical and physiological). It is given by [22–26]:

$$
\begin{aligned}
PMV = {} & [0.303 * \exp(-0.036 * M) + 0.028]\{(M - W) - 3.96 * 10^{-8} \\
& * f_{cl}[((T_{cl} + 273)^4 - (T_r + 273)^4) - f_{cl} * h_c(T_{cl} - T_a)] \\
& -3.05[5.73 - 0.007(M - W) - p_a] - 0.42[(M - W) - 58.15] \\
& -0.0173 * M(5.87 - p_a) - 0.0014 * M(34 - T_a)\}
\end{aligned}
\tag{1}
$$

With

$$T_{cl} = 35.7 - 0.0275(M - W) - 0.155I_{cl}\{(M - W) - 3.05[5.73 - 0.007(M - W)$$
$$-p_a] - 0.42[(M - W) - 58.15] - 0.0173 * M(5.87 - p_a) - 0.0014 * M(34 - T_a)\}$$

$$\tag{2}$$

$$T_r = [(T_g + 273.15)^4 + \frac{1.1 * 10^8 * V_a^{0.6}}{\varepsilon * D^{0.4}} * (T_g - T_a)]^{0.25} - 273.15 \tag{3}$$

If $V_a \prec 0.2\,\text{m/s}$ then $T_r = [(T_g + 273)^4 + 0.4 * 10^8(T_g - T_a)^{\frac{5}{4}}]^{\frac{1}{4}} - 273 \tag{4}$

$$h_c = \begin{cases} 2.38(T_{cl} - T_a)\,for\,2.38(T_{cl} - T_a)^{0.25} \succ 12.1\sqrt{v} \\ 12.1\sqrt{v}\,for\,2.38(T_{cl} - T_a)^{0.25} \prec 12.1\sqrt{v} \end{cases} \tag{5}$$

$$f_{cl} = \begin{cases} 1.00 + 1.290I_{cl}\,for\,I_{cl} \leq 0.078\,\text{m}^2 \cdot \text{C/W} \\ 1.05 + 1.645I_{cl}\,for\,I_{cl} \succ 0.078\,\text{m}^2 \cdot \text{C/W} \end{cases} \tag{6}$$

$$Pa = \frac{RH}{100} * Ps \tag{7}$$

$$Ps = \frac{760 * 6.05 * 10^{-7}[((T + 7.066) * T + 908.88) * T + 9567]}{1.013} \tag{8}$$

The PMV is an index that gives the average value of the votes of a group of people expressing their thermal sensation on a 7-level scale between -3 and $+3$ (Table 1):

Table 1. Thermal sensation scale as a function of PMV values [23]

Bedford ladder		The ASHRAE scale	
7	Very hot	7 (+3)	Very hot
6	Hot	6 (+2)	Hot
5	Comfortably warm	5 (+1)	Slightly warm
4	Comfortable	4 (0)	Neutral
3	Comfortably cold	3 (−1)	Slightly cold
2	Cold	2 (−2)	Cold
1	Very cold	1 (−3)	Very cold

The conditions for using the PMV index are such that the use of the PMV index is recommended when its value is between -2 and $+2$; the following six parameters must fall within the intervals:

- Metabolism M = 46 W/m² to 232 W/m² (0.8 met to 4 met);
- The ambient temperature T_a = 10 to 30 °C;
- The average radiant temperature T_r = 10 to 40 °C;
- Air speed V_a = 0 to 1 m/s;

- The partial pressure of water vapour $p_a = 0$ at 2700 P_a;
- The thermal insulation of the garment $I_{cl} = 0$ m^2. °C/W at 0.310 m^2. °C/W (0 clo to 2 clo) [27]

The PPD index (predicted percentage dissatisfied), according to the 2005 ISO 7730 standard, provides a quantitative prediction of the percentage of people who are thermally dissatisfied and likely to be too hot or cold. According to [12] the PPD index is linked to the PMV index by the following equation [12]:

$$PPD = 100 - 95 * \exp(-(0.03353 * PMV^4 + 0.2179 * PMV^2)) \qquad (9)$$

According to Humphreys, the comfort temperature in buildings using HVAC systems is given by

$$T_n = 20.1 + 0.0077T_m^2 \qquad (10)$$

with a coefficient of determination of 0.44. According to De Dear and Brager [28]

$$T_n = 22.2 + 0.003T_m^2 \qquad (11)$$

The operative temperature is a comfort index that expresses the relationship between the average radiant temperature of the walls and the temperature of the environment, considering heat exchange phenomena such as convection and conduction. It is, therefore, an index for assessing the radiative and convective effects on individual comfort. In moderate environments where the difference between the temperature of the walls and the air is less than 4 °C ($T_{mr} - T_a < 4$ °C), the operating temperature can be obtained using the relationship:

$$T_o = A * T_a + (1 - A) * T_{mr} \qquad (12)$$

$$A = \begin{cases} 0.5 \, si \, 0 \le V < 0,2 \, \text{m/s} \\ 0.6 \, si \, 0,2 \, \text{m/s} \le V \le 0,6 \, \text{m/s} \\ 0.7 \, si \, 0,6 \, \text{m/s} < V \le 1 \, \text{m/s} \end{cases} \qquad (13)$$

In naturally ventilated buildings, the atmosphere is not stationary but transient due to the variation of certain parameters over time. Obviously, in a naturally ventilated building, the speed of ambient air is often not controllable, and air can enter the building at any time and at different speeds. According to [29] the PMV-PPD model is not adequate for estimating thermal sensation inside naturally ventilated buildings because this model frequently overestimates or underestimates thermal sensation due to the non-inclusion of adaptation possibilities that a subject may have to maintain a comfortable condition.

The Fanger equations are not suitable for determining the thermal comfort state in naturally ventilated buildings.

Adaptation is modifying or adjusting something to make it suitable for something else. The adaptive model is a model that relates the interior design temperature or acceptable temperature ranges to external meteorological or climatological parameters [30]. There are three different categories of adaptation:

- Physiological adaptation
- Behavioural adaptation
- Psychological adaptation

The adaptive thermal comfort model compliant with standard EN 15251 provides a method for assessing thermal comfort in naturally ventilated buildings [31]. The adaptive thermal comfort model is based on the following principle: if a change occurs that leads to discomfort, people will react in such a way as to restore their comfort [6].

This approach is based on the results of thermal comfort surveys carried out in the field. These surveys focus on collecting data on the thermal environment and the simultaneous thermal response of subjects in real-life situations.

Comfort temperature results from the interaction between an individual, their building and the surrounding environment. According to [6] comfort temperature is strongly correlated with the average temperature measured. Several studies, such as [6, 32] give a thermal comfort equation close to:

$$T_n = 13.2 + 0.534T_m \qquad (14)$$

with a coefficient of determination of $R^2 = 0.94$.

According to de Dear & Brager, the comfort equation is given by

$$T_n = 13.5 + 0.546T_m \qquad (15)$$

with a coefficient of determination $R^2 = 0.91$ [28]

Several studies have been carried out to determine a thermal comfort index appropriate for naturally ventilated buildings. Fanger et al. (2002) developed the ePMV index, an extension of Fanger's PMV model.

$$ePMV = e * PMV \qquad (16)$$

where e is the expectation factor [34]

$$e = \begin{cases} 0.9 - 1 \; dans \; les \; régions \; où \; les \; bâtiments \; climatisés \; sont \; courants \; (saison \; estivale) \\ 0.7 - 0.9 \; dans \; les \; régions \; disposant \; de \; quelques \; bâtiments \; climatisés \; (saison \; d'été) \\ 0.5 - 0.7 \; dans \; les \; régions \; où \; il \; y'a \; peu \; de \; bâtiements \; climatisés \; (toute \; les \; saisons) \end{cases} \qquad (17)$$

We also have the aPMV index, which stands for

$$aPMV = PMV / (1 + \lambda * PMV) \qquad (18)$$

$$\text{With } \lambda = \begin{cases} 0.293 \; pour \; des \; climats \; chauds \\ -0.125 \; pour \; des \; climats \; froids \end{cases} \qquad (19)$$

The parameter λ represents the adaptation factor.

Treatment

The data analysed in this work is a time series consisting of a variety of quantitative data collected over a period of time. Hourly data for indoor air temperature, outdoor air temperature, mean radiant temperature, indoor wind speed, indoor relative humidity and outdoor relative humidity were taken from our study's areas in Yaoundé.

Data Collection

The wind speed values were collected using an anemometer, the components of which were designed and then printed using 3D printers with filaments made from carbon. Each time the anemometer turned, the magnet created a magnetic field that induced an electrical signal detected by the hall-effect sensor and caused the LED to glow, signalling the system consisting of the Arduino board that the anemometer had made a turn. The wind speed data were collected into the memory card within the box. The hall-effect sensor and the anemometer were connected to the box by female electrical wires.

The WBGT sensor contained an internal memory that provided values for the indoor or outdoor ambient temperature, indoor or outdoor relative humidity, black globe temperature and wet black globe temperature.

The DHT 11 gave outdoor temperature and relative humidity values. The female electrical wires enabled the DHT 11 sensor to be connected to the box and the temperature and relative humidity values to be saved on the memory card.

Processing with Excel

In the first case, processing consisted of eliminating bad data (data obtained during sensor bugs, power cuts, etc.).

Processing with Matlab

The MATLAB time series analysis tool was used to perform analyses on the data collected using the equations above.

Methodology

Our work initially consisted of calculating the PMV using Eq. 1 modelled in the MATLAB scientific calculator with the following input parameters: ambient temperature, mean radiant temperature, metabolism, clothing resistance, wind velocity and relative humidity. Secondly, we calculated the thermal comfort indices ePMV and aPMV respectively using Eqs. 15 and 17, and then compared these values with those of the thermal sensation experienced.

3 Results

Air temperature, mean radiant temperature, relative humidity and air speed are the four basic environmental variables that define the thermal state of the environment. Combined with the metabolic heat generated by human activity and the clothing worn by a person, they provide the six fundamental factors that define human thermal environments. These values are as follows (Table 3):

The comfort temperature in this building according to (Humphreys, 2002) (Eq. 14) is 26.66 °C, which corresponds to the average value of the operating temperature with a difference of 0.06 °C. According to the De Dear and Brager model (Eq. 15), it is 27.27 °C. The difference between the De Dear and Brager models and the operating temperature is 0.67 °C. The value obtained by Eq. 10 is identical to the operating temperature obtained in Table 2 to within 0.1, which means that the comfort temperature given by Eq. 10 is the one actually felt by the occupants.

We had a total of 8 volunteers to carry out this study in a naturally ventilated building. The volunteers ranged in height from 1.60 m to 1.80 m, in age from 14 to 31 and in weight from 45 kg to 75 kg.

Table 2. Environmental parameters

Parameters	Minimum	Higher	Mean
Indoor ambient temperature	22.8 °C	33.1 °C	26.56 °C
Mean radiant temperature	22.9 °C	33.25 °C	26.64 °C
Black globe temperature	22.9 °C	33.11 °C	26.60 °C
Operativ temperature	22.9 °C	33.11 °C	26.60 °C
Wet bulb globe temperature	20.8 °C	26.8 °C	23.6 °C
Outdoor temperature	20.9 °C	34.5 °C	25.22 °C
Indoor relative humidity	37.9%	83.6%	67.01%
Outdoor relative humidity	45%	95%	89.75°%
Air velocity	0 m/s	1.23 m/s	0.1 m/s

Table 3. Human-related parameters

Parameters	Minimum	Higher	Mean
Metabolism	41 W/m^2 of floor space	93 W/m^2 of floor space	67 W/m^2 of floor space
Clothing worn	0.016 m^2.K / W	0.155 m^2.K / W	0.0855 m^2.K / W

According to the ASHRAE standard, individuals are a priori in a state of thermal comfort when the PMV values are between −0.5 and 0.5 and the PPD less than 10% [30]. As a general rule, however, individuals are considered to be in a state of comfort when the PMV is between −1 and 1. In our case, the values obtained during the determination of their various thermal comfort indices for all the volunteers are contained in Table 4 and Table 5 below.

3.1 Real Environment

Analysis of the PMV/TSV ratio in the context of a real environment shows us that the PMV cannot be used to determine thermal sensation because the values obtained do not approach 1 to within 0.1. Using the values of the ePMV/TSV and aPMV/TSV ratios contained in Table 4 above, we can make the observations shown in the diagrams (Fig. 6) below in the case of a real environment.

3.2 Ideal Environment

Analysis of the PMV/TSV ratio in the context of an ideal environment shows us that the PMV cannot be used to determine thermal sensation because the values obtained do not approach 1 to within 0.1. Using the values of the ePMV/TSV and aPMV/TSV ratios contained in Table 4 above, we can make the observations shown in the diagrams (Fig. 7) below in the case of an ideal environment (Figs. 8 and 9).

Table 4. Thermal comfort index by volunteers for the real environment

Parameters											
	Volunteer	TSV	TSP	TSA	PMV	aPMV	PPD	ePMV	Tcl	PMV/TSV	aPMV/TSV	ePMV/TSV
Mean values	1	−1.000	1.000	0.000	−2.136	−2.914	82.511	−1.282	27.845	2.136	2.914	1.281
	2	−2.000	0.000	−1.000	−2.204	−3.043	85.072	−1.323	29.455	1.102	1.521	0.661
	3	−1.333	0.333	0.167	−0.791	−1.493	68.329	−0.474	27.175	0.593	1.119	0.355
	4	0.286	−0.286	−0.571	0.065	−0.490	45.831	0.039	24.997	0.227	−1.714	0.136
	5	−0.133	−0.067	−0.333	−1.557	−2.149	52.044	−0.934	30.894	11.707	16.117	7.005
	6	−0.556	0.444	0.333	−0.782	−2.167	75.589	−0.469	30.641	1.406	3.900	0.844
	7	0.000	0.500	0.750	−1.735	−2.293	61.198	−1.041	30.841	#DIV/0	#DIV/0	#DIV/0!
	8	0.385	−0.231	0.308	−1.650	−2.227	56.034	−0.990	30.849	−4.286	−5.790	−2.574

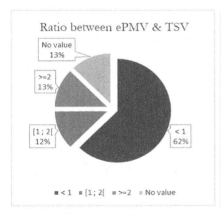
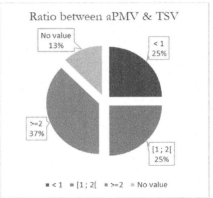

Fig. 6. Ratio between ePMV & TSV, aPMV & TSV for real environment

Table 5. Thermal comfort index by volunteers for ideal environment

	Parameters											
	Volunteer	TSV	TSP	TSA	PMV	aPMV	PPD	ePMV	Tcl	PMV/TSV	aPMV/TSV	ePMV/TSV
Mean values	1	−1.000	1.000	0.000	−3.189	−5.304	99.678	−1.914	28.671	3.189	5.304	1.914
	2	−2.000	0.000	−1.000	−2.692	−4.058	96.637	−1.615	29.853	1.346	2.029	0.808
	3	−1.333	0.333	0.167	−1.626	−2.782	77.993	−0.975	27.896	1.220	2.086	0.732
	4	0.286	−0.286	−0.571	−0.770	−1.603	64.673	−0.462	25.891	−2.692	−5.610	−1.617
	5	−0.133	−0.067	−0.333	−2.380	−3.573	80.298	−1.428	31.296	17.895	26.800	10.709
	6	−0.250	0.375	0.250	−2.582	−4.002	86.774	−1.549	32.421	10.328	16.006	6.198
	7	0.000	0.500	0.750	−2.354	−3.399	85.712	−1.413	31.197	#DIV/0	#DIV/0	#DIV/0!
	8	0.250	−0.333	0.250	−2.353	−3.451	83.047	−1.412	30.964	−9,412	−13.803	−5.647

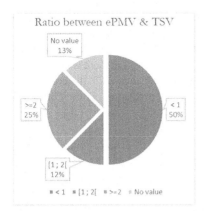
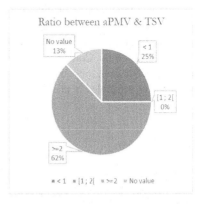

Fig. 7. Ratio between ePMV & TSV, aPMV & TSV for Ideal environment

In 1982, Fanger linked the values of PMV and PPD using Eq. 9. From this equation, he obtained a curve whose appearance is similar to that of our volunteers shown in the

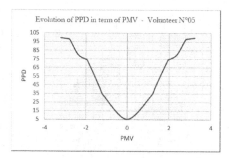
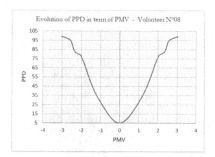

Fig. 8. Evolution of PPD in term of PMV in real environment

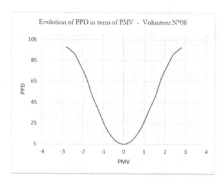
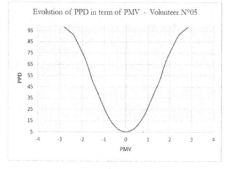

Fig. 9. Evolution of PPD in term of PMV in ideal environment

figures above. They represent some examples of changes in PPD as a function of PMV in the ideal and real environments of volunteers 5 and 9. These curves are in perfect agreement with the literature. They are similar to that obtained by [35].

The coefficient of determination is an index of the quality of the linear regression prediction. Its value lies between 0 and 1; the closer it is to 1, the better the linear regression matches the data collected. When this coefficient is 1, the correlation between the variables is total. Conversely, when it is close to 0, this means that there is virtually no correlation between the variables. For any value of R^2 greater than 0.25, the correlation between the variables is considerable, as we will have a correlation coefficient of 0.5 (Table 6).

3.3 Discussion

This table gives the values of the coefficient of determination obtained when plotting the TSV graph as a function of the ePMV, aPMV and PMV indices. We can see that with either the ePMV or PMV index, the coefficient of determination is the same in the case of an ideal environment as in a real environment. Given the values of these different indices, the most appropriate for estimating thermal comfort is the aPMV index in an environment considered ideal, but in a real environment, the most appropriate index is ePMV.

Table 6. R^2 values

Volunteer	R^2			
	Real environment		Ideal environment	
	ePMV = f(TSV)	aPMV = f(TSV)	ePMV = f(TSV)	aPMV = f(TSV)
3	0.0874	0.0702	0.0139	0.0111
4	0.4263	0.4504	0.2877	0.3123
5	0.184	0.2024	0.0952	0.0912
6	0.0236	0.0114	0.0279	0.0325
7	0.2745	0.2361	0.3502	0.3722
8	0.2754	0.2118	0.0119	0.0017
Average R^2	0.2118	0.1970	0.1311	0.1368
Average R	0.430	0.406	0.305	0.300

In a real environment, for 33.333% of the volunteers, the correlation between aPMV and TSV is considerable because R^2 is greater than 0.25, but for 50% of the volunteers, the correlation is considerable.

For 33.333% of the volunteers, the correlation between ePMV and TSV, between aPMV and TSV is considerable because R^2 is greater than 0.25 in an ideal environment. This implies a correlation greater than 0.5. The highest correlation coefficient value between the aPMV index and the TSV is 0.67, which corresponds to the highest value we obtained in our real environment. This value might lead us to believe that the PMV index would best approximate the thermal sensation felt by occupants. However, by calculating the average of this correlation coefficient for the majority of volunteers, we find that the ePMV index best approximates the thermal sensation felt, with an average of 0.430 in a real environment and 0.305 in an ideal environment.

4   Conclusion

The aim of this work was to study thermal comfort by determining three parameters PMV, aPMV and ePMV, to compare these parameters with the value of TSV in order to select the parameter that best approximates the thermal sensation experienced by the occupant. The second objective was to determine the thermal comfort temperature values. The results obtained in this work show that the Humphrey model is the most suitable for determining the thermal comfort temperature; neither the ePMV index nor the aPMV index can be used to assess thermal comfort in our work area. Based on the different values of the coefficient of determination, in an ideal environment, the most appropriate index is the aPMV, in a real environment it is rather the ePMV index. The relationship between the ePMV and TSV, aPMV and TSV indices shows that the ePMV index is the index that could be used to approximate the thermal comfort experienced by occupants.Further studies could be carried out at other times of the year to determine adaptive patterns of thermal comfort. This way, the "e" and "λ" factors could be re-evaluated to choose those corresponding to our context.

Author Contributions. Tsague Nguimatio Cathy Beljorelle—Conceptualization, methodology, software, validation, formal analysis, investigation, resources, data curation, writing—original draft preparation, writing—review and editing, visualization, project administration, funding acquisition.

Tchinda Rene—Conceptualization, validation, visualization, supervision,

Seutche Jean Calvin—Conceptualization, methodology, validation, investigation, formal analysis, investigation, writing—review and editing

Medjo Nouadje Brigitte—Validation, formal analysis, visualization, supervision

All authors have read and agreed to the published version of the manuscript."

Funding. "This research received no external funding".

References

1. Touzani, A.: Énergétique du bâtiment, BUREAU VERITAS (2017)
2. Vincelas, F.F.C., Ghislain, T., Robert, T.: Effects of the type of building materials on the thermal behavior of building in the hot dry climates: a case study of Maroua city, Cameroon. Int. J. Innov. Sci. Eng. Technol. **4**(13) (2017)
3. Dong, Q., Xing, K., Zhang, H.: Réseau de neurones artificiels pour l'évaluation de la consommation énergétique et du coût des immeubles de bureaux en bois stratifié par croix dans des régions froides graves. Sustainability (2017)
4. Kemajou, A., Tseuyep, A., Egbewatt, N.E.: Le confort thermique en climat tropical humide vers un réaménagement des normes ergonomiques. Revue des Energies Renouvelables **15**(13), 427–438 (2012)
5. Nematchoua, M.K., Tchinda, R., Ricciardi, P., Djongyang, N.: A field study on thermal comfort in naturally-ventilated buildings located in the equatorial climatic region of Cameroon. Renew. Sustain. Energy Rev. **136**, 381–393 (2014)
6. Nicol, J.F., Humphreys, M.A.: Adaptive thermal comfort and sustainable thermal standards for buildings. Energy Build., 4 (2002)
7. Kameni Nematchoua, M., Roshan, G., Tchinda, R.: Impact of climate change on outdoor thermal comfort and health in tropical wet and hot zone (Douala), Cameroon. Iranian J. Health Sci. **2**(12), 25–36 (2014)
8. Sikram, T., Ichinose, M., Sasaki, R.: Assessment of thermal comfort and building-related symptoms in air-conditioned offices in tropical regions: a case study in Singapore and Thailand. Front. Built Environ. (2020)
9. Nitcheu, M., Njomo, D., Meukam, P.: Experimental study of thermal comfort in traditional buildings in the region of Adamawa in Cameroon. J. Basic Appl. Sci. Res. **7**(111), 1–13 (2017)
10. Kuchen, E.: Variable thermal comfort index for indoor work space in office buildings: a study in Germany. Open J. Civil Eng., 670–684 (2016)
11. Kameni, N.M., Tchinda, R., Djongyang, N.: Field study of thermal comfort in naturally ventilated classrooms of Cameroon. Universal J. Environ. Res. Technol. **3**(15), 555–570 (2013)
12. Fanger, P.O.: Thermal Comfort. Danish Technical Press (1970)
13. Lee, D., Brenner, T.: Perceived temperature in the course of climate change: an analysis of global heat index from 1979 to 2013. In: The Influence of Perceived Temperature on Human Well-Being in the Context of Climate Change, p. 53 (2016)

14. Grosdemouge, V.: Proposition d'indicateurs de confort thermique et estimation de la température radiante moyenne en milieu urbain tropical. Contribution à la méthode nationale d'évaluation des ÉcoQuartiers (2021)
15. Belkhouane, H.: Etude de l'impact des modèles de confort sur la consommation énergétique pour les bâtiments NZEB's type bureaux (Cooling dominated) (2017)
16. Picard, C.F., et al.: Définition des indicateurs de confort (2020)
17. Fiorentini, M., Serale, G., Kokogiannakis, G., Capozzoli, A., Cooper, P.: Development and evaluation of a comfort-oriented control strategy for thermal management of mixed-mode ventilated buildings. Energy Build. (2019)
18. Simons, B., Koranteng, C., Adinyira, E., Ayarkwa, J.: An assessment of thermal comfort in multi storey office buildings in Ghana. J. Build. Constr. Plann. Res., 30–38 (2014)
19. Denker, A., El Hassar, S.M.K.: Guide pour une construction Eco-énergétique en Algérie, Alger: Deutche Gesellschaft für: Internationale Zusammenarbeit (GIZ) GmbH (2014)
20. Penu, G.: La thermique du batiment. Dunod, Paris (2016)
21. Zhao, Q., Lian, Z., Lai, D.: Thermal comfort models and their developments: a review. Energy Built Environ. 2(11), 21–33 (2021)
22. Albatayneh, A., Alterman, D., Page, A., Moghtaderi, B.: The impact of the thermal comfort models on the prediction of building energy consumption. MDPI Sustain. 10(13609), 5 (2018)
23. Fabbri, K.: Indoor Thermal Comfort Perception: A Questionnaire Approach Focusing on Children, Springer, Cham (2015). https://doi.org/10.1007/978-3-319-18651-1
24. Guo, H., Aviv, D., Loyola, M., Teitelbaum, E., Houchois, N., Meggers, F.: On the understanding of the mean radiant temperature within both the indoor and outdoor environment, a critical review. Renew. Sustain. Energy Rev. (2019)
25. Wu, Y.: Individual thermal comfort prediction using classification tree model based on physiological parameters and thermal history in winter. Build. Simul. (2020)
26. Deval, J.: Le confort thermique en climat tempéré. Revue Sci. Appl., 513–531 (1984)
27. ISO 7730:2005: Ergonomie des ambiances thermiques- Détermination analytique et interprétation du confort thermique par le calcul des indices PMV et PPD et par des critères de confort thermique local (2005)
28. Yang, L., Yan, H., Lam, J.C.: Thermal comfort and building energy consumption implications – a review. Appl. Energy, 164–173 (2014)
29. Thapa, S., Bansal, A.K., Panda, G.K.: Adaptive thermal comfort in the residential buildings of north east India—an effect of difference in elevation. Energy Built, 1 (2017)
30. Ramspeck, C.B.: Thermal environmental conditions for human occupancy. Atlanta (2004)
31. Roetzel, A., Tsangrassoulis, A., Dietrich, U., Busching, S.: On the influence of building design, occupants and heat waves on comfort and greenhouse gas emissions in naturally ventilated offices. A study based on the EN 15251 adaptive thermal comfort model in Athens, Greece. Build. Simul. 3, 87–103 (2010)
32. Humphreys, M.A., Nicol, J.F.: Outdoor temperature and indoor thermal comfort: raising the precision of the relationship for the 1998 ASHRAE database of field studies 106(1485), 5 (2000)
33. Fanger, P.O., Toftum, J.: Extension of the PMV model to non air-conditioned buildings in warm climates. Energy Build., 533–536 (2002)
34. Yao, R., Li, B., Liu, J.: A theoretical adaptive model of thermal comfort – adaptive predicted mean vote (aPMV). Build. Environ., 2089–2096 (2009)
35. Ekici, C.: A review of thermal comfort and method of using Fanger's PMV equation. In: 5th International Symposium on Measurement, Analysis and Modeling of Human Functions, Vancouver (2013)
36. Lee, D.: The influence of perceived temperature on human well-being in the context of climate change. Université de Marburg, Marburg (2016)

Classification Analysis of Some Cancer Types Using Machine Learning

Scott Ulrich Jemea Ebolo[1]([✉]), Olusola Samuel Makinde[2],
and Berthine Nyunga Mpinda[1]

[1] African Institute for Mathematical Sciences, 608 Crystal Garden, Limbe, Cameroon
scott.ebolo@aims-cameroon.org, bmpinda@aimsammi.org
[2] Department of Statistics, Federal University of Technology, 704, Akure, Nigeria
osmakinde@futa.edu.ng

Abstract. Cancer is a disease caused by changes in deoxyribonucleic acid, which attacks cells in the body, causing them to grow uncontrollably and spread to other parts of the body. Cancer can be deadly. The fact that it can develop anywhere in the body gives rise to many types of cancer. Because a good diagnosis increases the probability of administering a good treatment to save life. Therefore, to reduce the mortality rate from cancer, several diagnostic methods have been developed as the appropriate treatment option is highly dependent on the type of cancer. In this work, we address the issue of classification of some cancer types by using supervised learning methods to classify prostate cancer, lymphoma, leukaemia and small round blue cell tumour. To be more specific, we used five models: support vector machine, decision tree, random forest, K-nearest neighbours (KNN) and artificial neural network. Each cancer dataset was trained using each of the machine learning methods on the Google Colab graphics processing unit (GPU). The test samples were classified for each cancer type, and the performances of the five models were compared in terms of their percentages according to some metrics. To reduce the dimension of the data, we have incorporated a new approach that involves performing principal component analysis on our dataset. This new approach led to the discovery that the KNN method was the best according to our dataset, with 90% accuracy for the prostate and 100% for the others.

Keywords: Cancer · Classification · Machine Learning Techniques · Lymphoma · SRBCT · Prostate · Leukaemia

1 Introduction

Diseases that are mostly brought on by human activities can affect anybody, young or old, male or female [1]. These diseases have evolved over time claiming the lives of many people. In addition, the number of people affected by these deadly diseases is constantly on the rise. Cancer is certainly the most common and most complex one among these diseases.

© ICST Institute for Computer Sciences, Social Informatics and Telecommunications Engineering 2024
Published by Springer Nature Switzerland AG 2024. All Rights Reserved
F. Tchakounte et al. (Eds.): SAFER-TEA 2023, LNICST 566, pp. 216–233, 2024.
https://doi.org/10.1007/978-3-031-56396-6_14

A 3500-year-old disease, cancer, was discovered for the first time in Egypt, and it has grown steadily over the years, leading to the death of many. Cancer is caused by mutations to deoxyribonucleic acid (DNA) within cells in one part of the body. These mutations are also called genetic changes. It is a disease that attacks the cells of the body, causing them to grow uncontrollably and spread to other parts of the body thus affecting the whole body [2]. As it can develop itself anywhere in the body, doctors have given it different names coming from the organs or tissues of the body where cancer starts to develop itself. For example, lung cancer starts in the lungs, breast cancer starts in the breast, and brain cancer starts in the brain. Cancers can also be classified based on the type of cells that cause them, such as epithelial or squamous cells. There are a few categories of cancers that begin with the types of cells, such as sarcoma, carcinoma, leukemia, lymphoma, or multiple myeloma.

According to statistics, in 2018, 752,000 cases of cancer with more than 500,000 deaths were recorded, and this was just in Africa alone [3]. Therefore, for the successful implementation of any therapy, the accurate identification of the many forms of cancer is essential. Despite the fact that the categorization of cells into dangerous and non-cancerous categories has made tremendous progress in cancer diagnosis over the years as a consequence of the outcomes of many researchers' efforts, there is still much room for improvement in the diagnosis procedure. This is because carcinogenic tumours adapt and evolve as the world evolves. For example, the incidence of malignant melanoma, the most lethal type of skin cancer, has grown over the previous decade. In the United States, the fatality rate from melanoma increased by 3% between 2009 and 2010 [4]. Skin cancers have since become more common not only in America, but also in countries where the majority of the population is Caucasian, such as the United Kingdom and Canada, where 10,000 diagnoses and an annual mortality rate of around 1,250 people have been recorded [5]. From this, it is clear that the concern to reduce cancer mortality by improving methods of analysis and classification of cancer types is of great importance.

In recent years, microarrays have had a considerable impact on the identification of informative cancer-causing genes [6,7]. The main drawback of microarray data comes from the fact that the number of genes N far exceeds the number of samples M (that is $N \gg M$), which hampers the useful information of the dataset and leads to computational instability. Therefore, the identification of relevant cancer is a challenging task in classification analysis [8]. Feature (gene) selection has prompted many scientists to explore the field of functional genomics. As a result, a lot of algorithms and models have been developed to improve diagnosis [9–11]. The main objective of feature selection (FS) is to (a) improve classification accuracy by avoiding over-fitting or under-fitting of the model on the unseen data, (b) provide cost-effective models involving faster gene classification, and (c) obtain in-depth knowledge of the classification process of cancer types.

To identify illnesses, the classification approaches in the field of health employ computational methods, such as mathematical optimization, machine learning, and statistical methods. Among the many diseases, human cancers have been and will continue to be a major focus of research in classification analysis because of their permanent impact on human life. Breast cancer (BC) is the second greatest cause of mortality in women globally, just after lung cancer, with an expected 2,261,419 new cases and 684,996 new deaths in 2020 [12]. In the United States, 281,550 new instances of breast cancer were detected in 2021, with 43,600 fatalities recorded in women [13]. In order to save lives and reduce the number of deaths, many researchers have been pondering on the best ways to classify the different types of cancers in order to facilitate treatment or how they could improve the diagnosis of human cancers so as to choose the best therapy and thus reduce the number of deaths. We will present some of the key findings of the study in the subsequent lines.

In 2011, Idikio et al. [14] noted that human cancer categorization was now based on the notion of cancer cell genesis, light, and electron microscopic characteristics. The functional characteristics of cancer stem cells had not yet been included in cancer categorization. A proposed approach to cancer categorization might help to enhance future treatment. We agree with this conclusion because it is crucial to be able to classify different types of cancer to enable better treatment.

It is in that sense that in 2000 Furey et al. [15] presented their work, and they found that thousands of gene expression measurements were generated by DNA microarray investigations. Their study comprised both tissue sample categorization and data investigation for mislabelled or dubious tissue findings. Using support vector machines (SVM), they created an approach to analysing that type of data. They applied the SVM approach to ovarian cancer tissues, normal ovarian tissues, and other normal tissues. On several datasets of their analysis, they showed that different machine learning approaches performed better compared to statistical approaches.

Rasool et al. [16], found that forecasting analyses based on machine learning provided the possibility of early detection strategies for breast cancer diagnosis. They proposed data exploration strategies and created four alternative prediction models in their study to increase breast cancer detection accuracy. These suggested approaches and classifiers were tested on Wisconsin Diagnostic Breast Cancer and Breast Cancer Coimbra datasets. The diagnosis accuracy of their models increased with the data exploration strategies proposed, with 99.3% accuracy for polynomial SVM, 98.06% of accuracy for Logistic Regression, 97.35% and 97.61% accuracies for KNN and ensemble classifier respectively.

In view of the above, we can say that a lot of research has been done on improving the diagnosis of different types of cancer. However, despite the considerable advancement of these different diagnostic methods, there is still a large area to explore. This work is a synthesis and an improvement of the research conducted by the authors in [17]. It seeks to apply some machine learning methods in order to classify the different cancer types. It aims to identify the optimal classification method in the class of methods used, which can be used as an application by doctors, helping them to make better diagnoses, and then apply the best treatment to save cancer patients. Literature has shown that gene expression data are throughput data with a sample size of less than 50 while the number of features is in the thousands. Another intuitive feature of gene expression data is that the data are mostly unbalanced across cancer types. Unlike previous studies, this study will handle this problem to improve classification accuracy.

2   Methodology

2.1   Data

In this study, four cancer datasets were considered for the implementation of our classification approach. These datasets are available in R libraries. The data sets are prostate, lymphoma, leukaemia, and Small round blue cell tumour datasets. These data sets were also considered in Makinde [18] for some distance-based methodologies

The prostate is part of the male reproductive system, located just below the bladder, and in front of the walnut-sized rectum, it surrounds the urethra (the tube that drains urine from the bladder). The prostate dataset consists of 52 prostate tumour and 50 normal samples with 6033 genes. Normal and tumour classes are coded in 0 and 1, respectively, in the 'y' vector. Matrix 'x' is gene expression data and arrays were normalized, log-transformed, and standardized to zero mean and unit variance across genes as described in Detling et al. [19] and Chung et al. [20] comprehensively.

Lymphoma is a cancer that starts in the infection-fighting cells of the immune system, called lymphocytes. These cells are found in the lymph nodes, spleen, thymus, bone marrow, and other parts of the body. When you have lymphoma, the lymphocytes change and grow out of control. The lymphoma dataset consists of 42 samples of diffuse large B-cell lymphoma (DLBCL), 9 samples of follicular lymphoma (FL), and 11 samples of chronic lymphocytic leukaemia (CLL) with 4026 genes. DBLCL, FL, and CLL classes are coded in 0, 1, and 2, respectively, in the 'y' vector. Matrix 'x' is gene expression data and arrays were normalized, imputed, log-transformed, and standardized to zero mean and unit variance across genes as described in Detling et al. [19] and we can look at Chung et al. [20] for more details.

Leukaemia is cancer of the body's blood-forming tissues, including the bone marrow and the lymphatic system. Many types of leukaemia exist. The leukaemia dataset consists of two groups: group 1 of size 27 and group 2 of size 11 with 3051 genes (that is, 38 tumour mRNA expression levels) from the leukemia microarray study of Golub et al. [21].

Small round blue cell tumour is a group of childhood tumours that is characterized by a similar appearance under the microscope. The appearance is that of small, round, primitive cells that stain blue with conventional staining techniques for biopsy analysis. This dataset contains 83 samples with 2308 genes: 29 cases of Ewing sarcoma (EWS), coded 1, 11 cases of Burkitt lymphoma (BL), coded 2, 18 cases of neuroblastoma (NB), coded 3, 25 cases of rhabdomyosarcoma (RMS), coded 4. A total of 63 training samples and 25 test samples are provided in Khan et al. [22].

As we said, this section presents the way our data sets were prepared before applying the different classification methods. This consists in tidying our data and applying the PCA process.

2.2   Methodology

Tidying Data. This step presents the different procedures that we used to clear and prepare our different datasets.

Firstly, on the datasets that are unbalanced, we applied oversampling methods in order to get all of them balanced. Oversampling is used by survey statisticians to decrease variations in important statistics of a target subpopulation. Oversampling accomplishes this by increasing the sample size of the target subpopulation. We have two cases:

- The first case is on the binary dataset, that is, when the dataset has only two classes, we used the simple class imbalanced classification with the function **RandomOverSampler**. RandomOverSampler consists in giving a set of randomly selected minority instances in $Smin$, augmenting the original set S by reproducing the selected examples and adding them to S [23].
- In the second case, when the dataset has at least three classes, we used the multi-class imbalanced classification with the function **SMOTE**. SMOTE algorithm generates artificial instances based on similarities between existing minority cases in the feature space rather than the data space [23].

SMOTE is the most common and maybe most successful oversampling approach. Both of them can be found in the "imblearn.over_sampling" library.

Secondly, from the fact that the datasets have the input and output together, we need to split them in such a way that they can be easily used for the different machine learning algorithms. This process can be better observed through Fig. 1.

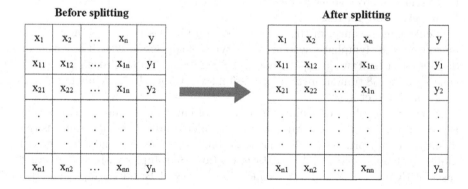

Fig. 1. Splitting the dataset process.

We obtained as a dataset, two sub-dataset such as the first for our input features (variables), and the second for our output (labels). After these steps, we applied the principal component analysis (PCA) to our input features.

Principal Component Analysis (PCA). PCA is an exploratory statistical method for a graphical description of the information present in large datasets [25]. The aim is to reduce the dimension of the data without losing too much information. This synthesizes the huge quantity of information into an easy and understandable form while following the different steps below:

- Standardization of the data;
- Correlation matrix between components and the initial variables;
- Eigenvalues and Eigenvectors;
- Selection of components using some criteria as Kaiser's rule or Scree test [24] (Fig. 2).

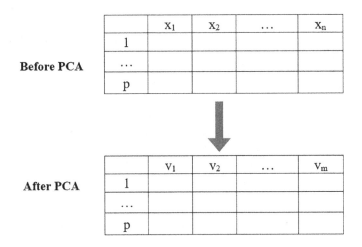

Fig. 2. Description of PCA process

where $\forall\, X_i$, $i = 1,..,n$, $\forall\, V_j$, $j = 1,...,m$, and $m \leq p \ll n$, with p number of observation such that:

$$V_j = \sum_{i=1}^{n} a_{ij} X_i \,.$$

(1)

We use principal component (PC) scores to reduce variables. Firstly, we carry out PCA on our parameters using a predetermined number of PCs sampled to describe at least 95% cumulative variation. In each PC, we chose the variable with the highest score as the most important variable. Since PCs are orthogonal in the PCA, selected variables will be completely independent (non-correlated).

2.3   Decision Trees (DT)

Decision tree, which borrows ideas from decision analysis, is a machine learning method which is used for both classification and regression. Decision trees can be used to visually and explicitly represent decisions and decision-making.

Entropy E is used to assess the impurity or randomness of a dataset. Entropy's value is constantly between 0 and 1, indicating that it is better when equal to 0 and worse when equal to 1. The entropy of the categorization of the training set S with regard to c_i states is determined if the target G is with varying attribute values. This is represented in Eq. 2 [26,27].

$$E(y, S) = \sum_{c_i \in V(y)} - \frac{|\sigma_{(c_i=y)}S|}{|S|} \cdot \log_2 \frac{|\sigma_{(c_i=y)}S|}{|S|} , \qquad (2)$$

where the expression $V(y)$ is the range of the target attribute y.

One metric for segmentation is information gain, often known as mutual information. This intuitively reveals how much knowledge we have of the value of a random variable. It is the inverse of entropy; the greater its value, the better. On the basis of the notion of entropy, data gain $Gain(a_i, S)$ is defined as follows in Eq. 3. Information Gain has been used in various classification studies such as and it is defined as:

$$Gain(a_i, S) = E(y, S) - \sum_{v_{i,j} \in V(a_i)} \frac{|\sigma_{(v_{i,j}=a_i)}S|}{|S|} E(y, \sigma_{(v_{i,j}=a_i)}S), \qquad (3)$$

where $V(a_i)$ is the range of the discrete attribute a_i and S is a training set equal to the attribute value of attribute $v_{i,j}$.

The Gini index is a criterion based on impurities that assess the differences in the probability distributions of the target attribute's values. The Gini index has been defined in several papers, including [27].

$$Gini(y, S) = 1 - \sum_{c_i \in V(y)} \left(\frac{|\sigma_{(c_i=y)}S|}{|S|} \right)^2 \qquad (4)$$

Therefore, we apply the likelihood-ratio and we obtain:

$$G^2(y, S) = 2 \cdot \ln 2 \cdot Gain(y, S) . \qquad (5)$$

This ratio is used to calculate the statistical significance of the information gain criteria.

2.4   Random Forest (RF)

Random Forest (RF) is a non-parametric model that is a collection of decision trees in which randomization is introduced into the training process of each individual tree using a bagging technique. During the training phase, it is a method of creating and averaging several decision trees [28].

The fundamental concept behind RF is to reduce the correlation between the trees in order to increase the variance of the bagging [28]. Each node is partitioned using the best predictors from a subset of predictors randomly selected at that node. Before each split, if p is the total number of input variables, RF picks $m \leq p$ of the input variables at random as candidates for splitting. Typically, m has a value of $\sqrt{p}$ or even as low as 1. Furthermore, this random selection yields trees with distinct structural characteristics. As a result, bias is typically not substantial; on the other hand, randomness increases variance, but this is wiped out later by averaging. This helps RF to avoid over-fitting and differentiate itself from other non-linear methods.

Given that B independent bootstrapped samples of the training set are obtained, each with its own model estimator T_i, averaging these results in a low-variance estimator model $\hat{F}_{avg}$, and we make a prediction at a new point x which is defined in Eq. 6 as follows [29]:

$$\hat{F}_{avg}(x) = \frac{1}{B} \sum_{i=1}^{B} T_i(x) , \tag{6}$$

where $\hat{F}_{avg}$ is the output of the ensemble of trees $\{T_i\}_B$ for the algorithm of random forest.

Here below, RF has special features that allow it to perform the out-of-bag estimate, of variables' importance.

Out-of-bag estimate is a strategy that consists in evaluating the prediction at (x_i, y_i) by using only the individual model whose bootstrap samples did not include (x_i, y_i). The generalized error of this is given by Eq. 7:

$$Err(\hat{F}_S) = \frac{1}{N} \sum_{(x_i,y_i) \in S} \mathcal{L}(\frac{1}{M^{-i}} \sum_{l=1}^{M^{-i}} f_{S^m_{m_{k_l}}}(x_i), y_i) , \tag{7}$$

where $m_{k_1}, ..., m_{k_{M-i}}$ refer to the indices of M^{-i} trees that do not include (x_i, y_i), $\mathcal{L}$ the loss, f_{S^m} the individual models. This method sometimes provides an accurate estimation of the generalization error of the ensemble that is even more precise than K-fold cross-validation.

2.5 Support Vector Machine (SVM)

Support vector machines (SVM) were first introduced by Vapnik [30]. Unlike DT and RF, SVM is a model-free method that provides efficient solutions without any assumption regarding the distribution and interdependency of the data [31]. SVM is known as the algorithm that finds a special kind of linear model, the maximum margin hyperplane which gives the maximum separation between the decision classes. The training examples that are closest to the maximum margin hyperplane are called support vectors, and we have SVM for binary classification and multi-class classification.

In binary case, the machine should classify an instance as only one of two classes; yes/no, 1/0, or true/false. Let the i-th input point $X_i = (x_1, x_2, ..., x_n)$ be the realisation of the random vector $X_i \in \mathbf{R}^N$ and this input point be labelled by the random variable $Sign \in \{-1, 1\}$. We have Φ a function defined as follows:

$$\Phi : I \longrightarrow F$$
$$X_i \longmapsto \Phi(X_i)$$

such that $I, F \subseteq \mathbf{R}^N$, where I is the input space and F is a feature space. We assume that a sample S of p labelled data points such that:

$$S = \{(x_1, y_1), (x_2, y_2), ..., (x_p, y_p)\}$$

The SVM learning algorithm finds a hyper-plane (θ^T, b) such that we want to maximize $\frac{2}{\|\theta\|}$, then we need to minimize $\|\theta\|$, hence the optimization solves:

$$\min_{\theta, b} \frac{1}{2} \|\theta\| \text{ , subject to} \begin{cases} Sign(\theta^T \Phi(X_i) - b) \leq -1, & \text{for negative class} \\ Sign(\theta^T \Phi(X_i) - b) \geq 1, & \text{for positive class} \\ \forall \ 1 \leq i \leq p. \end{cases} \quad (8)$$

The solution $\{\hat{\theta}, \hat{b}\}$ leads to a classification using $Sign(\hat{\theta}^T \Phi(X_i) - \hat{b})$.

The necessity to minimize the norm of θ is that it will help us to maximize $\frac{2}{\|\theta\|}$ which is the larger of the hyper-planes. That means, the separation between the two categories can be seen clearly and can be well classified with the lowest rate of error.

For multi-class classification, the same principle as binary classification is utilized after breaking down the multi-classification problem into multiple employed in binary classification problems [32]. The r-th SVM is trained with all of the instances in the r-th class with positive labels while the rest of the instances with negative labels. Thus, given n training data $(x_1, y_1), ..., (x_n, y_n)$; where, $x_i \in \mathbf{R}^n$, $i = 1, ..., n$ and $y_i \in \{1, \cdots, k\}$ is the class of x_i. We require a hyper-plane to separate every two classes in the One-to-One technique, ignoring the points of the third class. The i-vs-j classifier solves the following quadratic optimization problem:

$$\min \frac{1}{2} (\omega^{ij})^T \omega^{ij} + C \sum_{i=1}^{n} \xi_i^{ij} . \quad (9)$$

The equations of hyperplane separating the different i and j classes used here are defined as follows:

$$(\omega^{ij})^T \Phi(x_t) + b^{ij} \geq 1 - \xi_i^{ij}; \text{ if } y_t = i$$
$$(\omega^{ij})^T \Phi(x_t) + b^{ij} \geq \xi_i^{ij} - 1; \text{ if } y_t = j,$$

where $\xi_i^{ij} \geq 0$, and $t = 1, ..., n$.

The one-vs-one technique seeks to eliminate the one-vs-rest method's imbalance problem by training binary classifiers exclusively with data from the two initial classes indicated by each classifier. The one-vs-one technique generates $k(k-1)/2$, where k is the number of classes [33,34].

Following the construction of all classifiers, we may employ the following voting strategy: If the sign of the i-vs-j classifier indicates that x_t belongs to the ith class, the vote for the i-th class is increased by one. Otherwise, the jth class's vote is increased by one. Finally, we conclude that x_t has the most votes in the class. This voting tactic is known as the "Max Wins" strategy. If votes for two classes are tied, we simply choose the one with the lower index [35].

2.6 K-Nearest Neighbours (KNN)

The KNN algorithm used in our problem considered the output as a target class. The problem is solved or classified by the majority vote of its neighbours, where the value of K is taken as a small and real-valued positive integer. There are different methods for calculating the distance: Manhattan, Euclidean, Cosine, etc. However, this study applies to Euclidean distance only. Let (c_{x_j}, c_{y_j}) be the centroid and (xi, yi) be the data point. The Euclidean distance can be calculated as:

$$\sqrt{\sum_{i=1}^{N}(x_i - y_i)^2}. \tag{10}$$

2.7 Artificial Neural Network (ANN)

A neural network is a massive interconnection processor built up with simple computing nodes that have a natural aptness for storing experiential knowledge and making it ready for use [36]. The challenges created by its restriction have led to the development of a powerful neural network called Multilayer Perceptron (MLP) capable of overcoming the limitations of the previous single layer.

Globally, in MLP the input layers are connected to the hidden layers, which in turn connect to the output layers. The connection between layers uses a learning rule to optimize weights or parameters. This can be seen in Fig. 3.

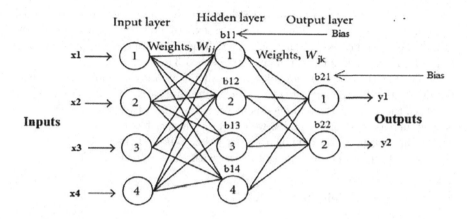

Fig. 3. Example of ANN with one hidden layer [37].

In general, the number of inputs is given by the feature spaces and the number of outputs by the number of categories. When few parameters are used the model is not able to learn enough and loses its ability to generalize [38]. So the big deal is how to operate a proper adjustment that would enable the model to best generalize. This problem is handled by the backpropagation algorithm in MLP. Backpropagation generally proceeds in two phases: forward and backward phases.

The forward phase principally propagated the input forward through the network. During this process, the network's synaptic weights are fixed, the weighted sum of the inputs to the node and the activation for the node is computed at each layer as showed by the following system 11:

$$\begin{cases} Z_k = \sum_i W_{i,k} X_k + b_k \\ X'_k = g(Z_k). \end{cases} \tag{11}$$

here, X is the input, X' is the output of the hidden layers which will be the input for the next hidden layer, b is a bias that always has an output of 1, W is the weight, i and k are the indices and g is the activation function.

The most commonly used activation function is Sigmoid used on the output layer when we have two classes, Relu is used on hidden layers, and Softmax is used on the output layer when we have at least three classes respectively defined as follow:

$$g(Z_k) = \frac{1}{1 + e^{-Z_k}} \; ; \; g(Z_k) = \max\{O, Z_k\} \; ; \; g(Z_k) = \frac{e^{Z_k}}{\sum_{i=1}^{k} e^{Z_i}}.$$

The forward phase helps to fix the network's synaptic weights and to proliferate the input values through the network; layer after layer until it reaches the output. In order to solve the misclassification problems, we use loss functions,

Binary Cross Entropy (BCE) for binary classification and Categorical Cross Entropy (CCE) respectively defined as follows:

$$\mathcal{L}_{BCE_p}(y) = -\frac{1}{N}\sum_{i=1}^{N} y_i \log(p(y_i)) + (1 - y_i) \log(1 - p(y_i)) , \qquad (12)$$

where y is the label and p(y) is the predicted probability of the point.

$$\mathcal{L}_{CCE}(s) = -\frac{1}{M}\sum_{p=1}^{M} \log\left(\frac{e^{s_p}}{\sum_{j}^{c} e^{s_j}}\right) , \qquad (13)$$

where each s_p is the convolutional neural network (CNN) score for each positive class, and M is the number of training examples.

The backward phase consists in propagating the errors backward through the network as follows: compute the error value in every node of the output layer, then compute the node's value error and update each node's weight of all the layers in the network. Particularly, in the regression task, the fit can be measured by the sum-of-squared errors [28].

$$R(W, b) = \sum_{k}\sum_{i}(y_{ik} - f_k(x_i))^2 \qquad (14)$$

where y and f are respectively the exact output and the predicted output.

Unlike other error functions, the goal while regularizing this function is not to obtain the global minimizer since it leads to overfitting. Hence, backpropagation relies on the gradient descent to minimize the error function $R(W, b)$. At the iteration, $(l + 1)$ the gradient descent [28] is defined by Eq. 15:

$$\begin{cases} W_{ki}^{(l+1)} = W_{ki}^{l} - \gamma_l \sum_i \frac{\partial R_i}{\partial W_{ki}^l} , \\ b_{ki}^{(l+1)} = b_{ki}^{l} - \gamma_l \sum_i \frac{\partial R_i}{\partial b_{ki}^l} \end{cases} \qquad (15)$$

where γ_l is the learning rate. Learning rate is the parameter that helps to modify the weights and the bias of the network.

Even though backpropagation has been proven to be the ideal tool for training MLPs, it has faced the major problems of long training.

2.8   Evaluation of Performance

In this study, testing data is utilized to assess the performance of the various procedures employed and accuracy and F1-score will be considered. The first set of metrics can be obtained through the confusion matrix similar to Fig. 4. The confusion matrix in itself is not a performance measure, but several useful performance metrics are based on the confusion matrix and the numbers inside.

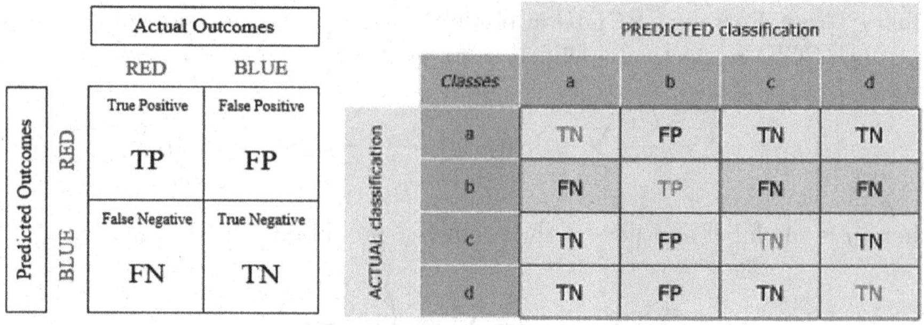

Fig. 4. The format of a confusion matrix for binary and multi-class classification [39].

In classification problems, accuracy A is defined as the number of correct predictions produced by the model divided by the total number of predictions made. If the classes in the dataset are roughly balanced, accuracy is a powerful statistic. We used Eq. 16 to compute our accuracy:

$$A = \frac{TP + TN}{FP + FN + TP + TN} \ .$$

(16)

The $F1\text{-}Score$ is defined as:

$$F1 - S = \frac{2 \cdot Precision \cdot Sensitivity}{Precision + Sensitivity} \ ,$$

(17)

with:

$$Precision = \frac{TP}{TP + FP} \ , \quad Sensitivity = \frac{TP}{TP + FN}.$$

3   Results and Discussion

3.1   Results

In this section, the results of the five machine learning algorithms performed on the four cancer types are presented. First, outcomes of each data pre-processing and classification approach are presented for each cancer type. For the analysis, we divided our dataset into two sub-datasets; 80% for the training sample, and 20% for the testing sample, we also split each dataset into input (which are numerical values of gene characteristics) and output (which are the different categories), this for each dataset. Finally, a discussion on the different machine learning techniques after performing PCA is presented based on the results given by each of them in a table, in order to identify the optimal classification methods.

Prostate. For the case of prostate cancer, we obtained after applying PCA on the input, the dimension which has reduced from (102, 6033) to (102, 101). Then, we performed the five classification methods.

Figure 5a displays a curve that allows us to find the optimal value of k that gives the best accuracy for the K-nearest neighbours classifier. It is observed that $k = 12$ is the optimal number of neighbours which gives us the lowest *value-error* $= 0$. That can be seen in Table 1, which also provides the results of other classification methods.

Lymphoma. The Lymphoma dataset was unbalanced, so an oversampling procedure was implemented on the dataset to make it a balanced dataset. After that, PCA has been applied to the balanced data to reduce the dimension from (62, 4026) to (62, 61).

Figure 5b presents a curve that allows us to get an optimal value of k that gives the best accuracy for the k-nearest neighbours classifier on lymphoma data. It is observed that kNN is of optimum performance at $k = 2$.

It can be observed that the kNN ($k = 2$), decision trees, random forest, and support vector machine with polynomial kernel achieved perfect classification. And we can see in Table 1 that 100% for accuracy and F1-score are obtained. We can conclude that all these classification methods can be appropriate for classifying lymphoma data.

Leukaemia. Similar to the lymphoma dataset, leukaemia data was unbalanced. so an oversampling procedure was implemented on the dataset to make it a balanced dataset. After that, PCA was applied to the balance data to reduce the dimension from (54, 3051) to (54, 37) with the aim of improving the performance and rapidity of classification methods.

Figure 5c presents the mean error associated with various values of k. It is observed that kNN is of optimum performance at some values of $k = 1, 2, ..., 10$, 14, 24, 26, 28, 29.

Once more, all classification methods performed competitively, except artificial neural networks. This can be observed through the Table 1.

SRBCT. SRBCT dataset was unbalanced. An oversampling procedure was implemented on the dataset to make it a balanced dataset. Once more, PCA was applied to the balance data to reduce the dimension of the data from (83, 2308) to (83, 71).

The optimal choice of k is observed, in Fig. 5d, to be $k \in [1, 9]$. By the principle of parsimony, KNN is of optimum performance at $k = 1$.

Table 1 provides a comparison of the performances of classification methods employed on SRBCT data in terms of accuracy and F1 score. KNN (at $k = 1$) performs well compared to other methods.

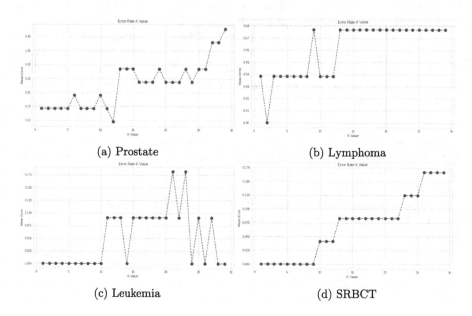

(a) Prostate

(b) Lymphoma

(c) Leukemia

(d) SRBCT

Fig. 5. Choice of the best value of k neighbours

Table 1. Comparison of the classification methods

| | | Cancer type | | | |
ML Technics	Evaluation	Prostate	Leukemia	Lymphoma	SRBCT
DT	Accuracy	86%	100%	100%	88%
	F1 Score	86%	100%	100%	88%
RF	Accuracy	76%	100%	100%	96%
	F1 Score	76%	100%	100%	96%
SVM	Accuracy	81%	100%	100%	96%
	F1 Score	81%	100%	100%	96%
KNN	Accuracy	90%	100%	100%	100%
	F1 Score	90%	100%	100%	100%
ANN	Accuracy	85.7%	77%	9%	87%
	F1 Score	82.35%	78%	70%	87%

3.2 Discussion

It is observed that the classical machine learning methods such as SVM, DT, RF, and KNN perform better than the ANN, which is a non-classical machine learning method. The poor performance of ANN may be attributed to the sample sizes. However, this requires further investigation. The performances of the support vector machines in classifying leukaemia and lymphoma are equivalent to results in Makinde [18], where classical statistical methods were considered for the classification of cancer types without oversampling procedure.

4 Concluding Remark

In this study, we applied machine learning techniques to classify some cancer types. The performance of five classification methods, namely decision tree (DT), random forest (RF), support vector machine (SVM), K-nearest neighbours (KNN), and artificial neural network (ANN) were investigated by analysing prostate, leukaemia, lymphoma, and small round blue cell tumour data. These datasets are highly dimensional and unbalanced. Each of the datasets was tidied and split before reducing the dimension of each of the competing classes by using PCA in order to optimize data analysis and oversampling was performed for datasets that were unbalanced. Then, machine learning techniques were performed on the cancer data and the results were tabulated for each of the cancer data. Lastly, it was found that the k nearest neighbour rule performs well for each of the datasets.

References

1. Sattenspiel, L.: Tropical environments, human activities, and the transmission of infectious diseases. Am. J. Phys. Anthropol. Official Publ. Am. Assoc. Phys. Anthropol. **113**(S31), 3–31 (2000)
2. Merola, R., et al.: PCA3 in prostate cancer and tumor aggressiveness detection on 407 high-risk patients: a National Cancer Institute experience. J. Exp. Clin. Cancer Res. **34**(1), 1–6 (2015)
3. Sharma, R.: Breast cancer burden in Africa: evidence from GLOBOCAN 2018. J. Public Health **43**(4), 763–771 (2021)
4. Hernandez, B.Y., Green, M.D., Cassel, K.D., Pobutsky, A.M., Vu, V., Wilkens, L.R.: Cancer research center hotline: preview of Hawai'i Cancer facts and figures 2010. Hawaii Med. J. **69**(9), 223 (2010)
5. Schadendorf, D., et al.: Melanoma. Lancet **392**(10151), 971–984 (2018)
6. Leung, Y.F., Cavalieri, D.: Fundamentals of cDNA microarray data analysis. Trends Genet. **19**(11), 649–659 (2003)
7. Flores, M., Hsiao, T.-H., Chiu, Y.-C., Chuang, E.Y., Huang, Y., Chen, Y.: Gene regulation, modulation, and their applications in gene expression data analysis. Adv. Bioinform. **2013** (2013)
8. Lee, G., Rodriguez, C., Madabhushi, A.: Investigating the efficacy of nonlinear dimensionality reduction schemes in classifying gene and protein expression studies. IEEE/ACM Trans. Comput. Biol. Bioinform. **5**(3), 368–384 (2008)

9. Lee, C.-P., Leu, Y.: A novel hybrid feature selection method for microarray data analysis. Appl. Soft Comput. **11**(1), 208–213 (2011)

10. Peng, Y., Li, W., Liu, Y.: A hybrid approach for biomarker discovery from microarray gene expression data for cancer classification. Cancer Inf. **2**, 117693510600200030 (2006)

11. Ye, J., Li, T., Xiong, T., Janardan, R.: Using uncorrelated discriminant analysis for tissue classification with gene expression data. IEEE/ACM Trans. Comput. Biol. Bioinf. **1**(4), 181–190 (2004)

12. Sung, H., et al.: Global cancer statistics 2020: GLOBOCAN estimates of incidence and mortality worldwide for 36 cancers in 185 countries. CA Cancer J. Clin. **71**(3), 209–249 (2021)

13. Siegel, R.L., Miller, K.D., Fuchs, H.E., Jemal, A.: Cancer statistics, 2022. CA Cancer J. Clin. (2022)

14. Idikio, H.A.: Human cancer classification: a systems biology-based model integrating morphology, cancer stem cells, proteomics, and genomics. J. Cancer **2**, 107 (2011)

15. Furey, T.S., Cristianini, N., Duffy, N., Bednarski, D.W., Schummer, M., Haussler, D.: Support vector machine classification and validation of cancer tissue samples using microarray expression data. Bioinformatics **16**(10), 906–914 (2000)

16. Rasool, A., Bunterngchit, C., Tiejian, L., Islam, M.R., Qu, Q., Jiang, Q.: Improved machine learning-based predictive models for breast cancer diagnosis. Int. J. Environ. Res. Public Health **19**(6), 3211 (2022)

17. African Institute for Mathematical Sciences (AIMS) Cameroon. Master's thesis, Classification analysis of some cancer types, 29 May 2022. https://library.nexteinstein.org/thesis/classication-analysis-of-some-cancer-types/. Accessed 17 Sept 2023

18. Makinde, O.S.: Gene expression data classification: some distance-based methods. Kuwait J. Sci. **46**(3) (2019)

19. Dettling, M., Bühlmann, P.: Supervised clustering of genes. Genome Biol. **3**(12), 1–15 (2002)

20. Chung, D., Keles, S.: Sparse partial least squares classification for high dimensional data. Stat. Appl. Genet. Mol. Biol. **9**(1) (2010)

21. Golub, T.R., et al.: Molecular classification of cancer: class discovery and class prediction by gene expression monitoring. Science **286**(5439), 531–537 (1999)

22. Khan, J., et al.: Classification and diagnostic prediction of cancers using gene expression profiling and artificial neural networks. Nat. med. **7**(6), 673–679 (2001)

23. Huang, P.J.: Classification of Imbalanced Data Using Synthetic Over-Sampling Techniques. University of California, Los Angeles (2015)

24. Raîche, G., Walls, T.A., Magis, D., Riopel, M., Blais, J.G.: Non-Graphical Solutions for Cattell's Scree Test. Hogrefe Publishing, Methodology (2013)

25. Saporta, G., Keita, N.N.: Principal component analysis: application to statistical process control. ISTE (2009)

26. Charbuty, B., Abdulazeez, A.: Classification based on decision tree algorithm for machine learning. J. Appl. Sci. Technol. Trends **2**(01), 20–28 (2021)

27. Rokach, L., Maimon, O.: Decision trees. In: Maimon, O., Rokach, L. (eds.) Data Mining and Knowledge Discovery Handbook, pp. 165–192. Springer, Boston (2005). https://doi.org/10.1007/0-387-25465-X_9

28. Hastie, T., Tibshirani, R., Friedman, J.H.: The Elements of Statistical Learning: Data Mining, Inference, and Prediction, vol. 2. Springer, New York (2009). https://doi.org/10.1007/978-0-387-84858-7

29. James, G., Witten, D., Hastie, T., Tibshirani, R.: An Introduction to Statistical Learning, vol. 112. Springer, New York (2013). https://doi.org/10.1007/978-1-4614-7138-7

30. Cortes, C., Vapnik, V.: Support-vector networks. Mach. Learn. **20**(3), 273–297 (1995)

31. Yu, W., Liu, T., Valdez, R., Gwinn, M., Khoury, M.J.: Application of support vector machine modeling for prediction of common diseases: the case of diabetes and pre-diabetes. BMC Med. Inform. Decis. Mak. **10**(1), 1–7 (2010)

32. Rathgamage Don, D.P.W.: Multiclass Classification Using Support Vector Machines (2018)

33. Knerr, S., Personnaz, L., Dreyfus, G.: Single-layer learning revisited: a stepwise procedure for building and training a neural network. In: Soulié, F.F., Hérault, J. (eds.) Neurocomputing. NATO ASI Series, vol. 68, pp. 41–50. Springer, Heidelberg (1990). https://doi.org/10.1007/978-3-642-76153-9_5

34. KreBel, Y.H.G.: Advances in Kernel Methods, Pairwise Classification and Support Vector Machines. MIT Press (1998)

35. Hsu, C.-W., Lin, C.-J.: A comparison of methods for multiclass support vector machines. IEEE Trans. Neural Netw. **13**(2), 415–425 (2002)

36. Haykin, S.: Neural Networks and Learning Machines, 3/E. Pearson Education India (2009)

37. Sanaei, A., Yousefi, S.H., Naseri, A., Khishvand, M.: A novel correlation for prediction of gas viscosity. Energy Sources Part A Recovery Utilization Environ. Eff. **37**(18), 1943–1953 (2015)

38. Duda, R.O., Hart, P.E., et al.: Pattern Classification. Wiley (2006)

39. Grandini, M., Bagli, E., Visani, G.: Metrics for multi-class classification: an overview. arXiv preprint arXiv:2008.05756 (2020)

Development of an Intelligent Safety Monitoring Device for Train-Track System in Cameroon

Tse Sparthan Azoh[1]($\boxtimes$), Wolfgang Nzie[2], Bertin Sohfotsing[3], and Tibi Beda[4]

[1] University of Bamenda, P.O Box 39, Bambili, Cameroon
sparthanazog@gmail.com
[2] University of Ngaoundere, P.O Box 455, Ngaoundere, Cameroon
[3] University of Dschang, P.O Box 134, Bandjoun, Cameroon
[4] University of Ngaoundere, P.O Box 454, Ngaoundere, Cameroon

Abstract. Valued as the best land transportation sector when it comes to the movement of heavy tons of freight and plenty of passenger's at a unique instant, the railway industries have flippantly registered series of accidents that accounted for economic and social deprivation. These accidents directly related to environmental changes, human mistakes and material damages, heavy speeding, overloading, absence of inspection before train departure has portrayed the inconsistency of current maintenance strategies design to guarantee the availability and reliability of traintrack transportation network recently. The important to have an observation platform to preview active and proactive failures in various industries is of great interest. This research paper focuses on suggesting with application a strategy for the design, manufacturing and installation of an intelligent observation tool (IOT) suitable to follow-up failures and repair activities in related industries. Therefore, to guarantee safety of travellers, welfare of freights and protection of infrastructures. However, the strategy uses an inductive technique for failures extraction and a deductive technique for ranking these failures. For real time authentication, the suggested strategy was later simulated to investigate failures on train-track holding system caused by fatigue as it contributes to about 90% of mechanical failures relating to accident in the rolling stock, aerospace, maritime, processing and other related industries.

Keywords: Safety · Monitoring · Maintenance · Intelligent Observation Tool (IOT) · Train-Track

1 Introduction

Acknowledgement as the society's most famous land transportation sector with an average capacity of about 10,000 billion tonne of freight for every one kilometer and 5 billion travelers annually worldwide (Pavithra et al. 2019), the rolling stock industry occupies a network of about 1.5 Million kilometers worldwide, 90406 km in Africa and Cameroon about 1000 km. Due to huge economic demand by Central African states, over 800 million USD was advocated in maintaining railway lines in Cameroon (Lezin

© ICST Institute for Computer Sciences, Social Informatics and Telecommunications Engineering 2024
Published by Springer Nature Switzerland AG 2024. All Rights Reserved

F. Tchakounte et al. (Eds.): SAFER-TEA 2023, LNICST 566, pp. 234–257, 2024.
https://doi.org/10.1007/978-3-031-56396-6_15

et al. 2013). The increment of per axle load over recent time, the need for improving the arriving time of freight, passengers and other services has hugely increased its traffic nature without putting in practice novel maintenance policies to accompany an optimum exploitation of this sector in developing countries. However, traffic increment has led to a handful of dramatic accidents. The Eséka train derailment in Cameroon on 21[st]october 2016 that accounted for about 79 deaths and 700 injured, freight misfortune, infrastructure damage and downtime of the entire network. According to the result of the investigations instructed by presidential decree signed on the 25th of October 2016, the experts established that, the drama was directly linked to an increment of a designated train speed from 40 km/h to an unacceptable speed of 96 km/h, train over loading and defective brakes associating to improper departure inspection[1].To mitigate on the current issues through the protection of infrastructure, freight and safety of travellers in future, the importance to have an observation platform to preview failures in related industries is a must (proposed by the experts). This mitigating action is an element of condition based maintenance plus which intergrate the use of intelligent observation infrastructures design to assist fault diagnostic and prognostic activities. Diagnostic involves discovery and extraction of fault on a specific component, meanwhile prognostic assist in forecasting the exact timeline for possible failure to occur (Sparthan et al. 2020). However, the complexity of industrial systems during real time exploration showcase a huge barrier for maintenance engineers and operators to detect, isolate and fine-tune the exact duration at which possible failures are predicted. This is because their design requires significant number of activities at a single instant which becomes complex to manage using human knowledge (Tse et al. 2020). The support of an intelligent infrastructure is therefore of huge significance. This study will focus on suggesting with application a methodology for the design, manufacturing and installation of an intelligent observation tool suitable to follow-up failures and repair activities in the railway industries and beyond.

Inclusively, a series of scholars and railway engineers have invested their time in providing relevant solutions relating to the rolling stock industry. Currently, the use of a low cost and zero repair smart sensing system for observing the attitude of brake forces on the disc during stoppage or slow down process of the train has been investigated (Socie and Barkan 2008). The authors achieved their goal as they segregate from sensors reading, non-contact interactive network and energy reaping modules during design and construction of the intelligent device. The device was authenticated with positive results as practically it grants the posibility to measure the evolution of brake forces under normal and heavy vibrative environment in real-time. Moreover, a concept that bring together an inbuilt sensing network system to measure vibration reading of a bogie and a GPS to identify train position on the railroad was further inaugurated with field appreciation. The proposed off-grid observation tool was able to register sensor reading related to velocity and acceleration level of the railroad individual components and the bogie element with respect to time and location of the train (Tsunashima et al. 2012). A software design for speculating the total length required to stop or slow down the rail-vehicle under different loading and environmental issues in accordance with European technical data sheet design for the connectivity of fast railway network has been put to practice. The intelligent tool grants the possibility to identify the influence of the

---

[1] Cameroon Radio Television (radio news of 23 may 2017).

brake pad frictional coefficient on the stopping length of the train (Pugi et al. 2013). The novel tool that intelligently combines a GPS (Global Position System) and GSM (Global System for Mobile Communication) to observe the speed, distance travelled, location of the train using sensor readings from remote areas with application was further introduced. The suggested online tool achieved it quality by segregating from bogie to railroad faults based on the modification of vibrating signals obtained during field work. For system auto-verification, the users were able to request the state of bogie and railroad components via an SMS (Short Message Service) send to the online observation tool, the system axiomatically reply via SMS to the mobile phone indicating the position of the vehicle (Ahmed et al. 2015). An important survey on the evolution and different solutions of railway network condition monitoring in the past decades with strong recommendation on how effective the use of strain gauges, accelerometers contributes in speculating train stopping length contrast to the use of optical fibers was further assessed under simulated and practical environments. The authors enumerate how the work of many researchers has contributed in boosting the design and maintenance activities in the rolling stock industry (Georges et al. 2015; Weston et al. 2015). Anap et al. (2016) designed and constructed an intelligent device to assist railway users in India on how to prevent train derailment within their rolling stock network. The tool outperforms its quality through the recognition of flames, water increment and physical obstacles found on the railway line using smart sensing elements. Their design incorporates the use of an ARM7 Microcontroller for the recieving and convention of analogue sensor reading into digital signals, a GSM unit to facilitate communication between the train, operator and top management on train stoppage as undesired scenario is identified during operation. An advance tool that intelligently observe the phase changes of railway component directly linked to train accidents was later inaugurated with reading gain from infrared, piezo and reed sensor. The novel device presented good quality, as it has features capable of estimating rail uncertainties, vehicle motion and availability of obstacles on the railway network using ATmega8 microcontroller for analogue to digital interpretation. For constant follow up by operator and management, the model integrates an LCD (liquid crystal display) module, Motor Leds and Buzzers as output units (Deepika et al. 2017). A collision protective system that has the quality to locate any hindrance using ultrasonic sensing readings, an Arduino microcontroller and a radar unit for the discovery of lengthy item on railway line using Proteus software showcases good attitude by characterise train exact location, velocity and interval using radio display signals to the operator and management in case of undesired circumstancies (Pavithra et al. 2019).

Despite the esteem interest and contribution from the above authors on the design, manufacturing and authentication of the monitoring tools, current challenges on train rapidity and fast repair intercession in remote areas do not require engineers and researchers to restrict their thinking on active measures and neglecting proactive measures. The expansion on innovative concepts for clever observation that does not restrict only on failure discovery and extraction, but is capable of combining the former with proactive intercession concepts such as RUL (Remaining Useful Life) estimation of individual components, the enforcement of possible repair and after damage action which protect infrastructure, travelers and freight is hugely needed. Therefore, the goal of this research paper is to develop with application a strategy that will guide engineers on the design, manufacturing, installation and exploration of an intelligent observation tool that is going to assist rolling stock operator in Cameroon and beyond the opportunity to monitor the degradation nature of train-track components. Therefore, to improve the safety of goods, passengers, infrastructure closer to the railway lines and also the welfare of the entire network. This paper is segregated from an introduction situating the state of arts on current methods used in monitoring train-track maintenance, the suggested methodology suitable to develop a safety monitoring tool with application to the train-track holding system. Lastly, the conclusion and future research programs.

2   Methodology

In practice, the damaged pattern of every component within a system defers even when they have equal material properties and operating under the same environmental conditions. The existing maintenance procedures and action plan developed to manage train-track systems in Cameroon and beyond mostly focused on complete downtime before repair interventions. Therefore, increase in the duration required to detect, isolate and carry out repair action on a given train or track along the network has been a challenging issue with human understanding. To identify the behavior of every component during field exploitation is of huge importance to company owners, engineers and researchers. This will help in reducing sudden break down, predict duration of possible failures and also prepare the maintenance engineer on the availability of spare parts. The need for an intelligent system is heavily required in other to reduce the cost of maintenance, guide the process of repairs, optimize the availability of spare parts and also the reliability of the train on the track. Figure 1 below is an extract that portrays the various stages and necessary tools to be used in the design and implementation of the Intelligent Observation Tool (IOT) platform. Segregating from the knowledge of the system that combines both inductive and deductive technologies to a global technique in referencing of material for construction. The modeling and simulation software for numerical assessment of the IOT before the manufacturing stage. An online observation platform for human interpretation with full authentication in the railway industry. Figures 2, 3, 4, 5 and 6 are elaborated organigrams that expresses how the IOT is scientifically developed for real time exploitation.

2.1   Knowledge of the System

This panel outlines the state of affair of the system to be observed. It grants the ability to the user to identify the system in question, give it required contribution, normal operating condition, mission and reactions to their working environment through an inductive/deductive technique. Regarding the rolling stock system, an inductive technology center on FME has been adopted as it grants the posibility to the developper to distinguish from component to human mistake which contains features that examine inclusively the internal and external state of affair related to failures, their effect and suggested mitigating actions (Chunling et al. 2016). To rank these failures, the Fault Tree Deductive Technique (FTDT) has been appraised. It's going grant the developper the ability to differentiate in a descending order, collective from non-collective failures

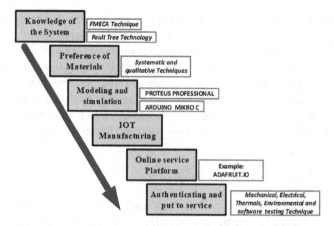

Fig. 1. Suggested methodology for intelligent base maintenance

either under linear or nonlinear nature of the system to be observed. To protect the safe mode of the train-track system, the FTDT focuses on a specific unpleasant happening, ranking this happening and designating an approach that is suitable to judge its causes. The happenings are then isolated and showcased on a graphical model using boolen operations to give the connection joining this happening and their hierarchy on the system. Figure 2 is the nature of FTDT executed to distinguish and perform miss match ranking of the systems using boolen operators (logic gates). The number of layers on the fault tree and the evolution of happenings depend on the size of the system (layer 1 to layer N). The technology shows the logical branches from a single fault at the summit of the tree to the origin of the cause(s) at the foot of the tree. Fault tree does not showcase all achievable deterioration state of affairs for the observable components in the precise system, but accommodate at most those deteriorations style whose survival donate to the existence of the happening at the summit for analysis and judgement for variation and insertion.

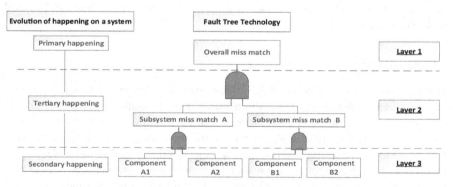

Fig. 2. The adopted approach for fault classification for rolling stock system

2.2 Preference of Components

One of the most complex event in the development of intelligent engineering systems is setting an appropriate preference for the components to be used. Therefore, in practice, there are in need of special material for their manufacturing, compatibility regarding different operating environment and the quality of the results requesting from them. The quality control techniques adopted in estimating if the choosen components match the general specification of the intelligent tool before further usage involves reason methodically in resolutions, segregate from one component and complete before a new component, indept study about the property of a material to formulate essential working conditions of the components, detail formulate of all the requirements of the component in question, check the consistency of the threshold signatures and test components that can operate within this signatories, and lastly give preferences on single components not on entire system level. Moreover, the most difficult activity on the quality control activity is designating the specifications of components through material preference criteria as the quality of any engineering system is centered on the state of affair of the individual components material properties. However, the preference of material adopted in selecting suitable components for this work relies on the cost of production, availability in the market, cost of usage, suitably for specific working conditions, size and shape, tolerancies, weight, process of production, privilege to failure, precision, stability, response time and external environmental influences. Figure 3 is an extract that summaries the interconnectivity within the considerable factors use in selecting material for constructing the IOT before field exploitation.

2.3 Modeling, Simulation and Manufacturing of the IOT

Figure 4a shows the suggested procedure adopted in modeling and simulating the IOT using Proteus professional software and Micro C Pro. Proteus is used for circuit design, simulation and debugging while Micro C Pro for developing the software code. For analysis and validation through human understanding, the Arduino IDE software is used to program the microcontrollers. After including the hardware peripherals and constructing the electronic circuit, next step is to test its working situation and debug if (when) it does not. The entire embedded system should be simulated at the press of a button and then interact with it in real time using light emitting diode (LED), LCD, switches and buttons on screen displays. Finally, when the testing and debugging is complete, next is to transfer the program onto the hardware after forming for practical authentication and put to service on the railway network. Figure 4b is a flow chart that shows the procedure respected in manufacturing the intelligent tool. The IOT is assembled using electromechanical forming techniques. The best performance of the IOT depends on the software package used. The operator simply plugs in the programming cable, configures the program and then presses a button to transfer the software program from the Proteus model to the hardware intelligent tool. Depending on the relative knowledge about programming languages, the user may also want to write code and control the hardware at a lower level. Finally, when the IOT has been manufactured in real-time, and the program has been deployed and tested, the final step is to authenticate the tool by implementing on a rolling stock holding system with strict considerations on the observation Platform.

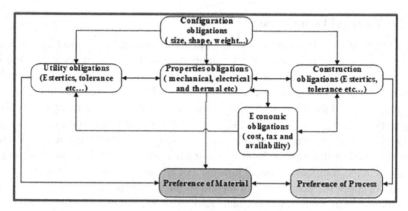

Fig. 3. Suggested obligations to be use for material preference IOT

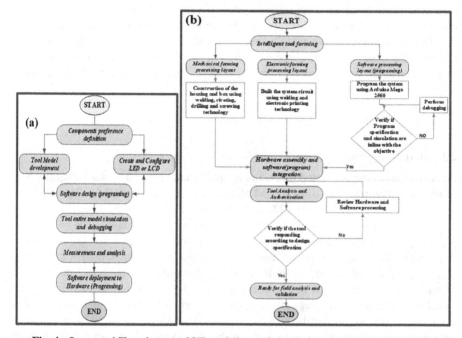

Fig. 4. Suggested Flowchart: (a) IOT modeling and simulating, (b) IOT Manufacturing

2.4 Observation Platform Development

One of the key ideas in this research is to follow up the attitude of railway systems both on city sites and remote areas. Human intervention and follow up is very difficult when a breakdown or collision occurs in remote areas. Therefore, a platform for distance communication is of huge interest. Figure 5 is a flow chart for the suggested procedure used to build the offline/online service platform. After the production of the IOT, the GPS/GSM and ESP module with microcontroller is added and the SIM card inserted (built system), powering on and initialise the GPS/GSM module, installing all programmable libraries, and also connect antennas for both GPS and GSM to verify if it can receive coordinates, able to receive and send SMS. Programming for both microcontroller and sim808 GPS/GSM module using Arduino IDE software, then the first phase of testing should be established with esteem checking of program for possible errors and corrections. For practical implementation of the online observation module, an iCloud service platform is used since it has the quality to receive from hardware systems, sending, display, storing and then retrieve technical readings that explain the attitude of each component on the entire train-track system via internet connection. Therefore, distance monitoring is further achieved through the design of a mobile app and a webpage intalled in phones/computers.

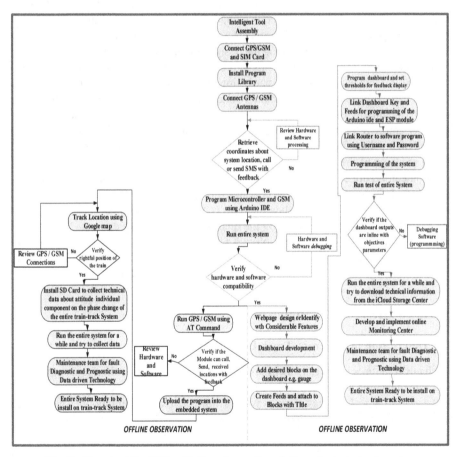

Fig. 5. Flowchart for Offline/Online observation platform for train-track system

2.5 Implementation of the Intelligent Observation Tool

Upon completion of the observation platform, to implement the IOT for condition base observation of railway systems requires indept authentication as the system will operate in both city sites and remote areas. Thus the working situation of the train generates several effects that are not favorable for the smooth testing and running of intelligence devices since they are required to operate with high precession, accuracy stability and robustness. Railway operators should place some strict considerations on mechanical, electrical, thermal and environmental pollutions during usage. To mitigate these pollutants, the following authentications are to be established with strict consideration on international standards and national regulations governing the installation and smooth running of IOT devices mounted on railway systems. The authentications processes should distinguish from hardware and software analysis in accordance to risk judgement and management, safety prerequisite and hazardous relating health conditions of the operators. There two distingue forms of testing adopted for the suggested IOT include the production tests to be done during the design and manufacturing phase to appreciate the goodness of individual components in relation to software requirements. A qualification test is executed to verify the perfection of the manufactured prototype hardware and software utilities on a train-track network that include electrical test which duty is to certify the quality of the cabling, printed circuit board (PCB), protect the wiring and hardness, improve on the selection of electronic components, physical injury, shocks, low and high voltage minimization etc. The functionality test, it aims at evaluating if the output readings of the IOT device grant quality results as in real-time, and if not optimisation can be done on the quality of the software. Mechanical test relating to stress analysis and vibration tests shall be conducted to determine the required resonance frequency the IOT can withstand when the train is on motion. The quality of any onboard condition monitoring device relies on the quality of its sensoring devices. Thermal and environmental test center on the evolution temperature, humidity, flow rate, pressure differencies and the manner of which the heat or cool energy is diffused (conduction, conversion and emission) both internal and external surfaces of the IOT (Fig. 6).

3 Application of the Suggested Strategy

3.1 Description of the Train-Track Holding System

Mechanical failures in the railway industry account for 44.7% to wheelset components, 36.7% to brake unit and 18.6% to the chassis. However, fatigue contributes to about 90% of these mechanical failures in railway, maritime, aerospace, automobile, processing and other related industries. The aim of this section is to put to practice the above suggested technology in other to follow-up the nature and evolution of fatigue related depreciations applicable to the train-track holding components. The train track holding system to be cross-examined. It involves an axel mounted 50CrV4 chromium vanadium steel suspension springs regularly exploited in the rolling stock sector in Cameroon. It portrays good qualities in shock resistant, high toughness and with its fatigue limits for reverses tension and torsion as $\left(\sigma_{-1}^T\right)_s = 482.63\,\text{MPa}$ and $\left(\tau_{-1}^T\right)_s = 278.64.65\,\text{MPa}$ single handedly, young modulus $\left(E^T\right)_s = 207000\,\text{MPa}$, modulus of rigidity $\left(G^T\right)_s =$

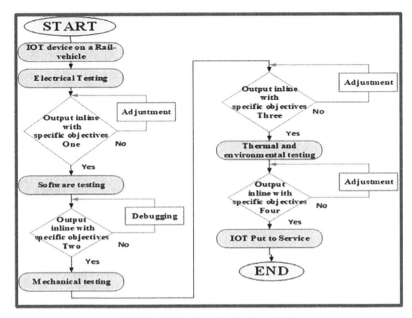

Fig. 6. IOT authenticating flow chart

79300 MPa, density $(\rho^T)_s$ = 7860 kg/m³ and poison ratio $(\vartheta)_s$ = 0.29 (Pavan 2013). Meanwhile, the track holding ingredients constitutes a **1084 structural medium carbon steel rail and hot rolled structural sleeper with** fatigue limits for completely reverses tension and torsion as $(\sigma^T_{-1})_R$ = 361.94 MPa and $(\tau^T_{-1})_R$ = 208.84 MPa². The UIC ballast with density of 2400 kg/m³, ultimate tensile stress 22 MPa, maximum allowable stress 130 MPa and Young modulus 200 MPa and poison ratio 0.25. Table 1 is an extract that portrays the failure mode effect analysis of the train track holding components subject to mechanical failures caused by multiaxial fatigue using numerical simulation study and literature. The attitude of mismatch for every given components has been attributed a code which is significantly link to the type, nature and mitigating action during field exploitation of the rolling stock system components.

Globally, the term threshold is a familiar statement used in the context of intelligence base maintenance. It distinguishes the state of affairs of any industrial system. Considered as an interval or value above which the train-track holding systems are going to record a failure and below or within which no failure is going to be recorded. Regarding the nature of affairs of our holding system, threshold signals are obtained when Eqs. 1 and 2 are simulated using system running variables. These threshold signals which interpret the quality when running the train-track holding systems are then used by the IOT maintenance tool to derivate and report at every given instance the deterioration rate from good state. Since our duty is to establish a stress-train oriented technique that will grant us the possibility to discover fatigue damage attitudes and a pattern to speculate the service life of mechanical parts put through recurrent loading scenarios, this panel

---

[2] British steel, 2020.

Table 1. Train-Track system decomposition matrix using FMEC Technology.

Train-Track System					
Ref	Holding System				
Designation Fault Code	Mission statement	Miss match attitude	Course of miss match	Effect of miss matches	Corrective plan
Suspension system (IS or OS or ES)	The duty of the suspension is to protect the wheelset and riding comfort of humans and freight	Crack and or broken axel A	Heavy stresses and above yield stresses	Noice and heavy vibration Reduces the fatigue life of the axel	Welding or replacement
		Buckle fracture B	Fatigue stresses	Spring deformation and miss alignments Reduces the fatigue life of the suspension	Replace according to UIC standards
		Deformed springs C	Heavy Fatigue stresses gain from wheel/rail irregularities Etc	Heavy vibration and discomfort to travellers and their goods Reduces the fatigue life of the suspension	
		Broken helical springs D	Heavy Fatigue stresses gain from wheel/rail irregularities Etc	Heavy vibration and discomfort to travellers and their goods Train derailment due to wheel unbalance	
Rail (R)	The rails provide smooth running surfaces for the train wheels and guide the wheel sets in the direction of the track. It also accommodate the wheel loads and distribute these loads over the sleepers	Rail Cracks	Heavy shear stresses gain from wheel/rail dynamic loading	Heavy material fatigue	Replace the rail

(*continued*)

Table 1. (*continued*)

Train-Track System					
Ref	Holding System				
Designation Fault Code	Mission statement	Miss match attitude	Course of miss match	Effect of miss matches	Corrective plan
		Rail deformation and Shear A		Heavy vibration Discomfort to travellers and their goods Train derailment due to wheel unbalance Wheel/rail contact misalignment Reduces the fatigue life of the rail and entired track components	Replace and alignment according to UIC standards
		Head Checks and Squats (RCF) B	Heavy material Fatigue	Train derailment due to wheel unbalance Reduces the fatigue life of the rail and entired track components	Control wheel/rail profile Reduce axel load and speed. Or Replace and alignment according to UIC standards
		Wear and Tear (corrugation) C	Heavy blow on the rail gain from wheel jumping Heavy Fatigue stresses	Reduces the fatigue life of the rail Wheel/rail contact misalignment Train derailment due to wheel unbalance Reduces the fatigue life of the rail and entired track components	Track alignment Replace the rail

Table 1. (*continued*)

Train-Track System					
Ref	Holding System				
Designation Fault Code	Mission statement	Miss match attitude	Course of miss match	Effect of miss matches	Corrective plan
Sleeper (S)	The main functions of these sleepers are to transfer and distribute the wheel loads transferred by the rails and fastening system to the supporting ballast, fix the track gauge, maintain adequate rail	Bending and fracture Cracks A	Dynamic loading gain from rail Irregularities Imperfection within wheel/rail contact Variation of track resonance	Reduces the fatigue life of the sleepers and also reduces mechanical resistance of the entire track Reduces the ability of the entire tract withstand dynamic stresses	Replace according to UIC standards
		Split Concrete Sleeper	Heavy stresses gain from rail Irregularities Lack/shortage of lubricant	Rail deformation and misalignment	
		Damaged Concrete Bearers B		Increase track resonances Reduces the fatigue life of the sleeper and entired track components	
		Abrasion C	Shrinkages due to drop in moisture content	Heavy stresses build up and possible Rupture of sleepers	
Ballast (B)	Provides a medium for uniformly distribution of loads transmitted via the sleepers from dynamic rail loading due to trafficking into the subgrade	Crack in Ballast A	Heavy repeated train loading	Reduces the fatigue life of the ballast	Maintain according to UIC standards

(*continued*)

Table 1. (*continued*)

Train-Track System					
Ref	Holding System				
Designation Fault Code	Mission statement	Miss match attitude	Course of miss match	Effect of miss matches	Corrective plan
		Plastic Deformation B	Heavy impact of axle load and wheel/rail irregularities Fines fill void developed with the aggregates		
		Shear Failure C		Reduces the fatigue life of the ballast Reduces rail stability	

stipulates a multi-axial recurrent stress-strain state series and put to service a unique pattern that serves as the multi-axial cycle counting identity, select from ltterature a unique multiaxial fatigue life criterion that favors the degradation parameter influenced either by external issues or internal stresses subdued to evaluative conditions, and lastly identify the service duration of every component in direct relation to their fatigue life cycle (Eq. 1) will be used to estimate the number of cycles for train holding components and Eq. 2 for the track components. Table 2. is an extract that showcases the characteristic properties adopted for estimating the required number of cycles needed with respect to their respective design periods (years).

$$(N)_i = (3600 * T_D * T_P * T_W * T_{NW} * R_L)/(T_N * T_S) \tag{1}$$

$$\left(N^T\right)_i = (3600 * T_D * T_{PN} * T_W * T_{NW})/(T_N * T_S) \tag{2}$$

where;

T_D:: allowable working duration(years)for each vehicle or track component
T_P: number of trips per day for a unique train
T_{PN}: number of train passes per day
T_W: number of a unique train travel per week
T_N: number of weeks a unique train travel per year
R_L:: length of the railroad(KM)
T_S: Train speed

The number of estimated cycles required for the train holding components defers from that of the track because train holding components are design to be used in a short duration as compare to the track components. Table 3 depicts the threshold values adopted for the developments of the IOT in this work to aid smooth active and proactive

Table 2. Properties adopted for estimating the required number of cycles $\left(N^{T}\right)_{i}$

Ref	Parameters	Train Components	Track Components	SI Units
1	TP	2	2	
2	TD	12	15	Years
3	TPN		8	
4	TW	4	4	
5	TNW	52	52	
6	RL	263		
7	TS	40	40	Km/h
8	TN	0.1	0.01	Seconds

maintenance activities on the holding system during real time exploitation as multiaxial fatigue failure and depreciation are to be investigated. Figure 7 is an extract that portrays the manner in which the failure due to fatigue for the train track holding system same to their increment. The Fault Tree analysis is extrapolated at first hand using the events showcased in the cause-effect analysis Table 3. This table expresses a detail on every related event associated to fatigue failures of the rolling stock holding components during field evaluation. Where the A, B, C, D…. Signifies specific causes related to a given component effect that enables a given failure that may lead to full fatigue damage and possible derailment of the entired system. The first layer of the fault tree expresses the highest-level at which possible downtime or train accident can occur when we have a combination of fatigue damage either from the train and/or the track. The second layer further separate the track/train subsystem relative fatigue failure and lastly, the third layer portrays the exact components that have huge contributions to the full fatigue damage and related accidents cause by derailment of the train from its track.

Rolling stock activities are the most delicate processes as far as train-track holding dynamics are concerned. The preference of material to be used for the IOT devices must integrate all the required working conditions of the rolling stock. This is going to be achieved when the black box nature of the sensor readings that defines the natural state of the holding system is transformed using if then statement for human understanding using on/off line interpretative display subsystems. Distinguished as hardware and software subsystems, the IOT device intergrates the following hardware modules; Data tracking, location tracking and SMS, Data storage, Power supply, indicating, internet, display and communication module and service center. Figure 8 shows how these hardware modules interact within themselves to perform the desired function requested from the suggested IOT devices when operating train track holding component. The software module involves programmable languages that will associate or link all hardware components to function and achieve a unique goal as it involves modeling and simulation of the IOT in a virtual environment before deployment in real time hardware system.

Table 3. Adopted threshold parameters for the suggested IOT

Train Track Holding System				
Components		Thresholds		
		Diagnostic (MPa)		Prognostic (Cycles)
Vehicle	Inner Spring	$\left(\tau^T_{hhmax}\right)_{is}$	$\leq 1003.76MPa$	3.50E + 06
		$\left(\tau^T_{hhmin}\right)_{is}$	$\geq 796.83MPa$	
	Outer Spring	$\left(\tau^T_{hhmax}\right)_{os}$	$\leq 296.95MPa$	3.50E + 06
		$\left(\tau^T_{hhmin}\right)_{os}$	$\geq 234.68MPa$	
	Edge Spring	$\left(\tau^T_{hhmax}\right)_{es}$	$\leq 214.49MPa$	3.50E + 06
		$\left(\tau^T_{hhmin}\right)_{es}$	$\geq 164.81MPa$	
Track	Rail	$\left(\tau^T_{hhmax}\right)_{R}$	$\leq 1497.07MPa$	240.0e + 9
		$\left(\tau^T_{hhmin}\right)_{R}$	$\geq 1259.41MPa$	
	Sleepers	$\left(\tau^T_{hhmax}\right)_{Sp}$	$\leq 1155.21MPa$	240.0e + 9
		$\left(\tau^T_{hhmin}\right)_{Sp}$	$\geq 58.32MPa$	
	Ballast	$\left(\tau^T_{hhmax}\right)_{B}$	$\leq 130MPa$	240.0e + 9
		$\left(\tau^T_{hhmin}\right)_{B}$	$\geq 22MPa$	

The suggested IOT for rolling stock condition monitoring intergrates data tracking sensing elements that has the ability to isolate physical quantities such as the minimum and maximum loading nature within components and the remaining useful life due to fatigue of respective component in months. The technical reading gained from these sensing elements works at a voltage that is compatible to trigger the interpritation of control and location tracking modules for human understanding through offline display module and the online communication modules via mobile network and wireless connections. The actual interpreted sensing readings from the control units is further accumulated in the off line data storage module and an online icloud account embedded in the communication modules (service center and mobile phone). As an intelligent electronic system, the entire IOT device is energised using an electric power supply module with strict considerations to the quality of the input electrical signals required by individual components. The hidden detail indicates the wireless nature within connection of the respective modules of the system during manufacturing, usage and maintenance.

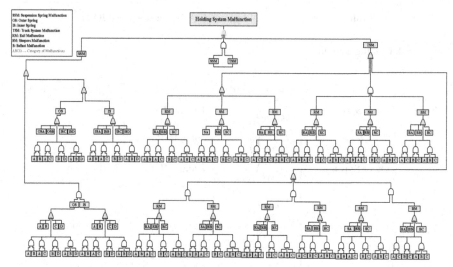

Fig. 7. Connection between system evolution and fault tree hierarchy for the Train-Track holding system

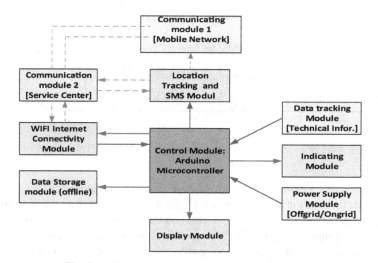

Fig. 8. IOT hardware interconnectivity block diagram

The Data Tracking Module: This module involves fatigue sensing, temperature sensing and the GPS elements. The function of these sensors is to provide the control module the attitude of individual components under the effect of fatigue stresses when put through changeable loading nature of the train and track holding systems at every instance with serverity in real-time. While the job of the GPS is focused on the exact position of the fault on the holding system components and a unique location of the entire train along the railroad network. The Ni FS Al 1100 sensor that constitute a stainless steel wire of thickness 0.0127 mm, analogue to digital signal converter, can resist a stress level greater than 919 MPa, young modulus of 200GPa and temperature rate of [−55 to 150] ^{0} C is adopted for fatigue damage estimation. The LM35 temperature sensor is to give exact measurement on how hot or cold the IOT internal and external components operate in real time. The LM35 is exactness coordinated circuit temperature sensors, whose field voltage is directly related to Celsius temperature. The LM35 is evaluate to work within a range of [−55 to 150] ^{0} C and a voltage rage [0–5.5] V which is compatible to that of the arduino microcontroller.

The Control Module: This module recieves technical readings that explains the attitude of individual components in a hidden nature from the data tracking module in analogues manner, convert to digital form for human comprehension in real time. Made of an Arduino Mega 2560 microcontroller, this module thus indicates the current state of every component and perhaps enforce the required maintenance action to be performed in real time. It is an open source programmable circuit board that can be integrated into the observation of both linear and nonlinear systems. This board contains a microcontroller which is able to be programmed to sense and control objects in the physical world. By responding to sensors and inputs, the Arduino is able to interact with a large array of outputs such as LEDs, displays and the data that the Arduino reads from a sensor as an input. Arduino MEGA 2560 have more sketch memory and RAM, with 54 digital I/O pins, 16 analogue inputs than the Arduino UNO with just 14 digital input/output pins [pins 0–13]. Within this research work, we are to receive the variation of sensor readings about nature of stresses, exact damage component, fatigue service life, IOT internal and external temperature nature, frequency of vibration, connect with GPS to get current location, interpret the information and send to the display unit and mobile phones for human understanding through GSM module and data storage for future access. The biggest advantage of Arduino is its ready-to-use structure, since they come in a complete package including a 5V voltage regulator, a burner, an oscillator, a microcontroller, serial communication interface, LED and headers for the connections.

The Location Tracking and SMS Module: Isolate by precision the unique position of the train along the railroad network and thus the location of failures or possible degradation rate of the holding system respective components using digital technical information's gained from the control module. As an offline approach, human comprehension is done using a mobile communication network. Made of SIM808 technology, it is a complete Quad-Band GSM/GPRS module which combines GPS technology for satellite navigation and a working voltage of [5.0 to 12] V. It has a SIM application toolkit where SIM is going to be for simcard insertion. The compact design which integrates GPRS and GPS in a SMT package significantly saves both time and cost for one to develop GPS enabled applications. Featuring an industry-standard interface and GPS function, it allows variable assets to be tracked seamlessly at any location and anytime with signal coverage. Further, it can send GPRS data (HTTP), receives GPS data, send and receive SMS messages and also capable of operating as a passive and active tracker. Passive because it stores technical sensor readings gained from the Arduino microcontroller such as GPS location, speed, heading and other trigger events. Once the monitoring device return to a predetermined point, the device is removed and the data downloaded to a computer for evaluation. The active trackers also collect the same information but mostly transmit the technical readings in real-time via cellular or satellite networks to a computer or service centre for evaluation. This technology is of high value because even in the absence of internet connection technical readings can still be obtained offline for evaluation in future need by the help of a mobile network communication system via SMS sent to the IOT device. Meaning if the operator needs to know the exact state of the entire holding system of a specific railcar, they need to send an SMS to the IOT through the number of the Simcard installed in SIM808 module, an automatic feedback SMS will be recieved on current status, and also the coodinates about the latitude and longitude which can be used to track the unique location of the train using Google Map. This GPS antenna draws about 10mA and will give you an additional 28 dB of gain. It got a 5-m-long cable so it will easily reach wherever it is needed to. The antenna is magnetic so it will stick to the top of a car or truck or any other steel structure. Its operating frequency range is $[1575.42^{\pm 1.023}]$ MHz and voltage range is [2.5 to 5.5] V and corresponding current range is [6.6 to 16.6] mA. With or without the presence of a clear sky it is capable of capturing the satellite. GPS Down/Up converter used for very long cable runs. This GPS antenna that receives the GPS signal, converts it to a lower frequency which is then sent down the cable. Next to the GPS receiver is an up converter that converts the signal back to the original frequency and delivers it to the GPS receiver and a response time of $\leq 2.0]$ ms. GSM (Global System for Mobile Communications) Module are dependent on antennas. The antenna is what allows communications signals to be sent and received. The antenna that we have used in our work provides operation at both GSM Quad Band Frequency with + 2dB gain. This antenna operates in Quad Band [890/960, 1710/1880] MHz Frequencies and its Omni-directional.

The Data Storage Module: Like other storage devices, this module is made of a Virtuabotix SD Card with SanDisk memory. This SD Card is compatible to the Arduino UNO for the accumulation of large quantity of technical readings and can be used for a broad range of applications from scientific perspective to statistical outreach outdoor. With an operating voltage of [3.3 to 5.0] V DC, easy wiring to any microcontroller. The technical sensor reading gain from the control module is stored offline on site using this SD card for future use (either for failure discovery or RUL speculation of the entire train track holding components and even the entired system). Within which VCC pin delivers power to the module and thus connected to 5V pin on the Arduino, meanwhile GND is also connected to the earth pin Arduino. The Master in Slave Out (MISO) is a serial peripheral interface (*SPI*) output from the SD Card Module. While the Master out slave IN (MOSI) is serial peripheral interface input to the SD Card Module. A Serial Clock (SCK) pin for the acceptance of clock pulses which synchronizes data transmission generated by Arduino. Finally, the Slave Select (SS) pin used to enable and disable specific devices on SPI bus by Arduino (Master). A DS3231 RTC precision low cost accurately real time clock chip that manages all time keeping functions is use for recording the time at which data was logged into the SD card. The date of the month is automatically adjusted for months with fewer than 31 days, including corrections for leap year (valid up to 2100).

The Display Module: This model guides the user with quality interpritation about the attitude of the train track holding components in real time. Made of a 20 × 4 liquid crystal display module, the device exhibits technical information visually on a screen processed from the Arduino microcontroller. It utilizes a I2C interface which means fewer pins (4 pins) are necessary to use this product than would be needed with a regular 16 × 2 LCD display. In this research work, information concerning the state of the rail, sleepers and springs and their current operation being performed by the IOT devices main module is exhibited to the operator via the LCD. The notation 20 × 4 denotes the fact that the LCD has the ability to exhibit technical information in 80 characters.

The Indicating Module: It comprises of both Light Emitting Diode (LED) and an alarm used to alert the driver or operator of the status of the system. The RGB LED is adopted in this section as it shares a common anode or cathode to set their color. It is made up of three internal LEDs (red, green, and blue) that when combined gives rise to every type of output color. In order to give rise to many colors, we need to set the intensity of each internal LED and combine the three color outputs. Made up of three colors that blink continuously till the operator is notified on the actual state of that system and they draw significantly less current than any other form of bulb. The alarm is placed at the disposal of both the operator and the control center; they produce significant noise or sirens that calls for server attention in conditions where a failure or downtime of the holding system and also when the components of the hardware section of IOT is malfunctioning. The continuation of this section will be associated to the Bursa type alarm for noise generation and common cathode LED.

The Power Supply Unit: This comprises the power cable and its accessories. It functions to provide the necessary electric power needed for the efficient functioning of the system components. Upon installation on the rail vehicle, the power supply will include the train battery for Ongrid and an accumulator for Offgrid purpose (in case of train failure). The train battery is used to charge the Offgrid accumulator or alternative sources such as Solar plants. The Arduino UNO needs a power source for it to operate and can be powered in a variety of ways. We can do so by connecting the board directly to a computer via a USB cable, USB cable which is also used to upload the program to the board. Because we want our research to be mobile, we considered using a 9V battery pack. The last method would be to use a 9V AC power supply. Battery will serve the purpose of accumulator and power the system when need arises. It is rechargeable and has maintenance-free operation and low discharge functionality as lead acid battery of 12V.

The WiFi Connection Module: This module grants the possibility of the IOT control system to connect with the communication module within city centers and remote areas to track the status and location of the rail vehicle. A Low cost ESP8266 module is adopted in this section as it allows microcontrollers such as Arduino to connect to a WiFi network and make simple TCP/IP connections using hayes-style commands, and also can be programmed like any other Arduino device. It operating voltage (VCC) is of the range [+3.3 to 3.6] V and a GND of [0] V, RX/TX data receiver and transmitters which is compatible to the setup of Arduino technology.

The Communication Module: Is a service center that involves a computer and mobile phone networking systems made of ESP8266 and SIM808 module. The link between the service center and the mobile phone with the IOT mounted on the train is done both off/on line. For the online connectivity, the service center also known as the control room of the rail way network is made up of series of computers interconnected together to interprete the status of the train-track system using an online iCloud service platform. The online app grants the ability to the users to create an individual account that will give them the access in monitoring the dashboards that shows measurable parameters. It also grants the quality in downloading technical readings that expresses the behavior of the holding system in real time. For the offline connectivity, a mobile telephone device that is capable of communicating with the GPS/GSM module to receive updates and display of any happenings faults or reminder of possible maintenance in the system. It is portable and capable of storing data and connecting to the internet to track exact location. Within the context of this research, this mode of communication with the IOT entails the offline and online approach. Regarding offline communication, the user will be able to send an SMS to the IOT device through the number of the SIM Card installed in the SIM808 Module. A feedback on the status of individual components will be recieved by the user with coodinates on the unique location of the train on the railroad network. This coodinates should be copied and displayed on Google map to track the exact location either on city sites or remote areas. To appraise the full version of the IOT, Fig. 9 is the hardware architectural diagram that portrays how the modules should be connected within each other during field development. The sensors for the track components should be segregated and labeled contrary to that of the train in other to reduce further complexity during maintenance of the IOT. Therefore, enables appropriate means of communication within the maintenance intervention team on site and the control room using a wireless mobile networking system.

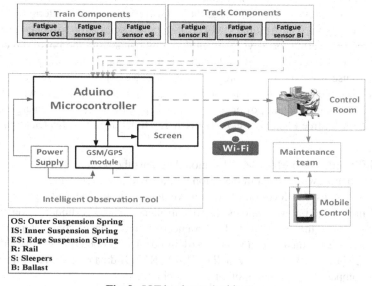

Fig. 9. IOT hardware Architecture

Figure 10 is the simulated model that demostrate detailly the various modules and working principle of the suggested intelligent observation tool when call to perform failure discovery and extraction. As the train is on motion, the stress sensors (OS, IS,

ES, R, S, B) will identify the level of stresses for every component and display their results on the LCD screen. The microcontrollers received the signals from the sensors and calculate the damage index using Fogue fatigue damage criterion. The calculated damage index is contrasted with the thresholds index ($E_{FB} = 1$) to generate residual signals and displayed on the LCD panel. Fault is discovered when the calculated damage index is greater than the threshold damage index. Fault is segregated when the values estimated stresses for every individual component as opposed to the threshold as shown on the LCD display module. Practical demonstration is available for appraisal.

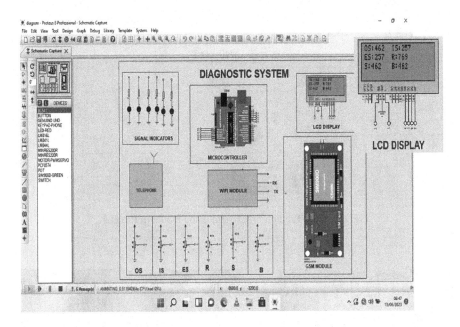

Fig. 10. Fault discovery and segregation IOT simulated model in Proteus

Figure 12 is the simulated model that demostrate how prognostics are done. After calculating the diagnostic index using fugue criterion and the Paris-miner cumulative damage theory, the number of cycles (N) for every respective component are being estimated and display on cycle counting visualization panel. The calculated damage index and remaining useful life (RUL in years) are contrasted with their respective thresholds values to generate residual signals. Fault prognostic is achieved when the calculated damage index is greater than the threshold index and its respective raining useful life below the it threshold RUL as shown on the duration visualization counter (track and suspension springs. Practical demonstration is available for understating. Figure 11 is the prototype version of the suggested maintenance observation device awaiting real time exploitation with individual components link to each other. The good aspect of this devices is its ability to control the on and off of the train, verifies the goodness of all operating parameters before any train travel, predict the remaining useful fatigue life of various holding components using cycle counting parameters, set a damage threshold value for fault discovery and segregation during field exploitation. Meanwhile, previous researchers focused on estimating rail uncertainties, vehicle motion, availability of obstacles on the railway, and the discovery of lengthy item (Deepika et al. 2017; Pavithra et al. 2019).

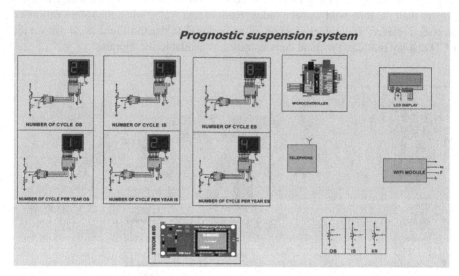

Fig. 11. Fault Prediction IOT simulated model in Proteus

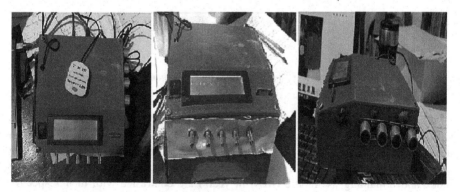

Fig. 12. Prototype of the Suggested intelligent observation tool

4 Conclusion

This portion of research has focused on suggesting a strategy which is going to aid maintenance personnel to establish a monitoring platform suitable to executing repairs on train-track holding components with application. A unique methodology that showcases the various steps required to put to action the intelligent observation tool has been elaborated. Segregated from knowledge about the observe system, preference of material, modeling and simulation, tool forming, online service platform, authenticating and put to service. A block diagram that clarifies how the IOT is inter-connected using different modules was further showcased with related material preferences. Though the full simulated model of the IOT showcases esteem interrelated qualities during and after prototype construction, field evaluation and application is still our object of interest in future. As it will aid rolling stock and other industries to appraised the novel strategies on one hand, and also grant an appraisal for the suggested intelligent observation tool for real time expansion worldwide. The furture of this research shall focus on the development of a multiaxial fatigue recording sensor, an extension of the novel methodology for full time mitigation of human inconsistence relating to the safety of passengers, welfare of freights and protection of the entire train-track infrastructure in Cameroon and beyond.

References

Pavithra, K., Tamil, S., Kowsalya, M., Dinesh, B.B.: Railway track monitoring and accident avoiding system. Int. J. Eng. Res. Technol. (IJERT), ISSN: 2278–0181 (2019)

Lezin, M.S., He, X., Robert, E.M.: Analytical model of underground train induced vibrations on nearby building structures in Cameroon: assessment and prediction. Leonardo Electron. J. Pract. Technol. **12**, 63–82 (2013). ISSN 1583–1078

Tse, S.A., Wolfgang, N., Bertin, S., Olivier, G., Tibi, B.: A proposed scheme for fault discovery and extraction using ANFIS: application to train braking system. Stud. Eng. Technol. **7**(1), 48–63 (2020). ISSN 2330–2038 E-ISSN 2330–2046

Sparthan, T., Nzie, W., Sohfotsing, B., Beda, T., Garro O.: A valorized scheme for failure prediction using ANFIS: application to train track breaking system. Open J. Appl. Sci. **10**, 732–757 (2020)

Darell, S., Christopher, B.: Design of a smart sensor system for monitoring railcar braking system. High-Speed Rail IDEA Project **51** (2008)

Chunling, G.: CRH 3 brake system failure modes, effects and critical analysis. In: 2nd Workshop on Advanced Research and Technology in Industry Applications (2016)

Weston, P., Roberts, C., Yeo, G., Stewart, E.: Perspectives on railway track geometry condition monitoring from in-service railway vehicles. Veh. Syst. Dyn. **53**(7), 1063–1091 (2015)

Deepika, G.J., Gurpreet, K., Neha, K., Suruchi, R., Sonal, D., Mahendra, S.M.: Railway accident monitoring. Int. J. Recent Innov. Trends Comput. Commun.**5**(5), 704–706 (2019). ISSN: 2321-8169

Tsunashima, H., Naganuma, Y., Akira, M., Takeshi, M., Hirotaka, M.: Condition monitoring of railway track using in-service vehicle. In: Perpinya, X. (ed.) Reliability and Safety in Railway (2012). ISBN: 978-953-51-0451-3

Pugi, L., Monica, M., Susanna, P., Gregorio, V.: Design and preliminary validation of a tool for the simulation of train braking performance. J. Mod. Transport.**21**(4), 247–257 (2013). https://doi.org/10.1007/s40534-013-0027-6

Georges, K., Christophe, C., Damien, K.t, Georgios, A. Olivier, V., Véronique M.: Review of trackside monitoring solutions: from strain gages to optical fibre sensors. Sensors **15**(4), 20115–20139 (2015). https://doi.org/10.3390/s150820115

Towards a Flexible Urbanization Based Approach for Integration and Interoperability in Heterogeneous Health Information Systems: Case of Cameroon

Moskolaï Ngossaha Justin[1]([envelope]) [iD], Ynsufu Ali[1], Batouré Bamana Apollinaire[2], Djeumen Rodrigue[1], Bowong Tsakou Samuel[1], and Ayissi Eteme Adolphe[2]

[1] Faculty of Science, University of Douala, PO BOX 24 157, Douala, Cameroon
jmoskolai@fs-univ-douala.cm
[2] University Institute of Technology, University of Ngaoundéré,
PO BOX 455, Ngaoundéré, Cameroon

Abstract. Ensuring seamless integration and interoperability in heterogeneous health information systems is a significant challenge in healthcare. This paper presents a methodological approach that leverages urbanization in information systems to address these challenges. Urbanization involves transforming existing infrastructure incrementally, anticipating constraint changes, and incorporating new technologies. By adopting this approach, healthcare organizations can quickly adapt their systems to meet evolving demands while preserving critical information assets. The study delves into the unique context of health information systems and provides insights into achieving semantic integration. The proposed approach effectively resolves interoperability issues without requiring extensive system reconstruction. It introduces the concept of an Emergence information system, enabling collaboration across diverse contexts, including inter-ministerial, decentralized state services, and non-governmental organizations. Case studies validate the approach, showcasing the benefits of a flexible and urbanized integration strategy. The Yaoundé Urban Information Systems Integration and Interoperability Platform (YUSIIP) serves as a tangible demonstration. The research underscores the importance of embracing the urbanization perspective to enhance the efficiency and effectiveness of healthcare information systems, ultimately leading to improved patient care and outcomes.

Keywords: Health · information systems · Urbanization of information systems · Interoperability · Ontology

1 Introduction

The integration and interoperability of health information systems have become critical challenges in the healthcare domain. As healthcare organizations increasingly adopt diverse and complex information systems, the need for seamless communication and

© ICST Institute for Computer Sciences, Social Informatics and Telecommunications Engineering 2024
Published by Springer Nature Switzerland AG 2024. All Rights Reserved
F. Tchakounte et al. (Eds.): SAFER-TEA 2023, LNICST 566, pp. 258–275, 2024.
https://doi.org/10.1007/978-3-031-56396-6_16

collaboration among these systems becomes imperative. The ability to exchange data effectively and ensure the interoperability of heterogeneous systems is essential for delivering high-quality patient care and improving healthcare outcomes [1].

In the context of developing countries in general, and Cameroon in particular, collaboration and information exchange between health institutions is increasingly complex, if not impossible. This situation is due to the fact that most of these institutions have their own autonomous information systems, specific to each institution and materialized by the absence of an operational framework. The result is a proliferation of autonomous, distributed and heterogeneous information systems, built independently or even incompatibly [2], making the task of integrating and interoperating data sources very complex. The lack and/or unavailability of reliable health data for good collaboration between health structures, the difficulty of clearly and precisely defining common objectives, and the difficulty of basing the decision-making process on reliable statistics in the health field can all be observed.

To address these challenges, flexible approaches are required that can accommodate the dynamic nature of healthcare systems and facilitate efficient data exchange. One such approach is the concept of urbanization in information systems. Urbanization emphasizes the incremental transformation of existing infrastructure while anticipating changes in internal and external constraints, as well as incorporating new technologies [3]. This approach offers a promising solution to the integration and interoperability issues faced by healthcare organizations. In this context, how urbanization of information system approach can be performed in order to tackle integration and interoperability challenges in the healthcare system in developing countries.

The primary goal of this paper is to establish the context and significance of this research, it is crucial to explore the existing state of the arts related to health information systems integration, interoperability, and urbanization in information systems. Then the second objective is to introduce a methodological approach that leverages the concept of urbanization to address the integration and interoperability challenges in the healthcare context. By adopting an urbanized approach, healthcare organizations can adapt their systems rapidly to meet evolving demands while preserving critical information assets. This approach enables semantic integration, reducing the need for extensive system reconstruction and ensuring the efficient exchange of information.

By exploring the unique context of health information systems and offering insights into achieving semantic integration, this paper contributes to the advancement of knowledge in the field. The effectiveness of the proposed urbanization approach is validated through case studies, demonstrating its potential to address interoperability issues and improve the efficiency and effectiveness of healthcare information systems. Ultimately, this research aims to provide healthcare organizations with practical guidance on embracing the urbanization perspective to enhance integration and interoperability in their heterogeneous health information systems. By doing so, it strives to contribute to the improvement of patient care and outcomes in the healthcare domain.

The rest of the paper is structure as follows: Sect. 2 presents a comprehensive review of the relevant literature, including studies on health information systems integration, interoperability, and the concept of urbanization in information systems. Section 3 outlines the methodological framework employed in this research and including the research design. Section 4 presents architecture of integration and interoperability proposed, discussing the effectiveness of the urbanization approach in addressing interoperability issues in heterogeneous health information systems. Finally, Sect. 5 concluded the paper.

2   Related Works

2.1   Overview of Information System Integration and Interoperability

With the advent of the Internet and Intranet, the exchange and sharing of information from various distributed, autonomous, and heterogeneous information systems have become a critical requirement [2]. In such a scenario, simultaneous access to multiple sources is often necessary, as they contain pertinent and complementary information, thereby emphasizing the importance of interoperability among these systems. The task of achieving interoperability and integrating data sources to offer users a unified access interface is challenging. This challenge encompasses three key aspects: data heterogeneity, source autonomy, and source evolution [4].

The integration of disparate information systems necessitates the consideration of interoperability issues arising from various forms of heterogeneity, including hardware platforms, diverse software systems, and particularly semantic heterogeneity. According to [5], interoperability encompasses the concept of collaboration among applications, specifically referring to the ability of independently developed tools to cooperate and function together. Interoperability implies that source A can request and receive services from source B and utilize their functionalities, establishing interoperability between sources A and B. Data exchange represents a limited form of interoperation, where system A periodically transfers data to system B. In general, two information systems are deemed interoperable if they fulfill certain conditions: the ability to exchange messages and requests or the capability to work together as a cohesive unit to accomplish a shared task [5].

These conditions imply that interoperable systems can utilize each other's functions, act as clients and servers, and communicate even if their internal components are incompatible. According to [5], interoperability can be observed at various levels: (i) The most internal level exists within the architecture of data management systems, where gateways serve as specific programs that establish connections between systems, enabling a given system (A) to access the data of another system (B). Gateways currently exist between multiple database management systems (DBMS). (ii) At the intermediate level, a multi-database system is installed. This software layer facilitates the definition of a persistent view or perspective on a collection of databases for each user. Such systems ensure appropriate connections based on the defined view, allowing access to distributed data but lacking support for consistency constraints between different data sources. (iii) At the highest level, a global system is developed on top of existing systems, ensuring overall consistency across the systems and providing the desired level of integration with a set of data sources.

The interoperability of information systems has garnered significant interest as a result of the ongoing need to integrate new and evolving systems, particularly within collaborative enterprise networks. Enabling distributed, autonomous, and heterogeneous applications to collaborate and interact poses a significant challenge. The requirement for interoperability is delineated across four levels: data, services, processes, and business [6, 7]. From a data perspective, the objective is to facilitate communication among different data models (such as hierarchical, relational, object-oriented) by employing various conceptual schemes (such as vocabularies, data structures, and types) associated with the supporting applications. This task involves the identification and sharing of information from heterogeneous sources, which may reside in different databases running on distinct operating systems supported by diverse machines.

From a service standpoint, the aim is to identify, consolidate, and integrate functions from separate applications that have been designed and implemented independently. This process entails addressing both syntactic and semantic differences, as well as establishing connections to diverse sources of information. Interoperability encompasses mechanisms that facilitate the linking of process description languages (such as workflow standards), as well as the coordination, distribution, training, and verification of processes [8].

The aforementioned levels of interoperability encounter three types of barriers [9]: (i) conceptual barriers stemming from the diverse presentation and communication of fundamental concepts; (ii) technological barriers arising from the utilization of different technologies for communication and information exchange. To facilitate collaboration, companies need integrated information and communication technologies (ICTs) and decision-making support tools. (iii) organizational barriers resulting from disparate work practices.

Typically, a decision support system can only be developed on the periphery of existing systems. Its construction necessitates a comprehensive understanding of operational information systems [10]. As the data sources of these systems become increasingly complex and distributed, integration is crucial to enable communication and cooperation among these sources. Some systems may require migration to a new version to address integration and interoperability challenges. The objective is to enhance system agility and responsiveness, ensuring rapid adaptation to new demands while preserving existing information assets. This constitutes the core issue of integrating and interoperating information systems [11]. The barriers, levels, approaches, and solutions to interoperability are summarized in Fig. 1 (see Fig. 1).

According to [12], three approaches exist to achieve interoperability between systems:

- The integrated approach, which consists of building a common format for all models in order to develop a single system (the interacting systems become one with a single model).
- The unified approach, which consists of keeping the own model of each communicating system and defining a common format at a meta-level to make correspondences (each system keeps its own structure before and after communication).
- The federated approach, which does not propose a common format for communication and requires dynamic adjustment and support efforts.

In the literature, other approaches such as the urbanization of information systems also help systems to evolve while ensuring interoperability between different systems. Information system urbanization takes into account of existing systems and helps to better

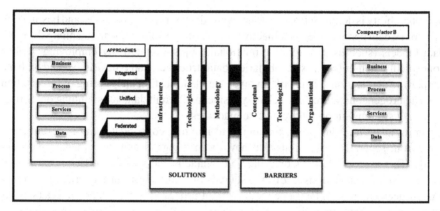

Fig. 1. Interoperability: levels, barriers, approaches and solutions.

anticipate changes and internal and external constraints impacting on the information system, using new technologies.

2.2 Urbanization of Information Systems

Primarily due to a highly competitive economic environment driven by globalization, organizations face the imperative to adapt to the changes brought about by this dynamic context. These changes encompass various forms, including technological advancements, organizational restructuring, and legal modifications. Business information systems, in particular, are significantly impacted by these transformations. When inadequately integrated within the organizational structure, these systems can burden stakeholders to the extent of detrimentally affecting their performance.

The process of urbanizing an information system entails organizing its transformation, aligning business objectives with technological opportunities, and simultaneously simplifying and enhancing its flexibility and responsiveness. By transforming constraints into opportunities, the resultant target information system can optimize the services provided. As outlined in [13], the goal of information system urbanization is to redesign or modernize the existing system, capitalizing on technological advancements without starting from scratch. This approach should be implemented within controlled cost parameters, avoiding disruptions to ongoing operations or compromising service quality.

On a practical level, the urbanization of information systems borrows from the metaphor of the urbanization of cities, a central feature of which is the definition of a set of coherent plans and actions helping to optimize the organization of spatial, economic, social, environmental and other functions. [14] suggests the definition of a coherent and modular structuring framework, based on the definition of various levels of representation to which common or specific rules are associated, including the planning of forecasts (e.g. Local Town Planning Scheme or PLU) and the definition of development authorizations (e.g. building or demolition permits).

Overall, both cadastral and IT mapping is based on the definition of several layers of urbanization corresponding to specific visions (as illustrated in Fig. 2): (a) a strategic vision providing the objectives and missions of urbanization; (b) a business vision describing the processes and activities; (c) a functional vision describing the functions and services organized into zones, districts, blocks, etc.; (d) an application vision describing the application elements (on the IS side), the buildings and associated equipment (on the cadastral side); (e) a technical or infrastructure vision describing the technical architecture, the infrastructure and the services provided. (e) a technical or infrastructure vision describing the technical architecture, for example transport networks, energy networks, etc. (on the cadastral side), telecommunications networks, computers, printers, etc. (on the information system side).

As mentioned in [9], common framework made up of various frames of reference is also developed during the urbanization process: the metaphor of general urbanization rules thus leads to the definition of general rules specific to IS (as described below).

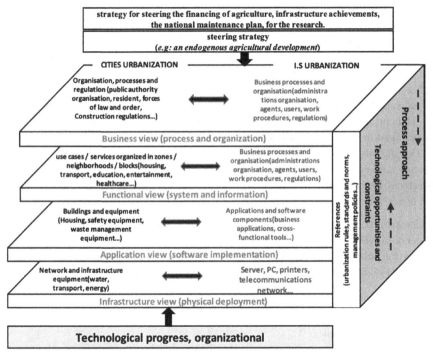

Fig. 2. Parallel between urbanization of cities and urbanization of IS (adapted from CIGREF, 2003).

Most African countries are faced with the following situations:

– Obsolescence of their ministerial departments' IT tools (where they have them);
– Frequent changes to legislation as a result of the gradual establishment of democratic institutions;
– The introduction of decentralization, with the creation of decentralized services designed to offer a range of local services to users (both individuals and businesses);
– Development strategies aimed at achieving Emergence, set out, for example, in documents such as the DSCE (Growth and Employment Strategy Paper) in Cameroon;

– Etc.

Alignment of information systems development strategies with a view to Emergence is therefore necessary. For maximum efficiency, as part of a decision-making aid and better monitoring of strategies, the urbanization of state information systems is ultimately essential, as it leads to relevant and efficient decision-making, better collaboration between administrations, between administrations and partners, and even between administrations and users. Health information systems in developing countries in general, and in the Cameroonian context, appear to be a good candidate for this technology.

2.3 The Urbanization Approach in Health Information Systems

As defined by the World Health Organization (WHO), the health information system (HIS) is a key enabler that must be aligned with health strategy. Although information technology (IT) applications in healthcare have been around for more than thirty years, methods for evaluating the outcomes of the use of IT-based systems in health informatics remain a challenge for policy makers, as well as for those wishing to measure the effects of ICTs in healthcare environments [15, 16]. However, with the adoption of technologies such as the Internet of Health Things [17, 18], cyber-physical systems [18], machine learning and Big Data [19], the healthcare sector has recognized the relevance of Industry 4.0. The concept of Big Data has offered many benefits and opportunities in this area. It has changed the way information is collected, shared and used.

Despite this considerable research, it can be observed in the field that the information systems deployed are generally imperfect, or even unsuitable for achieving strategic objectives. In the context of Cameroon, which is the focus of this study, the problems of HIS are as follows:

– Computerization of the healthcare system is not a genuine public project, defined and steered by the State. As in other sectors, there is no reference document emanating from the political authority, setting out the guidelines for computerization and defining the role of each party (State, ministry, ministry departments, hospitals, professionals, etc.);
– Health data is not recorded, or is often poorly archived when it is;
– The information available is that held by international organizations or international research institutions;
– Existing information is disparate, incomplete and difficult to access;
– Information systems are poorly interoperable, both internally and externally, compartmentalized, unstable in the face of internal (organizational) or external changes (regulations, governance, technical modifications), not very safe or secure, and difficult to use in collaborative processes between players with different profiles, and often supported by disparate infrastructures, etc.

Another concern of the healthcare system in Cameroon is to meet the challenges of setting up health information systems that are aligned with the strategy, interoperable, coherent, stable, secure, cross-territorial and cross-organizational. This is the challenge of urbanizing an information system [20]. Urbanization therefore involves creating a standardized, agile and scalable system. The SIS can therefore be compared to a city (Table 1).

Table 1. The analogy between the urban planning of a city and the urban planning of a health information system

Components	Description	Analogy with the urban development plan
Strategy	IT strategy for the organization aligned with the business strategy	A vision of the city based on the future needs of its residents
Principles	Criteria for choosing solutions and making investment decisions	Zoning and building codes to ensure quality and consistency
Mapping	Systems and user mapping	Infrastructure maps and diagrams (water, electricity, sewers, etc.)
Components	Key functional and information components	Description of prefabricated components for overall construction
Evaluation grid	Criteria for assessing solutions and standards	Component evaluation criteria (duration, cost, etc.)
Standards	Rules and standards to be respected by systems	Standards for electrical wiring and plumbing networks
Governance	Architecture modification process and rules	Rules for amending the town plan and decisions
Transition plan	Portfolio of prioritized and assessed projects	City improvement plan (green spaces, traffic, transport, etc.)

Overall, health indicators and care practices have improved since the 1970s. However, the objectives set by the Alma-Ata International Conference and the declaration in favor of primary health care, health for all in the year 2000, have not been achieved in Cameroon, as in most developing countries. The health situation remains characterized by high mortality, particularly among children, low life expectancy and a morbidity rate that continues to give cause for concern, linked to nutritional deficiencies and communicable diseases. The development of the health system is not harmonious.

A number of actions need to be taken to improve the health of the Cameroonian population, particularly the urban population:

– Organize the health system in such a way as to make it more effective and efficient.
– Evaluate the practices of health professionals.
– Evaluate the health programs put in place to ensure that they are effective.
– Assess the health needs of the population and establish public health priorities.
– To give priority to essential medicines and generics, by establishing effective policies for controlling medicines, from supply to marketing.
– Promote health education and prevention (role and responsibility of patients).
– Set up a permanent health data recording system.
– To ensure that the public and private health sectors complement each other, and to coordinate the actions of the various players.
– Combat inequalities in access to healthcare and poverty.
– Combat corruption.

- Put in place a legal framework for the practice of traditional medicine, and repressive measures against charlatans.
- Evaluate the need for healthcare personnel, train them accordingly, and introduce strict rules for the practice of medicine.
- Develop strategies to overcome persistent difficulties in the area of human resources (careers, assignment, continuing training).

According to [21], although some of these actions have already been undertaken, the results are slow in coming. Much remains to be done. In addition, the controlled implementation of appropriate, scalable (robust, sustainable) information systems is a prerequisite for care coordination. This is based on the sharing of data (particularly patient data), the essential prerequisites of which are the interoperability of healthcare information systems (political, organizational, semantic, technical, etc.) and the management of reference systems. [22] highlights that these issues are difficult not only because of their technical aspects, but also because they are political issues that need to be tackled at national level to ensure the necessary coherence (the steering of health information systems is the responsibility of the State). What's more, today's healthcare professionals, decision-makers and experts seem to share the same convictions:

- The performance of the healthcare system, which lies in its ability to improve the quality of care and ensure better patient management, requires the development of patient-centred information systems.
- The improvement of professional practices, which depends on the application of knowledge established by research, requires information systems to develop traditional communication functions and integrate decision support tools (secure use of clinical best practice guidelines, implementation of computerized protocols, introduction of alert systems based on patient records, etc.).

Patient information and empowerment play a very important role in the results of healthcare interventions (treatments, prevention campaigns, etc.). Implementing information systems can make it easier for patients to play an active role in managing their own state of health (improving links between patient records, patient assistance tools, documentation, educational programs, telehealth services, etc.).

The design of (healthcare) information systems must meet three requirements. They must:

- Be based on an open architecture that helps the scope of the system to evolve and allows functions and tasks to be shared across business processes;
- Manage data on the basis of semantic standards and repositories that are stable, durable, recommended and updated at national level, and adopted by all;
- Facilitate the work of professionals by integrating information gathering and processing into business processes as simply as possible. The software involved in these processes must share data and knowledge: they must be interoperable.

Health information systems in Cameroon are still a long way from meeting these requirements. In the context of this work, two approaches to information system urbanization can be envisaged: (i) a top-down approach, starting with urbanization strategies and moving on to technical deployment, helping to define a general urbanization framework at state level. (ii) a bottom-up approach, characteristic of the transformation of technological or organizational innovations and other changes into opportunities. This approach opportunistically integrates the many technological innovations, particularly in the context of ICTs (with the contributions of service-oriented technologies and social networks) not only to facilitate the definition of a catalogue of local services for users, but also to help them enrich the State Health Information System (as described in the next section). With this in mind, we need to define a methodological framework for putting them into operation.

3 Methodological Framework Proposed

The information systems urbanization approach is based primarily on the four levels described above [13]: business, functional, application and technical. Generally speaking, two operational principles guide a successful urbanization approach:

(1) while defining common frames of reference, the first concern is to deconstruct the existing system, by "de-imbricating" systems and the various business lines and activities, in order to avoid stacking up IT applications, which is generally the source of the "gas factory" effect;
(2) a second concern is to find the right balance between pooling and advanced specialization (i.e. delegating responsibility for a specific task to the smallest IT unit).

The approach must also help to find a balance between the following issues: (i) identifying the changes required to implement the company's or organization's strategy, (ii) safeguarding the consistency and improving the efficiency of the information system, and (iii) implementing a quality system more quickly, while limiting the risks and costs associated with communication between the various functions involved, and with the integration of new technologies, tools and methods. The approach (see Fig. 3) can be based (as recommended by [13]) on the following stages:

– Planning the study;
– Review of strategic axes (understanding of the company's business strategy, definition of the target vision);
– Analysis of the existing situation (mapping of the existing situation, study of technological opportunities, assessment of the existing situation, orientation and implementation of the strategy);
– Strategy definition (SOP, performance forecasts, target organization, evaluation of scenarios and choices);
– Convergence plan (finalization of the convergence plan, definition and implementation of the monitoring strategy);
– Publication of the strategy;
– Updating the strategy.

Inspired by this approach, an instance of the urbanization methodology is proposed in the following figure (see Fig. 4). The management of health data (storage, organization, search, manipulation) requires us to ensure that all the complex data can be integrated. It is generally proposed that integrated tools be developed [23–25]. The tool proposed in

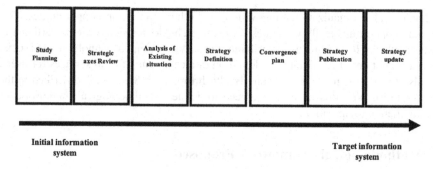

Fig. 3. Methodological approach to the urbanization of information systems

this work to provide the various stakeholders in the health sector with up-to-date, reliable data needed for the design and monitoring/evaluation of health strategies and/or programs is a platform for the interoperability of distributed and heterogeneous databases in the urban areas of developing countries [26, 27]. It is an open, integrated decision-making information system.

- A system that is open to its environment: the urban sector is totally open and evolving very rapidly. Openness to its environment is considered from two angles: firstly, the possibility opens to any producer and/or user of urban data (technical services, researchers, media, NGOs, donors, etc.) to make available and consult the data of interest to them; secondly, the possibility of hosting and/or referencing distributed and autonomous sources of information belonging to different urban bodies.
- Integrated system: the platform uses data from independent data sources. The integration operation makes it possible to create a coherent, consistent system.
- Decision support system: the information flows handled in the information system are indicators, synoptic tables, qualitative and quantitative statistical analyses, graphs, etc.

The urbanized system recommended in this study is based on the urbanization strategy for the health system in developing countries in general and Cameroon in particular. More specifically, the aim is to define a National Urbanization Plan through pilot projects involving the Ministries concerned by the ecosystem services involved in this development strategy. A schematic diagram of the general architecture of the proposed system is described below.

The Information System proposed as part of this study (cf. Figure 5), known as the Emergence Information System (EIS), is built according to a classic architecture: in addition to the strategic level, the various layers of the proposed system correspond to the urbanization visions described above (see Fig. 5), namely (i) the business level characterizing the processes and the organization, (ii) the functional level comprising the information assets, (iii) the application level translating the software implementations, and finally (iv) the infrastructure level which concerns the physical deployment of the system in question.

However, it is different (from the classic cases) in that it is built around 3 contexts of use: (1) the inter-ministerial context, (ii) the ministerial context and (iii) the context

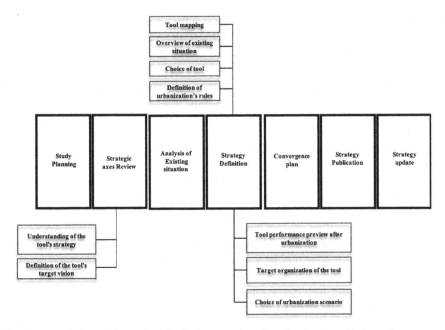

Fig. 4. Instantiation of the methodological approach to the urbanization of information systems in the interoperability tool for heterogeneous databases.

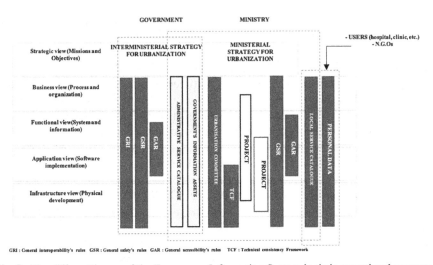

GRI : General interoperability's rules   GSR : General safety's rules   GAR : General accessibility's rules   TCF : Technical consistency Framework

Fig. 5. The different layers of the Emergence Information System in their operational contexts.

of the "singular" systems of non-state users (private individuals, economic operators, non-governmental organizations).

At the inter-ministerial level, the first step is to define a general urbanization framework based on the National Urbanization Plan (mentioned above), with a view to better coordinating specific ministerial actions (as part of the emergence strategies); the second step is to define General Interoperability Rules (GIR), General Security Rules (GRS) and General Accessibility Rules (GAR) for ministerial information systems and the government information system. The result should be a catalogue of government services accessible to ministerial departments, as well as a knowledge base constituting the state's information assets, fed by feedback from government actions.

At ministerial level, within the framework of the urbanization pilot projects, the aim is to define a general urbanization charter, framed by the RGA and RGS, as well as a Technical Coherence Framework (CCT) for ministerial Information Systems. In turn, the ministerial departments must define general accessibility and security rules, both for their decentralized services and for users, and even for non-governmental organizations or local or international development partners. Technological innovations can help non-state bodies to interact with decentralized government departments, for example to access or update their medical records (in the case of an individual), update their tax records (for an economic operator, a development partner), monitor the progress of projects financed (for a donor, a partner in the Emergence process), etc. These local services made available to non-state bodies, at ministerial level, are undoubtedly an interesting lever for materializing government efficiency and can have a strong decisive impact on the Doing Business indicator of African states.

Finally, the third context involves interconnecting the "unique" systems of non-state users with the information systems of ministries (or their decentralized departments). Hence the importance of general security and accessibility rules to be defined at ministerial level.

This outline of the Emergence Information System suggests, for its implementation, considering the problems of collaboration (inter-ministerial, intra-ministerial i.e. with decentralized services, extra-ministerial (i.e. with non-state systems), as well as the problems of interoperability as announced in the preamble to this communication. It is also suggested that, in defining the general rules (interoperability, security, accessibility), account should be taken of the specific problem of trust (as in supply chains), as States are supposed to share part of their information assets with external bodies.

The resulting architecture proposed (cf. Fig. 6) consists of implementing cooperation between autonomous healthcare information systems. A common platform that produces decision-making tools for decision-makers based on the data warehouse. Available data sources (heterogeneous databases) offer their data or the characteristics of their data in the format of these sources (CSV, DocSQL, SQL, XML, etc.). The common platform will retrieve the data from the available databases and carry out any processing it wishes, and will use this data to create one or more historical series for storage in the database warehouse (DW). The common platform will offer two access points: the first access is reserved for administrators of the common platform to carry out administrative tasks such as updating data, updating the data directory, etc. The second access is reserved for end users of the common platform to carry out administrative tasks such as updating the data directory. A second access point will be reserved for end users to consult and use the data. Figure 6 below illustrates the various players involved in the process.

Each participating data source uses its own technology within its information system. The interoperability tool will help to retrieve the necessary data and store it in the

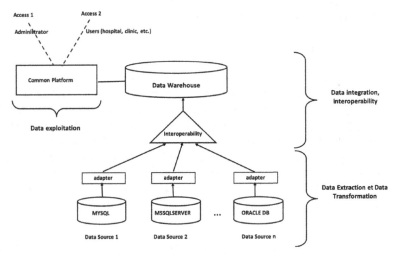

Fig. 6. Illustration of how the system and participants work.

warehouse. The common platform offers the different players the information they need. This difference in approach will help the common platform to put itself in contact with all the players in the urban sector.

Implementing this process will require the use of a number of technologies covering all aspects of intelligent business. The databases to be used come from several types (object, relational, etc.) available for use. Each database has an adapter which is considered to be the bridge between it and the decision support tool. (ODBC, OLEDB, NATIVE ACCESS, DIRECT ACCESS, PILOT, ETC.). Data is collected via these points.

– The interoperability tool: this mainly concerns the implementation of a decision support system for cooperation between urban bodies. Its task will be to bring together the extracted data, process it and store it in the data warehouse.
– The data warehouse: this is the heart of the integrated information system. The idea is to create an ideal model of the data available to a decision-maker. Such a database helps him to carry out retrospective analyses, which focus on the outcome of present and past events, and prospective analyses, which focus on forecasting future events or behavior based on historical data. It is in fact the mould, the filter that will help the interoperability and integration of data from different distributed and heterogeneous information systems.

To validate this architecture, a platform for the interoperability of information systems applied to the healthcare sector has been implemented. In the following part of this study, an implementation based on a service-oriented architecture and using Internet technologies is proposed.

4   Case Study of YUSIIP Platform

4.1   Context of the Case Study

Most urban areas in developing countries have an unorganized development system. Data management in these areas is not well managed. Hence the need for a professional data management system. Urban decision-makers and managers need consolidated, reliable information. In this context, the YUSIIP platform proposes mechanisms for integrating heterogeneous information systems in order to facilitate decision-making on the development of African cities, which are characterized by insufficient resources, a lack of consultation between the various stakeholders and a scarcity of reliable information. Inspired by the methodological approach proposed above, the YUSIIP prototype has been set up. It aims to support and help all the players involved in the city's development to work together effectively in the future.

The YUSIIP platform concerns the study of mechanisms for integrating heterogeneous and incomplete information systems in order to help decision-making in urban development, in a context of African cities marked by a lack of resources, insufficient consultation between the various stakeholders and information that is scattered, difficult to access and not very reliable. The heart of the YUSIIP platform is its Distributed Data Warehouse (DDW), which capitalizes on data and knowledge relating to the following urban themes: environment, health, transport, infrastructure, etc. for the city of Yaoundé. As part of this work, the schematic diagram of the platform presented above led us to the interoperability architecture for health information systems based on the sustainable integration model for urbanized health information systems.

4.2   Result and Discussions

The architecture proposed below (see Fig. 7) is the result of the urbanization of the YUSIIP platform. It presents a set of protocols that helps several database systems and application programs work together to improve urban mobility systems.

This architecture constitutes the following components:

Data sources (heterogeneous and distributed databases). These are the places where the data to be used comes from. They can be the places where the data was created or where the physical information was digitized. However, even the most elaborate data can be considered as sources, as long as another process accesses and uses it. In practical terms, a data source can be a database, a flat file, measurements taken directly from physical devices, data obtained by web scraping or one of the many static and streaming data services that abound on the Internet. In this work, the data sources will be distributed and/or heterogeneous databases. Databases remain the most widely used data sources as they are the primary data shops in universal relational or object database management systems (DBMS). Databases may be located locally or on a remote server, or represented on several different sites with different characteristics. The data to be processed will come from these different databases.

Datawarehouse. Datawarehouses are databases that help to store historical, structured, non-volatile, subject-oriented data for analysis. It is a relational database designed for data queries and analysis, decision-making and Business Intelligence activities, rather

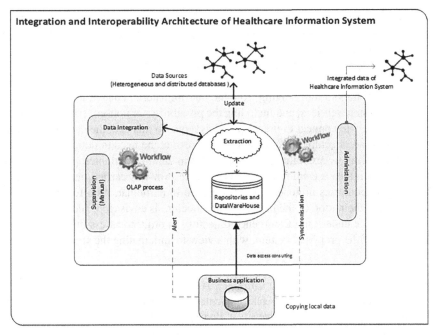

Fig. 7. Integration and interoperability architecture for healthcare information systems.

than for transaction processing or other traditional uses of databases. The information stored in the data warehouse is historical, providing an overview of the various transactions that have taken place over time. Redundant data is often included in Datawarehouses to offer users several views of the information. This is why the data stored in the Datawarehouse is often aggregated to help users access it more easily. In addition to a relational database, a data warehouse environment includes a tool for extracting, transporting, transforming and loading data (ETL). There is also an online analytical processing engine (OLAP), customer analysis tools and other applications to help manage the processing of the data collected.

Data federation platform. This platform helps urban players to access federated data for analysis and decision-making.

The YUSIIP platform is a functional platform. With a view to validating the integration and interoperability model for health information systems in Cameroon, the system is currently being implemented. Solutions for semantic interoperability based on artificial intelligence algorithms are also being considered.

5 Conclusion

With a view to the emergence of African countries, this study has helped to highlight the importance of defining an effective state information system, taken as a framework for observation and decision support to facilitate relevant and effective decision-making. The urbanization of health information systems is seen as a prerequisite for a successful trajectory, and has been chosen as the context for application, not least because of the complexity of managing the ecosystem services involved in this development strategy, but also because of the importance of public safety in any sustainable development strategy. At the IT level, the definition of an Emergence information system was proposed, aimed at implementing the recommended development strategy, which integrates various forms of collaboration, ranging from the interministerial context to the contexts of decentralized State services, and including the possibility for non-governmental organizations and users to connect to the proposed system. To this end, the description of the recommended architecture has also helped to illustrate the need to define general rules for interoperability, accessibility and security. An integration and interoperability architecture based on the case study of the YUSIIP platform was carried out in the context of developing countries in general and Cameroon in particular. As a follow-up to this study, an implementation of the urbanized architecture is envisaged, accompanied by a simulation of the underlying Emergence trajectory in order to assess the relevance and performance of the proposed system, with a view to anticipating the strategic decisions to be taken.

Acknowledgement. This work resulted from a Fellowship at the Hanse-Wissenschaftskolleg Institute for Advanced Study, Delmenhorst, Germany. We address our thanks to the team of Comnets Rechearch group of the University of Bremen for their expertise.

References

1. Chen, D., Doumeingts, G., Vernadat, F.: Architectures for enterprise integration and interoperability: past, present and future. Comput. Ind. **59**(7), 647–659 (2008). https://doi.org/10.1016/j.compind.2007.12.016
2. Eteme, A.A., Ngossaha, J.M.: The contribution of ICTs to sustainable urbanization and health in urban areas in Cameroon. In: I. Management Association (ed.), Waste Management: Concepts, Methodologies, Tools, and Applications, pp. 624–641. IGI Global (2020). https://doi.org/10.4018/978-1-7998-1210-4.ch030
3. Trabelsi, L., Abid, I.H.: Urbanization of information systems as a trigger for enhancing agility: a state in the Tunisian firms. Eur. J. Bus. Manage. **5**(5), 63–77 (2013)
4. Bellatreche, L., Dung, N.X., Pierra, G., Hondjack, D.: Contribution of ontology-based data modeling to automatic integration of electronic catalogues within engineering databases. Comput. Ind. **57**(8–9), 711–724 (2006)
5. Ploquin, N.: Etude des différents modes d'interopérabilité en génie logiciel (Doctoral dissertation, Master Thesis, University of Nantes (2001)
6. National Health development plan of Cameroon (NHDP) 2011–2015, https://www.uhc2030.org/fileadmin/uploads/ihp/Documents/Country_Pages/Cameroon/Cameroon_National_Health_Plan_2011-2015_French.pdf. Accessed July 2023
7. Berre, A.J., et al.: The ATHENA Interoperability Framework. In: Gonçalves, R.J., Müller, J.P., Mertins, K., Zelm, M. (eds.) Enterprise Interoperability II. Springer, London (2007). https://doi.org/10.1007/978-1-84628-858-6_62
8. Bruller, B.: Architectures de système d'information: modèles, services, protocoles. Vuibert Informatique (2003)

9. Eteme, A.A., Ngossaha, J.M.: Urban master data management: case of the YUSIIP platform. In: Faiz, S., Mahmoudi, K., (eds.), Handbook of Research on Geographic Information Systems Applications and Advancements, pp. 441–465. IGI Global (2017). https://doi.org/10.4018/978-1-5225-0937-0.ch018

10. Benson, T., Grieve, G.: Principles of health interoperability. Springer, Cham, pp. 21–40 (2021)

11. Liu, L., Li, W., Aljohani, N.R., Lytras, M.D., Hassan, S.U., Nawaz, R.: A framework to evaluate the interoperability of information systems–measuring the maturity of the business process alignment. Int. J. Inf. Manage. **54**, 102153 (2020)

12. Chen, D.: Framework for enterprise interoperability. Enterp. Interoperability Interop-Pgso Vis. **1**, 1–18 (2017)

13. Longépé, C.: Le projet d'urbanisation du SI: Cas concret d'architecture d'entreprise. Dunod (2009)

14. Manouvrier, B., Ménard, L.: Application Integration: EAI B2B BPM and SOA, vol. 130. Wiley, Hoboken (2010)

15. Rahimi, B., Vimarlund, V.: Methods to evaluate health information systems in healthcare settings: a literature review. J. Med. Syst. **31**, 397–432 (2007). https://doi.org/10.1007/s10916-007-9082-z

16. Dwivedi, R., Mehrotra, D., Chandra, S.: Potential of internet of medical things (IoMT) applications in building a smart healthcare system: a systematic review. J. Oral Biol. Craniofacial Res. **12**(2), 302–318 (2022)

17. Kouroubali, A., Katehakis, D.G.: The new European interoperability framework as a facilitator of digital transformation for citizen empowerment. J. Biomed. Inform. **94**, 103166 (2019)

18. Tamfon, B.B., Bilounga Ndongo, C., Bataliack, S.M., Ngoufack, M.N., Nguefack-Tsague, G.: Routine health information system in the health facilities in Yaoundé–Cameroon: assessing the gaps for strengthening. BMC Med. Inform. Decis. Mak. **20**(1), 1–11 (2020)

19. Samalna, D.A., Ngossaha, J.M., Ari, A.A., Kolyang.: Cyber-physical urban mobility systems: opportunities and challenges in developing countries. Int. J. Softw. Innov. (IJSI) **11**(1), 1–21 (2023). https://doi.org/10.4018/IJSI.315662

20. Saxena, A., MISRA, D., Ganesamoorthy, R., Gonzales, J.L.A., Almashaqbeh, H.A., Tripathi, V.: Artificial intelligence wireless network data security system for medical records using cryptography management. In: 2022 2nd International Conference on Advance Computing and Innovative Technologies in Engineering (ICACITE), pp. 2555–2559. IEEE, April 2022

21. Ondoua, J.P.B.: Le système de santé camerounais. Actualité et Dossier Santé Publique **39**, 61–65 (2002)

22. Ndlovu, K., Mars, M., Scott, R.E.: Interoperability frameworks linking mHealth applications to electronic record systems. BMC Health Serv. Res. **21**(1), 459 (2021)

23. Kurtev, I., Bézivin, J., Jouault, F., Valduriez, P.: Model-based DSL frameworks. In: Companion to the 21st ACM SIGPLAN Symposium on Object-Oriented Programming Systems, Languages, and Applications, pp. 602–616, October 2006

24. Shvaiko, P., Villafiorita, A., Zorer, A., Chemane, L., Fumo, T., Hinkkanen, J.: eGIF4M: eGovernment interoperability framework for mozambique. In: Wimmer, M.A., Scholl, H.J., Janssen, M., Traunmüller, R. (eds.) Electronic Government, EGOV 2009, LNCS, vol. 5693, pp. 328–340. Springer, Berlin (2009). https://doi.org/10.1007/978-3-642-03516-6_28

25. Bawack, R.E., Kamdjoug, J.R.K.: Adequacy of UTAUT in clinician adoption of health information systems in developing countries: The case of Cameroon. Int. J. Med. Informatics **109**, 15–22 (2018)

26. Kalé, L.V., Bhandarkar, M., Jagathesan, N., Krishnan, S., Yelon, J.: Converse: an interoperable framework for parallel programming. In: Proceedings of International Conference on Parallel Processing, pp. 212–217. IEEE, April 1996

27. Kumar, S.V., et al.: Land information system: an interoperable framework for high resolution land surface modeling. Environ Model Softw.Softw. **21**(10), 1402–1415 (2006)

Food Recommender System in Sub-Saharan Africa: Challenges and Prospects

Ephraim Sinyabe Pagou[1]([email]) , Vivient Corneille Kamla[1], Igor Tchappi[2] ,
Josiane Ngathic[1], Ludovic Tsakam[1], and Amro Najjar[3]

[1] ENSAI, University of Ngaoundere, Box 454 Ngaoundere, Cameroon
ephraimpagou@gmail.com, josianetheresa@gmail.com
[2] AI-Robolab/ICR, Computer Science Department, University of Luxembourg,
4365 Esch-sur-Alzette, Luxembourg
[3] Luxembourg Institute of Science and Technology (LIST),
5 avenue des Hauts-Fourneaux, 4362 Esch-sur-Alzette, Luxembourg

Abstract. Nutrition is one of the most important lifestyle components that can be altered, therefore even minor changes or bad food choices can have a huge impact on health. Food recommendation systems are especially useful for maintaining a balanced diet or preventing chronic diseases such as diabetes, cancer, and cardiovascular disease, which are responsible for 63% of deaths worldwide, according to the World Health Organization. The underlying problem with building a meal suggestion system is a lack of contextual information for creating a user profile. It is critical to consider the social, cultural, economic, political, and environmental facts relevant to certain regions of the world. Creating user profiles based on Artificial Intelligence (AI), on the other hand, need contextual information that takes into account social, cultural, economic, political, and environmental elements. In Sub-Saharan Africa, where diet is connected to ethnicity and climatic seasons, AI-based dietary advice can target healthy or malnourished individuals. This article examines the current status of food recommendation systems, obstacles, lessons learned, and future directions and open questions. The objective is to provide additional user and meal profile characteristics to future item and recipe suggestion systems, hence encouraging healthy eating for Sub-Saharan Africa.

Keywords: Sub-Saharan Africa · Recommender-system · Nutrition
e-coach · chronic diseases

1 Introduction

In the face of information overload, online recommendation systems have proven effective in a range of scenarios, enabling users to overcome it, accompanying them in their decision-making process, and assisting in the modification of their

© ICST Institute for Computer Sciences, Social Informatics and Telecommunications Engineering 2024
Published by Springer Nature Switzerland AG 2024. All Rights Reserved
F. Tchakounte et al. (Eds.): SAFER-TEA 2023, LNICST 566, pp. 276–287, 2024.
https://doi.org/10.1007/978-3-031-56396-6_17

behavior [1]. Food advice has historically gotten less attention, especially when compared to leisure and entertainment. This is remarkable considering the significance of food to human nutrition, the variety of options available, the difficulty of selecting food decisions [2], and the significant personal and social penalties of poor choices. Obesity and diabetes are lifestyle and diet-related disorders that account for 60% of all fatalities worldwide, according to [3]. Both illnesses are preventable and treated. Both illnesses can be avoided and, in some cases, reversed with the right die.

Both disorders can be avoided and, in some cases, reversed by making healthy dietary choices [4]. As a result, health-conscious food recommendation systems are frequently seen as an essential component of the answer to encourage healthy dietary choices [5,7]. However, there are several reasons why dietary recommendations are difficult to provide, not just to encourage healthy behavior, but also to forecast what individuals want to eat, as this is complicated, diverse, culturally driven, and context-dependent. Furthermore, practitioners and academics must address extra challenges that do not emerge in other fields of recommendation when designing food recommendation systems.

Indeed, user demands, such as allergies or lifestyle preferences, such as the desire to eat solely vegan or vegetarian cuisine, can be complex and constricting. In many circumstances, standard techniques perform poorly, and relevant data sources for filtering recipes are not easily accessible [8]. Other difficulties include the fact that foods can have multiple names, that ingredients can be prepared in a variety of ways, and that, unlike in areas where products or media are recommended, it is not always clear whether a recommended product can be prepared or consumed due to the availability of ingredients, culinary knowledge, or equipment.

This article contributes in two ways. To begin, we provide an overview of the state of the art in food recommendation systems, highlighting the most current approaches to the problem as well as significant specialties such as food recommendation systems for user groups or systems that promote healthy eating. We investigate the algorithms utilized in the food domain, how systems are normally appraised, and the resources accessible to people interested in developing or studying recommender systems in practice. In a second contribution, we examine the numerous obstacles ahead, as well as a recap of past research lessons gained and an outline of major future paths and open topics. We believe that by providing these contributions, we will provide a valuable resource for researchers in Sub-Saharan Africa context.

2   Existing Solutions

This chapter focuses on recent research in the field of customized nutrition using decision support systems. The analysis highlights two main categories of studies conducted in the past three years, excluding those related to genetic information. The first category involves the development of complex information models for tailored services, specifically focusing on the adaptive provision of nutritious meals to improve the quality of life for both healthy individuals and patients with diet-related chronic disorders [9]. These studies utilize block diagrams based on user responses to dynamic health surveys [10], a mobile social semantic framework for generating health recommendations [11], and ontologies to handle recipes, menus, and medical prescriptions [12]. Additionally, researchers have explored integrated modeling of nutrition knowledge to assist elderly users in creating their own healthy eating plans [13] and have encoded nutrition knowledge as an ontology for nutrition care processes [14]. Another study describes a distributed system that addresses home care in the context of self-nutrition and malnutrition prevention, utilizing bio-inspired algorithms for menu planning and ordering diet-controlled meals [15].

The second category of studies focuses on processing nutritional data from current sources rather than data modeling. These publications approach nutritional recommendations as an optimization problem in the context of healthy menu design, resolving menu planning issues. While menu planning problems have been addressed as optimization cases in the past, several research groups continue to utilize this approach using various optimization techniques such as genetic algorithms, ant colony optimization, and goal-oriented optimization (Fig. 1).

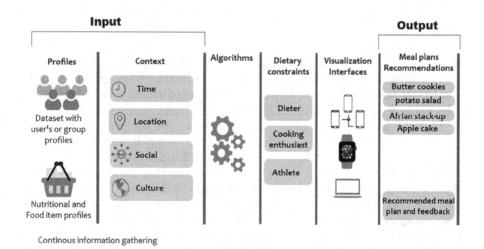

Fig. 1. The general architecture for food recommendation systems

Content generator algorithms can be categorized into pre-generated and real-time types. Pre-generated algorithms generate offline material through background jobs, while real-time algorithms use a context-based interface for quick retrieval. Pre-generated algorithms are preferred due to their faster performance and faster retrieval from storage. Real-time algorithms are used as a fallback for algorithms that cannot be pre-generated due to immediate context or excessive design costs. Real-time generated algorithms are often used to wrap existing legacy and third-party recommendation sources (Fig. 2).

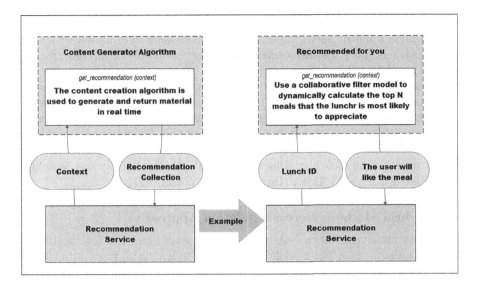

Fig. 2. Examples of real-time content generation algorithms

2.1   Content-Based Filtering Recommandation Approach

The text discusses two main categories of studies in the field of customized nutrition using decision support systems. The first category focuses on the development of complex information models for tailored services, such as adaptive provision of nutritious meals for healthy individuals and patients with diet-related chronic disorders [5]. This involves using block diagrams, mobile social semantic frameworks, and ontologies to handle recipes, menus, and medical prescriptions. Another study explores integrated modeling of nutrition knowledge for elderly users to create their own healthy eating plans. The second category of studies focuses on processing nutritional data from current sources, specifically addressing menu planning issues using optimization techniques like genetic algorithms and ant colony optimization. Additionally, content-based techniques have been used to personalize recommendations based on user preferences, utilizing ingredient complement and substitution networks, as well as visual cues [12] and automated feature learning [22].

2.2   Collaborative Filtering Recommandation Approach

Methods for meal recommendation systems based on communal filtering were also suggested and assessed. Freyne and Berkovsky used Pearson's correlation on a ranking matrix to evaluate a nearest-neighbor strategy and discovered that it was no match for the content-based approach mentioned above [5]. According to Harvey et al., SVD outperforms both the content-based and collaborative filtering algorithms presented in [7]. Ge, Elahi et al. [23] presented a matrix factorization (MF) technique for food recommendation systems that provides substantially greater prediction accuracy than content-based prediction accuracy and traditional matrix factorization by merging ranking information with user-provided labels. They also demonstrate the smart phone device interface for this method.

These examples demonstrate how labels, in addition to the normal binary and scaled ratings, may be used to provide a more precise degree of information to evaluations. Trattner and Elsweiler [24] have evaluated many collaborative filtering algorithms implemented in the LibRec2 framework on a huge dataset gathered from the web recipe portal allrecipes.com. The most effective CF techniques were Latent Dirichlet Allocation (LDA) (Griffiths, [26]) and Weighted matrix factorization (WRMF) (Hu, Koren, & Volinsky, [27]).

2.3 Hybrid Methods Recommandation Approach

Hybrid recommenders have been proposed by other scientists for the task of recommending recipes. For modeling, Frein and Berkowski [5] fused a user-based collaborative filtering method with a content-based method. Furthermore, in their subsequent work for user groups, they used a hybrid approach to combine three different recommendation strategies into a single model using a switching strategy. The switching was simply based on the ratio between the number of items reviewed by the user and the final total number of items. Another example of the hybrid approach can be found in the work of Harvey et al. [7] achieved the best results in their experiments by combining the SVD approach with user and item shifts.

2.4 Context-Aware Filtering Recommandation Approach

Numerous studies have identified factors such as context, gender, time, leisure, and food availability as relevant for improving recipe recommendations [29,30]. However, there is a lack of awareness of these factors and their effectiveness in improving recommendation accuracy [32], [?]. Harvey et al. analyzed data from a dataset with participants providing various variables, revealing that factors like cooking step description, nutritional quality, material availability, and weekday affected customers' thoughts on the suggestion.

2.5 Group-Based Filtering Recommandation Approach

Food choices are influenced by social settings, such as who is present, why they are present, and their preferences. Group recommendation systems consider these social settings when designing meal lists for groups of individuals. Research on group meal recommendation systems is sparse, with the first attempts dating back to the early 1990s. Berkowski and Frein's work presents four strategies for promoting recipes to groups, including generic, aggregate, aggregate prediction, and aggregate prediction strategies [5]. The tailored version performs better, but it is not practical to produce customized recommendations for all users. Elahi et al. suggest a mobile interface and algorithm for a meal recommendation system in a group scenario, using a group-based preference detection technique [34].

2.6   Health-Aware Filtering Recommandation Approach

When motivating research on food recommendation systems, health concerns and better eating habits are frequently emphasized (Freyne & Berkovsky [5]; Harvey et al., [7]). However, the incorporation of health in recommendations has recently gained a lot of attention (Elsweiler et al. [24]). One option to achieving this aim is to explicitly include nutritional components into the recommendation process. Ge, Ricci, and Massimo [35] employ this strategy in the recommendation algorithm by taking the quantity of calories into account. This was accomplished using a "calorie balance function," which compensates for the difference between the calories required by the consumer and the calories in the recipe. They highlight the trade-off that most customers face between endorsing what they want and what suits their diet.

This is a trade-off that most customers face (Harvey et al., [7]) and should be optimized (Elsweiler et al., [24]). The authors advise combining these two aspects linearly as a foundation for assessing alternative algorithmic ways to integrate health into the recommendation process.

3   Evaluation Metrics and Metholodgies

Evaluation methods used in food recommendation systems have improved over some time. The first concept papers found in the literature did not use any type of evaluation (Hinrichs & Kolodner, [36]). After a long time (Freyne & Berkovsky, [5]), researchers started to use evaluation methods that are now recognized by the community as standard practice (Herlocker [37]). The specifics of the experiments differ, but usually the datasets are subdivided into subsets for training and testing to simulate user profiles and recommendation feedback. As in other recommendation domains, historical datasets are usually split in such a way that 80% of the data is used for training and the remaining 20% is left for testing. A k-fold [6] testing procedure or a drop and pick protocol can also be employed. Collections may be obtained in a variety of methods, ranging from natural collections acquired from the internet or donated sources to performing user studies to collect tiny data sets. Different metrics are used by these systems to assess the performance of algorithms. These typically reflect the prediction error, such as mean absolute error (MAE) or root mean square error (RSME) (Freyne & Berkovsky (Freyne & Berkovsky)), or the quality of the ranked item list, such as extraction, precision, mean accuracy (MAP), and normalized cumulative diminishing gain (NDCG) [39]. Early work in the recommender systems field concentrated on the classification prediction problem, but more recent and present work considers recommendations as a classification problem [25].

4   Application Resources

This section outlines resources for building food recommender systems. We present a summary of (i) datasets typically used to investigate food consumption patterns and evaluate algorithmic techniques, as well as (ii) nutrition and health resources that may be utilized to construct health-aware recommender systems. Finally, the development frameworks that are often utilized are outlined.

4.1   Data Sets for Recipes, Meal Plans and Menus

Research generally relies on single item representations, such as those contained in the datasets given above, which are often recipes, to construct meal plan recommender systems. Dedicated meal plans, on the other hand, may be obtained as ground truth data from websites such as *Eatingwell*, *FitBit*, and many other popular health platforms [40]. These resources provide generic meal plan templates for a day or a week. Allrecipes has been utilized as a research resource in the context of meals, for example, a combination of an appetizer, main dish, and dessert [28]. In [24], the authors also provided a whole behavioral dataset, including user interactions.

4.2   Nutrition and Health Resources

Knowing more about a given food item, such as its energy content or other nutritional properties, is usually required in the context of food recommender systems. These are commonly necessary for building systems that aim for certain dietary limitations or goals, such as health-conscious food recommender systems. The most common way to measure and compute the nutrition of a specific food item is to map elements to standard databases. The USDA database is also used by Google's knowledge graph. The fact that food items can only be successfully mapped and calculated if they perfectly match the entries in the database is a typical difficulty with these direct mapping ideas [30].

Food labels and rules enforced by food safety organizations are utilized in the real world to inform consumers about how healthy a specific food item is. This is generally country-specific. So far, the Food Standards Agency (FSA) in the United Kingdom and the World Health Organization (WHO) [41] have effectively applied their standards in the context of food recommendations. Both criteria are based on a 2000kcal diet and take various nutritional properties of foods into account.

5   Research Challenges and Future Directions

Personal models for meal recommendation are often focused on the context of the user and intrinsic health parameters. However, achieving comprehensive and accurate personal models is challenging due to three sources: data ingestion, life event recognition, and pattern recognition [42]. Data ingestion involves using various sensors and preprocessing modules to extract relevant features from raw sensor information, but the reliability of information and the availability of different sensor methods can vary greatly. Additionally, the proliferation of recipe-sharing websites and social media platforms provides massive volumes of culinary data, making it difficult to aggregate heterogeneous multimedia data. Visual food analysis is crucial for meal suggestion, providing high-level knowledge of food categories, volume, and calorie [43]. However, accurate visual food analysis is challenging due to its flexibility and lack of firm structures.

The user's food choice has distinct qualities, including biological, psychological, social, cultural, and historical influences. Using publicly available food data to learn about a user's food preferences is straightforward, but it often focuses on modeling one or more components of the data. Approaches borrowed from other domains, such as psychology and neuroscience, are expected to offer new paths for accurate food preference learning.

Currently, no software package is available for creating a meal recommendation system. Previous research has either built their own systems or based their prototypes on existing recommendation frameworks, which may not be optimal for recommending healthy food products. The LibRec library, designed for food recommendations, has been developed but is only accessible in Java [?].

While AI has the potential to revolutionize the way we discover and enjoy culinary delights, it is essential to acknowledge the unique challenges faced in the African context. Here are a few limitations to consider:

- Cultural Diversity: Africa is a continent rich in cultural diversity, with each region boasting its own distinctive cuisines and culinary traditions [45], AI-based food recommender systems often struggle to capture the nuanced preferences and dietary habits of various African cultures accurately. The lack of comprehensive and localized data poses a challenge in providing personalized recommendations that align with the diverse tastes and dietary requirements of African populations.
- Limited Data Availability: AI algorithms thrive on vast amounts of data to make accurate predictions and recommendations [46]. However, the availability of structured. However, the availability of organized and comprehensive food-related data in Africa might be restricted, making it difficult to successfully train AI models. This lack of data limits recommender systems' capacity to comprehend local cuisine preferences and respond to the specific demands of African consumers.
- Connectivity and Access: While AI has enormous promise, it is critical to recognize the digital gap that exists in many regions of Africa [47]. Access to smartphones and computers, as well as limited internet availability, are significant impediments to the general adoption and use of AI-based food recommender systems. The benefits of such systems may be confined to select urban regions or privileged persons if they are not widely accessible.
- Regional products and Recipes: African food frequently relies on locally produced products and traditional recipes that aren't always well-documented or well known [48]. Because the data supplied may be few or insufficient, AI-based systems may struggle to propose dishes based on these regional components and recipes. In the lack of extensive information and resources, incorporating localized knowledge into AI models becomes difficult.

– Health and Nutritional concerns: Health and nutritional concerns are important in African cuisine choices [49]. Traditional African diets vary and can be
quite nourishing. However, AI-based food recommender systems may lack the
understanding of local dietary norms, cultural eating behaviors, and nutritional requirements essential to make reliable suggestions that fit with these
aspects.

While AI-based food recommender systems have limitations in Africa, it is
critical to acknowledge the continuous efforts to overcome these difficulties. User-
friendly interfaces, mobile applications, and offline functionality can all help to
improve accessibility and bridge the digital divide.

Africa's culinary treasures could continue to thrive and be cherished with the
help of AI, as we work to overcome these restrictions and build a more inclusive
and culturally sensitive food recommendation environment.

6   Conclusion

As a result, food recommendation is an essential domain for both people and
society. The work discussed in this paper demonstrates that, despite its relevance, food item recommendation is rather low in contrast to other categories.
The work done so far reveals that, while user taste predictions for food can
be produced using existing methods, the performance achieved is lower than in
other domains. This indicates that preference learning should remain a focus
for the food domain because trials presented in the literature have shown that
standard methods are only capable of providing rather unsatisfactory results
regardless of the form of user feedback used (i.e. ratings, tags, or comments).
Finally, another community element that has to be created is the assessment of
food recommenders and the techniques utilized to do so. Offline evaluation has
often been done with proprietary collections in the literature. We must work
together as a community to collect uniform data, establish common baseline
methodology, and, most critically, conduct more online research to understand
how our ideas work as live systems in naturalistic settings.

Acknowledgments. This work has been partially supported by the Chist-Era grant
CHIST-ERA19-XAI-005, and by (i) the Swiss National Science Foundation (G.A.
20CH21_195530), (ii) the Italian Ministry for Universities and Research, (iii) the Luxembourg National Research Fund (G.A. INTER/CHIST/19/14589586), (iv) the Scientific and Research Council of Turkey (TÜBİTAK, G.A. 120N680).

References

1. Ricci, F., Rokach, L., Shapira, B.: Introduction to recommender systems handbook.
In: Ricci, F., Rokach, L., Shapira, B., Kantor, P. (eds.) Recommender Systems
Handbook, pp. 1–35. Springer, Boston (2010). https://doi.org/10.1007/978-0-387-
85820-3_1

2. Scheibehenne, B., Greifeneder, R., Todd, P.M.: Can there ever be too many options? A meta-analytic review of choice overload. J. Consum. Res. **37**(3), 409–425 (2010)
3. Habib, S.H., Saha, S.: Burden of non-communicable disease: global overview. Diabetes Metab. Syndr. Clin. Res. Rev. **4**(1), 41–47 (2010)
4. Ornish, D., et al.: Can lifestyle changes reverse coronary heart disease?: The Lifestyle Heart Trial. Lancet **336**(8708), 129–133 (1990)
5. Freyne, J., Berkovsky, S., Smith, G.: Recipe recommendation: accuracy and reasoning. In: Konstan, J.A., Conejo, R., Marzo, J.L., Oliver, N. (eds.) UMAP 2011. LNCS, vol. 6787, pp. 99–110. Springer, Heidelberg (2011). https://doi.org/10.1007/978-3-642-22362-4_9
6. Siddik, M.B.S., Wibowo, A.T.: Collaborative filtering based food recommendation system using matrix factorization. Jurnal Media Informatika Budidarma **7**(3), 1041–1049 (2023)
7. Harvey, M., Ludwig, B., Elsweiler, D.: You are what you eat: learning user tastes for rating prediction. In: Kurland, O., Lewenstein, M., Porat, E. (eds.) SPIRE 2013. LNCS, vol. 8214, pp. 153–164. Springer, Cham (2013). https://doi.org/10.1007/978-3-319-02432-5_19
8. Stefanidis, K., et al.: PROTEIN AI advisor: a knowledge-based recommendation framework using expert-validated meals for healthy diets. Nutrients **14**(20), 4435 (2022)
9. Agapito, G., et al.: DIETOS: a dietary recommender system for chronic diseases monitoring and management. Comput. Methods Programs Biomed. **153**, 93–104 (2018)
10. Åström, K.J., Murray, R.M.: Feedback Systems: An Introduction for Scientists and Engineers. Princeton University Press, Princeton (2021)
11. Mata, F., Torres-Ruiz, M., Zagal, R., Guzman, G., Moreno-Ibarra, M., Quintero, R.: A cross-domain framework for designing healthcare mobile applications mining social networks to generate recommendations of training and nutrition planning. Telematics Inform. **35**(4), 837–853 (2018)
12. Bianchini, D., De Antonellis, V., De Franceschi, N., Melchiori, M.: PREFer: a prescription-based food recommender system. Comput. Stand. Interf. **54**, 64–75 (2017)
13. Espín, V., Hurtado, M.V., Noguera, M.: Nutrition for Elder Care: a nutritional semantic recommender system for the elderly. Expert. Syst. **33**(2), 201–210 (2016)
14. Cioara, T., et al.: Expert system for nutrition care process of older adults. Futur. Gener. Comput. Syst. **80**, 368–383 (2018)
15. Taweel, A., et al.: A service-based system for malnutrition prevention and self-management. Comput. Stand. Interf. **48**, 225–233 (2016)
16. Toledo, R.Y., Alzahrani, A.A., Martinez, L.: A food recommender system considering nutritional information and user preferences. IEEE Access **7**, 96695–96711 (2019)
17. Simon, D.: Biogeography-based optimization. IEEE Trans. Evol. Comput. **12**(6), 702–713 (2008)
18. Luan, J., Yao, Z., Zhao, F., Song, X.: A novel method to solve supplier selection problem: Hybrid algorithm of genetic algorithm and ant colony optimization. Math. Comput. Simul. **156**, 294–309 (2019)
19. Ghanbari, A., Kazemi, S.M., Mehmanpazir, F., Nakhostin, M.M.: A cooperative ant colony optimization-genetic algorithm approach for construction of energy demand forecasting knowledge-based expert systems. Knowl.-Based Syst. **39**, 194–206 (2013)

20. Galdieri, R., Longobardi, A., De Bonis, M., Carrozzino, M.: Users' evaluation of procedurally generated game levels. In: De Paolis, L.T., Arpaia, P., Bourdot, P. (eds.) AVR 2021. LNCS, vol. 12980, pp. 44–52. Springer, Cham (2021). https://doi.org/10.1007/978-3-030-87595-4_4

21. Milosavljevic, M., Navalpakkam, V., Koch, C., Rangel, A.: Relative visual saliency differences induce sizable bias in consumer choice. J. Consum. Psychol. **22**(1), 67–74 (2012)

22. Yang, L., Cui, Y., Zhang, F., Pollak, J. P., Belongie, S., Estrin, D.: PlateClick: bootstrapping food preferences through an adaptive visual interface. In: Proceedings of the 24th ACM International on Conference on Information and Knowledge Management, pp. 183–192, October 2015

23. Ge, M., Elahi, M., Fernaández-Tobías, I., Ricci, F., Massimo, D.: Using tags and latent factors in a food recommender system. In: Proceedings of the 5th International Conference on Digital Health 2015, pp. 105–112, May 2015

24. Elsweiler, D., Trattner, C., Harvey, M.: Exploiting food choice biases for healthier recipe recommendation. In: Proceedings of the 40th International ACM SIGIR Conference on Research and Development in Information Retrieval, pp. 575-584, August 2017

25. Hiriyannaiah, S., Siddesh, G.M., Srinivasa, K.G.: DeepLSGR: neural collaborative filtering for recommendation systems in smart community. Multimedia Tools Appl. **82**(6), 8709–8728 (2023)

26. Griffiths, T.: Gibbs sampling in the generative model of latent dirichlet allocation (2002). http://citeseerxist.psu.edu/viewdoc/summary

27. Hu, Y., Koren, Y., Volinsky, C.: Collaborative filtering for implicit feedback datasets. In: 2008 Eighth IEEE International Conference on Data Mining, pp. 263–272. IEEE, December 2008

28. Hamdollahi Oskouei, S., Hashemzadeh, M.: FoodRecNet: a comprehensively personalized food recommender system using deep neural networks. Knowl. Inf. Syst. **65**, 1–23 (2023)

29. Rokicki, M., Herder, E., Trattner, C.: How editorial, temporal and social biases affect online food popularity and appreciation. In: Proceedings of the International AAAI Conference on Web and Social Media, vol. 11, no. 1, pp. 192–200, May 2017

30. Kusmierczyk, T., Trattner, C., Nørvåg, K.: Understanding and predicting online food recipe production patterns. In: Proceedings of the 27th ACM Conference on Hypertext and Social Media, pp. 243–248, July 2016

31. De Choudhury, M., Sharma, S., Kiciman, E.: Characterizing dietary choices, nutrition, and language in food deserts via social media. In: Proceedings of the 19th ACM Conference on Computer-supported Cooperative Work & Social Computing, pp. 1157–1170, February 2016

32. Abbar, S., Mejova, Y., Weber, I.: You tweet what you eat: studying food consumption through twitter. In: Proceedings of the 33rd Annual ACM Conference on Human Factors in Computing Systems, pp. 3197–3206, April 2015

33. Wansink, B., Sobal, J.: Mindless eating: the 200 daily food decisions we overlook. Environ. Behav. **39**(1), 106–123 (2007)

34. Elahi, M., Ge, M., Ricci, F., Massimo, D., Berkovsky, S.: Interactive food recommendation for groups. In: Recsys Posters, October 2014

35. Ge, M., Ricci, F., Massimo, D.: Health-aware food recommender system. In: Proceedings of the 9th ACM Conference on Recommender Systems, pp. 333–334, September 2015

36. Sobek, R.P., Laumond, J.P.: Using learning to recover side-effects of operators in robotics. In: Proceedings of the Sixth International Workshop on Machine Learning, pp. 205–208. Morgan Kaufmann, January 1989

37. Herlocker, J.L., Konstan, J.A., Terveen, L.G., Riedl, J.T.: Evaluating collaborative filtering recommender systems. ACM Trans. Inf. Syst. (TOIS) 22(1), 5–53 (2004)

38. Chen, M., Jia, X., Gorbonos, E., Hoang, C.T., Yu, X., Liu, Y.: Eating healthier: exploring nutrition information for healthier recipe recommendation. Inf. Process. Manage. 57(6), 102051 (2020)

39. Pratama, D.E., Nurjanah, D., Nurrahmi, H.: Tourism recommendation system using weighted hybrid method in Bali Island. Jurnal Media Informatika Budidarma 7(3), 1189–1199 (2023)

40. Hemaraju, S., Kaloor, P.M., Arasu, K.: Yourcare: a diet and fitness recommendation system using machine learning algorithms. In: AIP Conference Proceedings, vol. 2655, no. 1. AIP Publishing, May 2023

41. Golagana, R., Sravani, V., Reddy, T.M., KavithaAssistant, C.H.: Diet Recommendation System Using Machine Learning

42. Min, W., Jiang, S., Jain, R.: Food recommendation: framework, existing solutions, and challenges. IEEE Trans. Multimedia 22(10), 2659–2671 (2019)

43. Zhao, Y., et al.: Biodegradable intelligent film for food preservation and real-time visual detection of food freshness. Food Hydrocolloids 129, 107665 (2022)

44. Lops, P., Polignano, M., Musto, C., Silletti, A., Semeraro, G.: ClayRS: an end-to-end framework for reproducible knowledge-aware recommender systems. Inf. Syst. 119, 102273 (2023)

45. Kohnert, D.: Machine ethics and African identities: perspectives of artificial intelligence in Africa (2022). Available at SSRN 4163096

46. Nakalembe, C., Kerner, H.: Considerations for AI-EO for agriculture in Sub-Saharan Africa. Environ. Res. Lett. 18(4), 041002 (2023)

47. Ade-Ibijola, A., Okonkwo, C.: Artificial intelligence in Africa: emerging challenges. In: Eke, D.O., Wakunuma, K., Akintoye, S. (eds.) Responsible AI in Africa: Challenges and Opportunities, pp. 101–117. Springer, Cham (2023). https://doi.org/10.1007/978-3-031-08215-3_5

48. Bul, K., Holliday, N., Bhuiyan, M.R.A., Clark, C.C., Allen, J., Wark, P.A.: Usability and preliminary efficacy of an artificial intelligence-driven platform supporting dietary management in diabetes: mixed methods study. JMIR Hum. Factors 10, e43959 (2023)

49. Nji, Q.N., Babalola, O.O., Mwanza, M.: Aflatoxins in maize: can their occurrence be effectively managed in Africa in the face of climate change and food insecurity? Toxins 14(8), 574 (2022)

50. Buzcu, B., et al.: Explanation-based negotiation protocol for nutrition virtual coaching. In: Aydogan, R., Criado, N., Lang, J., Sanchez-Anguix, V., Serramia, M. (eds.) PRIMA 2022. LNCS, Springer, Cham (2022). https://doi.org/10.1007/978-3-031-21203-1_2

Detection and Recognition of Cough Sounds Using Deep Learning for Medical Monitoring

Fabien Mouomene Moffo[1]([⊠]) [iD], Auguste Vigny Noumsi Woguia[1] [iD],
Joseph Mvogo Ngono[2] [iD], Samuel Bowong Tsakou[1] [iD],
and Nadiane Nguekeu Metepong Lagpong[1] [iD]

[1] Faculty of Science, Douala University, Douala, Cameroon
fmouomene@yahoo.fr
[2] Iut, Douala University, Douala, Cameroon

Abstract. Coughing is the most prevalent indication of respiratory illness. The importance of cough detection and classification as a preventive measure against infectious diseases cannot be overemphasized. The importance of cough testing is also relevant to public health. However, accurate classification of cough in noisy environments remains a major challenge. Pattern recognition algorithms can be adapted to work in noisy environments and real-time situations. Our cough detection and classification method is based on the analysis of the acoustic signature of coughs using artificial intelligence and deep learning. Before training the deep neural network model, the MFCC (Mel-Frequency Cepstral Coefficients) method is used to extract the acoustic characteristics of the sounds used. Our system uses a sensor attached to the neck to detect movements of the throat and trachea during coughing. The results of our study on the acoustic analysis of coughing were satisfactory. This model classifies coughs into three classes with an accuracy of 78.09%. We are developing state-of-the-art systems that can effectively detect and classify coughs, even in noisy environments. This means that hospitals, airplanes and noisy public places can use our technology to identify patients in need of medical attention or with symptoms of respiratory disease.

Keywords: Cough · Detection · Classification · Deep Learning · Sensor

1 Introduction

Coughing is an important indicator for assessing respiratory health and identifying Diseases of the respiratory tract. The new area of research called "cough pattern recognition" seeks to utilize technological advancements to recognize, assess, and group the sound characteristics of coughs [2]. This cutting-edge approach has promising implications for medicine, enabling remote monitoring of patients and early detection of respiratory problems and lung disease [1–3].

The assessment of respiratory problems has traditionally relied on subjective clinical techniques, such as careful listening by the clinician or the use of specialized monitoring

© ICST Institute for Computer Sciences, Social Informatics and Telecommunications Engineering 2024
Published by Springer Nature Switzerland AG 2024. All Rights Reserved
F. Tchakounte et al. (Eds.): SAFER-TEA 2023, LNICST 566, pp. 288–296, 2024.
https://doi.org/10.1007/978-3-031-56396-6_18

equipment. However, these approaches are often inadequate due to their subjectivity and lack of objectivity, which can lead to a slow or inaccurate diagnosis. New data-driven scientific approaches to assessing respiratory problems have emerged to overcome these limitations and detect abnormalities at an early stage. One of the most promising is the use of deep learning to detect and recognize tonal sounds. The scientific literature on deep learning is still developing. Background noise is one of the main challenges for automatic detection of sound and speech anomalies in this approach: the environment in which a person is located may contain a variety of background noises, such as conversations, music or other ambient sounds. It can be challenging to differentiate between a cough and other cough-like noises [4–7].

However, it is possible to differentiate and identify cough sounds in a real-world environment. Existing cough recognition algorithms can be modified to work effectively in more violent environments and real-time scenarios. Research laboratories have had to collect sound recordings for COVID-19 patients of all ages, in changing environments, symptomatic or asymptomatic. This data provides an opportunity for AI algorithms to learn pandemic-specific audio patterns for patients. Commonly collected auditory recordings to detect COVID-19 are coughs. Groups such as COUGHVID, collect data from cough recordings.

We propose a deep learning-based system for identifying Cough sounds. Our model is a variant of CONVNet. It classifies patients into three categories: healthy individuals, those showing symptoms of disease, and those carrying the Covid 19 virus. This model is designed to be integrated into wearable devices or home sensors to help monitor people's health and well-being. If the patient is in a difficult environment, the sensor must be attached to the neck using a harness. The performance of this model is 78.09% accurate.

2 Materiel and Methods

We conducted cross-sectional research in a descriptive, exploratory and diagnostic study. The Fig. 1 shows our general medical monitoring concept and Fig. 2 presents the methodology of our study.

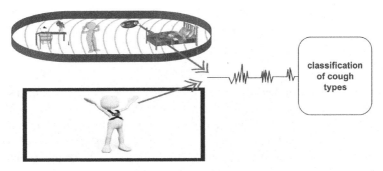

Fig. 1. Medical monitoring concept

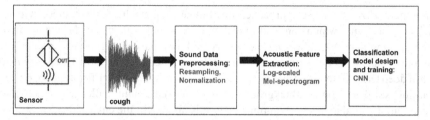

Fig. 2. Methodology for audio recognition

2.1 Dataset

This research originated in our laboratory before the COVID-19 pandemic. In collaboration with health care workers, we recorded cough samples from healthy patients and patients with respiratory diseases. The remaining data during the pandemic through the COUGHVID laboratory is public data. The COUGHVID dataset is a valuable resource designed to aid research on analyzing cough signals for early detection of respiratory illnesses, such as COVID-19. The metadata associated with this dataset provides crucial details about its characteristics and properties.

Below is a description of the metadata associated with our dataset: Cough audio recordings contains cough audio recordings of healthy subjects as well as subjects with COVID-19 and other respiratory diseases. The recordings are made using a variety of devices, such as mobile phones or special microphones, and are stored in audio formats. Each recording is accompanied by a label detailing the subject's health status. The collection also includes demographic metadata on the subjects, including age, gender, geographical and ethnicity origin. These details will allow the study of potential changes in the acoustic characteristics of the cough as a function of these factors. Clinical annotations included in the cough recordings include patient-reported symptoms, diagnostic test results (such as COVID-19 PCR results) and any relevant medical history. These clinical annotations provide further information about the relationship between sound characteristics and respiratory disease. The metadata also provides information about the data collection protocols used, such as the instructions given to the subjects, the recording parameters (such as background noise) and the distance between the subject and the microphone. These details can be crucial to understanding the results of the analysis (Fig. 3).

2.2 Preprocessing

First, the audio signal, like any other incoming signal, must be digitized into a sequence of numbers, called samples, each indicating the air pressure on the microphone at a given time. The raw data collected was in Ogg, Webm and Mp3 formats. We first developed an algorithm for the automatic conversion of lossless audio data into wav format. The Wav format, unlike the Ogg and Webm formats, offers the best listening quality and has the advantage of not compressing the audio file. A crucial stage in machine learning applied to signal processing is the preparation of audio data in WAV format.

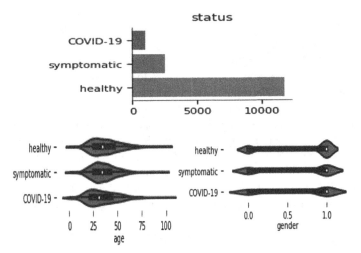

Fig. 3. Dataset Coughs.

There are several techniques to effectively manage the imbalance in the audio dataset before training a deep learning model. Subsampling has been used, which reduces the majority class by randomly taking a subset of samples from that class to match the size of the minority class. This creates a relative balance between the classes.

The aim is to prepare the raw audio data so that it is suitable for training an automatic learning model. The MFCC (Mel Frequency Cepstral Coefficients) procedure is commonly used to convert audio data into spectrograms. The pre-processing of WAV audio data generally involves a number of steps, which may vary depending on the particular requirements of the application [8].

This was achieved by dividing the audio epochs by their maximum value, resulting in a range of values. To facilitate analysis, the audio signals are broken down into small segments. This decomposition allows the audio stream to be viewed as a sequence of smaller units of time, a common representation used to capture the characteristics of the audio signal. The following steps are used to determine the MFCC: The audio signal is converted from the linear frequency scale to the Mel scale, a nonlinear scale that closely approximates the way humans perceive frequency. To minimize artefacts at the ends of the frames, the audio signal divided into frames is often multiplied by a window. To move the audio signal from the transient to the frequent domain, a Short-Term Fourier Transform (STFT) is applied to each frame. This gives the frequency distribution in each frame.

2.3 Architecture

Deep learning consists in: building the architecture of a multilayer network by arranging and connecting modules; training this architecture by gradient descent after computing this gradient by backpropagation. The following is a description of the architecture of our CNN, which uses ReLU activation, takes an MFCC (Mel-frequency cepstral coefficients) image as input, and produces three classes: three convolutional layers, three pooling layers with ReLU activation, one fully connected layer, and one fully connected layer for output, as shown in Fig. 4.

Our choice of CNN (Convolutional Neural Network) to classify cough types is motivated by several reasons: CNNs have been shown to be highly effective in image classification, especially since the input to our model is an image (spectrogram). CNNs are able to efficiently capture local spatial relationships in an image; this ability is essential for extracting discriminative features from cough spectrograms, which show significant variations in terms of patterns, intensities, and shapes. CNNs use convolutional and pooling layers to progressively reduce the dimensionality of the data, thereby better handling the complexity of cough spectrograms and avoiding the problem of the curse of dimensionality. The use of LSTM (Long Short-Term Memory) can be considered as part of a study to analyze the temporal sequence of coughing and its evolution over time [15].

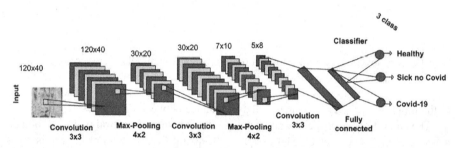

Fig. 4. Architecture.

2.4 Sensor

Our system uses a sensor attached to the neck to detect movements of the throat and trachea during coughing. The Non-Intrusive Cough Sensor (NICS) is a state-of-the-art device designed to accurately collect cough sounds from patients without causing discomfort or harm to their health. It consists of several key components:

Sensitive microphones: The NICS features highly sensitive microphones that employ advanced noise reduction technology to accurately capture coughs even in loud surroundings.

Comfortable harness: The device attaches to the patient's neck with a lightweight and ergonomic harness, which is adjustable to fit various neck sizes. The harness is made of hypoallergenic materials to prevent skin reactions.

Wireless connectivity: Data collected by the NICS is transmitted wirelessly to a central collection device, such as a smartphone or computer, via a secure Bluetooth or Wi-Fi connection.

Long-life battery: The sensor is equipped with a rechargeable battery that provides sufficient autonomy for continuous use for several days, minimizing interruptions in data collection.

Moisture Protection: Because coughing can be accompanied by saliva, the NICS is moisture protected to prevent damage to electronic components.

Intelligent analysis algorithms: Collected data is processed in real-time using advanced analysis algorithms to distinguish cough sounds from other ambient noise and quantify their intensity and frequency.

Data Security: Cough data is encrypted and stored securely to ensure patient confidentiality in accordance with privacy regulations.

2.5 Training and Build

Building the model: For multiclass classification, the category cross entropy function, often known as the loss function, was developed. Adam was specifically designed to adjust the weight of the model during training. Accuracy (precision) was included as an additional evaluation metric to monitor model performance during training.

Model training: The number of iterations (100 epochs) and the batch size (32 batches) were set to regulate the length of the training process and the amount of data processed at any one time. The training minimizes the loss function after the model has been adjusted for weight and bias using the provided optimizer.

Testing the model: After training, the performance of the model was evaluated on the test set containing previously unrecognized data.

We used the K-Fold Cross Validation technique to train and evaluate our model.

The K-Fold Cross Validation approach consists of dividing our data set into K equally sized subsets, called "folds". Then, at each iteration, we use K-1 folds for model training and the remaining fold for model validation. This process is repeated K times, so that each fold is used exactly once for validation. After applying this technique, we obtained impressive results.

Hyperparameter optimization is an iterative process with the goal of identifying the optimal hyperparameters for a machine learning model in order to achieve the highest possible accuracy. The iterative process entails identifying the potential range of values for each. Hyperparameter and evaluating model performance using the accuracy metric. Hyperparameters are model parameters that must be defined before the model is trained and are not learned from the data. Using the ADAM optimization method, we tested and evaluated various sets of hyperparameters to find the most effective combinations for increasing model performance. The main objective of the optimization process is to identify the optimal hyperparameters that could produce the desired results.

3   Results and Discussions

3.1   Results

Cough recordings are accompanied by acoustic metadata describing the characteristics of the audio signal. This metadata includes attributes such as torus length, number of frequency frames, spectral energy, harmonics and temporal moments. These details make it possible to analyze the specific characteristics of coughs associated with different respiratory diseases. The architecture of the convolutional neural networks exploited, gives an overall accuracy of the Cross validation using the cough data of 78.09%.

The utilization of MFCC coefficients was a smart decision in capturing the vital characteristics of coughs, allowing our deep neural network model to achieve precise and rapid classifications (Figs. 5 and 6).

```
381/381 [==============================] - 1s 3ms/step - loss: 0.6784 - accuracy: 0.7684 - val_loss: 0.6560
- val_accuracy: 0.7809

Epoch 00095: val_loss did not improve from 0.65575
Epoch 96/100
381/381 [==============================] - 1s 3ms/step - loss: 0.6780 - accuracy: 0.7684 - val_loss: 0.6560
- val_accuracy: 0.7809

Epoch 00096: val_loss did not improve from 0.65575
Epoch 97/100
381/381 [==============================] - 1s 3ms/step - loss: 0.6778 - accuracy: 0.7684 - val_loss: 0.6560
- val_accuracy: 0.7809

Epoch 00097: val_loss did not improve from 0.65575
Epoch 98/100
381/381 [==============================] - 1s 3ms/step - loss: 0.6778 - accuracy: 0.7684 - val_loss: 0.6559
- val_accuracy: 0.7809

Epoch 00098: val_loss did not improve from 0.65575
Epoch 99/100
381/381 [==============================] - 1s 3ms/step - loss: 0.6786 - accuracy: 0.7684 - val_loss: 0.6561
- val_accuracy: 0.7809

Epoch 00099: val_loss did not improve from 0.65575
Epoch 100/100
381/381 [==============================] - 1s 4ms/step - loss: 0.6778 - accuracy: 0.7684 - val_loss: 0.6561
- val_accuracy: 0.7809

Epoch 00100: val_loss did not improve from 0.65575
Training completed in time:  0:02:22.722375
```

Fig. 5. Results to Build model

3.2 Discussions

The results of our study on cough shape recognition using a convolutional neural network (CNN) model are consistent with other studies in this area. Cough recognition is of increasing interest, especially in light of the COVID-19 pandemic, where coughing was identified as a key symptom of infection. Several previous studies have investigated different approaches to automatic cough recognition. To categorize different types of Coughs, several studies have used models based on conventional machine learning, such as support vector machines (SVMs) and artificial neural networks (ANNs). These approaches have shown promising results, but can be limited by the complexity of the character representation and the need to manually create some descriptors. In this study, we used a CNN model for face recognition. CNNs are deep neural networks that have been successfully used in computer vision, particularly for image categorization. However, their use for sound recognition is very recent and still under development. Our results show that the CNN model is acceptable for classifying different types of coughs from audio recordings. Our overall accuracy was 78.09%, which is consistent with results reported in related studies. This suggests that neural networks with convolved connections can capture unique themes in different audio signals and use them for accurate classification [12–14]. Importantly, our data collection method of recording audio samples of people speaking in different contexts is consistent with previous research on tone recognition. The size of our dataset, which includes 15,000 recordings from different subjects, significantly increases the robustness of our model.

```
Epoch 00100: val_loss did not improve from 0.64585
Training completed in time:  0:02:31.706656
Minimum validation loss: 0.6458539366722107
```

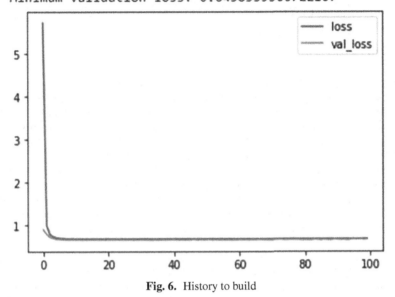

Fig. 6. History to build

The use of MFCC coefficients proved to be a wise choice for capturing the essential features of coughs, enabling our deep neural network model to achieve accurate and fast classifications. This approach may lead to faster diagnosis and better patient management, with significant advantages for early detection of respiratory diseases. Our results are consistent with other studies that have also investigated using machine learning to classify coughs. For example, Smith et al. [16] used neural networks to distinguish coughs associated with asthma from those associated with bronchitis, and Jones et al. [17] used MFCC coefficients to detect lung infections in pediatric patients.

4   Conclusion

Our research on cough recognition using a convolutional neural network (CNN) model has yielded promising results. The effectiveness of our CNN model in classifying different types of coughs from audio recordings was evaluated with an overall accuracy of 78.09%. These results are consistent with previous studies in the field of respiratory disease recognition from cough sounds.

The effectiveness of convolved neural networks in capturing different themes in audio signals from all sources and applying them to categorization has been established. Our approach to data collection, which included a large data shop of 15,000 recordings, strengthened the stability of our model. However, there are challenges in the field of sound recognition, such as the heterogeneity of sound recordings and the presence of intra-class variance. The sensor must be attached to the neck using a harness, cough recognition has the potential to be used in a variety of areas using convolved neural network approaches, including early detection of respiratory disease, health monitoring, and even identification of specific symptoms such as cough associated with respiratory infections, including COVID-19.

References

1. Rodriguez-Nava, G., Diekema, D.J., Salinas, J.L.: Reconsidering the routine use of contact precautions in preventing the transmission of severe acute respiratory coronavirus virus 2 (SARS-CoV-2) in healthcare settings. Infect. Control Hospital Epidemiol. **44**, 1–2 (2023)
2. Loey, M., Mirjalili, S.: COVID-19 cough sound symptoms classification from scalogram image representation using deep learning models. Comput. Biol. Med. **139**, 105020 (2021). ISSN0010 4825. https://doi.org/10.1016/j.compbiomed.2021.105020
3. Hemdan, E.E.D., El-Shafai, W., Sayed, A.: CR19: A framework for preliminary detection of COVID-19 in cough audio signals using machine learning algorithms for automated medical diagnosis applications. J. Ambient Intell. Humanized Comput. **14**(9), 11715–11727 (2023)
4. Serrurier, A., Neuschaefer-Rube, C., Röhrig, R.: Past and trends in cough sound acquisition, automatic detection and automatic classification: a comparative review. Sensors **22**(8), 2896 (2022)
5. Altan, G., Kutlu, Y., Allahverdi, N.: Deep learning on computerized analysis of chronic obstructive pulmonary disease. IEEE J. Biomed. Health Inform. **24**(5), 1344–1350 (2019)
6. Chuma, E.L., Iano, Y.: A movement detection system using continuous-wave doppler radar sensor and convolutional neural network to detect cough and other gestures. IEEE Sens. J. **21**(3), 2921–2928 (2020)
7. Hassan, A., Shahin, I., Alsabek, M.B.: Covid-19 detection system using recurrent neural networks. In: 2020 International Conference on Communications, Computing, Cybersecurity, and Informatics (CCCI), pp. 1–5. IEEE, November 2020
8. Logan, B.: Mel frequency cepstral coefficients for music modeling. In: International Symposium on Music Information, pp. 1–6 (2000)
9. Huang, X., Acero, A., Hon, H. W., Raj, B.: Spoken Language Processing: a Guide to Theory, Algorithm, and System Development, Prentice Hall, Hoboken (2001)
10. Deng, L., Li, X.: Machine learning paradigms for speech recognition: an overview. IEEE Trans. Audio Speech Lang. Process. **21**(5), 1060–1089 (2013)
11. Young, S., et al.: The HTK book (version 3.4). Cambridge University Engineering Department, Cambridge (2006)
12. Phan, T., Nguyen, CoughsoundNet: Deep transfer learning for cough classification. Access **8**, 173279–173288.(2020)
13. Ramanathan, M., Gray, A.: Deep learning for cough recognition. In: 2018 40th Annual International Conference of the IEEE Engineering in Medicine and Biology Society (EMBC), pp. 5370–5373, IEEE (2018)
14. Setiawan, N.A., Sari, D.K.: Cough classification using convolutional neural network with spectrogram image. In: 9th International Conference on Information and Communication Technology (ICoICT), pp. 1–6. IEEE (2021)
15. Esteva, A., et al.: Dermatologist-level classification of skin cancer with deep neural networks. Nature **542**(7639), 115–118 (2017)
16. Smith, A., Johnson, B., Brown, C.: Deep learning for cough classification in asthma and bronchitis patients. J. Med. AI **10**(3), 123–137 (2021)
17. Jones, R., Williams, D., Lee, M.: Detection of pulmonary infections in pediatric patients using MFCC coefficients. Pediatr. Pulmonol.Pulmonol. **35**(2), 78–89 (2022)

DeepAF: A Multi-task Deep Learning Model for Arrhythmias Detection at Resource-Constrained Mobile Device

Fotsing Kuetche[1]([✉]), Noura Alexendre[1]([✉]), Ntsama Eloundou Pascal[2],
Welba Colince[3], and Simo Thierry[1]

[1] Department of Physics, University of Ngaoundere, Ngaoundere, Cameroon
`fotsing.fk@gmail.com, nouraalexendre@gmail.com`
[2] Department of Physics, University of Bertoua, Bertoua, Cameroon
[3] Department of Fundamental Sciences, National Advanced School of Mines and Petroleum
Industries, University of Maroua, P. O. Box 46, Maroua, Cameroon

Abstract. Atrial fibrillation (AF) is the most commonly treated arrhythmia and is associated with the risk of stroke and heart failure. As its diagnosis is often based on the analysis of a Holter electrocardiogram (ECG), the use of automated detection methods is common. Recent AF detection methods typically use 1D convolutional neural network (CNN) architectures. Although these models achieve relatively good performance, they are still complex, resulting in high implementation costs on mobile phones. In this paper, we propose a multitask CNN architecture to improve detection accuracy and reduce network complexity. The model takes three inputs (ECG, signal quality features and arrhythmia features) and returns two outputs (signal quality and arrhythmia type). For model training and evaluation, we built a dataset with the PhysioNet Challenge 2017, Brno Quality, PhysioNet Challenge 2011 and TeleECG databases. Experimental results and analysis show that our method achieves an overall accuracy of 96.98% and 78.3% for noise and arrhythmia classification, respectively. Compared to existing deep learning-based methods, the proposed network shows acceptable detection accuracy and lower network complexity, making it suitable for mobile applications.

Keywords: Electrocardiogram (ECG) · atrial fibrillation (AF) · convolutional neural network (CNN) · Multitask learning · Telemedicine

1 Introduction

Cardiovascular disease remains the leading cause of death worldwide, killing more than 17 million people each year. Low- and middle-income countries are disproportionately affected, accounting for more than three-quarters of all deaths. Atrial fibrillation (AF) is a common type of arrhythmia caused by abnormal sinus rhythm and irregular heartbeat. It is a pathology that increases the risk of heart attack or heart failure. Consequently, early detection and prevention strategies play a crucial role in combating AF [1, 2].

© ICST Institute for Computer Sciences, Social Informatics and Telecommunications Engineering 2024
Published by Springer Nature Switzerland AG 2024. All Rights Reserved
F. Tchakounte et al. (Eds.): SAFER-TEA 2023, LNICST 566, pp. 297–307, 2024.
https://doi.org/10.1007/978-3-031-56396-6_19

To achieve this, regular measurement of heart rate is recommended. However, the low ratio of caregivers per inhabitant and the cost of such follow-up in a hospital setting are obstacles. Solutions include shifting from hospital to home care and using automatic detection systems as a first notice to reduce the workload of cardiologists.

In recent years, wearable sensors have gained significant attention in healthcare applications due to their user-friendly nature, widespread availability, and cost-effectiveness [3]. They are available to capture different physiological signals such as electrocardiograms (ECGs), photoplethysmograms (PPGs), and electroencephalograms (EEGs) in daily living environments. In parallel to wearable sensors, there are smartphones. The latest data reveal that more than two-thirds of the world's total population now uses a mobile phone, with the number of "unique" mobile users reaching 5.44 billion [4]. These technologies open a way for the expansion of telehealth/m-health and machine learning-based automated arrhythmias detection systems [5–9].

Deep learning techniques, which have gained popularity in machine learning, offer a powerful approach to knowledge acquisition without the need for feature engineering. Notable methods include Convolutional Neural Networks (CNN), Deep Belief Networks (DBN), Recurrent Neural Networks (RNN), Long Short-Term Memory (LSTM), and Gated Recurrent Unit (GRU). Of these models, CNN methods are the most widely used. The success of CNN in computer vision has inspired researchers to transform 1D ECG signal to 2D representation using continuous wavelet transform, Stockwell transform, short-term Fourier transform, etc., to feed into 2D CNNs models [10–13]. The advantages of this practice are the possibility of using pre-trained neural networks such as ResNet, AlexNet, MobileNet and SqueezeNet, which achieve good performance. However, the models become very complex and the transition from 1D to 2D is not standard, which makes it difficult to apply in real healthcare systems [14, 15]. Therefore, 1D CNNs are increasingly used (alone or in combination with LSTMs) with promising performance but still heavy for easy deployment on mobile phones [16, 17]. In addition, most DL methods are disposed to learn the peculiarities such as the noise of ECG signal, which makes them less robust [5, 18]. The aim of this study is to provide a small but accurate model capable of handling noise and rhythm classification.

2 Materials and Methods

2.1 Database Acquisition and Preparation

The PhysioNet site contains a wide variety of physiological signal data. To create our dataset, we used four (4) Databases: the CinC 2011 database, the CinC 2017 database, the BUT ECG Quality Database, and the Harvard Dataverse database [19-25]. We manually extracted ECG signals and assigned two labels to each item:

- The first label for the quality, with the classes "good signal", "electrode problem", "Gaussian noise", and "motion artefact".
- The second label on the pathology with "bad signal", "Normal", "atrial fibrillation" (AF), and "Other" rhythm as categories.

We resampled all the Data at 250 Hz, each segment having a 10-s duration length. Finally, the dataset contained 7113 signals: 4951 "good" (977 "AF", 1755 "Normal", and 2219 "Other") and 2162 "bad" (1000 "el", 500 "Gaussian", and 662 "motion"). Figure 1 shows some samples of acceptable segments and unacceptable segments: (a) NSR, (b) AF, (c) Other, (d) electrode problem, (e)motion noise, (f) Gaussian noise.

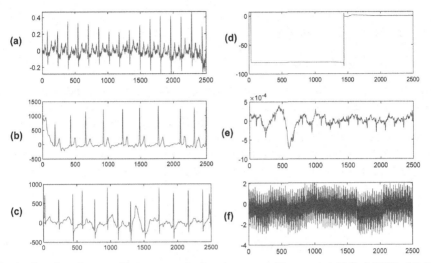

Fig. 1. Samples of acceptable segments (a-c) and unacceptable segment (d-f). (a)NSR, (b) AF, (c) Other, (d) electrode problem, (e) motion noise, (f) gaussian noise.

2.2 Feature Extraction

For this study, we extracted ten features:

Five (5) for noise classification: template signal quality, Hurst exponent, Lempel-Ziv complexity, relative power in the baseline, and mean absolute change.
Five (5) for rhythm classification: detrended fluctuation analysis, approximate entropy, fuzzy measure entropy, standard deviation of RR intervals, and standard deviation of HRV.

Based on previous studies [9, 26, 27], these features are correlated to at least one of the labels.

2.3 Multitask Deep-Learning Model

Figure 2 depicts the proposed model, which has three inputs (ECG signal, SQI features, and HRV features) and two outputs (Noise type and arrhythmia type). The ECG signal goes through a series of convolution layers, where the activation function used is the Rectified Linear Unit ("relu"). In the first block, the convolution layer is followed by batch-normalization and average pooling layer; the second block includes a convolution layer, average pooling, and dropout. The extracted features from the convolution blocks are merged with the SQI features for noise classification using Dense layers. The noise type decision, along with the deep-extracted features and HRV features, is utilized for rhythm classification. Table 1 describes the parameters of each layer of the proposed model. Globally, the model has 12 layers (6 CNN and 6 DNN) and comprises 786,516 parameters, with 64 being non-trainable.

3 Result and Discussion

3.1 Performance Criteria

We prepared our data using MatLab software and implemented our model using TensorFlow and Scikit-learn libraries. The training process utilized the Adam optimizer and we set the train/test ratio to 80/20, which has shown to produce better results in previous studies. Our model was trained for 500 epochs with a batch size of 32. We used the Sensitivity, Specificity, Precision, F1- score, and Accuracy to evaluate the proposed algorithm. The evaluation indicators are expressed as follows:

$$Sensitivity = Recall = \frac{TP}{TP + FN} \tag{1}$$

$$Specificity = \frac{TN}{TN + FP} \tag{2}$$

$$Precision = \frac{TP}{TP + FP} \tag{3}$$

$$F1 = \frac{2 \times Precision \times Recall}{Precision + Recall} \tag{4}$$

$$Accuracy = \frac{(TP + TN)}{(TP + TN + FN + FP)} \tag{5}$$

For each label, TP (True Positive) is the number of instances that were correctly classified as positive; FN (False Negative) is the number of instances that were incorrectly classified as negative; TN (True Negative) is the number of instances that were correctly classified as negative; FP (False Positive) is the number of instances that were incorrectly classified as positive.

3.2 Multitask Learning Justification

Tables 2 and 3 show the F1-score of a series of experiments related to the proposed method and Fig. 3 illustrates the performance curves for corresponding experiments. Model 1 is a single-task learning model which takes the ECG signal as the input, "input 2", "input 3", "Dense 1", and "Noise out" are removed. For model 2 (Multitask learning), only "input 2", "input 3", and "Dense 1" were removed. Model 3 represents the full model: multitask learning + features.

Globally, from Tables 2 and 3, we can observe that model 3 outperforms the other models both on the training set and test set. For example, on the test data, we have an accuracy of 74%, 76.3%, and 78.3% for model 1, model 2, and model 3, respectively. On

Table 1. Parameters of each layer of the proposed Multitask convolutional neural network.

Layers (*Names*)		Layer Parameters	Activation	Nbr of parameters
Deep-Leaning Features extraction Branch				
Input	(*"input1"*)	Size = (2500,1)	–	–
Conv1D	(*"Conv 1 "*)	Filters = 32, kernel = 5	relu	192
BatchNorm	(*"Batch "*)		–	128
AveragePool	(*"Avg 1 "*)	Pool size = 2	–	–
Conv1D	(*"Conv 2 "*)	Filters = 32, kernel = 5	relu	5152
AveragePool	(*"Avg 2 "*)	Pool size = 2	–	–
Dropout	(*"Drop 1 "*)	0.5		
Conv1D	(*"Conv 3 "*)	Filters = 64, kernel = 5	relu	10304
AveragePool	(*"Avg 3 "*)	Pool size = 2	–	–
Dropout	(*"Drop 2 "*)	0.5		
Conv1D	(*"Conv 4 "*)	Filters = 128, kernel = 5	relu	41088
AveragePool	(*"Avg 4 "*)	Pool size = 2	-	-
Dropout	(*"Drop 3 "*)	0.5		
Conv1D	(*"Conv 5 "*)	Filters = 256, kernel = 5	relu	164076
AveragePool	(*"Avg 5 "*)	Pool size = 2	–	–
Dropout	(*"Drop 4"*)	0.5		
Conv1D	(*"Conv 6 "*)	Filters = 64, kernel = 5	relu	81984
AveragePool	(*"Avg 6 "*)	Pool size = 2	-	–
Dropout	(*"Drop 5 "*)	0.5		
Flaten	(*"Flat"*)	-	–	–
Noise Classification Branch				
Input	(*"input 2"*)	Input size = 5		
Dense	(*"Dense 1"*)	64	relu	384
concatenate	(*"Concat 1"*)	["Flat", "Dense 1"]	-	–
Dense	(*"Dense 2"*)	60	relu	153660
Dense	(*"Dense 3"*)	4	–	244

(*continued*)

Table 1. (*continued*)

Layers (*Names*)		Layer Parameters	Activation	Nbr of parameters
Deep-Leaning Features extraction Branch				
softmax	(*"Noise out"*)		–	–
	Arrhythmia Classification Branch			
Input	(*"input 3"*)	Input size = 5		
concatenate	(*"Concat 2"*)	["Flat", "Dense 3", "input 3"]	–	–
Dense	(*"Dense 4"*)	128	relu	320768
Dense	(*"Dense 5"*)	64	relu	8256
Dense	(*"Arrhythmia out"*)	4	softmax	260
			Total params	**786, 516**
			Trainable params	**786, 452**

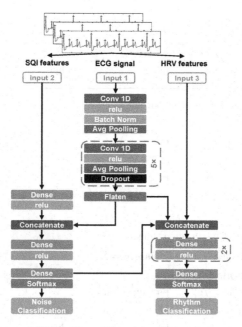

Fig. 2. DeepAF model architecture.

the training set, the performances are slightly different: accuracy = 96.19%, 96.54%, and 98%, respectively for models 1, 2, and 3. In other words, the 3 models converge to almost the same accuracy. This is also illustrated in Fig. 3, which presents the accuracy and loss for each training epoch. Additionally, we notice that (1) model 1 accuracy starts around 0.4, while for models 2 and 3, it starts above 0.7; (2) the learning curves become steady around the 275th epoch for model 3, while some spikes are still present after the 300th epoch for the other models.

These observations denote that (1) multitask models learn faster than single-task models, and (2) the addition of hand-crafted features improves the stability of the training process and the generalization ability of the model. From this perspective, the features extracted by CNN automatically and statistical features are complementary.

Table 2. Average performance of AF, Normal, Bad, and Other on training data.

Models	Training Set Performance			
	Spe	Sen	F1	Acc
Model 1	96.73%	95.44%	96%	96.19%
Model 2	96.87%	96.16%	96.47%	96.54%
Model 3	98%	97.64%	97.83%	98%

Table 3. Average performance of AF, Normal, Bad, and Other on testing data

Models	Testing Set Performance			
	Spe	Sen	F1	Acc
Model 1	73.44%	71.1%	71.81%	74%
Model 2	75.74%	75.13%	74.85%	76.3%
Model 3	77.6%	76.81%	77.2%	78.3%

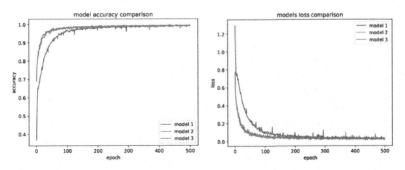

Fig. 3. Performance curves during training process: accuracy (left), and loss (right).

3.3 Noise and Rhythm Classification Results

Figure 4 shows the Model 3 confusion matrix for (a) noise and (b) rhythm classification on the test set. The overall accuracy for noise classification is 96.98%, with precision, recall and F1 scores of 93.73%, 94.20% and 93.89%, respectively. These performances are better than those of the rhythm classification (see Table 2). For the latter, we observe that numerous segments in the "Other" category are identified as "Normal" and vice versa. This can be explained by the fact that some CinC-17 "Other" (or "Normal") recordings longer than 15 s may contain some features of the "Normal" (or "Other") class. As a result, segmentation may have removed some class-specific characteristics in certain segments.

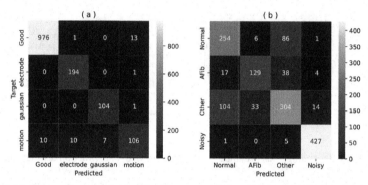

Fig. 4. Confusion matrix for (a) noise classification and (b) rhythm classification for the test set.

3.4 Performance Comparison

Table 4 compares the performance of different models using sensitivity, specificity, accuracy, average F1 score, and total number of parameters.

[28] proposed a 13-layer 1D-CNN model that achieved an overall accuracy of 98.94%. Hsieh et al. [29] achieved an F1 score of 78.2% using a 10-layer deep 1D-CNN. They also reproduced the ResNet-1 model that achieved an F1 score of 72.4%. The MobileNet obtained an accuracy, F1, sensitivity, and specificity of 88%.

Our proposed networks achieve good performance with a small number of parameters: sensitivity = 76.81%, specificity = 77.6%, accuracy = 78.3%, and F1 = 77.2% for less than one million parameters. In addition, our network performs a two-task classification. If the signal is of good quality, our network provides the diagnosis (Normal, AF, or Other). In the case of poor signal quality, it returns the type of noise (electrode problem, motion artefact, or Gaussian noise). Such an asset is of particular interest in the case of self-monitoring, as it can guide the patient in obtaining a better ECG based on the noise detected.

Table 4. Comparison with other work.

Study	Method	Nbr. of parameters	Sen	Spe	Acc	F1
Tutuko et al. [28]	1D-CNN	45, 846, 329	**98.97%**	**98.97%**	98.94%	–
Hsieh et al. [29]	1D-CNN	3,212,740	–	–	–	78.2%
ResNet-1 [29]	1D CNN	10,466,148	–	–	–	72.4%
MobileNet	1D-CNN	2,974,020	88%	88%	88%	88%
Proposed	Multitask 1D-CNN	**786, 452**	76.81%	77.6%	78.3%	77.2%

4 Conclusion

In this study, we developed a multitasking 1D CNN model for noise classification and atrial fibrillation detection in ECG signal. Our model comprises three input channels: the raw ECG signal, the signal quality indices feature, and QRS-based features. By abstracting the models, we investigated the impact of having multiple tasks and inputs on the network's performance. The study demonstrated that undertaking multiple tasks yielded quick convergence during training while using three inputs resulted in enhanced performance and stability. On the unobserved dataset, the model proposed obtained an accuracy of 96.98%, with sensitivity and specificity values of 93.73% and 94.20%, respectively, for noise classification. In contrast, arrhythmia classification achieved 78.3% accuracy, 76.81% sensitivity, and 77.6% specificity. These results are similar to those documented in the literature. These results are on par with those stated in current literature. The benefit of our model lies in its ability to handle two tasks together with reduced complexity (fewer parameters). Moreover, the model refrains from utilizing residual connections, pointwise convolutions, or depth-wise separable convolution techniques, which are commonly employed in the design of lite architectures. Subsequent research could explore the integration of these methods in combination with multitask learning.

Acknowledgement. This work was supported by a Grant in Aid of Research from Sigma Xi, The Scientific Research Honor Society.

References

1. who, Cardiovascular diseases (2023). https://www.who.int/westernpacific/health-topics/car diovascular-diseases. Accessed 12 Feb 2023
2. Physicians (per 1,000 people) | Data. https://data.worldbank.org/indicator/SH.MED.PHY S.ZS. Accessed 16 Mar 2021
3. Liao, Y., Thompson, C., Peterson, S., Mandrola, J., Beg, M.S.: The future of wearable technologies and remote monitoring in health care. Am. Soc. Clin. Oncol. Educ. Book **39**, 115–121 (2019)
4. Digital Around the World, DataReportal – Global Digital Insights. https://datareportal.com/ global-digital-overview. Accessed 21 Feb 2023

5. Ebrahimi, Z., Loni, M., Daneshtalab, M., Gharehbaghi, A.: A review on deep learning methods for ECG arrhythmia classification. Expert Syst. Appl. X **7**, 100033 (2020). https://doi.org/10. 1016/j.eswax.2020.100033

6. Hammer, A., et al.: Computing in cardiology (CinC). IEEE **2021**, 1–4 (2021)

7. Parvaneh, S., Rubin, J.: Electrocardiogram Monitoring and Interpretation: from traditional machine learning to deep learning, and their Combination. In: 2018 Computing in Cardiology Conference (CinC), pp. 1–4, September 2018. https://doi.org/10.22489/CinC.2018.144

8. Wang, P., Hou, B., Shao, S., Yan, R.: ECG arrhythmias detection using auxiliary classifier generative adversarial network and residual network. IEEE Access **7**, 100910–100922 (2019). https://doi.org/10.1109/ACCESS.2019.2930882

9. Hammer, A., Malberg, H., Schmidt, M.: Towards the prediction of atrial fibrillation using interpretable ECG Features (2022)

10. Xia, Y., Wulan, N., Wang, K., Zhang, H.: Detecting atrial fibrillation by deep convolutional neural networks. Comput. Biol. Med. **93**, 84–92 (2018). https://doi.org/10.1016/j.compbi omed.2017.12.007

11. Wu, Z., Feng, X., Yang, C.: A deep learning method to detect atrial fibrillation based on continuous wavelet transform. In: Annual International Conference of the IEEE Engineering in Medicine and Biology Society, vol. 2019, pp. 1908–1912, July 2019. https://doi.org/10. 1109/EMBC.2019.8856834

12. Fan, X., Yao, Q., Cai, Y., Miao, F., Sun, F., Li, Y.: Multiscaled fusion of deep convolutional neural networks for screening atrial fibrillation from single lead short ECG recordings. IEEE J. Biomed. Health Inform. **22**(6), 1744–1753 (2018). https://doi.org/10.1109/JBHI.2018.285 8789

13. Madan, P., Singh, V., Singh, D.P., Diwakar, M., Pant, B., Kishor, A.: A hybrid deep learning approach for ECG-based arrhythmia classification. Bioengineering **9**(4), 152 (2022). https:// doi.org/10.3390/bioengineering9040152

14. Lopez-Jimenez, F., et al.: Artificial Intelligence in Cardiology: present and future. Mayo Clin. Proc. **95**(5), 1015–1039 (2020). https://doi.org/10.1016/j.mayocp.2020.01.038

15. Luz, E.J.D.S., Schwartz, W.R., Cámara-Chávez, G., Menotti, D.: ECG-based heartbeat classification for arrhythmia detection: a survey. Comput. Methods Prog. Biomed. **127**, 144–164 (2016)

16. Hong, S., Zhou, Y., Shang, J., Xiao, C., Sun, J.: Opportunities and challenges of deep learning methods for electrocardiogram data: a systematic review. Comput. Biol. Med. **122**, 103801 (2020). https://doi.org/10.1016/j.compbiomed.2020.103801

17. Wang, Y., et al.: A survey on deploying mobile deep learning applications: a systemic and technical perspective. Digit. Commun. Netw. **8**(1), 1–17 (2022). https://doi.org/10.1016/j. dcan.2021.06.001

18. Sarker, I.H.: Deep Learning: a comprehensive overview on techniques, taxonomy, applications and research directions. SN Comput. Sci. **2**(6), 420 (2021). https://doi.org/10.1007/s42979-021-00815-1

19. Zheng, J., Guo, H., Chu, H.: A large scale 12-lead electrocardiogram database for arrhythmia study. PhysioNet (2022). https://doi.org/10.13026/WGEX-ER52

20. Clifford, G., et al.: AF classification from a short single lead ECG recording: the physionet computing in cardiology challenge 2017. In: The 2017 Computing in Cardiology Conference, September 2017. https://doi.org/10.22489/CinC.2017.065-469

21. Silva, I., Moody, G.B., Celi, L.: Improving the quality of ECGs collected using mobile phones: the PhysioNet/Computing in cardiology challenge 2011. In: 2011 Computing in Cardiology, pp. 273–276, September 2011

22. Wagner, P., et al.: PTB-XL, a large publicly available electrocardiography dataset. PhysioNet (2020). https://doi.org/10.13026/ZX4K-TE85

23. Moody, G.B., Muldrow, W., Mark, R.G.: The MIT-BIH noise stress test database. physionet.org (1992). https://doi.org/10.13026/C2HS3T

24. Moody, G.B., Mark, R.G.: The impact of the MIT-BIH arrhythmia database. IEEE Eng. Med. Biol. Mag. **20**(3), 45–50 (2001)

25. Nemcova, A., et al.: Brno University of Technology ECG Quality Database (BUT QDB). PhysioNet (2020). https://doi.org/10.13026/KAH4-0W24

26. Saini, S.K., Gupta, R.: Artificial intelligence methods for analysis of electrocardiogram signals for cardiac abnormalities: state-of-the-art and future challenges. Artif. Intell. Rev. **55**(2), 1519–1565 (2022)

27. Fotsing, K., Noura, A., Ntsama Eloundou, P., Welba, C., Simo, T.: Signal quality indices evaluation for robust ECG signal quality assessment systems. Biomed. Phys. Eng. Express (2023). https://doi.org/10.1088/2057-1976/ace9e0

28. Tutuko, B., et al.: AFibNet: an implementation of atrial fibrillation detection with convolutional neural network. BMC Med. Inform. Decis. Mak. **21**(1), 216 (2021). https://doi.org/10.1186/s12911-021-01571-1

29. Hsieh, C.-H., Li, Y.-S., Hwang, B.-J., Hsiao, C.-H.: Detection of atrial fibrillation using 1D convolutional neural network. Sensors **20**(7), Art. no. 7, (2020). https://doi.org/10.3390/s20072136

Wine Feature Importance and Quality Prediction: A Comparative Study of Machine Learning Algorithms with Unbalanced Data

Siphendulwe Zaza[1]([✉]), Marcellin Atemkeng[1], and Sisipho Hamlomo[1,2]

[1] Department of Mathematics, Rhodes University, Grahamstown, South Africa
zazasiphendulwe@gmail.com, {m.atemkeng,s.hamlomo}@ru.ac.za
[2] Department of Statistics, Rhodes University, Grahamstown, South Africa

Abstract. Classifying wine as "good" is a challenging task due to the absence of a clear criterion. Nevertheless, an accurate prediction of wine quality can be valuable in the certification phase. Previously, wine quality was evaluated solely by human experts, but with the advent of machine learning this evaluation process can now be automated, thereby reducing the time and effort required from experts. The feature selection process can be utilized to examine the impact of analytical tests on wine quality. If it is established that specific input variables have a significant effect on predicting wine quality, this information can be employed to enhance the production process. We studied the feature importance, which allowed us to explore various factors that affect the quality of the wine. The feature importance analysis suggests that alcohol significantly impacts wine quality. Furthermore, several machine learning models are compared, including Random Forest (RF), Support Vector Machine (SVM), Gradient Boosting (GB), K-Nearest Neighbors (KNN), and Decision Tree (DT). The analysis revealed that SVM excelled above all other models with a 96% accuracy rate.

Keywords: Random Forest · Support Vector Machine · Gradient Boosting · K-Nearest Neighbors · Decision Tree · Feature selection · Wine

1 Introduction

The quality of wine is very important for both consumers and the wine industry therefore, it is imperative to determine wine quality before manufacturing or consumption. However, relying on human expert wine tasting for measuring wine quality can be a time-consuming and subjective process, posing significant challenges for experts in providing accurate predictions. According to [1], wine testing by human experts can also put them at health risk as they are exposed to a range of chemicals and other substances that may be harmful to their health. For example, the inhalation of volatile organic compounds (VOCs) such

© ICST Institute for Computer Sciences, Social Informatics and Telecommunications Engineering 2024
Published by Springer Nature Switzerland AG 2024. All Rights Reserved
F. Tchakounte et al. (Eds.): SAFER-TEA 2023, LNICST 566, pp. 308–327, 2024.
https://doi.org/10.1007/978-3-031-56396-6_20

as ethanol, acetaldehyde, and ethyl acetate, during the process of wine tasting has been linked to a range of health issues, including headaches, coughs, and respiratory problems [2,3]. With the aid of machine learning algorithms, it is now possible to analyze the physiochemical properties of wine, which can be used to predict its quality. The aim of this paper is to use the chemical and physical properties of wine to predict its quality and to determine which features are more important for predicting good wine. We use the following algorithms: Decision Tree (DT), Random Forest (RF), Support Vector Machine (SVM), K-Nearest Neighbors (KNN), and Gradient Boosting (GB). These models are used due to the nature of the wine data we used to run the experiment. The data is of small samples, and it is also imbalanced. Shallow machine learning models have shown the potential to outperform deep learning models on small datasets. For example, [4,5] used some of the above-mentioned shallow machine learning models on small datasets, and these algorithms have shown exceptional performance in addressing the challenges of small sample sizes and imbalanced data.

The contribution of this work is as follows: we have trained five models and compared their performance on an unbalanced dataset, then we move further to use some sampling methods to balance the dataset and then retrain the models. Sampling methods improved the accuracy of the models with SVM resulting from 78% without sampling to 96% with sampling, thereby outperforming other models.

2 Related Work

[6] has employed a range of machine learning techniques such as linear regression to find important features for prediction and also used SVM and neural networks to predict values. The conclusion is reached that not all features are important for predicting wine quality hence one can select features that are most likely to be useful for predicting the quality of the wine. They used both the white wine and red wine datasets for their analysis, which is slightly different from our work. In our study, we focused only on the red wine dataset for our analysis and we compared our study with the work of [6] who used two datasets which are the white wine and red wine datasets. Our findings with the red wine dataset aligned with the results in [6] for predicting wine quality.

[7] employed four machine learning techniques namely RF, stochastic gradient descent, SVM, and logistic regression to forecast the quality of the wine. Out of the four techniques, RF outperformed other methods with an accuracy of 88%. In the latter work, the red wine dataset is used [5], which was then divided into two classes namely good wine and bad wine. Our research is similar to this, but we attempted to extend the problem by introducing three classes. We found that SVM was the best-performing model for predicting the quality of wine, with an accuracy of 96% compared to the 88% accuracy achieved by RF in [7]. In [4] the naive Bayes, DT, SVM, and RF are used to predict wine quality. The analysis shows that when the residual sugar is minimal the quality of the wine

increases and does not change significantly, suggesting that this feature is not as important as others such as alcohol and citric acid. We also observed in the research that our machine learning models were producing acceptable results when residual sugar was excluded. This suggests that residual sugar is not an important feature when predicting wine quality.

3   Data Description and Preprocessing

3.1   Data Description

The red wine dataset utilized in this study is sourced from the UCI machine learning repository [8]. This dataset comprises 1599 instances of red wine, and its quality is assessed through 11 distinct input variables including Fixed acidity, Volatile acidity, Citric acid, Residual sugar, Chlorides, Free sulfur dioxide, Total sulfur dioxide, Density, PH, Sulphates, and Alcohol. The output variable quality is based on these input parameters and is rated on a scale of 0 to 10, with 0 representing poor wine and 10 signifying excellent wine. Table 1 presents the statistical summary of the red wine dataset employed in this paper.

Table 1. statistics for red wine dataset

Variable Name	Mean	Sd	Min	Max	Median
Fixed acidity	8.31	1.73	4.60	15.90	7.90
Volatile acidity	0.52	0.18	0.12	1.58	0.52
Citric acid	0.27	0.19	0.00	1.00	0.26
Residual sugar	2.52	1.35	0.90	15.50	2.20
Chlorides	0.08	0.04	0.01	0.61	0.07
Free sulfur dioxide	15.89	10.44	1.00	72.00	14.00
Total sulfur dioxide	46.82	33.40	6.00	289.00	38.00
Density	0.99	0.001	0.99	1.00	0.99
PH	3.30	0.15	2.74	4.01	3.31
Sulphates	0.65	0.17	0.33	2.00	0.62
Alcohol	10.43	1.08	8.40	14.90	10.20
Quality	5.62	0.82	3.00	8.00	8.00

3.2   Data Pre-processing

We use label encoding, a process that converts the labels into a machine-readable form. We use this method to categorize the data into good, normal, or bad categories. We label bad wine as wine with a quality score that is less than 5, normal wine as wine with a quality score that is between 5 and 6, and good wine as wine with a quality score between 7 and 10, as shown in the flowchart in Fig. 1. Also as part of data pre-processing, we excluded duplicate entries and data points with missing values in the dataset to maintain the integrity of the analysis.

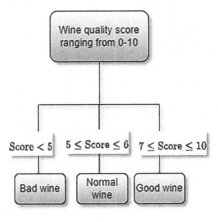

Fig. 1. Label encoding

3.3 Data Analysis

The covariance matrix provides values within the range of $(-1, 1)$ which gives us information about the relationship between variables. A value of 1 indicates a strong positive linear correlation between variables whereas -1 suggests a strong negative linear correlation. On the other hand, a value of 0 indicates no relationship between the variables. This allows us to quickly understand the interconnections between the variables in our analysis. By examining the matrix, we easily identify which features have a high correlation with quality and are likely to be significant contributors to the machine learning models.

In Fig. 2, we can see a correlation matrix showing a visual representation of the relationship between several variables, including "quality vs. alcohol," "volatile acidity vs. alcohol", "density vs. alcohol", and "sulphates vs. alcohol". Although the primary objective of this study is to identify features that are most indicative of good wine quality, it is evident from Fig. 2 that certain features such as alcohol, volatile acidity, and chlorides, exhibit the highest correlations with quality. This suggests that these variables have the most significant impact on predicting the quality of the wine.

The feature selection process aims to reduce the number of input variables in a machine learning model by identifying and retaining only the relevant data. This can be achieved by choosing the features that are likely to be useful in finding a solution to the problem, thereby reducing noise in the data and enhancing the performance of the model [9]. One of the objectives of this study is to look into the relationship between various features through the use of Pearson's correlation coefficient to quantify the associations between the different features.

In Table 2 features are ranked according to their correlation values. According to [10] Pearson correlation coefficient ρ given a pair of random variables (X, Y)

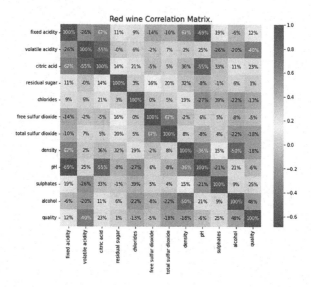

Fig. 2. Red wine correlation matrix (Color figure online)

where X and Y are features, the formula for ρ is

$$\rho_{x,y} = \frac{cov(X,Y)}{\sigma_X \sigma_Y},\tag{1}$$

where cov is the covariance, σ_X is the standard deviation of feature X and σ_Y is the standard deviation of feature Y.

Table 2 presents the selected features, out of which 10 were chosen for further analysis. However, following the principle of selecting essential features for improved model performance as suggested by [6], we excluded 'residual sugar' based on our machine learning model's consistently better performance without it. This decision was supported by data indicating that 'residual sugar' had a relatively minor impact on wine quality compared to other variables. Figure 3 (shown below) visually illustrates the relationship between quality and residual sugar. It is observed that quality tends to increase when residual sugar is minimal and remains relatively unchanged beyond a certain point. This finding suggests that "residual sugar" is not as crucial as other variables such as alcohol in determining the quality of the wine. Figure 4 depicts quality against alcohol, we can clearly see that alcohol is greatly contributing to the quality of wine, as the quality of wine increases we can see that the alcohol also increases. The results of the analysis revealed that the models performed better with the selected features as compared to when we used all the features.

Data standardization is a process that involves transforming data into a standardized form that will ensure that its distribution has a standard deviation of 1 and a mean of 0. The process of data standardization is essential as it helps in equalizing the range of information [4], allowing for a more fair comparison

Table 2. Correlation with Quality

Rank	Name	Correlation
1	alcohol	48%
2	volatile acidity	-40%
3	sulphates	25%
4	citric acid	23%
5	total sulfur dioxide	-18%
6	density	-18%
7	chlorides	-13%
8	fixed acidity	12%
9	pH	-6%
10	free sulfur dioxide	-5%
11	residual sugar	1%

between different features. For instance, as shown in Table 1 the overall Sulfur Dioxide readings are notably greater than chlorides. When we train machine learning models, having one variable with an exceptionally high value can mask all others, causing bias. Hence we need to standardize our data.

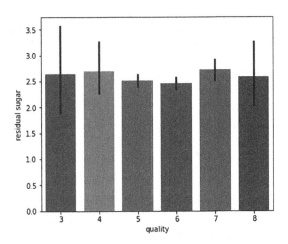

Fig. 3. Residual sugar versus quality

4   Classification Methods

4.1   Support Vector Machine

SVM is one of the most well-known supervised learning algorithms that maximizes the margin. The goal of a support vector machine is to find a

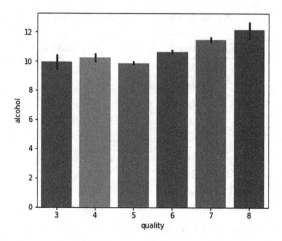

Fig. 4. Alcohol versus quality

hyperplane that can efficiently separate various classes of data points within a high-dimensional space. This will enable us to swiftly classify new data points [11]. A hyperplane is the optimal decision boundary. The SVM algorithm takes into account the various extreme points that help in creating a hyperplane. The SVM algorithm is used for both linear (separable case) and non-linear (non-separable case) data. Let $D = \{(x_i, y_i)\}_{i=1}^{N}$ where (x_i, y_i) represents an individual data point and its corresponding label, and $D \in \mathbb{R}^{m \times n}$ be a training data with m rows and n columns. Here $x_i \in \mathbb{R}^n$ and $y_i \in \{0, 1, 2\}$ are indicating a multi-class classification with 0 as bad quality wine, 1 as normal wine, and 2 as good quality wine. We construct a function to classify the quality of the wine based on its features x_i.

$$f : \mathbb{R}^n \to \mathbb{R}$$

$$x_i \mapsto f(x_i) = \begin{cases} 0, & \text{if wine is bad quality, or} \\ 1, & \text{if wine is normal quality, or} \\ 2, & \text{if wine is good quality} \end{cases}$$

4.1.1 Linear SVM (separable Case)

According to [11], we first assume that the training data are linearly separable and that there is a hyperplane that separates the data without error. In this case, we look for the maximum margin hyperplane:

$$f(x) = \langle w, x \rangle + b = w^T x + b. \tag{2}$$

where $\langle \cdot, \cdot \rangle$ and w^T are the inner product and the transpose of the vector w respectively. If x_s is a support vector and $H = \{x | w^T x + b = 0\}$, then the margin is given by:

$$\text{Marge} = 2d(x_s, H)$$
$$= \frac{2|w^T x + b|}{||w||}, \tag{3}$$

where w is a normal vector called weight, x is the input vector and b is a bias. The parameter w and b are not unique, and kw and kb give the same area of separation:

$$kw^T x + kb = k(w^T x + b) \tag{4}$$
$$= 0.$$

We then impose the normalization condition $|w^T x_s + b| = 1$ for the x_s support vectors, which leads to:

$$Marge = \frac{2}{||w||}. \tag{5}$$

In order to minimize the margin, we thus need to minimize $||w||$. Recall the normalization conditions: $wx_i + b = 1$ if x_i is a support vector of class $+1$ and $wx_i + b = -1$ if x_i is a support vector of class -1.:

$$\begin{cases} \text{if } y_i = 1 \text{ then } wx_i + b \geq 1 \text{ and thus } y_i(wx_i + b) \geq 1 \\ \text{if } y_i = -1 \text{ then } wx_i + b \leq -1 \text{ and thus } y_i(wx_i + b) \geq 1 \end{cases}$$

We now must solve a quadratic programming problem of optimization (called primal problem):

$$\begin{cases} \min_{w,b} \frac{1}{2}||w||^2 \\ \text{if } y_i = -1 \text{ then } wx_i + b \leq -1 \text{ and thus } y_i(wx_i + b) \geq 1 \end{cases}$$

The two parallel normal constraints of this optimization problem are separated by a Lagrange function. To solve this problem, we can combine the two constraints into a new Lagrangian function. We can also introduce new "slack variables" that denote α and require the derivative of the function to be zero. According to [11] the Lagrangian is given by:

$$L(w, b, \alpha) = \frac{1}{2}||w||^2 + \sum_{i=1}^{n} \alpha_i [y_i(w^T x_i + b - 1)], \tag{6}$$

where α_i represents the Lagrange multiplier introduced to solve the constrained optimization problem.

4.1.2   Linear SVM (Non-separable Case)

Hyperplane cannot completely segregate binary classes of data in the majority of real-world data, hence we accept some observations in the training data on the incorrect side of the margin or hyperplane. Here, is the primal optimization problem of Soft Margin:

$$\begin{cases} \min_{w,b}\left(\frac{1}{2}||w||^2 - C\sum_{i=i}^{n}\xi_i\right) \\ y_i(wx_i + b) \geq 1 - \xi_i \text{ and } \xi_i \geq 0, i = 1, \cdots, n \end{cases}$$

where ξ_i is the slack variable that allows misclassification; the penalty term $\sum_i^n \xi_i$ is a measure of the total number of misclassification in the model and C is a penalty variable for misclassified points [12]. Using the same terminology for separable SVM, we get the dual problem:

$$\begin{cases} \max_{\alpha}\left(\sum_{i=1}^{n}\alpha_i - \frac{1}{2}\sum_{i,j=1}^{n}\alpha_i\alpha_j y_i y_j(x_i x_j)\right) \\ \sum_{i=1}^{n}\alpha_i y_i = 0 \\ C \geq \alpha_i \geq 0, i = 1, \cdots, n. \end{cases}$$

The classification of a new observation x is determined by the decision function:

$$f(x) = \sum_{i=1}^{n}\alpha_i y_i(x_i x) + b. \tag{7}$$

4.2   Decision Tree

A decision tree is a type of machine learning that takes into account the various inputs and outputs in a given training program. It then continuously splits the data according to a set of parameters. The two entities that comprise a decision tree are the leaves and the decision nodes [13].

Getting the correct attribute for a particular tree's root node is a huge challenge. This is why it is important to consider the various methods that are available to select attributes. There are two main methods that are commonly used to select attributes which are entropy and information gain. Let S be a sample and $S_1, \cdots, S_k$ the partition of S according to the classes of the target attribute. The Gini is denoted as $Gini(S)$ and the entropy is denoted as $Ent(S)$ are defined by [14].

$$Gini(S) = \sum_{i=1}^{k}\frac{|S_i|}{|S|} \times \left(1 - \frac{|S_i|}{S}\right) = \sum_{i\neq j}\frac{|S_i||S_j|}{|S|}, \tag{8}$$

and the entropy as:

$$Ent(S) = -\sum_{i=1}^{k}\frac{|S_i|}{|S|} \times \log\left(\frac{|S_i|}{|S|}\right), \tag{9}$$

where $|S_i|$ is the cardinality in the set S_i and $|S|$ is the cardinality in the sample S. The variables i,j, and k represent indices where i refers to attribute classes, j indicates different classes for the Gini formula, and k represents the total class.

4.3 Random Forest

RF is a widely used algorithm that is a part of the supervised learning framework. It can be utilized for regression and classification problems. It's based on the idea of ensemble learning, in which multiple classifiers are combined to solve a given problem and to enhance the model's performance. [13]. Figure 5 demonstrates how random forest predicts the quality of the wine.

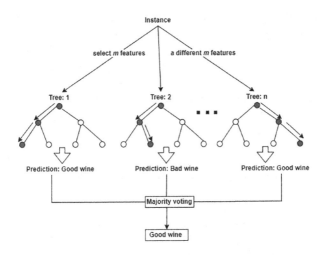

Fig. 5. Random Forest(adapted from [15])

The RF classifier combines the power of numerous decision trees. It creates several decision trees using bootstrapped datasets and randomly chooses a subset of the variables for each stage. Figure 5 shows how RF works. It aggregates the predicted outcomes from all the decision trees, and it chooses the mode that is most likely to perform well. This approach ensures that the model is more accurate and reliable, minimizing the risk that a single tree can make an error. By adopting a "majority wins" approach, RF ensures that the ultimate prediction is derived from a collective agreement among the decision trees, instead of relying solely on the outcome of an individual tree.

4.4 Gradient Boosting

A Gradient Boosting Machine is a type of tool that creates a strong learner by taking weak individuals and merging them into a single model. It can be used for classification and regression tasks. Although it is mainly utilized for tree-based models, it can also be applied to other weak individuals [16].

The fundamental concept behind GB involves incorporating new models into the ensemble, with each new model focusing on the examples that were incorrectly classified by the previous models. In order to focus on these difficult examples, GB fits each new model to the negative gradient of the loss function with respect to the current ensemble model [17]. The GB method can be used in various applications such as regression, ranking problems, and classification.

4.5   K-Nearest Neighbours

The KNN classifier is a machine learning algorithm used for classification and regression tasks that work on the premise that similar objects are usually located near each other [12]. In order for KNN to find the neighbors of a query point we need to calculate the distance between the query point and the other data points. These distance measures help in the formation of decision boundaries, which divide query points into distinct areas. One of the main drawbacks of the KNN algorithm is that it may be biased towards the majority class in datasets that are imbalanced, meaning that there are significantly more instances in one class than in another [18]. This is because KNN classifies query points by finding the k nearest neighbours in the training set and if the majority class dominates the neighbourhood of the test instance it is likely to be classified as the majority class.

Let's say we have a dataset with X representing a matrix that contains the features observed and Y representing the class label. Lets assume we have a point x which has coordinates $(x_1, x_2, \cdots, x_p)$ and point y with coordinates $(y_1, y_2, \cdots, y_p)$ [12]. The KNN algorithm is in this study because it categorizes new cases based on the Euclidean distance between the training data and the test observation. In k-NN, the optimal choice is determined by identifying the set of training data points that are closest to the given test observation in terms of Euclidean distance [19].

$$d(x_i, x_t) = \sqrt{\sum_{j=1}^{d} (x_{ij} - x_{tj})^2} = \|x_i - x_t\|, \tag{10}$$

where x_i represent the training data and x_t represent the test observation. Majority voting is the process of selecting the class that has the highest number of votes among the k-nearest neighbours in the K-nearest neighbours (KNN) algorithm. Majority voting is defined as follows according to [18]:

$$\hat{f}(x_t) = \operatorname*{argmax}_{c \in \{c_1, c_2, c_3\}} \sum_{(x_i, y_i) \in N_k(x_t)} I(y_i = c), \tag{11}$$

where x_t represent the test observation, $\hat{f}(x_t)$ represent a forecasted class label, $N_k(x_t)$ represent a set of training instances and I$(\cdot)$ represent an indicator function that takes a value as input and returns either 0 or 1 based on whether the input satisfies a certain condition [18].

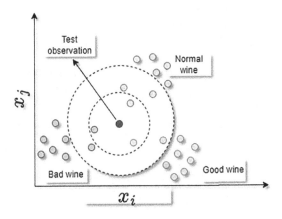

Fig. 6. KNN with different k-values (adapted from [12])

Figure 6 shows the KNN classifier with K= 3 and K= 7. We need to predict the class for the new observation (red circle) if it belongs to a class of Bad wine, Normal wine, or Class of Good wine respectively. If we choose k=3 (for a small dotted circle) then we have one observation in Class Bad wine, one observation in Class Normal wine, and one observation in Class Good wine. From this we have Pr(Bad wine)=$\frac{1}{3}$, Pr(Normal wine)=$\frac{1}{3}$ and Pr(Good wine)=$\frac{1}{3}$ respectively. We can clearly see that we have a tie among our classes where each class has one observation. Since the number of neighbours in class Bad Wine, class Normal, and class Good Wine are the same, we cannot determine the class of the new data point based on the number of neighbours alone. According to [20], we can use different tie-breaking techniques to determine the class in case of a tie. One common method is to choose the class that has the shortest average distance to the new data point. If we choose k=7 (for a big dotted circle) then we have two observations in Class Bad Wine, three observations in Class Normal Wine, and two observations in Class Good Wine. From this we have Pr(Bad wine)=$\frac{2}{7}$, Pr(Normal wine)=$\frac{3}{7}$ and Pr(Good wine)=$\frac{2}{7}$, so we can clearly see that the small red circle (test observation) belongs to class Normal wine based since class Normal wine has the highest probability as compared to other classes (majority voting). The value of a classier determines the performance of that class. However, selecting the correct different k values can be very challenging. This is because the value of k can have a huge impact on the accuracy of the predictive model [21].

5   Experimental Settings

5.1   Unbalanced Data

Fig. 7 demonstrates the red wine quality classes, the dataset's distribution can be seen with the most significant value being 5 with the class values ranging from 3 to 8.

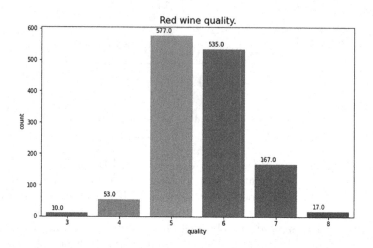

Fig. 7. Distribution of red wine quality (Color figure online)

The dataset depicts an unbalanced distribution of red wine with other classes not being fairly represented, the instances range from 10 in the minority class to 577. As suggested by [22], sampling techniques such as undersampling, oversampling, and SMOTE are used to handle unbalanced datasets. These are further discussed in Sect. 5.2.

5.2   Sampling Techniques

5.2.1   Undersampling and Oversampling

The oversampling method is an intuitive technique that increases the size of a minority class by creating duplicates of samples taken from the under-represented group. Undersampling on the other hand ensures that all of the data from the minority segment are kept and reduces the size of the majority segment to be the same as the minority segment. Undersampling is usually considered to be a disadvantage as it eliminates potentially useful data. Oversampling on the other hand is more likely to cause overfitting since it duplicates existing examples [23].

5.2.2 Synthetic Minority Oversampling Technique

According to [22], using the SMOTE filter proves to be a valuable approach in addressing imbalanced wine datasets. SMOTE employs a k-nearest neighbour method to create synthetic data points. SMOTE starts by selecting K nearest neighbours from the minority samples based on the desired level of oversampling and then randomly selecting a neighbour from K nearest neighbors [22]. The selection process is not deterministic as the K nearest neighbours are chosen randomly. The selection of the K neighbors is done randomly and the random data is combined to generate synthetic data. SMOTE utilizes synthetic data points to add diversity to the minority class, mitigating the issue of overfitting that arises from random sampling techniques. According to [22] SMOTE also creates a more balanced dataset which can help improve the performance of machine learning models when dealing with imbalanced data.

5.3 Hyper Parameter Tuning

In machine learning, the task of selecting a set of optimal hyperparameters for a learning algorithm is known as hyperparameter tuning. The simplest approach to tuning hyperparameters is undoubtedly grid search. Using this method, we simply construct a model for every possible combination of the supplied hyperparameter values and evaluate each model, and choose the model that yields the best results [24]. According to [25], hyperparameter optimization is expressed as:

$$x^* = \arg\min_{x \in X} f(x), \tag{12}$$

where $f(x)$ represents a score that we aim to minimize, such as the error rate evaluated on the validation set. x^* refers to the set of hyperparameters that produces the lowest score value while x can take any value within the X domain. With this, we want to determine the model hyperparameters that provide the highest score on the validation set metric.

5.4 Model Evaluation

To understand how well and efficiently the model performs, we measure and evaluate its performance. There are four techniques used to determine the accuracy of predictions:

- True Positive (TP): This indicates the percentage of samples that the model correctly identifies as positive.
- False Positive (FP): It represents the percentage of samples that the model mistakenly predicts as positive when they are actually negative.

– False Negative (FN): These are the samples that the model wrongly classifies as negative while they are positive in reality.
– True Negative (TN): These are the samples that the model accurately identifies as negative.

We use the following techniques to assess the model.

1. Accuracy: It can be characterized as either the proportion of all positive classes that the model correctly predicted to be true or the number of accurate outputs that the model provides. Its formula is:

$$Accuracy = \frac{TP + TN}{TP + TN + FP + FN}. \tag{13}$$

2. Precision: Precision refers to the ratio of predicted observations to the total number of expected positive observations. Its formula is:

$$Precision = \frac{TP}{TP + FP}. \tag{14}$$

3. Recall: Recall is known as the proportion of accurately predicted positive observations to all of the actual class observations. Its formula is:

$$Recall = \frac{TP}{TP + FN}. \tag{15}$$

4. F_1 Score: F_1 score is calculated as the balanced average of recall and accuracy. The test accuracy of the model is evaluated using the F_1 score. Its formula is [26]:

$$F_1 Score = 2 \times \frac{Recall \times Precision}{Recall + Precision}. \tag{16}$$

According to [27], accuracy is the primary metric used to evaluate models, but when dealing with skewed class distributions and imbalanced datasets, it becomes challenging to make accurate judgments. For instance, the recall rate for minority groups has typically dropped to zero. This indicates that the model is not able to properly classify them. The reduction in recall and precision scores for minority groups is due to how the model focuses more on the majority segment instead of the minority segments. This issue is caused by the preference of the accuracy model for the majority group. As a result, the classifier tends to perform poorly on the minority groups.

6   Results and Discussion

6.1   Results

For the purpose of this study, we are using five machine learning algorithms to predict the wine quality namely SVM, DT, KNN, GB, and RF. We implemented our models in an unbalanced dataset with default parameters and the results are shown in Table 3 below that our models performed poorly with support vector machine and random forest having the highest accuracy with 78% each. Table 3 provides a comprehensive overview of our models' performance across metrics such, as accuracy, precision, recall, and F1 score.

Table 3. Test results for the unbalanced dataset with default model parameters

Class	SVM			RF			KNN			GB			DT		
	Precision	Recall	F1 Score	Precision	Recall	F1 Score	Precision	Recall	F1 Score	Prescision	Recall	F1 Score	Precision	Recall	F1 Score
0	1.00	0.02	0.05	0.22	0.05	0.08	0.36	0.09	0.15	0.29	0.09	0.14	0.26	0.26	0.26
1	0.79	0.96	0.87	0.80	0.94	0.87	0.81	0.90	0.85	0.80	0.92	0.86	0.81	0.79	0.80
2	0.68	0.28	0.40	0.68	0.37	0.48	0.55	0.40	0.46	0.58	0.37	0.45	0.43	0.46	0.45
Accuracy	78%			78%			76%			77%			70%		

We also implemented our models on a balanced dataset with tuned parameters. The results are shown in Table 4, indicating that the models perform well compared to when the models were implemented in an unbalanced dataset with default parameters. As shown in Table 4 among the five machine learning algorithms used in this research to predict wine quality, SVM shows the best performance. As mentioned in Sect. 4.5 the KNN classifier in an unbalanced dataset tends to favour the majority class, this is evident in Table 3 as we can see that the precision, recall, and F1-score are high in the majority class (Class 1) as compared to other classes (Class 0 and Class 2). We can see that balancing the data and tuning your models increase the performance of your models as suggested by [22]. This is evident in Table 4 as we can see that the accuracy of our models increases as compared to when they were implemented our model in an unbalanced dataset with default parameters.

6.2   Feature Importance

We also graphed the feature importance based on our best-performing machine learning model which is in this case the SVM. As we can see the feature importance graphed in Fig. 8 alcohol is the most significant factor impacting wine quality, and this was also suggested by [28] that alcohol plays a crucial role in determining wine quality. Looking at the feature importance graph it suggests that tuning features such as "alcohol", "sulphates", and "volatile acidity" may

Table 4. Test results on the balanced dataset with tuned model parameters

	SVM			RF			KNN			GB			DT		
Class	Precision	Recall	F1 Score	Precision	Recall	F1 Score	Precision	Recall	F1 Score	Prescision	Recall	F1 Score	Precision	Recall	F1 Score
0	0.98	0.99	0.98	0.95	0.99	0.97	0.87	1.00	0.93	0.85	0.88	0.87	0.88	0.93	0.90
1	0.95	0.93	0.94	0.95	0.82	0.88	1.00	0.60	0.75	0.78	0.71	0.74	0.76	0.69	0.72
2	0.95	0.97	0.96	0.88	0.97	0.92	0.80	1.00	0.89	0.84	0.90	0.87	0.79	0.81	0.80
Accuracy	96%			92%			87%			83%			81%		

increase or decrease the wine scores. This information suggests that winemakers may benefit from tuning their models and playing around with the physiochemical properties of wine.

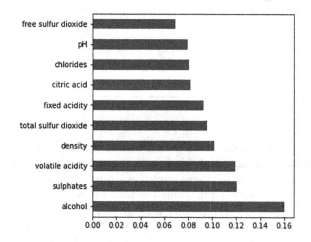

Fig. 8. Feature importance for our best performing model

6.3 Discussion

The objective of this research is to try and predict the quality of wine by analyzing the physico-chemical properties of the wine. It also looks into which features of the wine are most indicative of its quality. To achieve this goal we applied several machine learning algorithms as mentioned above, including Random Forest (RF), Support Vector Machine (SVM), Gradient Boosting (GB), K-Nearest Neighbors (KNN), and Decision Tree (DT). We chose to use these machine learning algorithms because they are widely used algorithms for classification problems and are effective for wine quality prediction. We also dug deeper into the data and we found an interesting relationship between our feature variables and the target variable (Quality). We used the correlation coefficient matrix as shown in Fig. 1 and features are ranked according to their correlation values. The results shown in Fig. 1 suggest that features like "alcohol", "volatile acidity", and "sulphates" have a high correlation with quality while features like "free sulfur dioxide" and "residual sugar" do not. In Table 2, features are ranked according to their correlation values, and the first 10 features are selected during the models' ultimate implementation.

We assessed the effectiveness of the algorithms by analyzing metrics, including precision, recall, accuracy, and F_1 score as presented in both Table 3 and Table 4. We then evaluated the performance of our model by applying it to both the imbalanced dataset with default parameters and to a balanced dataset with fine-tuned parameters. The results of the analysis are presented in Table 3 and Table 4 respectively. From the performance results it is evident that the best outcome is achieved with a balanced dataset with fine-tuned parameters. As mentioned above it is evident that balancing the data and tuning your model parameters enhances the models' performance.

7   Conclusion

This study showed the importance of feature selection in understanding the impact of analytical tests on wine quality. The results of the feature selection process showed that some input variables such as Alcohol had a more significant influence on predicting wine quality than others such as Residual sugar. Applying machine learning algorithms in conjunction with the results of the feature selection process presented a valuable opportunity to improve the wine production process.

We employed five machine learning models, namely Decision Tree (DT), Random Forest (RF), Support Vector Machine (SVM), K-Nearest Neighbors (KNN), and Gradient Boosting (GB). The Support Vector Machine (SVM) outperformed the other models with an accuracy of 96%. Therefore, we conclude that not all features were equally important for predicting wine quality and that tuning your models and balancing the dataset improved the performance of the models. We also saw that in Fig. 8 our feature importance graph suggested that tuning the models and playing around with physio-chemical properties such as "Alcohol" and "sulphate" may be beneficial in improving the prediction of wine quality.

Although this study presents promising results in predicting the wine quality using machine learning algorithms some limitations need to be addressed in future work, such as the small size of the dataset and we did not use all the algorithms. In future work using larger and more diverse datasets could enhance the machine learning algorithm's performance. This will help the algorithms generalize better and reduce the risk of overfitting, thus improving the wine production process. For our study, we only used Five machine learning algorithms and there are still many other algorithms that could be explored in future work. We can evaluate the performance of the algorithms using different metrics and we can explore the impact of different preprocessing techniques such as different feature scaling techniques on the performance of the algorithms.

References

1. Ádám, B., Molnár, Á., Bárdos, H., Ádány, R.: Health impact assessment of quality wine production in Hungary. Health Promot. Int. **24**(4), 383–393 (2009)
2. Saremi, A., Arora, R.: The cardiovascular implications of alcohol and red wine. Am. J .Ther. **15**(3), 265–277 (2008)
3. Meyer, M.: The subtle science of wine tasting (2019). https://winefolly.com/deep-dive/science-of-wine-tasting/
4. Dahal, K.R., Dahal, J.N., Banjade, H., Gaire, S.: Prediction of wine quality using machine learning algorithms. Open J. Stat. **11**(2), 278–289 (2021)
5. Dua, D., Graff, C.: UCI machine learning repository (2017)
6. Gupta, Y.: Selection of important features and predicting wine quality using machine learning techniques. Proc. Comput. Sci. **125**, 305–312 (2018)
7. Pawar, D., Mahajan, A., Bhoithe, S., Prasanna, M., Kumar, K.: Wine quality prediction using machine learning algorithms. Int. J. Comput. App. Technol. Res. **8**(9), 385–388 (2019)
8. Cortez, P., Cerdeira, A., Almeida, F., Matos, T., Reis, J.: Modeling wine preferences by data mining from physicochemical properties. Decis. Support Syst. **47**(4), 547–553 (2009)
9. Kira, K., Rendell, L.A.: A practical approach to feature selection. In: Machine Learning Proceedings 1992, pp. 249–256. Elsevier (1992)
10. Liu, Y., Yong, M., Chen, K., Li, Y., Guo, J.: Daily activity feature selection in smart homes based on Pearson correlation coefficient. Neural Process. Lett. **51**(2), 1771–1787 (2020)
11. Bin, Z.: Is the maximal margin hyperplane special in a feature space. Hewlett-Packard Research Laboratories, Palo Alto (2001)
12. LibreTexts, K nearest neighbors (2020). https://stats.libretexts.org/Bookshelves/Computing_and_Modeling/RTG%3A_Classification_Methods/3%3A_K-Nearest_Neighbors_(KNN). Accessed 25 Aug 2022
13. Chauhan, N.S.: Random forest vs decision tree: key differences (2022). https://www.kdnuggets.com/2022/02/random-forest-decision-tree-key-differences.html. Accessed 25 Aug 2022
14. Du, W., Zhan, Z.: Building decision tree classifier on private data (2002)
15. Johnson, K., Kuhn, M.: Comparison analysis of machine learning algorithms: Random forest and catboost (2020). https://rstudio-pubs-static.s3.amazonaws.com/740098_4d48bd29722f402abf662dd33fc67794.html. Accessed 25 Aug 2022
16. Natekin, A., Knoll, A.: Gradient boosting machines, a tutorial. Front. Neurorobot. **7**, 21 (2013)
17. Saini, A.: Gradient boosting algorithm: a complete guide for beginners (2021). https://www.analyticsvidhya.com/blog/2021/09/gradient-boosting-algorithm-a-complete-guide-for-beginners/. Accessed 03 June 2022
18. Liu, W., Chawla, S.: Class confidence weighted kNN algorithms for imbalanced data sets. In: Huang, J.Z., Cao, L., Srivastava, J. (eds.) PAKDD 2011. LNCS (LNAI), vol. 6635, pp. 345–356. Springer, Heidelberg (2011). https://doi.org/10.1007/978-3-642-20847-8_29
19. Tamamadin, M., Lee, C., Kee, S.-H., Yee, J.-J.: Regional typhoon track prediction using ensemble k-nearest neighbor machine learning in the GIS environment. Rem. Sens. **14**(21), 5292 (2022)
20. Reddy, A.: K nearest neighbors conceptual understanding and implementation in python (2020). https://www.citrusconsulting.com/k-nearest-neighbors-conceptual-understanding-and-implementation-in-python/

21. Ling, Y.L., Zhang, X., Zhang, Y.: Improved kNN algorithm based on probability and adaptive k value. In: 2021 7th International Conference on Computing and Data Engineering, pp. 34–40 (2021)
22. Chawla, N.V.: Data mining for imbalanced datasets: an overview. In: Data Mining and Knowledge Discovery Handbook, pp. 875–886 (2009)
23. Shelke, M.S., Deshmukh, P.R., Shandilya, V.K.: A review on imbalanced data handling using undersampling and oversampling technique. Int. J. Recent Trends Eng. Res. 3(4), 444–449 (2017)
24. Zahedi, L., Mohammadi, F.G., Rezapour, S., Ohland, M.W., Hadi Amini, M.: Search algorithms for automated hyper-parameter tuning. arXiv preprint arXiv:2104.14677 (2021)
25. Jia, W., Chen, X.-Y., Zhang, H., Xiong, L.-D., Lei, H., Deng, S.-H.: Hyperparameter optimization for machine learning models based on Bayesian optimization. J. Electron. Sci. Technol. 17(1), 26–40 (2019)
26. Kumar, K., Mandan, N.: Red wine quality prediction using machine learning techniques. In: 2020 International Conference on Computer Communication and Informatics (ICCCI), pp. 1–6. IEEE (2020)
27. Guo, X., Yin, Y., Dong, C., Yang, G., Zhou, G.: On the class imbalance problem. In: 2008 Fourth International Conference on Natural Computation, vol. 4, pp. 192–201. IEEE (2008)
28. Mor, N.S.: Wine quality and type prediction from physicochemical properties using neural networks for machine learning: a free software for winemakers and customers (2022)

Covid-19 Data Preprocessing Approach in Machine Learning for Prediction

Samuel Kotva Goudoungou[1]([envelope]), Paul Dayang[1], Naomi Dassi Tchomte[1,2], Justin Moskolaï Ngossaha[3], Fabien Mouomene Moffo[3], and Nathalie Mitton[4]

[1] Department of Mathematics and Computer Science, Faculty of Science, The University of Ngaoundere, PO BOX 454, Ngaoundere, Cameroon
`kotvagou@gmail.com, pdayang@univ-ndere.cm`
[2] Department of Mathematics and Computer Science, University Institute of Technology, The University of Ngaoundere, PO BOX 454, Ngaoundere, Cameroon
[3] Department of Computer Science, Faculty of Science, The University of Douala, PO BOX 24 157, Douala, Cameroon
`jmoskolai@fs-univ-douala.cm`
[4] National Institute for Research in Digital Science and Technology, University of Lille, PO BOX, 59650 Villeneuve D'ascq, France
`nathalie.mitton@inria.fr`

Abstract. Artificial Intelligence (AI) is a vast field that allows the development of programs capable of simulating human intelligence. One of the most used AI techniques that is very important the preparation of raw data which is called data preprocessing in Machine Learning. Data preprocessing is a technique that makes the data clean for machine learning and improves the performance of the model. With the different steps that we found already defined we set up a simpler architecture for data preprocessing. For that purpose, we worked with 5644 data simple of Covid-19. After analyzing the contours of our data; we have as steps of this architecture first the collection of data, the cleaning of these data, the encoding, the normalization of the data, the imputation to manage the missing values, then the selection of variables and finally the selection of features. We obtain an accuracy of 78% as a result of our experimentation with a very small error rate. This Covid-19 detection prediction result shows that data preprocessing plays an important role in Machine Learning.

Keywords: Data preprocessing · intelligent system · model · Machine Learning · support vector machine · accuracy

1 Introduction

Nowadays, the amount of data generated is increasing exponentially due to the emergence of the Big Data phenomenon [1]. This data requires data preprocessing in oder to improve the performance of the machine learning model. Data preprocessing is a technique used to convert raw data into a clean dataset. Data preprocessing is one of the major phases

© ICST Institute for Computer Sciences, Social Informatics and Telecommunications Engineering 2024
Published by Springer Nature Switzerland AG 2024. All Rights Reserved
F. Tchakounte et al. (Eds.): SAFER-TEA 2023, LNICST 566, pp. 328–344, 2024.
https://doi.org/10.1007/978-3-031-56396-6_21

of the knowledge discovery process [2]. Raw data is usually accompanied by many imperfections such as inconsistencies, missing values, noise and/or redundancies. The performance of subsequent learning algorithms will therefore be compromised if they are presented with low data quality. Thus, by conducting appropriate preprocessing steps, we are able to significantly influence the quality and reliability of the knowledge. The preprocessing of numerical variables is highly dependent on the quality of the received data [3]. Thus, preprocessing of objects, textures, audio, fingerprints and characters are among the common applications. Covid-19 is a disease that has caused so many murders. This disease has had an impact on several sectors, particularly on the socio-economic level. The approach will be based on the target variable, which is covid-19. In Machine Learning (ML), does data preprocessing play an important role when these data were entered by the non-specialist? Can it improve the quality of the result in ML? In fact, the data introduced by the non-specialist of the domain are sometimes unstructured; non-conform and with missing values, therefore the preprocessing comes to make the structuring and discretion to have a format conform to Machine Learning. After the definition of the problem, a fundamental question emerges: How to preprocess the data to make it in a format suitable for decision making in ML; How to do the imputation in the dataset so that it is ML compliant? The main objective of this work is to propose a data preprocessing approach for improving the performance of the prediction model applied to COVID-19. This work aims to make it easier for non-specialists in the field to use Machine Learning, thus simplifying the input of data into the system. We will review the existing approaches, propose the architecture of the model for preprocessing sample of COVID-19, and present the design and test results of our work.

2   Related Work on Data Preprocessing

Data preprocessing is a technique for making data suitable for ML [3–5]. Abstract data come from a multitude of sources, and collecting them is no longer really a challenge. It's what you do with it. Data science is about understanding how to collect and analyze data, allowing users to be informed and to appropriate decisions. Data preprocessing is an essential technique for any data scientist[6]. Indeed, in some cases, data preprocessing is the essential part of any data science project.

According to work carried out among others on data preprocessing we can list some below:

- **Data preprocessing in data mining** allows to improve the data quality submitted to the data mining algorithms. Data preprocessing consists of several successive steps (Cleaning, Integration, Transformation, Reduction, Discretization) [7];
- **Data preprocessing and mortality prediction, the Physionet/Computing in Cardiology Challenge**: the focus has been on the application of sophisticated machine learning algorithms; little attention has been paid to preprocessing performed on the data a priori. Four standard preprocessing methods have been compared with a new Box-Cox outlier rejection technique and analyze their effect on machine learning classifiers to predict mortality for critical care patients [8];

- **Data preprocessing techniques in a convolutional neural network based on fault diagnosis of rotating machines:** In conventional fault diagnosis, data preprocessing is usually used to accomplish feature extraction using preprocessing methods. However, the necessary data preprocessing can improve the diagnostic performance;
- **Data preprocessing used in the microplastics identification process:** after measuring a vibrational spectrum of microplastics, in many cases the resulting raw data should not be evaluated directly, due to numerous inconsistencies that may interfere with the signals of the analytics [9].
- In all these cases, the processing of the spectra becomes very important. All these mentioned disturbances can also be removed digitally, hence the preprocessing of the data.

3 Proposal for a Data Preprocessing Architecture

In order to propose a new architecture, we will draw lessons from the existing literature mentioned above in order to identify the weaknesses and suggest another solution approach. In the above approaches we find that data preprocessing no longer solves the problems in a general way but in a specific domain, a standard approach could be the object of data preprocessing for ML. We can list as limitations:

- Deleting huge data can lead to the drop in performance in the ML model;
- We note that the imputation of data is no longer taken into account;
- The mean square error in some models is high;
- The models were not evaluated to determine performance;

To solve the above-mentioned limitations, we propose the following approach. We need to implement a preprocessing tool which allows to preprocess data before their input into the Machine Learning. This preprocessing will be able to improve the performance and the execution time. We propose this preprocessing architecture according to Fig. 1.

The collected data needs preparation for good decision making in ML. This architecture of data preprocessing illustrated above follows a logic summarized in the following important steps.

3.1 Data Cleaning

Data cleaning is the operation of detecting and correcting (or removing) errors in data stored in databases or files [10]. The incorrect part of the processed data can be replaced, modified or deleted. The cleaning process identifies the erroneous data and automatically corrects it with a computer program or offers it to a human to make the changes.

3.2 Encoding

The inconding involves transforming categorical or qualitative data into numerical values [11]. This step is sometimes optional because you may have a dataset with categorical data already coded. In this case, you will not need to do another encoding. Machine learning models are based on mathematical equations, so intuitively the presence of categorical data will cause a problem because you can only keep numbers in the equations. So, this categorical data has to be coded into numerical data.

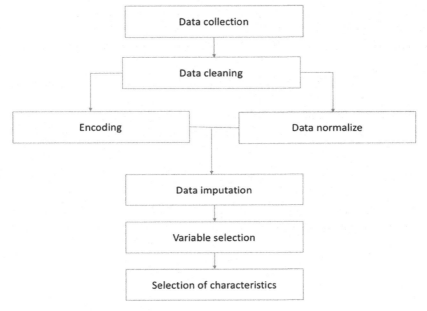

Fig. 1. Architecture of data preprocessing

3.3 Data Normalization

The data normalization allows us to reduce the complexity of the model. In our work we opt for the standardisation of the mean and standard deviation of any type of data distribution, which allows us to simplify the learning problem by freeing ourselves from these two parameters. Standardisation, also called Z-Score normalization) can be applied when the input features correspond to normal distributions (Gaussian distributions) with different means and standard deviations. Therefore, this transformation will have the impact of having all our features respond to the same normal distribution:

- The formula for standardizing the training functionality is as follows:

$$X_{Normalise} = \frac{X_{Train} - m}{\sigma} \tag{1}$$

- The formula for standardizing the test functionality is as follows:

$$X_{Normalise} = \frac{X_{Test} - m}{\sigma} \tag{2}$$

3.4 Data Imputation

This is a process of replacing missing data with substituted values. Missing data can introduce a significant amount of bias, make data processing and analysis more laborious, and reduce the efficiency of statistical methods. A dataset consists of quantitative variables (Y1,…, Yp) observed on a sample of n individuals; M denotes the matrix of missing values by $m_{i,j} = 1_{y_{i,j} missing}$.. There are several algorithms that can solve the problem of missing data, among which we have opted for the Singular Value Decomposition (SVD) algorithm in our architecture. This algorithm is subdivided into two cases:

- **Data intensity**: In the case where the observed data is much more than the missing data, we separate the dataset Y into two groups: on the one hand Y^c with the complete observations and on the other hand Y_m comprising the individuals for whom some missing data[9]. We then consider the truncated singular value decomposition (SVD) of the complete set:

$$Y_J^c = U_J D_J V_J^T \qquad (3)$$

where D_J is the diagonal matrix comprising the first J singular values of Y^c. The missing values are then imputed by regression:

$$min_{B \in R^j} \sum_{i\ observe} (Y_i - \sum_{j=1}^{J} v_i \beta_j)^2 \qquad (4)$$

Or V_j^* the truncated version of V_J, i.e. for which the rows corresponding to the missing data in row Y_1 are deleted. A solution to the problem given by:

$$\beta = (V_j^{*T} V_j^*)^{-1} V_j^{*T} V_j^* \qquad (5)$$

The prediction of missing data is therefore given by:

$$Y_j^* = V_j^* \beta \qquad (6)$$

- **Insufficient data**: If too many missing values are observed, this will lead to a significant bias in the calculation of the decomposition base. In addition, it happens that there is at least one missing data for all observations. In this case, the following problem must be solved;

$$min \left\| Y - m - U_J D_J V_J^T \right\| * \qquad (7)$$

where $||.||^*$ sums the squares of the elements of the matrix, ignoring missing values, m is the vector of the means of the observations. The solution of this problem follows the SVD completion algorithm:

Completion algorithm by SVD

Begin
1. To create a matrix $Y^{\wedge}0$ for which the missing values are filled in with the mean,
2. Calculate the SVD solution of the problem for the completed matrix Y i. This creates Y i+1 by replacing the missing values of Y plots in the regression;
3. To Repeat the previous step until $\| Y^i - Y^{i+1} \| / \| Y^i \| < \epsilon$, arbitrary threshold (often at 10^{-6});
End.

The complexity of this algorithm is O(n) in the best case and Ω(n) in the worst case.

3.5 Variable Selection

Variable selection is a process that selects a subset of variables that the process considers relevant. The input data for the process are the initial set of variables that form the representation space and the set of training data for the problem under study [11]. This is a method that allows us to specify how the independent variables are entered into the analysis. The process of variable selection can be broken down as shown in Fig. 2:

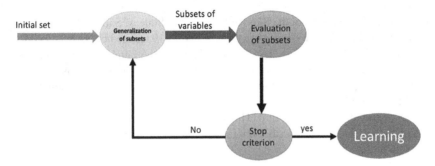

Fig. 2. Process of variable selection

3.6 Feature Selection

This is a process used in ML and data processing. That is, we try to minimize the loss of information from removing all other variables. After creating the architecture of our data preprocessing model, we also create a pipeline for the model [12]. Figure 3 describes the architecture of our pipeline:

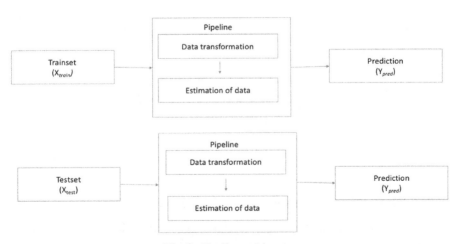

Fig. 3. Pipeline architecture

4 Model and Implementation

To implement our model of data preprocessing in case-based reasoning we will first collect and analyze the data, transform the categorical variables into numerical variables, normalize the data, impute missing values and then train and evaluate the model.

5 Data Collection and Analytical Exploration

The dataset is collected from the São Paulo Hospital, State of São Paulo in Brazil, The World Health Organization (WHO) qualified COVID-19, caused by SARS-CoV-2, as a pandemic on 11 March, as the exponential increase in the number of cases threatened to overwhelm health systems around the world, with demand for intensive care unit beds far outstripping existing capacity, with regions in Italy being prominent examples [67]. This dataset has 111 attributes and 5644 cases which are the diagnostic results of COVID-19 and its clinical spectrum. The SARS-Cov-2 exam result is the target variable to be predicted. They are described in Table 1. Figure 4 shows the distribution of the second target variable.

Table 1. Extract from the dataset

	Patient ID	Patient age quantile	SARS-Cov-2 exam result	Patient addmited to regular ward(1 = yes, 0 = no)	Patient addmited to semi-intensive unit(1 = yes, 0 = no)	Patient addmited to intensive care unit(1 = yes, 0 = no)	Hemotocrit	...	CtO2(arterial blood gas analysis)
0	44477f75...	13	negative	0	0	0	NaN	...	NaN
1	126e9dd13...	17	negative	0	0	0	0.236515	...	NaN
2	a46b4402a...	8	negative	0	0	0	NaN	...	NaN
3	f7d619a94f...	5	negative	0	0	0	NaN	...	NaN
4	d9e414657...	15	negative	0	0	0	NaN	...	NaN
...	...	...	...	...	...	...	...	...	...
5639	ae66feb9e...	3	positive	0	0	0	NaN	...	NaN
5640	c354f3d2a...	17	negative	0	0	0	NaN	...	NaN
5641	5c6789ed...	4	negative	0	0	0	NaN	...	NaN
5642	c20ae6bd0...	10	negative	0	0	0	NaN	...	NaN
5643	3c53456d...	19	positive	0	0	0	NaN	...	NaN

The different steps of the machine learning process are:

- Define Problem: identify the problem and clearly defineh the objective to be achieved;
- Collect Data: gathering the data we will need for ML;
- data analysis: detecting the target variable, knowing the structure of these data in order to normalize them;

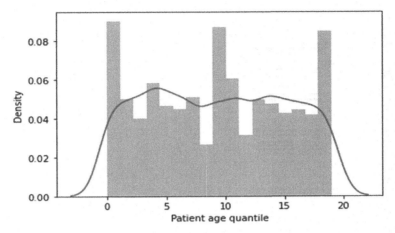

Fig. 4. The distribution of the variable Age patient quantity

- Train Model: training the model against a set of training and validation data.
- Evaluate: evaluate the model by comparing the accuracy of the results to the test dataset.

After the collection, the data are saved in a CSV file. We proceed to the analysis of this data by visualizing with matplotlib all the attributes of the dataset and we notice several columns that have no value in Fig. 5.

- Each line corresponds to an observation on a patient. It is the set of data obtained on a patient; an employee, the speed of a car are quantitative variables;

- Qualitative variable: takes on values called categories, modalities or levels that do not have a quantitative meaning. For example, the SARS-Cov-2 exam result of a patient is a categorical variable with two modalities: negative and positive;

Table 2 provides a detailed description of the dataset.

Cleaning is the process of checking the integrity and consistency of data. This step involves cleaning the data by column (feature) looking for anomalies, such as instances with missing or inconsistent features. It is important to identify missing data in a dataset before applying an ML. We look for the correlation between the target column (the value you are trying to predict) and the evaluation. If it has a high correlation, then leave the column otherwise we delete the column. This is because many of these algorithms are based on statistical methods that assume that they receive a complete dataset as input. Otherwise, the ML algorithm may provide a poor predictive model or simply not work. Thus, dealing with missing data and eliminating outliers is a necessary phase for any data science project[13]according to the correlation that shows us the outliers in Fig. 6. This correlation is plotted from the attributes to the target variables.

5.1 Data Pre-processing and Prediction

ML algorithms take the input data in matrix form, each row is an observation, and each column represents a feature of the patient. An observation (row of the data matrix) is said to have missing data if there is a feature for which its value is not filled in.

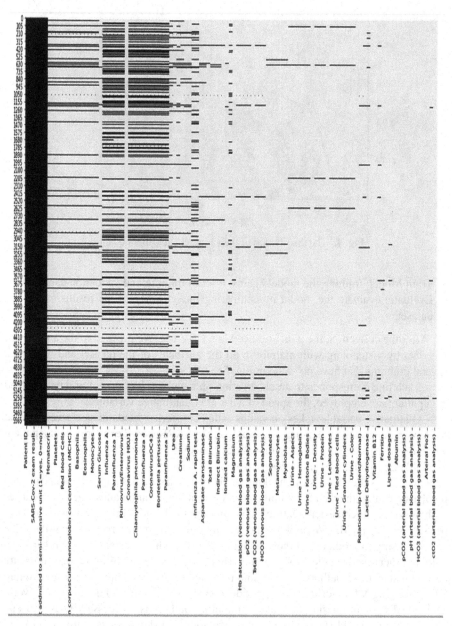

Fig. 5. Visualization of the datasets

Obviously, there can be several missing data for the same observation. However, the concern remains the same. Namely, how to process these missing data in order to fill in the missing information without significantly altering the initial dataset [14].

Table 2. Description of the dataset attributes.

Columns	Description	Type of data	Type of variables
Patient ID	Patient Identifiant	Alphanumeric	String
Patient age quantile	this variable represents the age of the patient who effected the tests	Numeric	Real
SARS-Cov-2 exam result	the result of the Covid-19 test	Categorical	string of characters
Patient addmited to regular ward	Patient admitted to the ordinary ward	Numerical	Real
Patient addmited to semi-intensive unit	Patient admitted to semi-intensive ward	Numerical	Boolean
Patient addmited to intensive care unit	Patient transferred to intensive care unit	Numerical	Boolean
Hematocrit	Red cell level in blood	Digital	character string
Hemoglobin	protein in each red blood cell	Digital	Character string
Platelets	platelet in blood	Digital	character string
...	...	...	...
CoronavirusOC43	Viral test	Categorical	string of characters

Dealing with the missing data then consists of repairing the dataset so that it can be used by the ML algorithms [15]. This allows the data to follow a common law. To deal with the missing data in our case, the following options are applied:

- When 90% of the values in a column are missing, the column is eliminated;
- Otherwise, the missing data are replaced by artificial values which are obtained by calculating the average of each column. Figure 7 shows an extract of the dataset after cleaning. In Fig. 7, we and observe in cleaned the dataset that the numbers of columns are reduced (from 111 columns to 35 columns).

At the end of the cleaning process, we get a complete dataset where all the characteristics of each observation are filled in. To see this contribution of this cleaning, we create an attribute that allows us to analyze the state of a patient. Figure 8 tells us, according to the attributes, in which status the patient can be. And each attribute is a component of blood or cough.

A dataset contains a huge amount of data. The larger and more diverse the dataset, the better the model will be able to predict accurate results. After the cleaning phase, our dataset consists of 5086 negative cases and 558 positive cases. These data are divided into 2 sets:

- **The training dataset**: It is composed of 80% of the available data, i.e. 4068 negative cases and 447 positive cases. It is therefore the most voluminous in terms of data [15, 16]. Indeed, it is on this dataset that the neural network will iterate during the

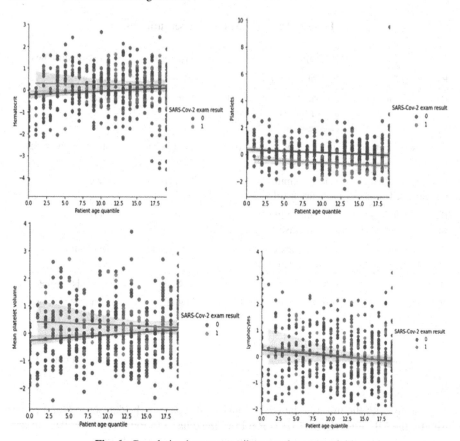

Fig. 6. Correlation between attributes and target variables

learning phase to be able to appropriate the parameters and adjust them. This set will be called up only once, at the end of each training iteration. It will allow the system to be balanced. This is the adjustment phase. Validation data is what we use to check the performance of the model during the regular training cycle. It ensures that the model will be applicable to other datasets than the one used for training.

- **The test dataset:** This is composed of 20% of the available data, i.e. 95 negative cases and 16 positive cases. Unlike the other sets, it will not be used to adjust the network but rather to evaluate the network in its final form, and to see how well it predicts. This is why it must be composed exclusively of new samples, never used before. This aims to avoid biasing the results by sending it data that it already knows and used during the training phase.[16].

This involves preparing the data in a format that works with the tools and techniques we use to train the model. The treatment by ML algorithms of numerical variables is simpler because they can be used directly without the need for transformation. However, the presence of categorical variables in the data generally complicates the training. Indeed, most ML algorithms take numerical values as input.

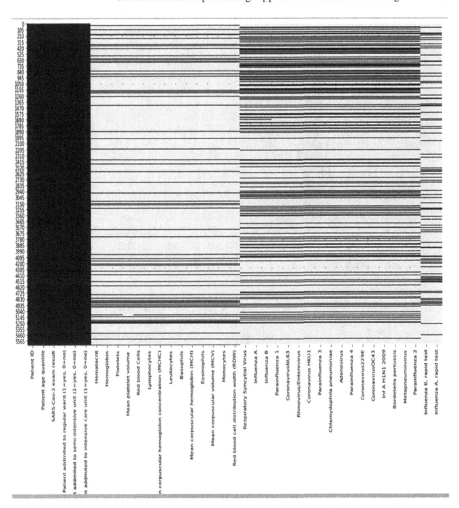

Fig. 7. Removal of unnecessary columns

Thus, we need to find a way to transform our modalities into numerical data. Moreover, the way in which this transformation is carried out is very important because the coding of categorical variables generally hinders the performance of learning algorithms.

In our dataset, the features *positive*, *negative*, *detected*, *not_detected* are represented as a string [17]. To map them into numerical values, we use the built-in functions of TensorFlow. They provide a way of representing strings as a one-hot vector which consists of encoding an n-state variable to n bits, only one of which takes the value of 1, the number worth 1 being the number of the state taken by the variable. The vocabulary set of states is transmitted as a list. However, when the number of states is large as in our case, it becomes impossible to train a neural network using one-hot encoding. Instead of representing the data as a single multi-dimensional vector, we instead use a lower-dimensional dense vector in which each cell can contain only 0 or 1.

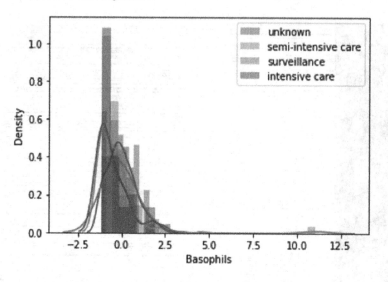

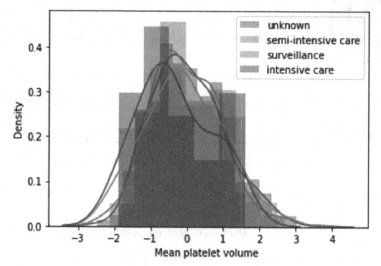

Fig. 8. Status of the patient

A model is the result of analyzing the data with an algorithm and any given combination of parameters, assuming that the model is a mathematical function y = f(x), where x represents the characteristics, y the label and f(x) the model [14]. It represents what an ML system has learned from the training data. This complex term can have one of two associated meanings:

- Pandas graph that expresses the structure of a prediction calculation;
- Particular weights and biases of this TensorFlow graph.
- In TensorFlow, a graph represents the specifications of the calculation. The nodes of the graph represent operations. The edges are oriented and represent the passage of

the result of an operation (a Tensor) as an operand to another operation. A Tensor is a main data structure of TensorFlow programs [18]. Tensors are N-dimensional data structures (the value of N can be very large), usually scalar quantities, vectors or matrices. The elements of a Tensor can contain integer, floating point or string values. The steps for implementing the model are: creation, training, evaluation and saving of the model.

- We have created a model based on machine vector support. In this model we will create a pipeline that takes into account the following parameters:
- Polynomial feature;
- selectKbest;
- standardscaler;
- svc (support vector machine);

```
Pipeline(steps=[('polynomialfeatures', PolynomialFeatures(include_bias=False)),
                ('selectkbest', SelectKBest()),
                ('standardscaler', StandardScaler()),
                ('svc', SVC(random_state=0))])
```

Training is a process to determine the best model. The model is trained with the training dataset and adjusted using the test dataset. Training is performed in 5 iterations (epoch). An iteration corresponds to a complete training cycle on the entire dataset so that each example has been seen once. A batch is a set of examples used in one iteration (i.e. gradient update) of the model training. The following Fig. 9 shows the evolution of the different accuracies (accuracy, Val_accuracy) during the training.

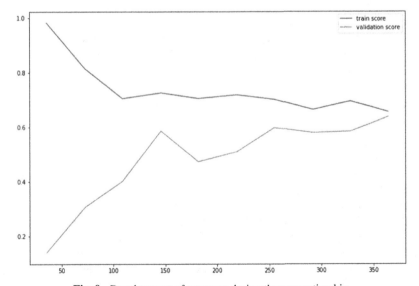

Fig. 9. Development of accuracy during the apprenticeship.

Accuracy is the proportion of correct predictions of a classification model. The accuracy value increases during training, which means that the accuracy of the model increases with each training step. The final accuracy value is 0.78. Table 3 summarises the performance of our model:

Table 3. Model performance

	Precision	Recall	F1-score	Support
0	0.91	0.96	0.94	95
1	0.78	0.44	0.56	16
Accuracy			0.90	111
Macro avg	0.84	0.71	0.75	111
Weighted avg	0.89	0.90	0.89	111

The purpose of model evaluation is to determine the performance, i.e. the accuracy of the predictions made by the model. This accuracy corresponds to the margin of error obtained by our model on a test sample. The confusion matrix is the tool used to measure the performance of a model by checking how often its predictions are accurate compared to reality in classification problems. A confusion matrix is an NxN table that summarises the success of a classification model's predictions, i.e. the correlation between the labels and the classifications of the model. One axis of a confusion matrix is the label predicted by the model, and the other is the actual label. N is the number of classes. In a binary classification problem, N = 2. To calculate a confusion matrix, it is necessary to have a set of test data with the expected outcome values. A prediction is then made for each row in the test dataset [19]. From the expected results and predictions, the matrix shows the number of correct and incorrect predictions for each class organised according to the predicted class. Each row of the table corresponds to a predicted class, and each column corresponds to an actual class. In the rows below the actual classes, the predictions or results are entered [18]. To understand how a confusion matrix works, it is important to understand the four main terminologies: TP, TN, FP and FN. The precise definition of each of these terms is as follows:

- True Positive (TP) Cases where the prediction is positive, and the actual value is effectively positive. Example: the doctor tells you that you have SARS-Cov-2 and you do indeed have it. True Negative (TN) This is where the prediction is negative and the actual value is negative. Example: the doctor tells you that you are not pregnant, and you are indeed not pregnant.
- False Positive (FP): A case where the prediction is positive, but the actual value is negative. Example: the doctor tells you that you are pregnant, but you are not pregnant.
- False Negative (FN) Cases where the prediction is negative and the actual value is positive. Example: the doctor tells you that you are not pregnant, but you are pregnant [20].

The evaluation of the model is carried out on the test dataset consisting of 1352 examples. The following Fig. 10 represents the confusion matrix obtained in graphic form on our test sample.

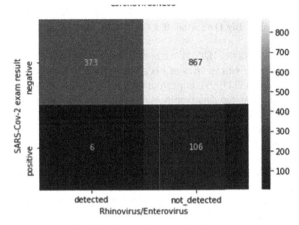

Fig. 10. Confusion matrix diagram

We observe in the figure below that out of 1352 examples, 1346 were correctly predicted and 06 were incorrectly predicted. TP = 106, TN = 373, FP = 867 and FN = 6. The evaluation produced very satisfying results with an accuracy of 0.78 and a very low loss as can be seen in Fig. 9.

6   Conclusion

In sum, to help ML gains performance and minimized runtime, this work focused on pre-processing data in order to improve the ML model. To obtain this model we used Pandas, Numpy, TensorFlow and Scikit-learn. We worked with COVID-19 dataset containing 111 attributes and 5644 cases. We first performed data collection, cleaning, encoding and normalization, then performed variable and feature selection, then trained the model on the training data (487 cases) and finally evaluated the model on a test sample (111 cases). This model takes as input the Covid-19 results, the patient's age and the diagnostic results of the blood and viral variables. Specifically, it predicts the future status of Covid-19. The performance of the model has been evaluated on a test dataset, on which it provides satisfactory results with an accuracy of 0.78. We can also consider designing models for data structuring and developing a platform or a data pre-processing application with a graphical interface for different Machine Learning approaches such as Case-Based Reasoning, Genetic Algorithm, Fuzzy logic.

References

1. García, S., Luengo, J., Herrera, F., García, S., Luengo, J., Herrera, F.: Introduction. Intell. Syst. Ref. Libr. **72**, 1–17 (2015). https://doi.org/10.1007/978-3-319-10247-4_1
2. Adedoyin, A., Kapetanakis, S., Petridis, M., Panaousis, E.: Evaluating case-based reasoning knowledge discovery in fraud detection. CEUR Workshop Proc. **1815**, 182–191 (2016)
3. "Prétraitement des données, données textuelles — papierstat. http://www.xavierdupre.fr/app/papierstat/helpsphinx/lectures/preprocessing.html. Accessed 28 Sep 2021

4. Alcalde-Barros, A., García-Gil, D., García, S., Herrera, F.: DPASF: a flink library for streaming data preprocessing. Big Data Anal. **8**, 1–17 (2019). https://doi.org/10.1186/s41044-019-0041-8

5. Gutierrez-Osuna, R., Nagle, H.T.: A method for evaluating data-preprocessing techniques for odour classification with an array of gas sensors. IEEE Trans. Syst. Man Cybern. Part B (Cybern.) **29**(5), 626–632 (1999). https://doi.org/10.1109/3477.790446

6. Shi, W., et al.: An integrated data preprocessing framework based on apache spark for fault diagnosis of power grid equipment. J. Signal Process. Syst. **86**(2–3), 221–236 (2016). https://doi.org/10.1007/s11265-016-1119-4

7. Munk, M., Kapusta, J., Švec, P.: Procedia computer science data preprocessing evaluation for web log mining : reconstruction of activities of a web visitor. Procedia Comput. Sci. **1**(1), 2273–2280 (2012). https://doi.org/10.1016/j.procs.2010.04.255

8. Johnson, A.E.W., Kramer, A.A., Clifford, G.D.: Data preprocessing and mortality prediction : the Physionet/CinC 2012 challenge revisited, pp. 157–160 (2014)

9. Renner, G., Nellessen, A., Schwiers, A., Wenzel, M., Schmidt, T.C., Schram, J.: Trends in analytical chemistry data preprocessing & evaluation used in the microplastics identi fi cation process: a critical review & practical guide. Trends Anal. Chem. **111**, 229–238 (2019). https://doi.org/10.1016/j.trac.2018.12.004

10. Jun, S.: A big data preprocessing using statistical text mining. J. Korean Inst. Intell. Syst. **25**(5), 470–476 (2015). https://doi.org/10.5391/JKIIS.2015.25.5.470

11. Kaabi, Y.N.M.: Chapitre 2 La sélection de variables, pp. 1–23 (2015)

12. Zhbannikov, I.Y., Hunter, S.S., Foster, J.A., Settles, M.L.: SeqyClean : A Pipeline for High-throughput Sequence Data Preprocessing, pp. 407–416 (2017)

13. Kalra, V.: Importance of Text Data Preprocessing and Implementation in RapidMiner, vol. 14, pp. 71–75 (2018). https://doi.org/10.15439/2018KM46

14. Mention : Ingénierie Informatique Modèle du prétraitement des données dans le Raisonnement à Partir des Cas (RàPC ou CBR) (2021)

15. Ren, B., et al.: Using data imputation for signal separation in high-contrast imaging. Astrophys. J. **892**(2), 74 (2020)

16. Fürnkranz, J., Gamberger, D., Lavrač, N.: Foundations of Rule Learning. Springer, Heidelberg (2012). https://doi.org/10.1007/978-3-540-75197-7

17. Humain, V., Discr, F., Principales, C.: Codage par Transformation Quelques Transformées …," no. 2, pp. 1–5

18. Grafberger, S., Stoyanovich, J., Schelter, S.: Lightweight Inspection of Data Preprocessing in Native Machine Learning Pipelines (2020)

19. Chaofeng, L.: Research and Development of Data Preprocessing in Web Usage Mining 3 Data Preprocessing in Web Usage Mining, pp. 1311–1315 (2006)

20. Cannas, B., Fanni, A., See, L., Sias, G.: Data preprocessing for river flow forecasting using neural networks: wavelet transforms and data partitioning. Phys. Chem. Earth, Parts A/B/C **31**(18), 1164–1171 (2006). https://doi.org/10.1016/j.pce.2006.03.020

Evaluation of Machine Learning and Deeplearning Algorithms Applied to Earth Observation Data for Change Detection in Polarimetric Radar Images

Nadiane Nguekeu Metepong Lagpong[1]($\boxtimes$) (iD), Joseph Mvogo Ngono[1],
Pierre Ele[2](iD), Vigny Noumsi[1](iD), Jean-Paul Rudant[3](iD),
and Fabien Mouomene Moffo[1](iD)

[1] University of Douala, Douala, Cameroon
`nguekeunadiane18@yahoo.fr`, `joseph.mvogo@gmail.com`
[2] University of Yaounde, Yaounde, Cameroon
[3] University Paris-Est-Marne-la-Valee, Paris, France

Abstract. The aim here is to detect changes in polarimetric radar images (VV and VH) from the Sentinel 1A and 1B satellites. These changes are of a general nature, and can be linked to natural disasters. They include earthquakes, flooding, sea water pollution, deforestation, crop evolution, land surveying and climate change. In our work, we are interested in changes in the city of Douala. We used a stack of two images, one taken before the change and the other taken after the change. Our contribution is to set up a method based on the fusion of machine learning, deeplearning and algebraic methods in order to obtain more efficient results. This model involves firstly applying machine learning methods such as random forest and algebraic methods based on Minkowski and Kolmogorov algorithms in parallel to our pre-processed images. The second step is to generate a deep learning model based on convolutional neural networks, which will take the images from the algebraic and machine learning methods as input in order to generate two output classes (changed and not-changed).

Keywords: Radar · polarimetric Radar · changes detection · deeplearning

1 Introduction

Change detection is at the heart of the human ecosystem. It helps to improve living conditions on earth.

Since December 2015, the sentinel satellite has been covering Cameroonian soil, enabling us to make remote observations [1]. This satellite is a product of COPERNICUS, which distributes radar images free of charge. Radar imagery enables us to observe the atmosphere, the ground [2] and the subsoil, in order to improve living conditions for mankind. Detecting these changes will enhance

© ICST Institute for Computer Sciences, Social Informatics and Telecommunications Engineering 2024
Published by Springer Nature Switzerland AG 2024. All Rights Reserved

F. Tchakounte et al. (Eds.): SAFER-TEA 2023, LNICST 566, pp. 345–358, 2024.
https://doi.org/10.1007/978-3-031-56396-6_22

security, boost agricultural production and significantly control climate change. Radar imagery is complex, with a capacity of around 1 GB already compressed, and its handling requires a high-performance machine. Also, radar imagery can sometimes cause confusion between targets with similar backscatter characteristics.

Radar signals are based on two actions, penetration and reflection. One part penetrates the ground, and the other is reflected by the target in the upper half of space. So extracting the characteristics of these signals becomes complicated. In the past, several methods using signal backscatter have been developed, including the Otsu algorithm [3], the gamma distribution [4], the statistical analysis [5], the hybrid method [6] and the algebraic method [7].

Note that these methods were not completely automatic. So, in order to obtain more convincing results, we used the supervised classification [8]. Convolutional Neural Networks have also been shown to provide better results in this domain [9–11].

The general objective is to automatically detect changes in a stack of two radar images taken on different dates in order to anticipate certain phenomena and locate and rescue people in danger. We will carry out the following tasks for its processing:

- Presentation of a stack of two images taken before and after the change;
- Perform pre-processing on our images, namely: satellite location correction, thermal noise correction, on-board noise correction, radiometric correction, coregistration, noise filtering (speckle) and geometric correction;
- Implement the machine learning algorithm: random forest;
- Implement algebraic method algorithms (minkowski and kolmogorov) and use Otsu's algorithm to binarize our images;
- Design a learning model based on CNN and deeplearning, which will take as input images from the machine learning method and algebraic methods to generate two classes (changed and not-changed);
- Perform sufficient tests on our model;
- Automatically detect changes in new images.

2 Data Presentation and Methods

2.1 Data Presentation

Thanks to sentinel's Data Hub, we've been able to download a number of images of the city of Douala, all free of charge. We are working with a series of two images:

- The 04/09/2017 image taken before the change;
- The 05/12/2020 image taken after the change.

These are sentinel images taken in a North-South (up-down) ascending node, of the sentinel1A and 1B satellites located in the same orbital plane but 180° apart, at an altitude of 700 km and with a repeat cycle of 6 days.

Our products are of the GRD (Ground Range Detected) type. These are the products most commonly used for land and sea monitoring applications. The mode used is IW (Interferometric Wide-Swath Mode) with a swath width of 250 km. The decomposition techniques used include Cloude-Pottier, Freeman-Durden, Pauli, Van Zyl, Yamaguchi and Touzi.

Given that the volume of our data is approximately 1 GB per image, it is important for us to reduce this size in order to better manipulate our data. The coordinates of the extracted area are shown below (Fig. 1).

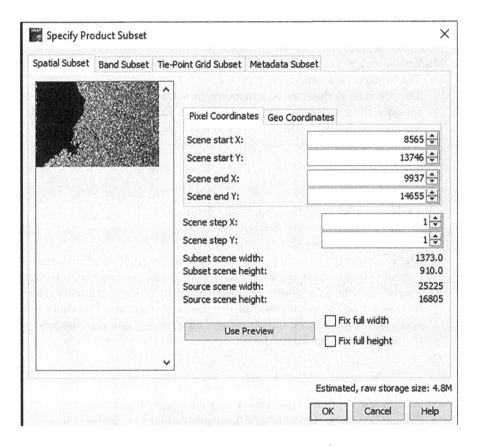

Fig. 1. Extraction coordinates of the area of interest.

Following pre-processing, we end up with a georeferenced image comprising 4 bands. These are the vv and vh bands of the images before and after the change.

2.2   Methodology

This phase consists of recovering the radar image from pre-processing, and applying the following methods:

– Machine learning algorithms such as random forest: A random forest is a supervised machine learning algorithm. It is one of the most widely used algorithms because of its accuracy, simplicity and flexibility. This algorithm is called a "forest" because it generates the growth of a forest of decision trees. The data from these trees is then merged to ensure the most accurate predictions.

With traditional data processing, a lot of valuable time is spent cleaning up the data. Random forests minimise this processing, as they deal well with missing data. Tests carried out to compare predictions resulting from complete and incomplete data have shown almost identical levels of performance. Outliers and non-linear features are essentially eliminated.

– Difference algorithm between two images using the algebraic methods of Minkowski and Kolmogorov:

- The Minkowski method
  The Minkowski distance is a distance in a Euclidean space that can be considered as a generalisation of both the Euclidean distance and the Manhattan distance. The general formula is as follows:

$$D_p(x, z) = (\sum_{i=1}^{n} d_i(x_i, z_i)^p)^{1/p} \tag{1}$$

  * For p=1 we have the Manhattan distance
  * For p=2 we have the Euclidean distance

- The Kolmogorov method
  The Kolmogorov test compares the observed distribution of a statistical sample with a theoretical distribution. It is used in preference to the chi-square test when the observed characteristic can take continuous values. It is based on the comparison of distribution functions. The concept of neighbourhood, which is important and more closely linked to the concept of proximity, is highlighted here.

$$V(p, q) = \frac{1}{2} \int |p - q| \tag{2}$$

  With p and q representing the vv and vh polarisations.

- Application of the Otsu method for thresholding our algebraic images.
  This method is used to perform automatic thresholding based on the shape of the image histogram, or the reduction of a greyscale image into a binary image. The algorithm assumes that the image to be binarised contains only two classes of pixels (i.e. the foreground and background) and then calculates the optimum threshold separating these two classes so that their intra-class variance is minimal. The threshold that minimises the intra-class variance is sought using all the possible thresholds:

$$\sigma_w^2(t) = w_1(t)\sigma_1^2(t) + w_2(t)\sigma_2^2(t) \tag{3}$$

The weights wi represent the probability of being in the i class, each separated by a threshold t. Finally, the variances of these classes are the σ_i^2.

- Image classification with the fusion of machine learning, algebraic methods and deeplearning.

As input to our model, we have images derived from machine learning methods, algebraic methods such as Minkowski and Kolmogorov, to which we have applied a threshold, using the Otsu method.

In image processing, the convolutional neural network (CNN) is at the top of the list of machine learning algorithms [12] and has been growing steadily since 2015. This algorithm is currently the most widely used due to its convincing results. We use medium-resolution satellite images (pixel 20 m x 20 m) with VH polarisation (vertical transmission and horizontal reception) and VV polarisation (vertical transmission and vertical reception). To do this, we need to classify each pixel according to numerical values that are good enough to drive a machine learning model.

The model selected is as follows:

This is a seven-layer model, chosen for the good accuracy of its results. The confusion matrix stands out from the other methods, with good results [13] with a P-Score of 0.94, R-Score of 0.93 and an F-Score of 0.93.

3   Results and Discussion

3.1   Results

Since we are working on two images, before and after the change, the preprocessing was carried out on these two images. Applying our machine learning algorithms, algebraic methods and deeplearning, we obtained the following results:

- Application of the Machine Learning Method: Random Forest
- Application of algebraic methods
  - Méthode de Minkowski
    The pixel values are almost zero.
    The Otsu threshold here has two values: 0 and 255. The number of pixels at 255 is reduced.
  - Méthode de Kolmogorov
    This method simply shows that the pixel values tend towards 0.
    Applying the Otsu threshold, we have the histogram above with two pixel values, 0 and 255. The number of pixels at 255 is slightly higher here than at Minkowski.
- Application of the Fusion of Machine Learning, Algebraic Methods and Deeplearning
  In this figure, we can simply see that our image has been binarised, with pixels in white showing areas of change, and those in black showing areas that have not changed. This is verified by the histogram below.

```
from tricks import *
import sys
import os
import numpy

nclasses = 2


def myModel(x):
    # input patches: 16x16x2
    conv1 = tf.layers.conv2d(inputs=x, filters=16, kernel_size=[5, 5], padding="valid",
                             activation=tf.nn.relu) # out size: 12x12x16
    conv2 = tf.layers.conv2d(inputs=conv1, filters=16, kernel_size=[3, 3], padding="valid",
                             activation=tf.nn.relu) # out size: 10x10x16
    conv3 = tf.layers.conv2d(inputs=conv2, filters=16, kernel_size=[3, 3], padding="valid",
                             activation=tf.nn.relu) # out size: 8x8x16
    conv4 = tf.layers.conv2d(inputs=conv3, filters=32, kernel_size=[3, 3], padding="valid",
                             activation=tf.nn.relu) # out size: 6x6x32
    conv5 = tf.layers.conv2d(inputs=conv4, filters=32, kernel_size=[3, 3], padding="valid",
                             activation=tf.nn.relu) # out size: 4x4x32
    conv6 = tf.layers.conv2d(inputs=conv5, filters=32, kernel_size=[3, 3], padding="valid",
                             activation=tf.nn.relu) # out size: 2x2x32
    conv7 = tf.layers.conv2d(inputs=conv6, filters=32, kernel_size=[2, 2], padding="valid",
                             activation=tf.nn.relu) # out size: 1x1x32

    # Features
    features = tf.reshape(conv7, shape=[-1, 32], name="features")

    # Neurons for classes
    estimated = tf.layers.dense(inputs=features, units=nclasses, activation=None)
    estimated_out = tf.reshape(estimated, shape=(1,nclasses), name="probably")
    estimated_label = tf.argmax(estimated, 1, name="prediction")

    return estimated, estimated_label, estimated_out, features
```

Fig. 2. Deeplearning model.

Our histogram shows two abscissa values: 0 and 1. What's more, the 0 largely dominates the 1, confirming that there are changes between these two dates. Changes were detected here at two levels:

- Changes linked to the presence or absence of objects. In our case, our object represents the boat parked at sea.
  The figure above shows the detection of boats at sea. Image a) is that of 04 September 2017, and on this image we can see in red the presence of two boats. our image b) of 05 December 2020 shows the absence of boats in the same area. And finally, our image c) is simply the result of merging the methods. The presence of boats at sea can be seen in red.
- Changes linked to the presence or absence of buildings. The buildings here represent the stadium.
  The figure above shows the presence or absence of the stadium. Image a) is that of 04 September 2017, and on this image we note in red the absence of the Japoma stadium, since on that date the stadium did not

yet exist. our image b) of 05 December 2020 shows the presence of the stadium in the same area. And finally, our image c) shows the Japoma stadium in red as an area of change.

It should be noted that apart from these two changes, there are also changes linked to deforestation, pollution of sea water, oil and gas, the installation of military bases, and so on.

3.2   Discussion

By comparing our results with the literature, we can see that our results are more relevant, with high accuracy, which is why we have chosen to merge our methods. Nevertheless, the execution time of our learning algorithms is high with the use of CPUs, which is why we are moving more and more towards the GPU for fast, parallel execution. It is clear that the use of full polarimetry will lead to better results [14]. For future work, we propose to add to our fusion method the topographical data of the environment, as well as the algebraic Kullback Leibler method based on probability distributions (Figs. 1, 2, 3, 4, 5, 6, 7, 8, 9, 10, 11, 12, 13, 14).

The pixel values are almost zero.

Fig. 3. Detection of changes using the Random forest method.

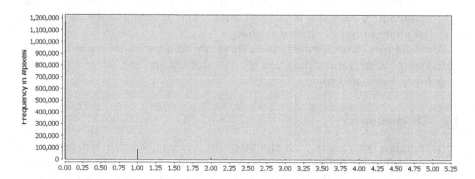

Fig. 4. Histogram of change detection using the random forest method.

Fig. 5. Detection of changes using the Minkowski method.

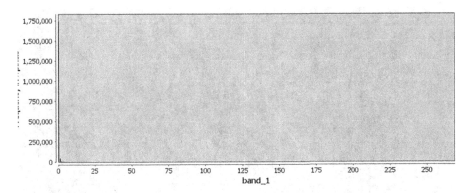

Fig. 6. Histogram of change detection using the minkowski method.

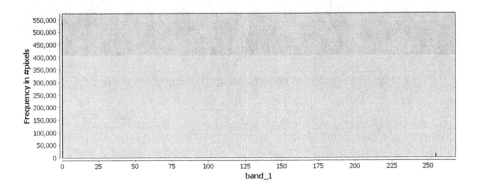

Fig. 7. Histogram of Minkowski method with threshold.

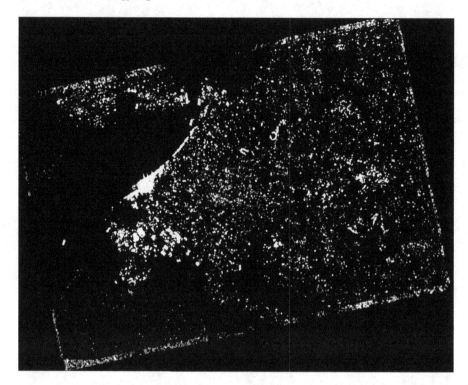

Fig. 8. Detection of changes using the kolmogorov method.

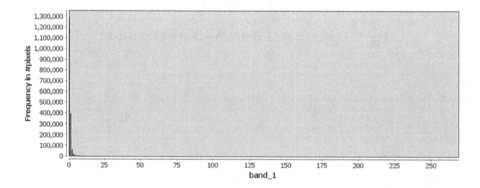

Fig. 9. Histogramme de la méthode de Kolmogorov.

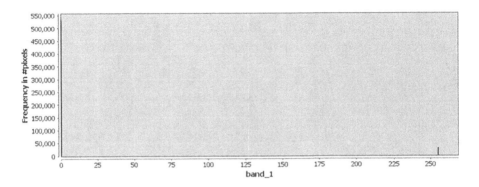

Fig. 10. Histogram of kolmogorov method with threshold.

Fig. 11. Detecting changes using the machine learning fusion method, algebraic methods and deeplearning.

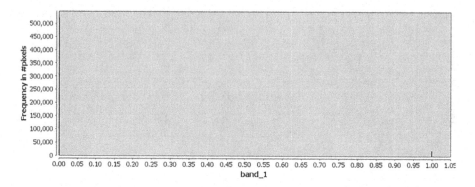

Fig. 12. Histogram of change detection using the machine learning fusion method, algebraic methods and deeplearning.

Fig. 13. Detection of boats at sea.

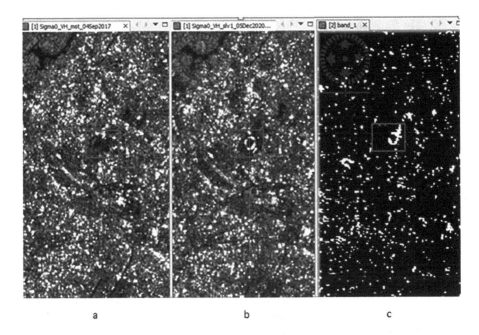

a   b   c

Fig. 14. Stadium detection.

4   Conclusion

An automatic change detection algorithm based on polarimetric radar images from the sentinel-1 satellite was developed in this work. Our work was divided into two main phases, namely the pre-processing phase and the data processing phase. In the pre-processing phase, we carried out operations such as: satellite location correction, thermal noise correction, on-board noise correction, radiometric correction, coregistration, noise filtering (speckle) and geometric correction. In the processing phase, we used the fusion of machine learning, algebraic methods and deeplearning to classify our images into two classes (pixels that have changed and pixels that have not). In comparison with previous change detection approaches, the fusion method proposed here is among the best in terms of the satisfactory results it achieves. In order to improve our work, we are going to use the topographic data of the environment, also, we will work on the complete polarization (VV, VH, HH). Also, as our sentinel-1 images are not very high resolution, we will be looking at ways of obtaining high-resolution images, which are not free at the moment.

References

1. Jacob, X.K., Bisht, D.S., Chatterjee, C., Raghuwanshi, N.S.: Hydro dynamic modeling for flood Hazar dassessment in a data scarce region: a case study of Bharathapuzha river basin, Environmental Modeling and Assessment (2020)

2. Elbialy, S., Mahmoud, A., Pradhan, B., Buchroithner, M.: Application of space borne synthetic aperture radar data for extraction of soil moisture and its use in hydrological modelling at Gottleuba Catchment, Saxony, Germany. J. Flood. Risk. Manage. **7**, 159–175 (2013)
3. Li, J., Wang, S.: An automatic method for mapping inland surface water bodies with Radarsat-2 imagery. Int. J. Rem. Sens. **36**, 1367–1384 (2015)
4. Liang, J., Liu, D.: A local thresholding approach to flood water delineation using Sentinel-1 SAR imagery. ISPRS J. Photogramm. Rem. Sens. **159**, 53–62 (2020)
5. Bolanos, S., Stiff, D., Brisco, B., Pietroniro, A.: Operational surface water detection and monitoring using Radarsat 2. Rem. Sens. **8**, 285 (2016)
6. Matgen, P., Hostache, R., Schumann, G.J.-P., Pifster, L., Hoffmann, L., Savenije, H.H.: Automated towards an automated SAR-based flood monitoring system: lessons learned from two case studies. Phys. Chem. Earth **36**, 241–252 (2011)
7. Jordi, I.L.: Contributions à lánalyse dímages dóbservation de la Terre pour la production de cartes dóccupation des sols et le suivi des changements dans des contextes opérationnels. Remote, Sens (2018)
8. Huang, W., et al.: Automated extraction of surface water extent from sentinel-1 data. Rem. Sens (2011)
9. Amin, A.M.E., Liu, Q., WangandA, Y.: Uthor Two. Convolutional neural network features based change detection in satellite images. In: First International Workshop on Pattern Recognition (2016)
10. Hu, F., Xia, G.-S., Hu, J., Zhang, L.: Transferring deep convolutional neural networks for the scene classification of high-resolution remote sensing imagery. Rem. Sens. **7**, 14680–14707 (2015)
11. Nogueira, K., Miranda, W.O., DosSantos, J.A.: Improving spatial feature representation from aerial scenes by using convolutional networks. In: 2015 28th SIBGRAPI Conference on Graphics, Patterns and Images (2015)
12. Wang, S., Chen, W., Xie, S.M., Azzari, G., Lobell, D.B.: Weakly supervised deeplearning for segmentation of remote sensing imagery. Rem. Sens. **12**, 207 (2020)
13. Duro, D.C., Franklin, S.E., Dubé, M.G.: A comparison of pixel based and object-based image analysis with selected machine learning algorithms for the classification of agricultural landscapes using SPOT-5 HRG imagery. Rem. Sens. **118**, 259–272 (2012)
14. Morandeira, N., Grings, F., Facchinetti, C., Kandus, P.: Mapping plant functional types in flood plain Wetlands: an analysis of C-band polarimetric SAR data from RADARSAT-2. Rem. Sens. **8**, 174 (2016)

Reviews

Reviews

Machine Learning Techniques for the Management of Diseases: A Paper Review

Ngolah Kenneth Tim[1]([✉]), Vivient Kamla[2], and Elie T. Fute[1]

[1] Computer Engineering Department, University of Buea, Buea, Cameroon
timngolah@yahoo.com
[2] Mathematics and Computer Science Department, ENSAI-University of Ngaoundéré, Ngaoundere, Cameroon

Abstract. The advancement in Artificial Intelligence has led to the improvement in human lives. Machine learning algorithms in particular and Artificial Intelligence in general have become very useful in today's activities. One of the sectors that has benefited from the new technology is the health sector. Machine learning techniques have been useful in the diagnosis and prediction of rare diseases. Many health sectors are using the techniques for the diagnosis and prediction of diseases thereby improving on the health situations of the patients in record time. Artificial Intelligence-based methods help in reducing the doctor to patients' ratio gap by providing machine learning alternatives in the prediction of diseases. In this paper, we give an overview of different machine learning techniques and their relevance in the diagnosis of particular diseases. Machine learning algorithms such as Support Vector Machine (SVM), Naïve Bayes, K Nearest Neighbor (KNN), Decision Tree (DT), Random Forest (RF), Artificial neural network (ANN), Convolution Neural Network (CNN), Logistic Regression and Linear Regression used for the diagnosis of diseases have been reviewed. A collection of most non-communicable diseases diagnosed using machine learning has been examined. A comparative analysis of the accuracy performance to diagnose diseases with different machine learning algorithms has also been presented.

Keywords: Artificial Intelligence · Machine Learning Techniques · Management of Diseases · Diagnosis of Diseases · Prediction of Diseases

1 Introduction

Machine learning (ML) is a branch of artificial intelligence that allows the machines to make use of dataset and make a judgment without the intervention of human beings [20].

A number of machine learning techniques based systems have been examined by some researchers for the management of diseases. Supervised, unsupervised, semi-supervised and reinforcement learning techniques or algorithms [14, 20] are some of

© ICST Institute for Computer Sciences, Social Informatics and Telecommunications Engineering 2024
Published by Springer Nature Switzerland AG 2024. All Rights Reserved
F. Tchakounte et al. (Eds.): SAFER-TEA 2023, LNICST 566, pp. 361–379, 2024.
https://doi.org/10.1007/978-3-031-56396-6_23

the useful machine learning algorithms used for the management of diseases. In comparative terms, supervised learning technique makes use of input and output data to predict similar circumstances, while in unsupervised learning, the algorithm learns only from input data and predicts the outcome from the input data. Semi-supervised learning on its part depends on both the supervised and unsupervised techniques while, in reinforcement learning technique, the system makes use of the environment to get the desired results [20] (Fig. 1).

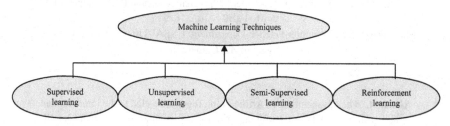

Fig. 1. Machine learning techniques

Machine learning techniques use machine learning algorithms to conduct their task by predicting output values from given input data [13]. Some of the algorithms are classified as regression or classification algorithms. Pijush Dutta et al. [13], gave a comparative analysis of machine learning algorithms. The main difference between Regression and Classification algorithms is that Regression algorithms are used to predict the continuous values whereas Classification algorithms are used to predict or classify the discrete values [13].

1.1 Motivation and Research Queries

As the population increases, there is adequate shortage of health facilities as well as health personnel to cater for the health needs of the people [16]. To bridge this gab there is high need of technology to assist the available health personnel. Artificial intelligence has been useful in many areas of life such as robotics, language translation etc. Using Artificial intelligence or machine learning techniques in health sector will go a long way to reduce the mortality rate of population. Machine learning plays a great role in epidemiological decisions in the health sector. Whereas epidemiology lays great emphasis on the causes (causation) [17], machine learning focuses on providing risk factors, health care gaps and improves risk score accuracy to the health providers. This risk score accuracy can be used to make predictions on health situations. These predictions are sometimes used by the government agencies to take health related decisions.

According to FarrukhSaleem et al. [16], a research conducted in India using data collected between February 2020 to March 2021 estimated that the epidemic doubled in size every 1.7 days to 46.2 days depending on the number of infected cases. Thus the use of machine learning techniques can go a long way to improve on the health situations of people as well as limit the spread of diseases.

1.2   Research Highlights

This paper review highlights the following:

- Presentation of machine learning techniques for the management of diseases.
- Logical review of machine learning algorithms or techniques used for the management of diseases.
- Analysis and review of existing works related to machine learning techniques for the management of diseases.
- Presentation of the analysis and analytical discussion of the previous work done.
- Identification of the research challenges for the implementation of machine learning techniques for the management of diseases.

1.3   Paper Organization

This review paper is organized as follows: Section 1 gives the introduction of machine learning techniques and the motivation. Section 2 presents different machine learning algorithms and the related works done using each technique. Section 3 highlights the different paper reviews on the same work. Section 4 discusses the analysis of different machine learning techniques for the diagnosis and prediction of different diseases as seen in related works. Section 5 focuses on challenges and open issues and we conclude with Sect. 6. The figure below shows the outflow of the paper (Fig. 2).

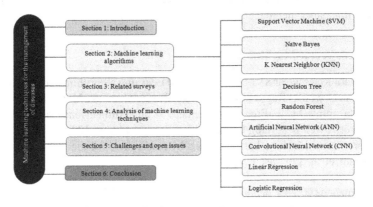

Fig. 2. Paper outflow

2   Machine Learning Algorithms

To implement machine learning algorithms, the following factors or metrics are taken into consideration:

Speed: The costs involved in generating and using the model.

Scalability: The ability to construct the model efficiently given large amount of data.

Interpretability: The level of understanding that is provided by the model.

Predictive accuracy: The testing tool to correctly predict the class label or value of new or previously unseen data, and the confusion matrix which uses True Negative (TN), False Negative (FN), False Positive (FP), and True Positive (TP).

Where True Negative means the Model has given a No prediction, whereas the real or actual value was also No, True Positive indicates that the model's prediction is yes while the actual value was also true, False Negative (also known as Type-II error) shows that the model's prediction is No, while the actual value was Yes, and False Positive (also known as Type-I error) shows that the model's prediction is Yes, while the actual value was No.

Using the confusion matrix properties, Machine Learning can measure performance [1, 3] of a classifier as recall, precision, accuracy and f1 as represented below:

i. Classification Accuracy (Accuracy) $= \frac{TP+TN}{TP+FP+FN+TN}$

ii. Miscalculation rate (Error rate) $= \frac{FP+FN}{TP+FP+FN+TN}$

iii. Positive prediction (Precision) $= \frac{TP}{TP+FP}$

iv. Negative prediction $= \frac{TN}{TN+FN}$

v. Sensitivity (Recall) $= \frac{TP}{TP+FN}$

vi. Specificity $= \frac{TN}{TN+FP}$

vii. F-measure $(f1) = \frac{2*Recall*Precision}{Recall+Precision}$

Some researchers have examined machine learning algorithms for the management of diseases [20]. Some useful machine learning algorithms used for the management of diseases in this paper include:

2.1 Support Vector Machine (SVM)

Support Vector Machine or SVM is a Supervised Learning algorithm that helps in solving Classification as well as Regression problems. The idea behind SVM [14] is to distinctly classify data points by finding a hyper plane in an n-dimensional space. The SVM approach works well in solving linear and nonlinear problems [20].

Support Vector Machine has been used by researchers for the management of diseases. Sriram et al. [29] used SVM algorithm amongst other algorithms to develop intelligent Parkinson's disease diagnosis systems. Their result shows that, SVM had the best performance (90.26% accuracy).

Otoom et al. [21] proposed a system for the monitoring of heart disease using SVM and other algorithms. The system used UCI dataset which consisted of 303 cases. At the end, SVM had the best performance with an accuracy of 88.3%.

Kumari and Chitra [21] carried out an experiment to predict diabetes disease using SVM with the help of Pima Indian diabetes data set and their accuracy was 78%.

An experiment was carried out by Fathima and Manimeglai [21] to detect dengue disease with the use of King Institute of Preventive medicine and Survey dataset in India. The resulting accuracy was 91%.

SVM was also used to predict liver disease by Vijayarani and Dhayanand [21] with the help of ILPD data set obtained from UCI. The dataset has 560 instances and the performance was 79.66%.

Charleonnan et al. [30] in order to predict kidney disease, used publicly available datasets and evaluated support vector machine (SVM), and received the accuracy of 98.3%.

2.2 Naïve Bayes Algorithm

Naïve Bayes algorithm is based on Bayes theorem. It is a supervised learning algorithm used in solving classification problems. It is very useful in text classification [3] that includes a high-dimensional training dataset. Naïve Bayes algorithm can be used for the filtering of spam emails and classifying documents [20]. It is a probabilistic classifier and used Bayes theorem which states that:

$$P(A|B) = \frac{P(B|A)P(A)}{P(B)} \tag{1}$$

where $P(A|B)$ is the posterior probability, $P(B|A)$ is the likelihood, $P(A)$ is prior probability and $P(B)$ is the marginal probability.

Vembandasamy et al. [21], conducted a research on heart disease using Naive Bayes algorithm. The data-set of about 500 patients obtained from one of the leading diabetic research institute in Chennai was used. The experiment resulted to a performance accuracy of 86.4%.

The diagnosis of heart disease was also carried out by Parthiban and Srivatsa [21] using a dataset of 500 patients from the research Institute in Chennai. The results from the Native Bayes had an accuracy of 74%.

Iyer et al.[23] on the other hand worked on diagnoses of diabetes disease using Naive Bayes with data set from Pima Indian diabetes data set and the accuracy recorded was 79.5%

Vijayarani and Dhayanand [22] used Naive bayes Classification algorithms to predict liver disease. The ILPD data set used comprising of 560 instances came from UCI. The implementation gave and accuracy of 61.28%.

Ba-Alwi and Hintaya [23] suggested a comparative analysis of different ML algorithms. In their analysis, they had an accuracy of 95% for Naive Bayes.

Sriram et al. [29], used KNN, SVM, Naive Bayes, and RF algorithms to develop intelligent systems for the diagnosis of Parkinson's disease. In comparative terms, Naive Bayes demonstrated poor performance (69.23% accuracy).

2.3 K-Nearest Neighbour

K-Nearest Neighbor is a Supervised Machine Learning algorithm useful for both Regression as well as for Classification problems. The algorithm makes use of k nearest data points in the training set to the data point for which a target value is unavailable and assigns the average value of the found data points to it [24].

To implement a diagnosis for kidney disease, Charleonnan et al. [30] used publicly available datasets for the evaluation of K-nearest neighbors (KNN) and received the accuracy of 98.1%.

Kandhasamy and Balamurali [31] compared ML algorithms such as DT, KNN, RF, and SVM for classifying patients with diabetes mellitus. The experiment was conducted using UCI Diabetes dataset, and the KNN ($K = 1$) obtained 100% accuracy although they used a very simplified diabetes dataset with few parameters. The size of the dataset still questions the 100% accuracy result obtained in the experiment.

Shouman et al. [32] used KNN to predict heart disease using a dataset of 712 from UCI Machine learning repository. The performance result was 97.4%

Lubaib and Muneer, [33] with the help of dataset of Michigan University used KNN to predict the diagnosis of heart disease and their performance accuracy was 99.8%.

Elmasri et al., [34] with the help of private data used KNN to detect and quantify the severity of abdominal aortic calcification and got 95.2% accuracy.

Femina, [35] used KNN for the diagnosis of hepatitis disease and obtained a score of 84.5% accuracy with the help of UCI Machine repository.

Kayaaltı et al. [36] with the help of private data used KNN to determine chronic hepatitis. The result was 95% accuracy.

Gardezi et al. [37] and Sayed et al. [38] used KNN to predict breast cancer. Their results were overwhelming as 92.81% and 99.72% with the help of dataset from UCI Machine learning.

2.4 Decision Tree

A Decision Tree is a supervised machine learning algorithm used for classification and Regression problems [13]. It uses a tree-like structure with leaf node representing the outcome, internal nodes representing the dataset and branches represent the decision rules. A decision tree uses yes or no questions to split the tree into sub trees and ends when no more split is possible.

Neelaveni and Devasana [38] proposed a model that can detect Alzheimer patients using DT, and achieved an accuracy of 83%.

Dengue is a severe contagious disease [20] and creates trouble in those countries where weather is humid for example Thailand, Indonesia and Malaysia.

Tarmizi et al. [39] used Decision Tree (DT), to predict dengue disease with data set from Public Health Department of Selangor State. By using 10-Cross fold validation DT offered 99.95% accuracy,

Seyedamin Pouriyeh et al. [40], Amir Hussain et al. [41] used DT to predict heart disease and had worst performance of 77.55% and 42.89% respectively as compared to other algorithms.

Acharya et al. [42] and Tayefi et al. [43] used DT to predict coronary artery disease (CAD) using a private dataset of 2346 individuals and had an accuracy of 98.99% and 91% respectively.

El Houby, [44] with the help of DT predicted the patients' response to hepatitis C virus treatment using private data. The accuracy of 92% was obtained.

Guo et al. [45] and Khalilabad et al. [46] predicted breast cancer using DT with private dataset and obtained a performance accuracy of 70% and 95.23% respectively.

2.5 Random Forest Algorithm

Random Forest is a popular supervised machine learning algorithm useful for both Classification and Regression problems. It provides predictive models for classification and regression [14]. Random Forest is composed of a large number of Decision Tree blocks used as individual predictors. Random forest takes prediction from each tree and uses the majority positive results to make the final prediction.

Kandhasamy and Balamurali [31] compared different ML in classifying patients with diabetes mellitus using UCI Diabetes dataset, and RF obtained 100% performance accuracy although the size of the dataset was too small that the 100% is questionable.

Sriram et al. [29] used Random Forest algorithms amongst other algorithms to develop intelligent Parkinson's disease diagnosis systems. In their results, Random Forest shows the best performance of 90.26% accuracy.

Vidushi and Shrivastava [47] used Random Forest (RF) algorithm for Alzheimer disease diagnosis and achieved an accuracy of 84.21%.

2.6 Artificial Neural Network (ANN)

Artificial neural network is a branch of computing with a powerful tool for modeling data [12]. It is able to capture and represent complex input/output relationships. ANNs are built from multi-layer of nodes linking each other. The number of neurons in a layer and the number of layers depends strongly on the complexity of the studied system. The neurons in the input layer receive the data and transfer them to neurons in the first hidden layer through the weighted links. The data are mathematically processed and the result is transferred to the neurons in the next layer (Fig. 3).

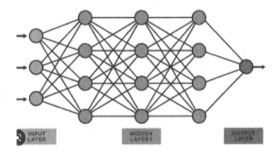

Fig. 3. Artificial Neural Network

Samuel et al. [12] used Artificial Neural Network (ANN) to predict heart risk. They obtained an accuracy of 91.1% with the help of dataset from UCI Machine learning repository.

Thomas et al. [48] classified cardiac arrhythmais using ANN with a dataset from ECG arrhythmia database and obtained an accuracy of 94.64%.

Rau et al. [12] predicted liver cancer using ANN using dataset from National Health Insurance Research database ce of Taiwan.

Kaya and Uyar, [49] used ANN to identify if patients suffering from hepatitis are predicted to be alive or not. The dataset used was from UCI Machine learning repository and their result was 100% accuracy.

Jilani et al. [50] and Resino et al. [51] used ANN for the diagnosis of hepatitis C virus using UCI Machine repository and obtained a score of 99.1% and 94.9% respectively.

2.7   Convolutional Neural Network

A convolutional neural network (CNN or convnet) is a subset of machine learning algorithms that can take an image as input, assigns attributes to the image, differentiates one from the other [26]. The pre-processing required in a ConvNet is much lower as compared to other classification algorithms. The architecture of a ConvNet is analogous to that of the connectivity pattern of Neurons in the Human Brain and was inspired by the organization of the Visual Cortex (Fig. 4).

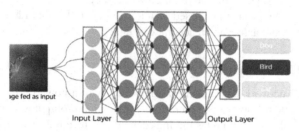

Fig. 4. Convolutional Neural Network

Rayan Alanazi [26] proposed a system using the CNN algorithm for the prediction of chronic disease and had 96% accuracy result. He then used other machine learning algorithms like Naive Bayes, Decision tree, and Logistic regression with the same data for the prediction of chronic disease and found out that CNN had the best accuracy performance of 96% as compared to other algorithms.

Farrukh Saleem et al. [16] in a paper review indicated that CNN has been widely used in different articles for the model and prediction of COVID-19 pandemic as compared to other algorithms.

Rashid Amin, [53] presented the use of CNN for the diagnosing of mild depression by processing EEG signals. The model used four functional connectivity metrics (coherence, correlation, PLV, and PLI) and obtained a classification accuracy of 80.74%.

Wejdan L et al. [27] in a paper review for Diabetic retinopathy detection through deep learning techniques observed the highly use of CNN with the use of Diabetic retinopathy datasets. As indicated in the review, most researchers have used the CNN for the classification and the detection of the Diabetic retinopathy images due to its efficiency [27].

Ibrahim Mahmood Ibrahim, Adnan Mohsin Abdulazeez [20] in a paper review indicated the use of GitHub and Kaggle dataset for the modeling of COVID-19 detection mechanism using CNN. This modeled system had a 94% accuracy performance.

2.8   Linear Regression

Linear Regression or Simple Linear Regression is a type of Regression algorithm that models the relationship between a dependent variable and a single independent variable. The relationship produced by linear regression is linear or a sloped straight line. It is considered to be the most conventional machine learning technique [14]. Its general form is written as:

$$y = a_0 + a_1 x + \varepsilon \qquad (2)$$

where $\mathbf{a_0}$ and $\mathbf{a_1}$ are constants, y is the variable to be predicted and x the variable used to predict. a_0 is the slope of the regression while a_1 represents the intercept and ε represents the error term.

2.9 Logistic Regression

Logistic Regression is much similar to the Linear Regression except that it is instead used for classification problems rather than regression problems. In Logistic regression we use an "S" shaped logistic function, which predicts two binary values (0 or 1). It is based on the sigmoid predictive function defined as:

$$y(x) = \frac{1}{1 + e^x} \qquad (3)$$

where x is a linear function [14]. The function returns a probability score P between 0 and 1. In order to map it to two discrete classes (0 or 1), a threshold value ε is fixed and the predicted class is equal to 1 if P $\geq \varepsilon$ and 0 otherwise.

To predict kidney disease, Charleonnan et al. [30] evaluated logistic regression (LR) using public dataset and received the accuracy of 94.8%.

Vidushi and Shrivastava [53] adopted and tested a ML based Alzheimer disease diagnosis. Using Logistic Regression (LR) and achieved an accuracy of 78.95%.

3 Related Surveys

This section presents the different paper reviews on machine learning techniques or algorithms related to the management of diseases:

Enas M.F. El Houby [12] presented a paper review on the diagnosis of some diseases using machine learning techniques. The author however indicated the difficulties of comparing different machine learning techniques under different conditions citing that for optimal results, the used data should be the same.

Yassine Merihi et al. [14] did a paper review principally on COVID-19 detection using machine learning based approach. The authors did a detailed analysis of different techniques used in relation to COVID-19. However, the paper did not use the accuracy metric to indicate the effectiveness of the different techniques.

Pijush Dutta et al. [13] did a comparative analysis review on various supervised machine learning techniques for the diagnosis of COVID-19. The authors presented the different symptoms for COVID-19 and worked on KNN, RF for its diagnosis. Their work focused on identification of COVID-19 using yes or no bases. The limitation on this research is that no metric was used to determine the accuracy of the results.

Amir Yasseen et al. [28] presented a paper review on automatic extraction of knowledge for diagnosing COVID-19 disease based on text mining techniques. Their observation was the fact that very few authors had carried out research on COVID-19. Their main bottleneck was on the choice of the classification algorithm to use.

V.V. Ramalingam et al. [24] also did a paper review on Heart disease prediction using machine learning techniques. In the paper, they indicated the usefulness of machine learning techniques for the prediction of heart disease. The limitation on the research was that there is still much research to be done on how to handle high dimensional data and over fitting.

C. Zhang et al. [48] produced a paper review on machine learning techniques for disease prediction in which the authors discussed the strengths and limitations of different methods and provided recommendations for future research.

A. Korolev et al. [54] worked on a paper review for Alzheimer's disease predictive modeling. The authors developed a model that uses neuroimaging data and clinical features to predict disease progression.

L. Chen et al. [55] did a paper review on Deep learning for healthcare in which the authors discussed the benefits and challenges of using deep learning in healthcare.

S. Shah et al. [56] presented a paper review on machine learning techniques for the diagnosis of COVID-19 in which they discussed the potentials of the techniques in predicting disease severity and identifying high-risk patients.

Meherwar Fatima, Maruf [57] presented a survey of Machine learning algorithms for disease diagnostic. In the paper, the authors did a comparative analysis of different diseases with their corresponding most suitable machine learning techniques.

4 Analysis of Machine Learning Techniques

4.1 Analytical Discussion

In this section, we give the analysis of the different previous works related to machine learning techniques in healthcare. The analysis is based on the review of different machine learning techniques, diseases tested using the techniques, the accuracy performance and the authors.

Table 1 shows some different machine learning techniques that have been used in the diagnosis of some diseases, their accuracy ratio and the authors of the articles. The reviewed articles covered the period from 2015 to 2022. A good number of researchers have worked on machine learning techniques as indicated in Table 1. The percentage of publications in SVM is higher than any other technique, this can be due to the number of diseases easily tested using SVM while the percentage of publications for Linear Regression is zero. COVID-19 has not been widely tested using many of the machine learning techniques, this can be due to its occurrence as it is not a regular disease. Some machine learning techniques as seen in Table 1 show different accuracy ratios for the same disease tested in different experiments.

Table 2 presents disease prediction accuracy for different Machine learning techniques with the corresponding column chart in Fig. 5. It can be seen that SVM or KNN is the best learning technique for Parkinson's disease because of the highest performance accuracy of 90.26% recorded using the techniques. For Diabetes, the most suitable learning technique is KNN or RF because of the 100% accuracy obtained. Heart disease had a good score for most of the machine learning techniques but KNN is the most suitable with 99.8% accuracy. Dengue disease performed very well with DT learning technique

Table 1. Machine Learning Techniques for the diagnosis of diseases

Machine Learning Techniques	Disease tested	Accuracy	Reference
Support Vector Machine (SVM)	Parkinson's disease	90.26%	Sriram et al., [29]
	heart disease	88.3%	Meherwar Fatima et al., [57]
	diabetes disease	78%	Meherwar Fatima et al., [57]
	dengue disease	91%	Meherwar Fatima et al., [57]
	liver disease	79.66%	Meherwar Fatima et al., [57]
	kidney disease	98.3%	Charleonnan et al., [30]
Naïve Bayes algorithm	heart disease	86.4%	Meherwar Fatima et al., [57]
	heart disease	74%	Meherwar Fatima et al., [57]
	diabetes disease	79.50%	Iyer et al., [23]
	liver disease	61.28%	Vijayarani et al., [22]
	Parkinson's disease	69.23%	Sriram et al., [29]
K Nearest Neighbour (KNN)	kidney disease	98.1%	Charleonnan et al., [30]
	diabetes mellitus	100%	Kandhasamy et al., [31]
	heart disease	97.40%	Shouman et al., [32]
	heart disease	99.8%	Lubaib and Muneer, [33]
	abdominal aortic	95.20%	Elmasri et al., [34]
	hepatitis disease	84.50%	Femina, [35]
	breast cancer	92.81%	Gardezi et al., [36]
Decision Tree	Alzheimer	83%	Neelaveni and Devasana, [38]
	dengue disease	99.95%	Malaysia. Tarmizi, [39]
	heart disease	77.55%	Seyedamin Pouriyeh, [40]
	coronary artery disease	98.99%	Acharya et al., [43]
	hepatitis C	92%	El Houby, [44]
	breast cancer	95.23%	Guo et al., [45]

(continued)

Table 1. (*continued*)

Machine Learning Techniques	Disease tested	Accuracy	Reference
Random Forest Algorithm	diabetes mellitus	100%	Kandhasamy et al., [31]
	Parkinson's disease	90.26%	Sriram et al., [29]
	Alzheimer disease	84.21%	Vidushi and Shrivastava, [48]
Artificial neural network (ANN)	heart risk	91.10%	Samuel et al., [12]
	cardiac arrhythmais	94.64%	Thomas et al., [48]
	hepatitis C	100%	Kaya and Uyar, [49]
Convolution Neural Network (CNN)	chronic disease	96%	RayanAlanazi, [26]
	COVID-19	92%	Farrukh Saleem et al., [16]
	mild depression	80.74%	Rashid Amin, [52]
	COVID-19 modeling	94%	Ibrahim et al., [20]
Logistic Regression	Alzheimer disease	78.95%	Vidushi and Shrivastava, [53]
Linear Regression	None		

with an accuracy of 99.95% and therefore DT can be used for its diagnosis. Liver disease did not do very well with any of the techniques as it had less that 80% score, however, SVM is had the higher score of 79.66%. For Kidney disease, the most suitable learning techniques are SVM and KNN because of the high performance of above 98% accuracy for both techniques. ANN learning technique, recorded a 100% accuracy with Hepatitis disease and hence can be considered as the most suitable learning technique. For Breast cancer, KNN and DT are suitable learning techniques because of the 92.5% and the 95.23% recorded respectively. RF is suitable for Alzheimer disease because of the 84.21% accuracy. CNN is a suitable learning technique for COVID-19, Depression and Chronic diseases because of their accuracy performance of 94%, 80.76% and 96% respectively.

Figure 6 shows the diseases tested using Support Vector Machine (SVM). The techniques produced good results with kidney disease giving the highest accuracy of 98.3%.

Figure 7 indicates the results from the testing using Naïve Bayes algorithm. This technique produced its highest accuracy score in heart disease testing with an accuracy of 86.4%.

Figure 8 presents the effectiveness of KNN in testing of diseases. Heart disease and diabetes mellitus and kidney disease had an accuracy of more than 97%.

Figure 9 portrays the used of DT in disease diagnosis and prediction. The technique produced excellent results for dengue disease, coronary artery disease and breast cancer with more than 95% accuracy results.

Table 2. Disease prediction accuracy for different Machine Learning techniques

Machine Learning Techniques	Diseases prediction %accuracy											
	Parkinson	Diabetes	Heart	Dengue	Liver	Kidney	Hepatitis C	Breast Cancer	Alzheimer	COVID	Depression	Chronic disease
SVM	90.26	78	88.3	91	79.66	98.3						
Naïve Bayes	69.23	79.5	86.4		61.28							
KNN	90.26	100	99.8			98.1	84.5	92.8				
DT			77.55	99.95			92	95.23	83			
RF		100							84.21			
ANN			91.1				100					
CNN										94	80.74	96
LR									78.95			

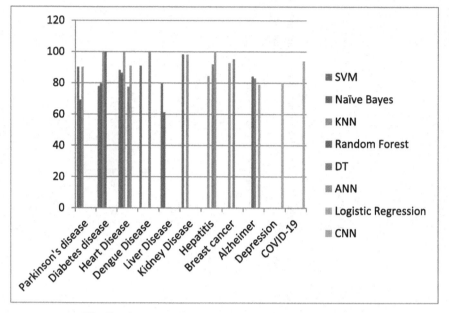

Fig. 5. Diseases Vs appropriate Machine learning technique

Figure 10 shows how RF technique was used in the diagnosis of some diseases. This technique was not used in testing many diseases but it gave a very good score for diabetes mellitus with an accuracy of 100%.

Figure 11 concentrates on the prediction of some rare diseases and pandemics using CNN technique. This is the only technique that elaborated on COVID-19 prediction and modeling. The technique how ever performed poorly in diagnosis and prediction of depression cases with the lowest accuracy of 81%.

Figure 12 indicates how Logistic Regression has not been widely use in the testing of diseases. In this paper, the technique was used only for Alzheimer and recorded 78.95% accuracy.

Figure 13 shows the percentage of different disease prediction modeled by different machine learning techniques. The figure indicates that the prediction or diagnosis of many diseases have been modeled using KNN and that only few diseases have been predicted using Logistic regression. The figure also indicates zero usage of linear regression.

Figure 14 focused on mainly heart related diseases with the use of ANN as the testing technique. The technique how ever did not produce high accuracy score for the heart related diseases.

5   Challenges and Open Issues

In this section, we present some challenges and open issues in diagnosis and prediction of diseases using machine learning techniques:

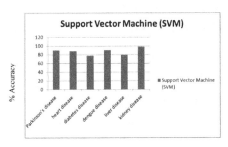

Fig. 6. SVM Accuracy for some diseases

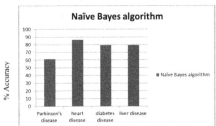

Fig. 7. Naïve Bayes Accuracy for some diseases

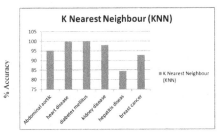

Fig. 8. KNN Accuracy for some diseases

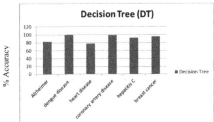

Fig. 9. DT Accuracy for some diseases

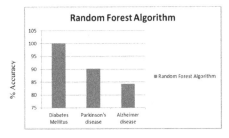

Fig. 10. RF Accuracy for some diseases

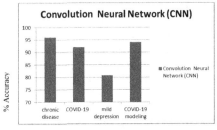

Fig. 11. CNN Accuracy for some diseases

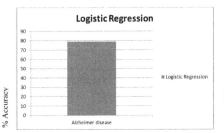

Fig. 12. Logistic Regression Accuracy for some diseases

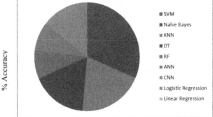

Fig. 13. Percentage of diseases predicted by different techniques.

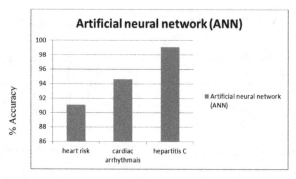

Fig. 14. ANN Accuracy for some diseases

5.1 Data Set

Diagnosis or prediction of diseases using machine learning techniques involves the use of data set. This data is first cleaned, trained and tested with machine learning software before use as the case may be. Wrong dataset will lead to wrong results. Because of environmental factors, some predicted results may differ from the reality. In our implementation of machine learning techniques we used a real world well simplified dataset for all the techniques.

5.2 Data Accessibility

Data in health sector is considered to be private. Machine learning techniques need real data to get good diagnosis. Gaining access to sensitive data about patients in the health sector always has a lot of bottlenecks. Fortunately, there are some firms with ready to used dataset that helps in most cases.

5.3 Data Quality and Availability

The performance of machine learning techniques heavily depends on the quality and quantity of data available for analysis. In many cases, the healthcare data is incomplete, inaccurate, and difficult to obtain due to privacy concerns.

5.4 Generalizability

Machine learning models trained on one patient population or health system may not generalize well to other populations or systems.

5.5 Regulatory and Legal Considerations

The use of machine learning models in healthcare is subject to regulatory and legal requirements, such as data privacy and liability concerns. These requirements can vary by jurisdiction and can be complex to navigate.

6 Conclusion

In this paper, we have provided a survey of different machine learning techniques such as Support Vector Machine (SVM), Naive Bayes Algorithm, K Nearest Neighbour (KNN), Decision Tree, Random Forest Algorithm, Artificial neural network (ANN), Convolution Neural Network (CNN), Logistic Regression and Linear Regression used for the diagnosis of diseases. We have equally provided a comparative analysis of the different algorithms suitable for the management of particular diseases. From analysis of results in Table 1, many of the algorithms have shown good results for the diagnosis and management of certain diseases. SVM and Naive Bayes have been widely used and their accuracy performance for the diagnosis of diseases has also been very good. However, a good number of machine learning techniques were not exploited for the diagnosis and prediction of COVID-19. The most suitable machine learning technique for each disease reviewed has been presented in Table 2. From Table 1, CNN was useful for the modeling and diagnosis of COVID-19 with accuracy performance of 94%. ANN gave a 99.1% accuracy for hepatitis C disease. Random Forest Algorithm did well for diabetes mellitus though the 100% accuracy is questionable because the dataset was very small. From the survey, it can be observed that Logistic and Linear Regressions are not useful for the diagnosis of diseases. Analysis in Table 1, shows that Machine learning techniques play a key role in the management of many diseases. The existing literature highlighted that the accuracy performance is relative and not absolute as it depends on the size of the dataset. It is therefore necessary to exploit other techniques' accuracy performance in predicting COVID-19 as many of the algorithms are still to be exploited for the prediction and diagnosis of COVID-19 pandemic.

References

1. Chui, K.T.: Disease diagnosis in smart healthcare: innovation, technologies and applications. Sustain. Health J. (2017)
2. Ardabili, S.F., et al.: COVID-19 outbreak prediction with machine learning. MDPI (2020)
3. Khanday, A.M.U.D., et al.: Machine learning based approaches for detecting COVID-19 using clinical text data. (2020)
4. Khader, K.: Machine learning systems in epidemics: in the AI of the storm. Int. J. Comput. Appl. (2020)
5. Laudanski, K., et al.: What Can COVID-19 teach us about using AI in pandemics? MDPI (2020)
6. Syeda, H.B., et al.: The role of machine learning techniques to tackle COVID-19 crisis: a systematic review. medRxiv (2020)
7. Almagooshi, S.: Simulation modelling in healthcare: challenges and trends. Sci. Dir. (2015)
8. Shinde, S.A., Rajeswari, P.R.: Intelligent health risk prediction systems using machine learning. Int. J. Eng. Technol. (2018)
9. Matthes, E.: Python Crash Course, A Hands-On, Project-Based Introduction to Programming. 2nd Edition (2023)
10. Cho, G., et al.: Review of machine learning algorithms for diagnosing mental illness. US National library of medicines (2019)
11. Ahsan, et al.: Machine learning based disease diagnosis. Eng., Biomed. Technol. (2021)

12. El Houby, E.M.F.: A survey on applying machine learning techniques for management of diseases (2017)
13. Dutta, P., et al.: Comparative analysis of various supervised machine learning techniques for diagnosis of COVID-19. ScienceDirect (2021)
14. Merihi, Y., et al.: Machine learning-based research for COVID-19 detection, diagnosis, and prediction: a survey (2022)
15. Syeda, H.B.: Role of machine learning techniques to tackle the COVID-19 crisis: systematic review. NIH (2021)
16. Saleem, F., et al.: Machine learning, deep learning, and mathematical models to analyze forecasting and epidemiology of COVID-19: a systematic literature review. Int. J. Environ. Res. Publ. Health (2022)
17. Broadbent, A., et al.: Can robots do epidemiology? Machine learning, causal inference, and predicting the outcomes of public health interventions (2022)
18. Yost, J., et al.: Tools to support evidence-informed public health decision making. BMC Publ. Health (2014)
19. Rose, S.: Intersections of machine learning and epidemiological methods for health services research. Int. J. Epidemiol. (2020)
20. Ibrahim, I., Abdulazeez, A.: The role of machine learning algorithms for diagnosing diseases. JASTT (2021)
21. Fatima, M., Pasha, M.: Survey of machine learning algorithms for disease diagnostic. Sci. Res. Publ. (2017)
22. Vijayarani, S., Dhayanand, S.: Liver disease prediction using SVM and Naïve Bayes algorithms. Int. J. Sci., Eng. Technol. Res. (IJSETR) (2015)
23. Iyer, A., Jeyalatha, S., Sumbaly, R.: Diagnosis of diabetes using classification mining techniques. Int. J. Data Min. Knowl. Manage. Process (2015)
24. Ramalingam, V.V. et al.: Heart disease prediction using machine learning techniques: a survey. IJET (2018)
25. Pouriyeh, S., et al.: A comprehensive investigation and comparison of machine learning techniques in the domain of heart disease. In: 22nd IEEE Symposium on Computers and Communication (ISCC 2017): Workshops - ICTS4eHealth (2017)
26. Alanazi, R.: Identification and prediction of chronic diseases using machine learning approach. J. Healthc. Eng. (2022)
27. Wejdan, L., et al.: Diabetic retinopathy detection through deep learning techniques: a review (2020)
28. Yasseen, A., et al.: Automatic extraction of knowledge for diagnosing COVID-19 disease based on text mining techniques: a systematic review. Periodicals Eng. Nat. Sci. (2021)
29. Sriram, et al.: Intelligent parkinson disease prediction using machine learning algorithms. IJEIT 3 (2013)
30. Charleonnan, et al.: Predictive analytics for chronic kidney disease using machine learning techniques. MITiCON (2016)
31. Kandhasamy, J.P., Balamurali, S.J.P.C.S.: Performance analysis of classifier models to predict diabetes mellitus 47 (2015)
32. Shouman, et al.: Applying k-nearest neighbour in diagnosing heart disease patients. ICKD (2012)
33. Lubaib, P., Muneer, K.A.: The heart defect analysis based on PCG signals using pattern recognition techniques. In: ICETEST, vol. 24, pp. 1024–1031 (2016)
34. Elmasri, K., et al.: Automatic detection and quantification of abdominal aortic calcification in dual energy X-ray absorptiometry 96 (2016)
35. Femina, B., Anto, S.: Disease diagnosis using rough set-based feature selection and K-nearest neighbor classifier. Int. J. Multi. Res. Dev. 2(4), 664–668 (2015)

36. Gardezi, S.J.S., et al.: Mammogram classification using deep learning features. In: IEEE, International Conference (2017)

37. Sayed, A.M., et al.: Automatic classification of breast tumors using features extracted from magnetic resonance images **95** (2016)

38. Neelaveni, J., Devasana, M.G.: Alzheimer disease prediction using machine learning algorithms. In: 2020 6th International Conference on Advanced Computing and Communication Systems (ICACCS) (2020)

39. Tarmizi, et al.: Classification of dengue outbreak detection using data mining models. JNIT 4, 96–107

40. Seyedamin, P., et al.: A comprehensive investigation and comparison of machine learning techniques in the domain of heart disease. In: IEEE, International Conference (2017)

41. Hussain, A., et al.: Heart disease diagnosis using the brute force algorithm and machine learning techniques. In: CMC 2022, vol. 76, no. 2

42. Acharya, U.R., et al.: Application of higher-order spectra for the characterization of Coronary artery disease using electrocardiogram signals **31** (2017)

43. Tayefi, M., et al.: hs-CRP is strongly associated with coronary heart disease (CHD): a data mining approach using decision tree algorithm **141** (2017)

44. El Houby, E.M.: A framework for prediction of response to HCV therapy using different data mining techniques. NIH (2014)

45. Guo, J., et al.: Revealing determinant factors for early breast cancer recurrence by decision tree (2017)

46. Khalilabad, N.D., et al.: Fully automatic classification of breast cancer microarray images. J. Electr. Syst. Inf. Technol. (2016)

47. Vidushi, A.R., Shrivastava, A.K.: Diagnosis of Alzheimer disease using machine learning approaches. Int. J. Adv. Sci. Technol. **29** (2020)

48. Thomas, M., et al.: Automatic ECG arrhythmia classification using dual tree complex wavelet based features **59** (2015)

49. Kaya, Y., Uyar, M.: A hybrid decision support system based on rough set and extreme learning machine for diagnosis of hepatitis disease **13** (2013)

50. Jilani, T.A., et al.: PCA-ANN for classification of Hepatitis-C patients. Int. J. Comput. Appl. **14** (2011)

51. Resino, S., et al.: An artificial neural network improves the non-invasive diagnosis of significant fibrosis in HIV/HCV coinfected patients **62** (2011)

52. Amin,R.,: Machine learning algorithms for depression: diagnosis, insights, and research directions. MDPI (2022)

53. Zhang, C., et al.: Prediction of shield tunneling-induced ground settlement using machine learning" techniques (2019)

54. Korolev, A., et al.: 3D DenseNet ensemble in 4-way classification of Alzheimer's disease (2020)

55. Chen, L., et al.: Synthetic data in machine learning for medicine and healthcare. Nat. Biomed. Eng. (2021)

56. Shah, S., et al.: Diagnosis of COVID-19 using CT scan images and deep learning techniques (2021)

57. Fatima, M., Pasha, M.: Comparative analysis of meta learning algorithms for liver disease detection (2017)

Support to Interaction Between Medical Practitioners and Patients: A Systematic Review

Ezekiel Olayide Tolulope[1]([✉]) [ID] and Franklin Tchakounte[2] [ID]

[1] Modibbo Adama University Yola, Girei, Adamawa State, Nigeria
Olayide.babalola@aun.edu.ng
[2] University of Ngaoundere, Ngaoundere, Cameroon
f.tchakounte@cycomai.com

Abstract. Effective interaction between medical practitioners and patients is critical in ensuring positive health outcomes. The primary goal of this systematic review is to identify different strategies for improving medical practitionerpatient interaction and to analyze their effectiveness in enhancing patient satisfaction, adherence to treatment, and health outcomes. A systematic review of the literature was conducted using electronic databases including IEEE, ACM Digital Library, Springer, Science Direct and Wiley Online Library, using keywords such as "doctorpatient communication," "physician-patient interactions," and "Patient-doctor interaction + Technology." "Patientdoctor interaction + Technology + Issues."Articles were included if they were published in English and contained strategies for improving medical practitioner-patient interaction. A total of 34 articles were included in this systematic review. The strategies identified were categorized into four themes: training programs, communication skills, patient-centered care, and technology-based interventions. Technology-based interventions, such as virtual consultations and electronic health records, were shown to enhance communication and information sharing between medical practitioners and patients. Improving medical practitioner-patient interaction is crucial in achieving positive health outcomes. The strategies identified in this review can be used to design interventions that improve communication skills, promote patient-centered care, and incorporate technology-based solutions to enhance communication and information sharing in clinical settings.

Keywords: Doctor-patient interaction · Technology-based intervention ·
Patient-doctor · Patient satisfaction · Patient-centered care · Trust ·
Communication · Patient-doctor interaction · Technology Issues · Patient doctor interaction and Technology

1 Introduction

Interaction according to [1], is the transferring of information between organizations, individuals, and society. Depending on the communication tool or medium, the engagement may be made easier or more difficult, losing meaning or goals. In the context of this

© ICST Institute for Computer Sciences, Social Informatics and Telecommunications Engineering 2024
Published by Springer Nature Switzerland AG 2024. All Rights Reserved
F. Tchakounte et al. (Eds.): SAFER-TEA 2023, LNICST 566, pp. 380–408, 2024.
https://doi.org/10.1007/978-3-031-56396-6_24

study, the definition of [1] will be adopted. Interactions between providers and patients can be considered a structural element of health care systems that affects how patients perceive their treatment. According to [2], challenges to effective interaction with medical personnel have been discovered in larger healthcare facilities despite increased accessibility to interpretation services [3] Exploring these interactions is necessary to identify broader influences from a historically racist and patriarchal system because they serve as a crucial conduit for women feeling supported in their care experience [4]. Given the significant influence these structural factors have on how care is received [5, 6].

In hospital settings, language barriers have contributed to disparities in care for individuals with language limitations, including longer hospital stay and increased likelihood of readmission after discharge [7, 8]. According to the study by the [9]. It was discovered that most doctors' participants and patients believe that language barrier affects their interaction as a result of doctor-centered approach. Study have it that maternal women with language barrier issues are likely to have poor health and more pregnancy-related problems, resulting in an increased risk of maternal and perinatal mortality [10, 11]. According to [11], this increased risk is because these women cannot provide a full medical history, resulting in inappropriate clinical decision-making. When a health care provider is unable to understand the nature of a patient's complaints, or the patient does not understand the treatment, serious health consequences can result [12]. The communication between a medical practitioner and a patient has long been recognized to be not only of diagnostic importance but good communication and positive interactions between patient and physician which can have a therapeutic benefit, unfortunately, because of language barriers and communication problems, many patients do not benefit from this interaction [13, 14] For the doctor to recommend adequate prescriptions and vice-versa for the patients to effectively follow the doctor recommendations, the dialogue between the patients and doctors should be clear on both sides. However, Language barriers and other communication issues prevent many patients from reaping the benefits of this interaction [14]. Many studies have linked language obstacles to inequality, health issues, worsening poverty, disadvantage, and unemployment when utilizing healthcare services [15, 16] Schinkel and others explained this further by saying that patients with language difficulties who get basic healthcare services are less likely than patients in the general population to actively participate in their treatment, to share their concerns, to ask more questions, and to be verbally domineering [14]. This increased risk is caused by the fact that these women are unable to give a complete medical history because they struggle to connect with their healthcare providers due to their complex social risk factors, leaving many of their needs unmet and leading to inappropriate clinical decision-making because of a language barrier [10, 11]. Medical assistance and diagnosis are crucial elements of healthcare that assist people in recognizing and treating a variety of medical disorders. Medical assistance is the provision of necessary medical care and treatment to a person and may entail rendering emergency care, dispensing medication, conducting diagnostic tests and treatments, and keeping track of the patient's progress [17, 18]. Patients receive medical assistance from medical professionals like doctors, nurses, and physician assistants. According to a study by Busto et al., a precise diagnosis is necessary for successful treatment and better patient outcomes [19].

Additionally, getting medical assistance and getting a proper diagnosis are essential for treating chronic illnesses including diabetes, hypertension, and cardiovascular disorders e.t.c. According to [20, 21], the definition of diagnosis is the process of determining a disease from its signs and symptoms to determine its pathology. Unfortunately, not all physicians are highly knowledgeable in every area of medicine. As a result, an automatic diagnosis system that benefits from both human expertise and machine precision was required [22, 23]. To get precise results from the diagnosis process at a lower cost, a good decision support system is required. To effectively diagnose illnesses, a variety of AI techniques are currently applied in the field of medicine [24–26]. AI is a crucial component of computer science that enables the advancement of computer intelligence. Any intelligent system must have the ability to learn. Deep learning, machine learning, and other learning-based AI techniques are only a few examples. The core components of healthcare are medical help and diagnostics. They are crucial to delivering efficient care and enhancing patient outcomes. To create effective treatment regimens, manage chronic diseases, and enhance patients' quality of life, accurate diagnosis is essential. Therefore, the purpose of this study is to conduct a systematic review on how to enhance patient-doctor communication in a medical context.

2 Related Review

Several proposals concerning investigation about medical practitioners–patient's interactions are proposed in literature. Reviews about application of technologies to improve such interaction as well as reviews about understanding characterization of such interaction are found in literature and are presented in the next lines. Cleaned interactions between medical practitioners and patients are required to sustain reliable application of recommendations from the patient side for a good health [27]. However, due to several considerations such as cultural barriers, language constraints and bidirectional attitudes, the interaction is constrained. The [2] explored different strategies for communication concerning nurse-patient interaction. They also studied incidences of these strategies on the patient participation in the care process in sub-Saharan Africa. They found that the topic of nurse-patient interaction is not broadly studied in SSA countries and that different aspects of health should be studied. They recommend to include capacity building about communication skills to strengthen nurses. The [28] realized a study on barriers related to nurse-patient clinical interactions from the previously mentioned constraints. From this interesting study, authors have been able to propose PC4, an approach of communication that healthcare professionals can use to mitigate these barriers during interactions. However, this model is subjective and thus not proven effective. In the same vein, [29] made a specific literature review concerning challenges and perspectives during intercultural communication between patients and health professionals about sexual health. He found some challenges between patients with immigration profiles and health practitioners. In this specific study, the author does not outline technological aspects to support interactions. [30] investigated 348 papers to explore interactions between health practitioners and lesbian, gay and bisexual (LGB) patients. At the end of this study, they found that health practitioners ignore key knowledge about LGB issues and other LGB attitudes which explain negative attitudes throughout interactions. This review does not consider technological attempts to cover interactions issues. Authors investigate increasingly the place of technology to sustain interactions between patients and practitioners. [31, 32] provides a review of exploitation of metaverse for healthcare in general. They have not focused on the interaction's aspects. However, this review is only specific to metaverse and does not touch several aspects of technologies to cover interactions.

Within this vision, [33] studied how mobile health (mHealth) is integrated in the whole process so that the interaction is realized autonomously and intelligibly. They advocated that the digitization with mHealth can be helpful to deal with interaction in different health sectors. However, this comes with some risks such as security, fault-tolerance, privacy that are not deeper evoked in this study. [34] systematically investigated the impact of Online Health Information (OHI) seeking behavior on the physician-patient relationship. This study only focuses on the OHI and not patientdoctor interaction in general. However, the authors inveterate that improvement of people's health information literacy and the quality of OHI are important factors that promote the positive impact of OHI on the physician-patient relationship. [35] investigated the adoption of block-chain to preserve secure and safe communication between patient and practitioners. Although it is an interesting solution, this technology remains under-studied in automated interaction health systems within the IoT context. Telemedicine has increasingly been a complementary alternative for interactions. After a review of 21 papers, [36] suggest that telemedicine should be considered as a long-term sustainability tool for keeping patient in touch with the practitioner in orthopedic surgery. This case is however not applicable in countries with no infrastructures available and patients not ready to exploit it. [37] confirmed that several technical, educational, infrastructure, legal, and economic issues must be addressed and solved for effectiveness of telemedicine.

As communicating risk is a challenging, yet essential, component of shared decision-making (SDM) in surgery, [38] reviews literature's with the aim to explore the current use of AI and VR in doctor-patient surgical risk communication, in other to improve the shared decision-making in surgery and the risk of communication to personalize doctor-patient surgical risk communication to individual patients and healthcare contexts. However, this study is only limited to Surgery and not Doctor-Patient interaction in general. [39] provide a literature review of in-depth information on their advantages and importance of IoT healthcare. The literature review compares various systems' effectiveness, efficiency, data protection, privacy, security, and monitoring. Additionally, the authors talk about IoT wearables in healthcare systems. However, this review does not consider interactions issues.

3   Review Methodology

The main steps included in this review can be summarized as follows:

Planning the review and developing a review protocol; Formulating research questions; Designing the strategy of search; Defining exclusion and inclusion criteria and Data selection.

In the following subsections, the methodology points are described.

3.1 Research Questions

The following research questions are studied in this paper.

RQ1: What approaches have been developed to deal with patient - health practitioner interactions?

RQ2: What are the open issues, that research oriented to patient - health practitioner interactions should focus on?

3.2 Search Strategy

Once the research questions are identified, the next step is proceeding with the search. For that, the following digital libraries have been exploited: IEEE, ACM Digital Library, Springer, Science Direct and Wiley Online Library. The proposed searching keywords in Table 1 are constructed for crawling purposes. For sake of consistency, citation engines such as Google scholar and Web of Knowledge have been further exploited. This additional search was meant to ensure that there is no relevant work overlooked. In addition, we also performed forward research on the collection of authors who cited the identified papers. This way has been able to get more and recent works (Table 1).

Table 1. Search keywords

Group	Keywords		
1	Patient Doctor Interaction		
2	Patient Doctor Communication		
3	Patient AND Health Practitioner AND Interaction OR Communication		
4	Patient AND Health Practitioner AND Interaction OR Communication Technology OR Language OR Issues OR Software	AI	OR
5	1 AND 2 AND 3 AND 4		

3.3 Inclusion Criteria

Only studies from the last 2019 years were included (i.e. 2019 onwards) and only those in English are considered. During the search, literature review and surveys concerning patient-health practitioner interactions and communication are collected. The reason is that they will be exploited in the "related reviews" part. The presence of the term "patient-doctor interaction" and "patient-practitioner" and "nurse-practitioner" guided the retention of the paper.

3.4 Exclusion Criteria

The following types of papers will be excluded.

Papers published in predatory journals; Papers not specific to patient-practitioner interaction and communication based on title and abstract; Papers not subject to peer-review.

3.5 Data Selection Process

Only those studies related to interactions and communication between patient-health practitioner have been considered for further review based on inclusion criteria. Mendeley has been used to save and organize the papers. We eliminated duplicates using its tool for that. Therefore, any extracted work that meets the proposed exclusion criteria has been considered as irrelevant and excluded from the result list. Since collecting relevant papers – that is – those which meet the inclusion criteria does not guarantee that the quality of all selected papers is met. To cover this situation, the quality of each paper is assured by reading the full text. After these steps, we finally obtained 33 papers, which are listed in the appendix section. PRISMA [85] has been followed for selecting the papers. Figure 1 depicts the different steps.

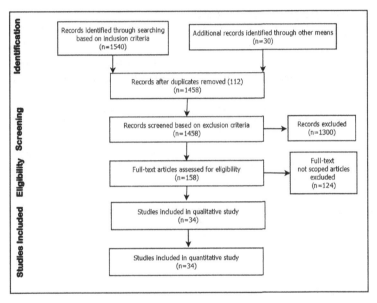

Fig. 1. PRISMA steps [81]

Figure 1 shows the repatriation of selected works over time. Obviously, the number of publications related to patient-practitioner interactions increasingly increases since 2019. Considering the number of selected papers in 2023 demonstrates that the health topic is gaining attention and therefore illustrates the critical need for structured and comprehensive review paper which summarize the prior work and current research trends. In addition, the distribution of journal papers for these 34 papers has been investigated (See Fig. 2). According to Fig. 2, it is obvious all the studies from 2019-date are 100% Journal and none were presented in any conference (0%). The results also revealed that most of these are carried out in developed countries. Concerning the year of publications, we found the proportion of gathered works published in 2020 and 2021 are equal with at about 100%. After counting the frequency of all reviewed papers, the results showed that more studies were done in the 2022 as compared to the other previous years.

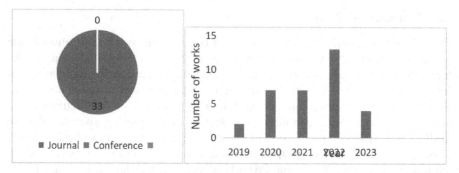

Fig. 2. Distribution of Journal and conference paper and the Year

4 Taxonomy and Result Analysis

In eights taxonomies, we have collated and discussed the various interventions to promote patientdoctor communication in this section. These taxonomies were primarily developed based on observations, knowledge, and some literature (See Fig. 3).

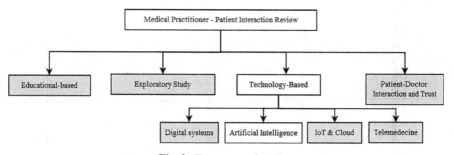

Fig. 3. Taxonomy of studies

4.1 Educational Based

Education, most especially the nursing curriculum has an important role to play in improving the medical practitioners and patient's interaction [38]. This session will review and analyze few literature with respect to the above subject matter. According to [39] nurse's capacity for good communication is crucial for building therapeutic bonds with their patients and achieving higher patient satisfaction. Additionally, it reduces treatment errors and raises the standard of nursing care. In this study, the authors claimed that nursing students develop therapeutic ties with their patients and that, as future nursing practitioners, they should be given communication skills training. This systematic review's goal was to determine how educational interventions affected nursing students' ability to communicate with patients. The review offers preliminary proof of the efficacy of the interventions used to teach patientcentered communication skills to nursing students. Although all interventions had a considerable impact on communication skills, the most effective approach has not yet been identified. It was found that non-English publications were not included in the study, which may have constituted bias by excluding items written in other languages. Additionally, a meta-analysis was not possible due to the variability of the intervention techniques and methodologies used to measure the outcomes of the investigations. To address the likelihood of bias resulting from the use of self-report measures and other potential kinds of bias, the studies require more evidence. Due to the nature of the educational intervention studies, the instructors who carried out the interventions were not blinded, which increases the likelihood of bias in the studies. However, it is also crucial to take into account that over 50% of the research were conducted in the setting of mental health, where communication is a crucial component of the nurse-patient connection. Future study should, according to the authors, be able to more thoroughly analyze the themes and areas in which communication skills development is included in the nursing curriculum.

Meanwhile, [40] claim that difficulties with the nursing curriculum contribute to the poor nursePatient connections in maternal and child health care. An investigation using a human-centered approach was conducted in a rural area of Tanzania with nine focus groups with nurses-patients and 12 key informant interviews with Maternal and Child Healthcare(MCH) administrators were used as part of a multi-step HCD method to first investigate the causes of strained nurse-client interactions. The results highlighted the significance of nursing curricula as agreed by both the nurse-patients that it will creating a welcoming learning environment for clinical practice on strengthening interpersonal relationships. Also, the author, states that, it serves as a crucial starting point for fostering these connections, which in turn improves patient satisfaction with nurses' competencies, trust in the formal healthcare system, healthcare-seeking behaviors, continuity of care, and MCH outcomes. Furthermore, [41] claim that the Extension for Community Healthcare Outcomes program (ECHO) is a successful example of a shared-learning capacity-building initiative. This study outlines the development, implementation, and assessment of a virtual educational COVID-19-focused ECHO program to assist healthcare professionals in providing mental health treatment for people with intellectual and developmental disabilities during the COVID-19 pandemic using a rapid design thinking approach. Moore's evaluation framework's initial five outcome levels, which center on participation, satisfaction, learning, self-efficacy, and change in practice was used. However, the open text feedback revealed that participants believed the ECHO program increased their knowledge and competency, created a sense of being a part of a community of practice, provided value for the COVID-19 innovations, supported resource sharing within and outside of program participants, and enabled changes to participants' approaches to client care in practice. Participants also felt that the program increased their confidence in helping clients and families.

According to [42], teaching healthcare practitioners Design Thinking (DT) can assist patientcentered care, which can be accomplished by identifying patient/care provider needs and empathizing with them. To increase clinical researchers' comprehension of the challenges associated with dementia caring that are largely unexplored and understudied, the study investigated the Design Thinking (DT) process model. The active participants in this study are the family cares of dementia patients. To increase clinical researchers' comprehension of the caregiving problem and solution space through pre- and post-surveys, a workshop and training methodology was adopted for this study. The results of an evaluation highlighted the researchers' general perception of design thinking, their thorough understanding of the difficulties faced by dementia caregivers, and their hypotheses regarding caregiver-specific therapies. This study made a contribution to the field of health design by investigating the value of design thinking in understudied areas, identifying critical issues in healthcare, identifying hidden needs through shared knowledge and expertise, and producing original health care research and contributions.

Also, [43] found in a qualitative study titled "Reflective based learning for nursing ethical competency during clinical practices" that learning and acquiring ethical competencies in care involve a blend of theoretical and practical approaches. The authors ascertained that sometimes, reflecting on practical activity is different from learning theory. Since they cause conflict among nursing students, topics like ethical values can be discussed in the context of reflective learning. As a result of the examination of the ethical reflections, three major types were found: (1) Professional performance and patient care evaluation; (2) the student as the central character in the conundrum; and (3) student coping. Problems and worries that students have to do with their ignorance, patient-student dialogue, mistakes they've made, and self-assurance. Some circumstances, which interfere with patients' autonomy and rights, can make patients feel stressed. The study concluded that all ethical problems identified by the students begin with the professional-patient relationship, including those related to bad news, errors, or malpractice. Stress factors include hospital routines that the patient cannot modify and asymmetric relationships with staff that encourage passivity. Students can build a higher ethical awareness of care and improve their decision-making abilities in ethical situations by reflecting on the ethical values of nursing in both the classroom and in clinical settings.

4.1.1 Discussion

Despite the several educational interventions employed to enhance the medical practitioner-patient interaction, the necessity of creating interventions to enhance nursing curricula to create patientcentered healthcare systems is acknowledged by all research. However, the key findings show that most of the examined studies used the design thinking approach as their training intervention methodology. Except for [40,42 and 43] the rest of the articles did not explicitly specify the nations in where most of the study were conducted. Only [43] of the research used theoretical frameworks to direct the intervention in terms of theoretical and conceptual frameworks for the intervention investigations. To design experimental investigations, however, that allow the variables and their relationships to be developed, as detailed in prior studies, theoretical and conceptual frameworks are crucial. The conceptual frameworks give details about the participants, the data collection process, and statistical analysis of the data, allowing for the direction of experimental study interventions and assisting in the interpretation of the results. Also, most of the interventions in the study reviewed are specifically focused on mental health in intellectual and developmental disabilities populations, dementia caregiver's specific intervention, nurse–patient relationships in Maternal Child and Health Care using the Human Centered Design approach. As such, their findings may not be generalizable to other cycles or settings. It is also discovered that the use of Artificial intelligence and other emerging technologies is lacking in all the papers reviewed above. In addition, the evaluation of implementation outcomes would be helpful to understand the impact of this educational intervention. However, the exploitation of the reviewed studies can be helpful to automate the identification of educational aspects to improve during the learning process. Gamified systems in this case are also in demand to develop games to support educational for interactions between patient and doctor.

4.2 Exploratory Study

The major goals of doctor-patient interactions are to uphold human health, advance medical science, and advance society. The possible doctor-patient relationship and its effect on doctor-patient interactions online were studied by [27]. The study specifically used text mining and econometrics analysis technology to explore the effects of social support from doctors in the online doctor-patient interaction on patient satisfaction. Text data for the study was collected from a large online health community in China (http://haodf.com) from January 2015 to December 2016, including a total of 276,728 consultations with 961 doctors, i.e., on average, each doctor provided online consultation services for 287 patients. The study's findings showed that patient satisfaction is significantly impacted by doctor-patient communication over the internet. Higher levels of patient satisfaction were indicated by those who had high-quality online consultations compared to those who received low-quality consultations. Furthermore, patient satisfaction is positively impacted by the doctor's informative and emotional assistance. Significantly more than informative support, emotional support has a greater impact on patient satisfaction. The degree of the patient's illness according to the authors also contributes to the relationship between the doctor's emotional and educational assistance and patient satisfaction. The findings of this study also support online doctor-patient communication and unstructured text data mining for medical services. Although text mining and econometrics analysis technology were used in this study to develop the genuine mechanism of online doctor-patient contact, the study only largely supported their hypothesis. Additionally, because the online medical community protects patients' anonymity and obscures their names, the study could not account for closely monitoring each patient's development and was unable to determine whether or not a patient had seen numerous doctors concurrently. Therefore, future studies could gather more specific data to compare the service mindsets and medical quality of other doctors. This study also reveals that, despite the stringent testing, only two types of disorders (such as cardiovascular and infertility) had data collected; therefore, additional diseases could be included in future research to broaden the applicability of the results. Also it is discovered that the study's optimum classifier for text categorization was employed, so certain errors were found during the text analysis process. Additionally, the study's sole method of gauging patient activity was the electronic medical record. Actually, information about patient activity is included in the text information that the patient provides during doctor-patient communication. As a result, the exploration of this work could aid future researchers in enhancing the algorithm to increase the classifier's accuracy and increase the accuracy of patient activeness, and also evaluate patient activity using all information (EMR + text information) supplied by the patient.

The findings of a study [44] sought to determine the impact of implementing a flipped learning strategy built on ASQ in nursing school. The study employed a quasi-experimental approach and involved 94 nursing students who participated in the study and were split into the experimental group and the control group. The control group received the conventional lecture-based teaching method, while the experimental group got the ASQ-based flipped learning technique. The study's utilization of videos, quizzes, and online discussions to increase students' engagement and learning is thoroughly described by the authors in addition to the flipped learning strategy itself. The article's ability to give a clear and succinct summary of the study's findings is one of its merits. The results showed that the ASQ-based flipped learning strategy was successful in enhancing nursing students' abilities, successes, and learning views. Students in the experimental group specifically outperformed those in the control group on a skills test, scoring much higher. Additionally, it was discovered that the flipped learning strategy improved student engagement, motivation, and involvement in the learning process. It is unclear, however, if the findings can be applied to other groups of learners or other subject areas because the study only focused on one category of learners (practitioner learners) in one field (nursing education). Additionally, because the study's sample size was too small, it might not be appropriate to extrapolate the findings to every learning scenario. Moreover, the analytical results may vary slightly due to the limits of the instruments. The efficacy of the ASQ-based flipped learning approach in a wider range of settings could be investigated in future studies also,the future behaviors and academic performance of nursing learners can also be investigated using various teaching styles in flipped learning.

One of the most crucial dynamics in healthcare is doctor-patient interaction, which has an impact on how patients are treated and how satisfied they are. Even though technical skills could receive more focus in physician school, communication is crucial in practice. However, it was suggested by [45] to investigate whether communication models used in the West are appropriate in Southeast Asia and to identify crucial elements of doctor-patient communication that ought to be included in a model for training in Vietnam. According to the study's findings, most patients (75.2%) found their consultations to be satisfactory, therefore both patients and doctors saw the majority of the list's components as essential for effective doctor-patient communication. Only 4.2% of respondents were dissatisfied, and none were extremely dissatisfied, while 20.6% of respondents said they were very satisfied. Almost all patients (75.6%) or were very satisfied (19.2%) when questioned about their overall satisfaction with the doctors' communication, and no one was very dissatisfied. However, even though real dialogue was largely positive, both parties agreed that there was still space for growth. Additionally, patients' expectations were lower than those of the professionals. Four components of the Western paradigm for doctor-patient communication—all of which support their partnership relationship—appeared to be of lower priority in Vietnam for both patients and doctors. The fact that this study was conducted in an outpatient clinic, where most patient-doctor interactions would occur at the first encounter and where not all patients could require a discussion of the appropriate course of treatment, could have an effect on the study's findings. Due to variables that were excluded from the study, such as whether the patient knew the doctor from a prior visit and whether they were primary care or specialty consultations, certain responses to survey items may have varied and due to the cross-sectional survey's questionnaire-based approach, inaccurate response choices could result from misunderstandings of language. The actual performance was not reviewed; the goal was to determine their perceptions of what a competent doctor should do.

Furthermore, according to [46] in the article "How Communication Can Help Women Experience a Maternal Near-Miss: A qualitative study from Tanzania" details a study on how communication can enhance the experiences of Tanzanian women who have had maternal near-misses. This study sheds emphasis on the communication difficulties faced by female victims of life-threatening situations. The female participants revealed a variety of both good and bad experiences. They stated that they felt more confident and trusted in the healthcare system when healthcare personnel kept them well-informed, engaged, encouraged, and involved. The study also underlines the necessity for health-care professionals to work effectively with one another in order to provide care, under-scoring the significance of this for policy and practice. Although the article's topic is pertinent and significant, there are a few places where the study's presentation may be strengthened. First of all, the paper fails to include any preventative measures for mater-nal near-misses in Tanzania also the study's sample size is modest, which could restrict how broadly the results can be applied. Furthermore, just one region of Tanzania was studied, which may limit the study's application to other locations or nations. Over-all, this article makes a significant contribution to the literature on maternal health and offers insightful information about the function of communication in Tanzania's efforts to reduce maternal near-miss events. The results indicate that educating women who pass out while they are there has to be a higher priority. Training to raise the standard of emergency treatment should include instruction in communication and information delivery. Such communication training may take into account the unique requirements of women and families where there were unconsciousness episodes.

4.2.1 Discussion

The doctor-patient interaction is one of the crucial and important topic that cannot be over emphasis. There are numerous study that has been explored in this field. However, It is discovered that most of these studies were carried out in developing country and mostly in China, Asian, United state and only a study in Tazania based on our understanding. For this reason, it is unclear if these review studies can be replicated in other developing country. Additionally, it was discovered that most of the study's sample size was too small, this might not be appropriate to extrapolate the findings to every learning scenario. Moreover, the analytical results may vary slightly due to the limits of the instruments.

4.3 Technological Based

This section explore some technological based intervention according to the literature:

4.3.1 Artificial Intelligence

Artificial intelligence is exploited to reason information collected and populated by digital systems [47, 48] Some technologies such as Internet of medical thin [49] or big data [48, 50] produce data as input to AI which will automatically retrieve decisions concerning interactions between patients and practitioners. In healthcare, AI is always associated to another technology used to collect and store data. For instance, several advancements have been proposed using the couple AI and cloud computing to support diagnostic procedures [51]. The different techniques encountered in research include classification, clustering, association rule mining and text mining whereas the focus of studies include (i) health management (ii) assistance to treatment and diagnosis (iii) risk control and disease prevention (iv) wearable sensors exploitation for virtual assistant and (v) drug characterization. In [27], a large textual dataset has been collected in China from January 2015 to December 2016 to understand patient satisfaction from online doctor-patient interaction. They exploited text mining to retrieve knowledge from the text. Results suggested that activeness and emotional support are two key features to consider for effective satisfaction. In [52], IoT sensors connected to the patient and to the surroundings are exploited to remotely collect data and the cloud for storage of data. The latter are exploited for a continuous monitoring of the following types of patients: accident victims, elderly people, preterm children, and chronically sick patients. Machine learning algorithms are exploited to classify a new patient based on his/her collected features and alerts on their current condition. Authors in [51] proposed a doctor recommendation method based on extracted interactive features from the knowledge graph and interpretable deep learning techniques. The proposed scheme gives as output the status of interactions between patients and doctors and the individual features that trigger the quality of the doctors' service. In [53], a multimedia interaction system has been designed and developed exploiting computer vision and deep learning technologies for hospital admitted, bedridden and immobile patients. The data manipulated include hand gestures, nose teeth-based interaction and voice-based interaction taken from sensor technologies.

Discussions

[53] study lacks standardized AI procedure to deal with clinical tasks. Also, the ethical and legal frameworks generic to cover such tasks are not considered in the paper. However, the study considered the exploitation of AI for interactions between patient and practitioners. Furthermore, the framework and guidelines for anyone who would like to develop AI systems for healthcare was lacking in their study. Health is so sensitive that just an error conducts directly could lead to death. In [54] the study lacks research designing schemes to automatically confer responsibility when errors induced in AI systems happen during virtual interactions. Likewise, the reinforcement learning and associated techniques are not covered in studies despite its relevance to deal with real-time systems. This study [54] also lack classification of interactions as providing satisfaction or dissatisfaction based on selected features. Recommendation systems should also be the objective after exploitation of AI. It means that the finality should be to effectively put in place these systems for online assistance and for feeding data.

4.3.2 Telemedicine

Due to the Covd-19 pandemic, telemedicine has revived since it does prone contact-less during diagnosis and treatment. In this context, this form of remote medical practice using information and communication technologies to connect patients and practitioners, has been recommended by authors to support patient professionals' interactions[56]. According to [56], clinicians in Australia see telehealth as an enabler for communication with patients when there is a considerable distance to find a specialist and when the road is not practicable. [57] made an analysis to know the effects of telemedicine in regards to orthopaedic patients and surgeons. In terms of patient satisfaction when interacting, results revealed no difference between interaction with telemedicine and interaction inperson. These results have been related to the satisfaction to the treatment and no other process during the communication between patient and surgeon. Also,[51] did not find real difference when using telemedicine than in-office visit concerning patient and physician experiences. These two studies show how complementary teleconsultation and face-face are complementary. Discussing Serious News Remotely: Navigating Difficult Conversations During a Pandemic concerning cancer care, telemedicine has also been applied via videoconference and telephone despite the fact live discussions with patients are preferable. SPIKES ((Setting, Perception, Invitation, Knowledge, Empathy/Emotion, and Strategy/Summarize)) is proposed by [58] as a protocol to consider serious discussions. They also proposed WIRE-SPIKES to encounter technological aspects such as the communication mean, the way of pausing, exchanging, …. Etc. [59] studied the added value of video consultations during communications concerning continuity in cancer care. They did it cross-sectoral wise between cancer patients, oncologists and general practitioners and results proved that multidisciplinary video consultations are feasible and supportive for cancer care.

Discussions

During the twenty-first century, telemedicine has without any doubt become an adjunct to classical health services. More particularly, it is considered as a support to interactions between patients and practitioners. The research area about telemedicine is crowded with proposals but within the scope of this review, the interest is focused on interactions. The aforementioned works showed its acceptance to both the patient and practitioners sides. However, it is also necessary to outline pitfalls which come with this technological mechanism. First, the infrastructures to put it in place are too expensive for deployment and for maintenance. Health services in developing countries can afford this, and therefore not exploiting it. Also, patients need money for a certain technological standing to conform (Internet, devices,..). In countries where the people hardly find food, telemedicine can be seen as a mystery. Second, people are not ready to use such technologies [56] Patients and even professionals need to be fully educated to make use of telemedicine objects. Even working on computer with basic software remains unaccomplished for quite a large population in Africa. Third, privacy issues due to manipulation of confidential data have unprecedently appeared [58]. There are questions related to the guarantee for the preservation of data and access control to authorized entities. Fourth, the physical contact during which the doctor can feel the patient emotions and see some other intrinsic signs is absent. The face-to-face presence sometimes triggers patient revealing information that he/she can't behind telemedicine screens. Agreements and sharing information between the both sides are not reliable since no one really feels the other. As a consequence, decision making concerning diagnosis becomes complex. Fifth, there is no confidence in using such tools [56]. Indeed, this situation is a consequence from the fourth one.

Culturally speaking, people like contact and have reserve to artificial [56]. The doctors need to enhance their trust to these technologies and for that, real demonstrations during training can be necessary. Likewise, how can the patient be in situation to trust a process performed by a virtual agent who even not speaks the common language. Last, the communication effectiveness is rare using telemedicine [56].

4.3.3   Digital Systems

In Sect. 4.3.2, we have explored the exploitation of telemedicine as a complement of interactions between patients and practitioners. In this section, we explore the use of some specific applications used to facilitate this interaction. Internet is the core support underlying digitalization associated with the widespread of smartphones which host the software developed for this objective. Some studies investigated the relationship between the use of smartphones by practitioners and means to communicate with patients [60]. They reveal that physicians are subject to higher stress when they overuse Internet to communicate with patients and that the quality of healthcare is negatively impacted as well as the relationships with patients. In this context, doctors deliver poorer patient care with critical mistakes [61]. Despite this situation, authors find helpful to get the patients closer to the health professionals.[62], developed a mobile application relying on Internet which procures interactions among patients, doctors and general practitioners for healthcare services and delivery. Functionalities include taking appointments, prescription management and patient data management. A standalone application is implemented by [63] to overcome insufficient access to specialized medical care by the rural populations. This application allows interaction between patients and several doctors and generates educational reports which guide on health education based on inputs about the disease. An investigation about three general practitioners (GP) service apps has been realized relying on explicit and implicit factors [64]. GP services improve availability of GP services, but they are constrained to the following: requirements of clearer exclusions, appropriate use via decision-making tools, additional rural-tailored interfaces, and possibility to possibility to combine appointment periods and costs with patient habits.

Discussions

These applications have been proved so helpful to connect patients with practitioners. However, the problem of continuity and coordination of care is clearly posed. After the first contact with the patient, how do permanently and temporally continue with the follow-up through the application. This imposes the application to be dynamic, evolution and intelligent. Moreover, if several doctors are involved in the process, how to assure the coordination to provide the confidence to the patient is one question to answer. There is also a problem of formal ownership of the application guaranteeing any responsibility either in negative or positive cases. In this case, the official instance should validate the utilization of the application. There is also the problem of privacy concerning information of stakeholders involved in the processes. Last but not least, the language of communication is a problem. The application should be designed considering the context in which it will be used.

4.3.4 IoT and Cloud

Healthcare has been re-invented with the huge opportunities provided by IoT [65, 66]. One big opportunity which came with the global health crisis CoVid-19 is the self-diagnosis replacing physical interaction with practitioners. Through objects such as sensors in wearable sensor devices interconnected through wireless sensor network or IoT, people collect data which can be processed by (mobile) applications to assist users in diagnosis. The collection of data is realized through IoT and their storage is done in the cloud for resilience purposes. In this context, the doctor is interfaced by the results from the processing of data provided by IoT. Sometimes, the computing related to data is also done in the cloud when resources are limited. After the storage the AI algorithms (as discussed in Sect. 4.3.1) take over for decision making such as prediction, diagnosis, and treatment. Coupling IoT with the cloud enables monitoring health status and it improves the quality of service. The paper [67] made a deep review of IoT-based healthcare systems and sufficiently demonstrated the place IoT.

For instance, in [67], the wearable device monitors some physiological parameters such as body temperature (BT), electrocardiograph (ECG), and heart rate (HR). It is possible to obtain ECG and PPG using Pulse Arrival Time (PAT) and therefore to estimate blood pressure (BP). The parameters are wirelessly transmitted to a gateway using a BLE module and then transferred to the cloud for further processing. A smart IoMT based architecture for E-healthcare is proposed in [68] for patient monitoring. The system disposes a cloud repository where the information acquired from sense devices is stored. It can therefore be extracted, preprocessed and refined by AI algorithms. The system developed in [69] measures the following patient's parameters: body temperature, heartbeat, and oxygen saturation (SpO2) in the blood and send the data to a mobile application using Bluetooth. The patients can visualize their health state after this information is sent to the LCD panel. In [70], a IoT based framework for remote monitoring of covid-affected patients is proposed. The biomedical parameters collected include PPG, ECG, accelerometer and temperature from bio wearable sensor devices. [71] provided a framework covid-affected patients may be remotedly monitored. For early covid detection, the model offered was an Internet of Things-based, remotely accessible, alert system bio-wearable sensor system.[72] described the methods to monitor patients with cardiovascular illness and recommend them the use of wearable smart devices to collect data and cloud stores for storing and processing of data. In another study [73], IoT is exploited to design a system for monitoring student health. Students' valuable metrics are monitored to identify behavioral and biological changes in students. The proposed approach includes three levels: identifying the required data for the student using biological and behavioral factors, capturing the information using biosensors and intelligent IoT devices, and pre-processing the data. A IoT system is proposed to detect for the presence of an arrhythmia by monitoring electrocardiogram (ECG) signal and processing heart data [74]. An alert is generated in case of arrhythmia. Similarly, a system is designed for heart disease risk prediction [75].

4.3.5   Discussions

Although IoT and the Cloud offer opportunities, there are some requirements to fulfil form their exploitation. First, Internet is indispensable to succeed the different processes from collection to process on the cloud. In just few cases where the wearable smart device has minimal resources, mobile applications locally make computations through a wireless sensor network. Additionally, the user is sometimes obliged/forced to accept permissions to let her/his data get stored somewhere in the cloud, without any privacy information. Unlike physical interactions during which the counterparties can manage privacy aspects, IoT and Cloud come with possible privacy leaks. Different equipment involved in the IoT are energy consuming. The different IoT architecture should be designed to minimize consumption of energy. Likewise, the designed system should provide the result as quickly as possible similarly to when the doctor is physically communicating with the patient. The current systems take 3 to 5 min and can take more depending on dataset size and the heterogeneity of complete system [70]. One crucial problem is the consistency of information. During physical interactions with the practitioners, the patient comments and replies in a complete way. But using IoT, due to limited resources devices, information is truncated and only few parts are taken. Consequently, the result from processing will also be incomplete. The environment in which the IoT app is installed should be safe to ensure that there is no infiltrated code or that the application is the real one. Otherwise, fake information will be sent and biased the output results. According to [75], environments of IoT are subjects to Distributed Denial of Service (DDoS) and Denial of Service (DoS) attacks.

4.4   Patient-Doctor Interaction and Trust

As of February 2019, China has 829 million active Internet apps, and the country's Internet penetration rate stood at 59.6%, according to data provided by the China Internet Network Information Center (CNNIC). According to [76], Chinese Internet users are more likely to use Internet applications to get health information than they are to consult with doctors, family members, or friends. Reported to studies, the enhancement of the patient-physician relationship is positively impacted by patients' online access to health information. The primary source of health information for the general people in China is now the Internet. According to certain research, 74.9% of medical staff members have a poor opinion of the existing patient-physician interaction. Medical conflicts have also frequently been the source of violent riots, attacks, and protests in Chinese hospitals [76]. In a quantitative study, it was determined whether online medical advice from doctors and patient health information literacy had an impact on patient-physician communication and trust in China. A web-based survey was used in this study to gather information from online applications with health issues. The data was analyzed using structural equation modeling to test the hypotheses. The investigation, however, reveals that the usefulness of online medical information and doctor advice both have a considerable impact on patients' trust in doctors and their interactions with them. Furthermore, the interaction between the patient and the doctor also significantly affects their level of trust in one another. The function of doctors as online advisors is also examined in this study, as is the question of how communication between doctors and patients would alter both parties' levels of trust. The study's practical applications include a better knowledge of how online health information works as well as possible effects on patient-physician interactions and physician trust that may be utilized to settle disputes between patients and doctors. This study only identified a few of the variables that influence patient-physician contact and trust; however, other pertinent studies have revealed that other variables, such as self-efficacy, perceived risk, perceived benefit, etc., still need to be explored. Additionally, this study only looked at one theory; however, additional theories, like the social exchange theory and the social capital theory, might be merged to look at patient-physician trust. In addition, the study did not address the effect that the participants' educational backgrounds may have had on their perception of the study's value. However, in order to increase the validity of this study model, other aspects and alternative theoretical viewpoints will be taken into account.

China has gradually developed a hierarchical diagnosis and treatment system that categorizes diseases according to severity and urgency, enabling medical institutions at various levels to handle diseases of various types and stages in accordance with various institutions' functions. This system was established to meet the needs of the people with regard to their health [50] This cross-sectional study looked at the factors that affect patients' trust in primary care physicians in China. Only 25.2% of Chinese citizens, according to the results, have confidence in medical services. If there wasn't a strong level of public trust in local government, there would be even less hope for the benefits of public's trust in the health system. Being a component of the doctor-patient relationship, trust played a significant role in the patient's medical journey. Since people's socioeconomic and demographic characteristics cannot be changed and faith in government has historically been strong, improving public perception of health care is the best—if not the only—way to boost public confidence in the health care system. This study discovered a positive relationship between residents' trust in doctors and their self-reported health status and FDCS. These two factors had the greatest influences, according to the standardized coefficients. Primary care physicians in PCIs are well recognized to perform a less significant role than specialists in hospitals in China and other nations[77] Chinese citizens, particularly those with bad health, have very little faith in the skills of primary care physicians, so when they become ill, they will go straight to hospitals for medical assistance. Family doctor contracts give patients better access to and more time with their preferred general practitioners, which enhances their perception of the quality of primary care and increases their happiness and confidence in PCIs. There may have been a failure to discover all potential factors impacting patients' trust because this study concentrated on sociolectdemographic parameters and just a few health and medical experience elements were examined. Additionally, because this study used a cross-sectional study design, it was impossible to assess the temporality and causality of the correlations that were found. Finally, since the sampling design and "mandatory" questionnaire introduced selection bias, the findings should be carefully interpreted. The samples in this study were younger, had a smaller sex ratio, and were significantly more educated than the national population in 2020, although their urban-rural ratios were similar. The authors claim that despite decades of government healthcare reform initiatives, China's low level of trust in PCIs and primary care physicians remains a significant problem. The study's findings pointed to a potential increase in trust among youthful, less educated, and generally unhealthier community members. However, further study is needed to better understand the underlying causes of their lower level of trust in primary care providers than other populations.

By examining the effects of social cue design and privacy concerns on two types of trust—trust in physicians and trust in the applications and by comprehending how these two types of trust influence behavioral intention in mobile medical consultations, [78] attempted to facilitate impersonal patientphysician interactions. The authors used online survey data from 429 users of mobile medical consultations to build the research model, and the partial least squares approach was used to examine the structural model. The findings demonstrated that social cue design elements not only have a variety of effects on the two categories of trust but also lessen privacy worries. Both sorts of trust are hampered by privacy concerns. It is also shown how the two levels of trust affect patients' intentions to use the service in the future, to share information, and to heed medical advice. Although the authors acknowledged that patients can seek health support more conveniently through mobile platforms, they also raised the issue of how to foster trust between patients and doctors in MMCs because most patients don't already know the doctors who treat them for their symptoms. By building a research model using PLS, this study also identified the predictors of two forms of trust (confidence in physicians and trust in the applications) and examined the effects of the two categories of trust on behavioral intention in mobile medical consultations. The findings indicated that three behavioral intentions in mobile medical consultations were predicted by physician trust: the intention to use constantly, the intention to share information, and the intention to heed medical advice.The results of this study provided recommendations for future research into the development of trust in the setting of impersonal interaction and implications for practitioners to enhance mobile medical consultation services.

[79] used a mixed method research methodology to investigate the idea of communicative trust in therapeutic encounters in public healthcare facilities and neighborhood pharmacies in Maputo, Mozambique. The study's goal was to comprehend how patients perceived and experienced communicative trust in their interactions with healthcare professionals. The investigation concentrated on relational processes and communicative rituals surrounding practices of diagnosis, prescription, or therapeutic recommendation, which are crucial in medical practice and, as shown in this analysis, are indicative of various levels of care, competence, and reliability. The results showed that patients highly valued healthcare professionals' communication abilities and saw it as a crucial component of trustbuilding strategies. The results also imply that therapeutic encounters for healthcare service consumers in these settings depend heavily on communicative trust. Participants talked about a lack of faith in public healthcare institutions due to bad communication, protracted wait times, and subpar facilities. Contrarily, individuals discussed establishing trust with neighborhood pharmacists through individualized attention, meticulousness, and continuity of service. However, the author argues that in order to establish trust in therapeutic interactions, a communication-focused strategy that is catered to the unique requirements and preferences of each user is necessary. Additionally, they contend that establishing trust necessitates ongoing efforts to address structural problems that influence users' experiences and perceptions of treatment. This

study demonstrates that, despite the many competence and authority traits of health-care practitioners, it is primarily their communicative behaviors during interactions that determine whether (symbolic) trust has the space to develop or to solidify. Additionally, while engaging in certain rituals may be a useful method of communication, the absence of other verbal and nonverbal communication during the contact may reduce the patient' trust in the recommendations or prescriptions being given. Users' viewpoints should be taken into consideration, and particular emphasis should be paid to these communica-tive and relational components, in efforts to enhance the quality and responsiveness of healthcare services centered around citizens' needs.

[79] in article "Interacting with Medical Artificial Intelligence: Integrating Self-Responsibility Attribution, Human-Computer Trust, and Personality" explores the mech-anism of patients' acceptance of medical AI following AI service failure from the per-spective of self-responsibility attribution. This study investigates the possible effects of interacting with medical artificial intelligence (MAI) on selfresponsibility attribu-tion, human-computer trust, and personality in healthcare using data from 249 patients in China. According to research, patients' self-responsibility attribution is positively correlated with human-computer trust (HCT), which in turn increases patients' accep-tance of medical AI for independent diagnosis and treatment. The moderating effect of personality factors is also examined in this article. In particular, agreeableness and conscientiousness weaken the relationship between HCT and acceptability of AI for assistive diagnosis and treatment while conscientiousness and openness improve the relationship between HCT and acceptance of AI for independent diagnosis and treat-ment. The authors debate that it is crucial to comprehend the psychological impact and integration of medical artificial intelligence (AI) on the healthcare industry, particularly in terms of the interaction between human users and AI systems, as advances in artificial intelligence continue to transform healthcare. The essay emphasizes the significance of self-responsibility attribution, which refers to how much people hold themselves or an AI system accountable for decisions. Even if assisted by AI, the authors contend that it is crucial for people to be in charge of their healthcare decisions in order to assure accountability and prevent any drawbacks. The paper also highlights the need of human-computer trust in interactions between people and AI. According to the author, elements like the AI's accuracy and the transparency of its decision-making process can have an impact on trust, which is important in influencing how people perceive and use AI. Personality qualities like openness and agreeableness may have an impact on how people view and use AI, which could have repercussions for the use and efficacy of AI in the healthcare sector. The exploration in this study provides useful tips for healthcare practitioners and technology developers on how to encourage responsible and produc-tive communication between people and medical AI systems. The necessity of striking a balance between the advantages of AI and the requirement for human accountability and trust in healthcare decisionmaking is emphasized.

4.4.1 Discussion

In the patient's medical journey, trust, as a component of the doctor-patient interaction, was crucial [50]. Only [80] concentrate on the mechanism of patients' acceptance of medical AI, despite the extensive literature on doctor-patient interaction in therapeutic contexts and increased attention to the significance of trust in such interactions. Since only one of the articles we studied was done in Mozambique and the bulk were done in China, their conclusions might not apply to other cycles or situations. The main study's findings suggested that younger, less educated, and generally unhealthier community members might become more trustworthy. To fully comprehend the reasons why they have less trust in primary care physicians than other demographics, more research is necessary. However, other pertinent studies have shown that additional variables, such as self-efficacy, perceived risk, perceived benefit, etc., still need to be examined. It is found that only a few of the variables that influence patient-physician contact and trust were identified in the studies. Only a small number of research examined more than one theory, but other theories, such the social exchange theory and the social capital theory, might be combined to study patient-physician trust. Additionally, the majority of the study did not discuss how the participants' educational backgrounds may have influenced how valuable they thought the study was. However, other factors and various theoretical stances should be taken into consideration in order to strengthen the validity of these study model.

In an effort to improve the caliber and responsiveness of healthcare services oriented around citizens' demands, users' perspectives should also be taken into account. Particular emphasis should be placed on these communicative and relational components. With AI systems in mind, the investigation in these studies offers us practical advice for healthcare professionals and technology developers on how to promote ethical and fruitful dialogue between people and medical practitioners. It is stressed how important it is to strike a balance between the benefits of AI and the need for human accountability and confidence in healthcare decision-making.

5 Open Issues, Challenges and Research Directions

Results from exhaustive investigation about interactions between patients and practitioners revealed some open issues for the progress of this research area. The following issues are concerns for the research and industry alike. Some orientations are proposed for interested people.

Trust: This aspect is essential for patients to really consider the recommendations from practitioners. For that, cultural aspects, identities as well as reputations of practitioners must be known and proved. In the other way, the practitioner needs to trust the patient arguments. Studies reveal that trust remains a concern, interfering the whole process of interactions. Surveys conducted are coarse-grained meaning that they determine factors which explain absence of trust but they lack to find fine-grained factors explained these coarse-grained factors. For example, they find that culture affects interactions but do not reveal generic cultural aspects to be considered. Explorative investigations should be performed to complete the current ones about this aspect. Some authors argue that trust can be brought with the help of technology such as artificial intelligence. In this case, owners/developers of applications lack to create a trust environment in patients are able to prove the identity of practitioners and the reverse way. Authors can look to build cooperative and third authority approaches to guarantee this aspect. Artificial intelligence comes with its own ethical problems which bias diagnoses giving advantage to a certain category of patients. Explainability and interpretability theories should be coupled to these applications to guarantee inclusivity.

Security, Privacy: Privacy is a key concern concerning health. Information relative to a patient shouldn't be release to anyone else. IoT or the cloud are using Internet that is a place where anything is found. Human speaking, privacy is applicable more easily than when technology/Internet comes into play. Authors should accentuate proposals to guarantee this aspect to bring a certain confidence to the application's users. Applications designed to abstract the interactions manipulate health data, confidential to the patient. Risks to leaking such data is higher. Risk management techniques should be investigated to determine risks associated to resources and to applied adequate countermeasures. The host systems should be healthy, so that the flows between host and the application. Static and dynamic analyses are recommended in this regard to observe normal and abnormal activities from the flows. In addition, there is a challenge concerning the information storage. Proposals do not integrate it. The support for storage should be alterable-free. It means that a diagnostic shouldn't for instance be modified by a third person without any privilege to do that. Countermeasures are to be proposed against deny of service (DoS) attacks, based on rigid access controls and authorization.

Fault-Tolerance: Availability of the proposed systems has been left behind. Imagine a patient remotely being listened and threated by a doctor and suddenly the connection is lost and loopholes appear. The practitioners will therefore misunderstand the patient and will bias diagnoses. The life of the patient is risky in this case. To this example, issues like optimization of battery of equipment in IoT, permanent electricity supply for terminal devices etc. Virtual infrastructures should be designed relying on costly cloud services and adapted to the context. Local centers should replicate minimal cloud services to be exploited by peers. Multi-agent systems can be exploited to mimic infrastructure architecture functionalities. Models for Internet of Medical Things (IoMT) should be designed to leverage energy consumption. Maintenance is also a key for fault-tolerant systems. Automatic approaches should be proposed to get those systems updated through a local and cloud server of updates. Recommendation techniques based on machine learning approaches are also often exploited in these cases to alert the administrator for any update to apply.

Education/Training and Language: Authors have recommended the option the pre-pare people in the use of technological solutions facilitating any interaction. Practitioners as well as patients should take trainings for these systems to efficiently manipulate them and even maintain them in the long term. This will be effective in case educative solutions well designed are given to users. Gamified/gaming systems can be of interest for this specific for successful interactions patient-practitioners. Such systems can be integrated in the curricula from lower to upper levels of education. Here, there is an issue which is not taken in account into proposals. Users of the applications are from different languages and from different cultures. This poses a problem of designing an interpreter depending on where the application will be exploited. The same issue also exists concerning the application proposed to support interactions. The patient must be able to see information in his/her own language to be able to interpret results and recommendations. Interpretation can be based on voice or text. Deep learning algorithms will therefore be exploited to recognize a language from voice or text and then to propose corresponding translated. In this case, large language model (LLM) theories can be exploited to the proposed systems.

Knowledge Management: The systems proposed in literature takes information for patients and practitioners and store them in a server. The preoccupation here is how to structure this information so that they can be re-use later for a diagnosis. To do that, ontological models need to be designed to formalize use cases and represent knowledge. Incremental learning is also a solution to add knowledge to the previous memory state. In so doing, health professionals can gain in time to prescribe new recommendations based on a different patient case.

Continuity and Coordination: A big issue is to have an evolutive and temporal inter-action. Different works only consider a one step interaction. In reality, we counter muti-stage interactions. In other words, after a t interaction made how to pass to a $t + 1$ interaction to follow-up the previous interaction: we called this a continuous interaction. A continuous interaction should be characterized so that memory shouldn't be lost. This requires a certain coordination between stakeholders such as generalized and special-ist doctors, patients and other actors. This situation can be modeled with multiagents, reinforcement learning and implicitly Markov Chains.

Artificial Intelligence: We noted that every research comes with its own way of exploit-ing AI algorithms to deal with healthcare. Since health is a sensitive area that should be well controlled, we should set a framework to follow when one wants to design AI solutions. In so doing, security, privacy will be easily ensured and the development of health products will be better regulated. Similarly, ethical aspects will be investigated more formally. The frameworks will be based on layered-based architecture. The first layer will be dedicated specifically risks related to AI such as ethics, responsibility, etc. The second layer will be for knowledge representation and processing and also for core processes. The third layer will be for core processes. A middleware can be designed man-age all the communications involved in the framework including libraries manipulated between the lower and the upper levels. A challenge using AI is to be able to characterize an interaction as complete or incomplete because it requires a dataset well constituted to be used in supervised or unsupervised learning. What can be done is to design rein-forcement and imitation learning schemes which take knowledge from an environment or from an expert guiding on different actions to take during interactions. A possibility is also to start collecting data with a form including variables/features to patients who will express their satisfaction about interactions with doctors/nurses or other professionals. This dataset could not contain target variable at start but later be given to unsupervised learning which will offer large possibilities for data mining and supervised learning. An idea could also be to capture gestures of patient and practitioners during the interactions and to call deep learning for sensing this information. The type of dataset can be textual and, in this case, Natural Language Processing (NLP) can be applied. AI responsibility should be deeply studied in case of adverse events induced by errors in AI systems.

6   Conclusion

Improving medical practitioner-patient interaction is crucial in achieving positive health outcomes. The strategies identified in this systematic study can be used to design interventions that improve communication skills, promote patient-centered care, and incorporate technology-based solutions to enhance communication and information sharing in clinical settings. It is stressed however, the important of striking a balance between the benefits of technological based systems such as AI and the need for human accountability and confidence in healthcare decision-making.

References

1. Mutudi, M., Iyamu, T.: An information systems framework to improve the issuance of identity documents through enhanced data quality in the Republic of Angola. Electr. J. Inf. Syst. Dev. Countries **86**, e12111 (2020). https://doi.org/10.1002/ISD2.12111
2. Kwame, A., Petrucka, P.M.: Communication in nurse-patient interaction in healthcare settings in sub-Saharan Africa: a scoping review. Int. J. Afr. Nurs. Sci. **12**, 100198 (2020). https://doi.org/10.1016/J.IJANS.2020.100198
3. Kwame, A., Petrucka, P.M.: Universal healthcare coverage, patients' rights, and nurse-patient communication: a critical review of the evidence. BMC Nurs. **21**, 1–9 (2022). https://doi.org/10.1186/S12912-022-00833l/PEER-REVIEW
4. Allice, I., Acai, A., Ferdossifard, A., Wekerle, C., Kimber, M.: Indigenous cultural safety in recognizing and responding to family violence: a systematic scoping review. Int. J. Environ. Res. Publ. Health **19**(24), 16967 (2022). https://doi.org/10.3390/ijerph192416967
5. Altman, M.R., McLemore, M.R., Oseguera, T., Lyndon, A., Franck, L.S.: Listening to women: recommendations from women of color to improve experiences in pregnancy and birth care. J. Midwifery Womens Health **65**, 466–473 (2020). https://doi.org/10.1111/jmwh.13102
6. Altman, M.R., Oseguera, T., McLemore, M.R., Kantrowitz-Gordon, I., Franck, L.S., Lyndon, A.: Information and power: Women of color's experiences interacting with health care providers in pregnancy and birth. Soc. Sci. Med. **238**, 112491 (2019). https://doi.org/10.1016/J.SOCSCIMED.2019.112491
7. Odonkor, C.A., et al.: Disparities in health care for black patients in physical medicine and rehabilitation in the united states: a narrative review. PM and R. **13**, 180–203 (2021). https://doi.org/10.1002/PMRJ.12509
8. Schrot-Sanyan, S., et al.: Language barrier as a risk factor for obstetric anal sphincter injury - A case-control study. J. Gynecol. Obstet. Hum. Reprod. **50**, 102138 (2021). https://doi.org/10.1016/J.JOGOH.2021.102138
9. Huang, C.W., et al.: Emotion recognition in doctor-patient interactions from real-world clinical video database: Initial development of artificial empathy. Comput. Methods Programs Biomed. **233**, 107480 (2023)
10. Panayiotou, A., et al.: The perceptions of translation apps for everyday health care in healthcare workers and older people: a multi-method study. J. Clin. Nurs. **29**, 3516–3526 (2020). https://doi.org/10.1111/JOCN.15390
11. Panayiotou, A., et al.: Language translation apps in health care settings: expert opinion. JMIR Mhealth Uhealth 7(4), e11316 (2019). https://mhealth.jmir.org/2019/4/e11316. https://doi.org/10.2196/11316
12. Fair Id, F., Raben, L., Watson Id, H., Vivilaki, V., Van Den Muijsenbergh, M., Soltaniid, H.: Migrant women's experiences of pregnancy, childbirth and maternity care in European countries: a systematic review (2020). https://doi.org/10.1371/journal.pone.0228378

13. Timmermans, S.: The engaged patient: the relevance of patient–physician communication for twentyfirst-century health. J. Health Soc. Behav. **61**, 259–273 (2020). https://doi.org/10.1177/0022146520943514

14. Schinkel, S., Schouten, B.C., Kerpiclik, F., Van Den Putte, B., Van Weert, J.C.M.: Perceptions of barriers to patient participation: are they due to language, culture, or discrimination? Health Commun. **34**, 1469–1481 (2019). https://doi.org/10.1080/10410236.2018.1500431

15. Haj-Younes, J., Abildsnes, E., Kumar, B., Diaz, E.: The road to equitable healthcare: a conceptual model developed from a qualitative study of Syrian refugees in Norway. Soc. Sci. Med. **292**, 114540 (2022). https://doi.org/10.1016/J.SOCSCIMED.2021.114540

16. Grand-Guillaume-Perrenoud, J.A., Origlia, P., Cignacco, E.: Barriers and facilitators of maternal healthcare utilisation in the perinatal period among women with social disadvantage: a theory-guided systematic review. Midwifery **105**, 103237 (2022). https://doi.org/10.1016/J.MIDW.2021.103237

17. Tozour, J.N., et al.: Application of telemedicine video visits in a maternal-fetal medicine practice at the epicenter of the COVID-19 pandemic. Am. J. Obstet. Gynecol. MFM **3**, 100469 (2021). https://doi.org/10.1016/j.ajogmf.2021.100469

18. Haleem, A., Javaid, M., Singh, R.P., Suman, R.: Telemedicine for healthcare: capabilities, features, barriers, and applications. Sens. Int. **2**, 100117 (2021). https://doi.org/10.1016/J.SINTL.2021.100117

19. Bustos, N., Tello, M., Droppelmann, G., García, N., Feijoo, F., Leiva, V.: Machine learning techniques as an efficient alternative diagnostic tool for COVID-19 cases. Signa Vitae **18**, 23–33 (2022). https://doi.org/10.22514/SV.2021.110/HTM

20. Kaur, S., et al.: Medical diagnostic systems using artificial intelligence (AI) algorithms: principles and perspectives. IEEE Access **8**, 228049–228069 (2020). https://doi.org/10.1109/ACCESS.2020.3042273

21. Desai, F., et al.: HealthCloud: a system for monitoring health status of heart patients using machine learning and cloud computing. Internet Things **17**, 100485 (2022). https://doi.org/10.1016/J.IOT.2021.100485

22. Swire-Thompson, B., Lazer, D.: Reducing health misinformation in science: a call to arms. Ann. Am. Acad. Polit. Soc. Sci. **700**, 124–135 (2022). https://doi.org/10.1177/00027162221087686

23. Landolsi, M.Y., Hlaoua, L., Ben Romdhane, L.: Information extraction from electronic medical documents: state of the art and future research directions. Knowl. Inf. Syst. **65**, 463–516 (2023). https://doi.org/10.1007/S10115-022-01779-1

24. Chidambaram, S., Sounderajah, V., Maynard, N., Markar, S.R.: Diagnostic performance of artificial intelligence-centred systems in the diagnosis and postoperative surveillance of upper gastrointestinal malignancies using computed tomography imaging: a systematic review and meta-analysis of diagnostic accuracy. Ann. Surg. Oncol. **29**, 1977–1990 (2022). https://doi.org/10.1245/S10434-02110882-6

25. Awotunde, J.B., Folorunso, S.O., Ajagbe, S.A., Garg, J., Ajamu, G.J.: AiIoMT: IoMT-based SystemEnabled artificial intelligence for enhanced smart healthcare systems. Mach. Learn. Crit. Internet Med. Things., 229–254 (2022). https://doi.org/10.1007/978-3-030-80928-7_10

26. Sawhney, R., Malik, A., Sharma, S., Narayan, V.: A comparative assessment of artificial intelligence models used for early prediction and evaluation of chronic kidney disease. Dec. Anal. J. **6**, 100169 (2023). https://doi.org/10.1016/J.DAJOUR.2023.100169

27. Chen, S., Guo, X., Wu, T., Ju, X.: Exploring the online doctor-patient interaction on patient satisfaction based on text mining and empirical analysis. Inf. Process. Manag. **57**, 102253 (2020). https://doi.org/10.1016/J.IPM.2020.102253

28. Kwame, A., Petrucka, P.M.: A literature-based study of patient-centered care and communication in nursepatient interactions: barriers, facilitators, and the way forward. BMC Nurs. **20**, 1–10 (2021). https://doi.org/10.1186/S12912-021-00684-2/FIGURES/1

29. Zhao, X.: Challenges and barriers in intercultural communication between patients with immigration backgrounds and health professionals: a systematic literature review. Health Commun. **38**, 824–833 (2021). https://doi.org/10.1080/10410236.2021.1980188

30. McNeill, S.G., McAteer, J., Jepson, R.: Interactions between health professionals and lesbian, gay and bisexual patients in healthcare settings: a systematic review. J. Homosex. **70**, 250–276 (2021). https://doi.org/10.1080/00918369.2021.1945338

31. Chengoden, R., et al.: Metaverse for healthcare: a survey on potential applications, challenges and future. IEEE Access **11**, 12764–12794 (2023). https://doi.org/10.1109/ACCESS.2023.3241628

32. Chengoden, R., et al.: Metaverse for healthcare: a survey on potential applications, challenges and future directions **4**, (2022). https://doi.org/10.1109/ACCESS.2017.DOI

33. Hamberger, M., et al.: Interaction empowerment in mobile health: concepts, challenges, and perspectives. JMIR Mhealth Uhealth **10**(4), e32696 (2022). https://mhealth.jmir.org/2022/4/e32696. https://doi.org/10.2196/32696

34. Luo, A., et al.: The effect of online health information seeking on physician-patient relationships: systematic review. J. Med. Internet Res. **24**(2), e23354 (2022). https://www.jmir.org/2022/2/e23354. https://doi.org/10.2196/23354

35. Merlo, V., Pio, G., Giusto, F., Bilancia, M.: On the exploitation of the blockchain technology in the healthcare sector: a systematic review. Expert Syst. Appl. **213**, 118897 (2023). https://doi.org/10.1016/J.ESWA.2022.118897

36. Melian, C., Kieser, D., Frampton, C., C Wyatt, M.: Teleconsultation in orthopaedic surgery: a systematic review and meta-analysis of patient and physician experiences. J. Telemed. Telecare **28**, 471–480 (2022). https://doi.org/10.1177/1357633X20950995

37. Nittari, G., Savva, D., Tomassoni, D., Tayebati, S.K., Amenta, F.: Telemedicine in the COVID-19 era: a narrative review based on current evidence. Int. J. Environ. Res. Publ. Health **19**, 5101 (2022). https://doi.org/10.3390/IJERPH19095101

38. Sezgin, E., Noritz, G., Hoffman, J., Huang, Y.: A medical translation assistant for non-english-speaking caregivers of children with special health care needs: proposal for a scalable and interoperable mobile app. JMIR Res. Protoc. **9**, e21038 (2020). https://doi.org/10.2196/21038

39. Gutiérrez-Puertas, L., Márquez-Hernández, V.V., Gutiérrez-Puertas, V., Granados-Gámez, G., AguileraManrique, G.: Educational interventions for nursing students to develop communication skills with patients: a systematic review. Int. J. Environ. Res. Publ. Health **17**, 2241 (2020). https://doi.org/10.3390/IJERPH17072241

40. Isangula, K.G., Pallangyo, E.S., Ndirangu-Mugo, E.: Improving nursing education curriculum as a tool for strengthening the nurse-client relationships in maternal and child healthcare: Insights from a humancentered design study in rural Tanzania. Front. Publ. Health (2023). https://doi.org/10.3389/fpubh.2023.1072721

41. Thakur, K.T., et al.: COVID-19 neuropathology at Columbia University Irving Medical Center/New York Presbyterian Hospital. Brain **144**, 2696–2708 (2021). https://doi.org/10.1093/brain/awab148

42. Aflatoony, L., Wakkary, R., Neustaedter, C.: Becoming a design thinker: assessing the learning process of students in a secondary level design thinking course. Int. J. Art Des. Educ. **37**, 438–453 (2018). https://doi.org/10.1111/jade.12139

43. Font Jiménez, I., Ortega Sanz, L., González Pascual, J.L., González Sanz, P., Aguarón García, M.J., Jiménez-Herrera, M.F.: Reflective based learning for nursing ethical competency during clinical practices. Nurs. Ethics, 096973302211405 (2023). https://doi.org/10.1177/09697330221140513

44. Lin, H.C., Hwang, G.J., Hsu, Y.D.: Effects of ASQ-based flipped learning on nurse practitioner learners' nursing skills, learning achievement and learning perceptions. Comput. Educ. **139**, 207–221 (2019). https://doi.org/10.1016/J.COMPEDU.2019.05.014

45. Tran, T.Q., Scherpbier, A.J.J.A., van Dalen, J., Van Do, D., Wright, E.P.: Nationwide survey of patients' and doctors' perceptions of what is needed in doctor - patient communication in a Southeast Asian context. BMC Health Serv. Res. **20**, 1–11 (2020). https://doi.org/10.1186/S12913-020-05803-4/TABLES/5

46. Kwezi, H.A., Mselle, L.T., Leshabari, S., Hanson, C., Pembe, A.B.: How communication can help women who experience a maternal near-miss: a qualitative study from Tanzania. BMJ Open **11**, e045514 (2021). https://doi.org/10.1136/BMJOPEN-2020-045514

47. Ognjanovic, I.: Artificial intelligence in healthcare. Stud. Health Technol. Inform. **274**, 189–205 (2020). https://doi.org/10.3233/SHTI200677

48. Jiang, L., et al.: Opportunities and challenges of artificial intelligence in the medical field: current application, emerging problems, and problem-solving strategies. J. Int. Med. Res. **49**, (2021). https://doi.org/10.1177/03000605211000157

49. Kakhi, K., Alizadehsani, R., Kabir, H.M.D., Khosravi, A., Nahavandi, S., Acharya, U.R.: The internet of medical things and artificial intelligence: trends, challenges, and opportunities. Biocybern. Biomed. Eng. **42**, 749–771 (2022). https://doi.org/10.1016/J.BBE.2022.05.008

50. Li, W., et al.: A comprehensive survey on machine learning-based big data analytics for IoT-enabled smart healthcare system. Mob. Netw. Appl. **26**, 234–252 (2021). https://doi.org/10.1007/S11036-020-017006/TABLES/4

51. Yuan, H., Deng, W.: Doctor recommendation on healthcare consultation platforms: an integrated framework of knowledge graph and deep learning. Internet Res. **32**, 454–476 (2022). https://doi.org/10.1108/INTR-07-2020-0379/FULL/PDF

52. Dhinakaran, M., Phasinam, K., Alanya-Beltran, J., Srivastava, K., Babu, D.V., Singh, S.K.: A system of remote patients' monitoring and alerting using the machine learning technique. J. Food Qual. **2022** (2022). https://doi.org/10.1155/2022/6274092

53. Islam, M.N., Aadeeb, M.S., Hassan Munna, M.M., Rahman, M.R.: A deep learning based multimodal interaction system for bed ridden and immobile hospital admitted patients: design, development and evaluation. BMC Health Serv. Res. **22**, 1–26 (2022). https://doi.org/10.1186/S12913-022-08095Y/TABLES/8

54. Verdicchio, M., Perin, A.: When doctors and AI interact: on human responsibility for artificial risks. Philos. Technol. **35**, 1–28 (2022). https://doi.org/10.1007/S13347-022-00506-6/METRICS

55. Mishra, S., Sharma, D., Srivastava, S.P., Raj, K., Malviya, R., Fuloria, N.K.: Telemedicine: the immediate and long-term functionality contributing to treatment and patient guidance. In: Choudhury, T., Katal, A., Um, J.S., Rana, A., Al-Akaidi, M. (eds.) Telemedicine: The Computer Transformation of Healthcare. TELe-Health, pp. 267–281. Springer, Cham (2022). https://doi.org/10.1007/978-3-030-99457-0_17

56. White, J., Byles, J., Walley, T.: The qualitative experience of telehealth access and clinical encounters in Australian healthcare during COVID-19: implications for policy. Health Res. Policy Syst. **20**, 1–10 (2022). https://doi.org/10.1186/S12961-021-00812-Z/TABLES/1

57. Chaudhry, H., Nadeem, S., Mundi, R.: How satisfied are patients and surgeons with telemedicine in orthopaedic care during the COVID-19 pandemic? A systematic review and meta-analysis. Clin. Orthop. Relat. Res. **479**, 47–56 (2021). https://doi.org/10.1097/CORR.0000000000001494

58. Holstead, R.G., Robinson, A.G.: Discussing serious news remotely: navigating difficult conversations during a pandemic. JCO Oncol. Pract. **16**, 363–368 (2020). https://doi.org/10.1200/op.20.00269

59. Trabjerg, T.B., Jensen, L.H., Søndergaard, J., Sisler, J.J., Hansen, D.G.: Cross-sectoral video consultations in cancer care: perspectives of cancer patients, oncologists and general practitioners. Support. Care Cancer **29**, 107–116 (2020). https://doi.org/10.1007/S00520-020-05467-0/TABLES/4

60. Veiga, M.G., Tadeu Felizi, R.T., Fernandes, C.E., Oliveira, E.: Whatsapp and Gynecologist-patient interaction: development and validation of a questionnaire to assess the stress perceived by the doctor. Revista Brasileira de Ginecologia e Obstetrícia **44**(5) (2022)

61. Petruzzi, M., De Benedittis, M.: WhatsApp: a telemedicine platform for facilitating remote oral medicine consultation and improving clinical examinations. Oral Surg. Oral Med. Oral Pathol. Oral Radiol. **121**(03), 248–254 (2016). https://doi.org/10.1016/j.oooo.2015.11.005

62. Nwabueze, E., Oju, O.: Using mobile application to improve doctor-patient interaction in healthcare delivery system. E-Health Telecommun. Syst. Netw. **8**, 23–34 (2019). https://doi.org/10.4236/etsn.2019.83003

63. Alazzam, M.B., Alassery, F., Almulihi, A.: Development of a mobile application for inter-action between patients and doctors in rural populations. Hindawi, Mob. Inf. Syst. (2021). https://doi.org/10.1155/2021/5006151

64. O'Sullivan, B., Couch, D., Naik, I.: Using mobile phone apps to deliver rural general practi-tioner services: critical review using the walkthrough method. JMIR Form. Res. **6**(1), e30387 (2022). https://doi.org/10.2196/30387

65. Ray, P.P.: A survey on internet of things architectures. J. King Saud. Univ. Comput. Inf. Sci. **30**, 291–319 (2018). https://doi.org/10.1016/j.jksuci.2016.10.003

66. Rejeb, A., Rejeb, K., Zailani, S.H.M., Abdollahi, A.: Knowledge diffusion of the internet of things (IoT): a main path analysis. Wirel. Pers. Commun. **126**(2022), 1177–1207 (2022). https://doi.org/10.1007/s11277022-09787-8

67. Wu, T., Wu, F., Qiu, C., Redouté, J.M., Yuce, M.R.: A rigid-flex wearable health monitoring sensor patch for IoT-connected healthcare applications. IEEE Internet Things J. **7**(8), 6932–6945 (2020). https://doi.org/10.1109/JIOT.2020.2977164

68. Ahila, A., et al.: A smart IoMT based architecture for E-healthcare patient monitoring system using artificial intelligence algorithms. Front. Physiol. **14**, 1125952 (2023). https://doi.org/10.3389/fphys.2023.1125952

69. Khan, M.M., Alanazi, T.M., Albraikan, A.A., Almalki, F.A.: IoT-based health monitoring system development and analysis. Secur. Commun. Netw. (2022). https://doi.org/10.1155/2022/9639195

70. Sharma, N., et al.: A smart ontology-based IoT framework for remote patient monitoring. Biomed. Sig. Proc. Control **68** (2021). https://doi.org/10.1016/j.bspc.2021.10271

71. Qureshi, M.A., Qureshi, K.N., Jeon, G., et al.: Deep learning-based ambient assisted living for selfmanagement of cardiovascular conditions. Neural Comput. Appl. **34**, 10449–10467 (2022). https://doi.org/10.1007/s00521-020-05678-w7

72. Souri, A., Ghafour, M.Y., Ahmed, A.M., Safara, F., Yamini, A., Hoseyninezhad, M.A: New machine learning-based healthcare monitoring model for student's condition diagnosis in Internet of Things environment. Soft Comput. **24**, 17111–17121. https://doi.org/10.1007/s00500-020-05003-6

73. Cañón-Clavijo, R.E., Montenegro-Marin, C.E., Gaona-Garcia, P.A., Ortiz-Guzmán, J.: IoT based system for heart monitoring and arrhythmia detection using machine learning. J. Healthc. Eng. (2023). https://doi.org/10.1155/2023/6401673

74. Nancy, A.A., Ravindran, D., Raj Vincent, P.M.D., Srinivasan, K., Gutierrez Reina, D.: IoT-cloud-based smart healthcare monitoring system for heart disease prediction via deep learning. Electronics (2022). https://doi.org/10.3390/electronics11152292

75. Džaferović, E., Sokol, A., Almisreb, A.A., Mohd Norzeli, S.: DoS and DDoS vulnerability of IoT: a review. Sustain. Eng. Innov. **1**(1), 43–48 (2019)

76. Peng, Y., Yin, P., Deng, Z., Wang, R.: Patient–physician interaction and trust in online health community: the role of perceived usefulness of health information and services. Int. J. Environ. Res. Publ. Health **17**, 139 (2019). https://doi.org/10.3390/IJERPH17010139

77. Wu, T., Deng, Z., Zhang, N., Buchanan, P.R., Zha, N., Wang, R.: Seeking and using intention of health information from doctors in social media: the effect of doctor-consumer interaction. Int. J. Med. Inform. **115**, 106–113 (2018). https://doi.org/10.1016/j.ijmedinf.2018.04.009.-DOI-PubMed

78. Zhang, W., Zhou, F., Fei, Y.: Repetitions in online doctor–patient communication: frequency, functions, and reasons. Patient Educ. Couns. **107** (2023). https://doi.org/10.1016/j.pec.2022.11.007

79. Rodrigues, C.F.: Communicative trust in therapeutic encounters: users' experiences in public healthcare facilities and community pharmacies in Maputo. Mozambique. Soc. Sci. Med. **291**, 114512 (2021). https://doi.org/10.1016/J.SOCSCIMED.2021.114512

80. Huo, W., Zheng, G., Yan, J., Sun, L., Han, L.: Interacting with medical artificial intelligence: integrating self-responsibility attribution, human–computer trust, and personality. Comput. Hum. Behav. **132**, 107253 (2022). https://doi.org/10.1016/J.CHB.2022.107253

81. Page, M.J., McKenzie, J.E., Bossuyt, P.M., et al.: The PRISMA 2020 statement: an updated guideline for reporting systematic reviews. Syst. Rev. **10**, 89 (2021). https://doi.org/10.1186/s13643-021-01626-4

Author Index

© ICST Institute for Computer Sciences, Social Informatics and Telecommunications Engineering 2024
Published by Springer Nature Switzerland AG 2024. All Rights Reserved
F. Tchakounte et al. (Eds.): SAFER-TEA 2023, LNICST 566, pp. 409–410, 2024.
https://doi.org/10.1007/978-3-031-56396-6

Printed in the United States
by Baker & Taylor Publisher Services